KINGDOM OF
OLIVES AND ASH

KINGDOM OF
OLIVES AND ASH

WRITERS CONFRONT
THE OCCUPATION

AYELET WALDMAN AND
MICHAEL CHABON, EDITORS

MORIEL ROTHMAN-ZECHER, ASSOCIATE EDITOR

HARPER  PERENNIAL

NEW YORK • LONDON • TORONTO • SYDNEY • NEW DELHI • AUCKLAND

FIRST EDITION

Designed by Jamie Lynn Kerner

Library of Congress Cataloging-in-Publication Data has been applied for.

ISBN 978-0-06-243178-3

HB 12.11.2023

CONTENTS

INTRODUCTION

AYELET WALDMAN AND
MICHAEL CHABON

W E DIDN'T WANT TO EDIT THIS BOOK. WE DIDN'T WANT TO write or even think, in any kind of sustained way, about Israel and Palestine, about the nature and meaning of occupation, about intifadas and settlements, about whose claims were more valid, whose suffering more bitter, whose crimes more egregious, whose outrage more justified. Our reluctance to engage with the issue was so acute that for nearly a quarter of a century we didn't even visit the place where Ayelet was born.

We had gone to Israel in 1992, a few months after we met. Though raised primarily in the United States and Canada, Ayelet had been born in Jerusalem, the daughter of immigrants from Montreal, and had lived and studied in Israel on and off over the years; it was Michael's first time. The Oslo accords were fresh and untested; it was a time of optimism, new initiatives, relative tranquility. We visited family and friends, made the requisite tourist pilgrimages to Yad Vashem, the Western Wall, Masada, the Dead Sea. We also spent time in the Muslim quarter in the Old City of Jerusalem, and visited celebrated mosques there, including the al-Aqsa, and in Akko. Some of what Michael saw during that time found its way, after undergoing a sea change, into the pages of *The Yiddish Policemen's Union*. It was a memorable visit, the first, we imagined, of many we would be making together.

We didn't go back for twenty-two years.

Over the course of that period, the tentative hope that followed Oslo vanished. Yitzhak Rabin was murdered. A second intifada, long and bloody, arose and was violently put down. The pace and extent of settlement construction in the territories increased, and the military occupation grew more entrenched, more brutal, more immiserating. Horrified and bewildered by the blur of violence and destruction, of reprisal and counter-reprisal and counter-counter-reprisal, put off by the dehumanizing rhetoric prevalent on both sides, we did what so many others in the ambivalent middle have done: we averted our gaze. We opted out of the debate, and stayed away from the country.

But in 2014, at the invitation of the Jerusalem International Writers' Festival, Ayelet went back to Israel. While she was there, she met with some of the courageous members of Breaking the Silence (BTS), a nonprofit organization composed of former Israeli soldiers whose service in the occupied territories has inexorably led them to work vigorously and courageously to oppose the occupation and bring it to an end. BTS took Ayelet on a tour of the city of Hebron. They introduced her to Issa Amro, the founder of a grassroots group called Youth Against Settlements, whose nonviolent actions and campaigns are among the most prominent and creative in the West Bank. For the first time she had a clear, visceral understanding of just what occupation meant, of how it operated, and of the decades of Israeli strategic planning that had gone into creating the massive, often brutal, always dehumanizing military bureaucracy that oversees and controls it.

Then Ayelet went to Tel Aviv and spent some time in the company of writers, filmmakers, artists, and intellectuals who live in that cosmopolitan city, where gay couples walk hand in hand in the streets, where chic restaurants put their own creative spin on traditional Middle Eastern cuisine, and where the pace and tenor of life is *sababa* (an Israeli slang term, of Arabic origin, whose meaning is akin to the American slang term "chill"). The city sparkles; it hums. And it averts its gaze. One would never know, on the streets of Tel Aviv, that an hour's drive away, millions of people are living and dying under oppressive military rule.

Ayelet had a wonderful time in Tel Aviv, and therein lay the problem. She felt so at ease in the country of her birth, so at *home*. But if she felt that way—that somehow she belonged to this country, by virtue of birth and temperament and upbringing, by virtue of being Jewish—then so too did she bear some measure of responsibility for the crimes and injustices perpetrated in the name of that home and its "security."

Once Ayelet had come to that conclusion, however, she was immediately confronted with a new problem: she felt powerless. How could she do anything to effect meaningful change, no matter how small, in this intractable morass that had defeated the best and worst efforts of dozens of presidents and prime ministers, secretaries of state, Nobel Prize winners and NGOs, statesmen and diplomats and peace activists, not to mention generations of violent extremists of every stripe who had sought their own twisted solutions?

When Ayelet came home from that trip she told Michael what she had seen in Hebron. She described the steel bars that had been welded across townspeople's front doors, sealing them in their homes. She related the frightening moment when a couple of young Palestinian boys had dared to set foot on the main street of their own city, a street on which Palestinians are barred from walking, putting themselves at risk and at the mercy of heavily armed IDF troops, out of some combination of boredom, bravado, and desperation. She described how disgusted she had been by graffiti scrawled on walls across Palestinian Hebron calling, in Hebrew, for the death of Arabs. She told him the story of the things she had seen and heard, and as Michael listened, his reluctance, the product of decades of disenchantment and disengagement, began to fade.

As it faded we both began to realize that storytelling itself—bearing witness, in vivid and clear language, to things personally seen and incidents encountered—has the power to engage the attention of people who, like us, have long since given up paying attention, or have simply given up.

Storytelling—that was a territory, free and unrestricted, that we knew well. More important, we knew a lot of story*tellers*: creative writers and novelists whose entire job consists, according to Henry James, of being "one on whom nothing is lost." Professional payers of attention, they had the skill and the talent, if we could engage them, to engage others, using their mastery of language and eye for telling detail to encourage people to stop averting their gazes, to take another look, and maybe see something that fifty years of news reports, white papers, and propaganda had missed.

So, conscious of the imminence of June 2017, the fiftieth anniversary of the occupation, we put the word out—to writers on every continent except Antarctica, of all ages and eight mother tongues. Writers who identified as Christian, Muslim, Jewish, and Hindu, and writers of no religious affiliation at all. Some had already made clear and public their political feelings on the subject of Palestine-Israel, but most had not, and many acknowledged from the outset that they had never really given the subject more than a glancing consideration. For many it was their first visit to the area; some were returning to a place they knew well. The Palestinian and Israeli writers were writing about home. They all came away, as we'd only dared to hope, brimming over with the vividness of the things they had seen, and the need to put it into words, to share the story.

Over the course of 2016, the writers in this volume, in small parties that ranged from a single person to as many as seven individuals, came to Palestine-Israel, on delegations organized by Breaking the Silence. Once there, they spent most of their time in the occupied territories, in East Jerusalem neighborhoods like Silwan, Sheikh Jarrah, and the Shuafat refugee camp; in West Bank cities like Hebron, Ramallah, Nablus, Jericho, and Bethlehem; in West Bank villages including Nabi Saleh, Susiya, Bili'in, Umm al-Khair, Jinba, al-Wallajeh, Kufr Qaddum; and in the Gaza Strip. In these places, the writers met with Palestinian community organizers and nonviolent protest leaders, among them Issa Amro, as well as with shop owners, artists, intellectuals, and laborers, women's rights advocates and journalists, businesspeople and farmers, grandparents, parents, and children. They also met with Israeli settlers and with

Israeli and Palestinian antioccupation activists, human rights law-yers, academics, and writers. In each case, the individual inclination and interest of the writer drove his or her itinerary—some slept over at families' houses in Palestinian refugee camps, villages, and cities, while others explored soap factories and archeological sites. Some visited the military court, others spent time with bereaved Palestinian and Israeli families. The subjects chosen by the authors were diverse and varied; this breadth of experience, perspective, and narrative is reflected in the pages of this book.

We want to be clear: we had no political expectations of these writers. We invited them to participate in this project based on their literary excellence and their influence over wide and devoted reader-ships in their own countries and in many cases all around the world. We did not censor them or try to restrict their words in any way. What they saw is what they wrote is what you'll read. A team of scrupulous fact-checkers labored for months to confirm the veracity and factual basis of each of these essays.

Finally, as with all the other writers involved in this project, neither of us has or will ever receive payment of any kind for our work. All royalties from the sales of *Kingdom of Olives and Ash*, after expenses, will be divided between Breaking the Silence and Youth Against Set-tlements, whose hard, unremunerated, twilit work will go on long, long after the reader has turned the last page.

THE DOVEKEEPER

GERALDINE BROOKS

THEIR PLANS WERE QUITE PRECISE: THEY WOULDN'T ATTACK WOMEN, or the elderly, or children like themselves. Their targets, they agreed, would be men in their late teens and early twenties— young men of military age. All this was settled between them before they left the house.

Hassan Manasra, fifteen, took a carving knife from his mother's kitchen, but his cousin Ahmed, thirteen, couldn't find the long, daggerlike knife he'd intended to use for his weapon. It took him a while, but finally he located it, concealed in a cupboard, where his father had hidden it for safekeeping.

The Manasras live in a compound of multifamily homes occupying almost a block in the Jerusalem hillside neighborhood of Beit Hanina. In the shared courtyard, half a dozen bicycles of various sizes are propped against a tree or lie in the dirt by the tall entry gate. Ten brothers and their families share the compound, and the children move fluidly through each other's apartments. Uncle or father, sibling or cousin: it makes little difference. While the stairwells have the provisional, still-under-construction look of dwellings in a constant state of addition, the rooms inside are furnished rather formally: prints of alpine landscapes, velvet-covered sofas, lacy tablecloths. In Ahmed's bedroom, the sheets have cartoon figures of astronauts. It's the home of a modestly prosperous clan whose breadwinners run a family-owned grocery store, or work in trades or in transportation.

Until October 12, 2015, Hassan and Ahmed followed the same schedule as all the school-age cousins in the household: go to class, come home, eat, change clothes, and then go play in an area that their uncles had cleared for them on the unused land beneath the highway overpass that separates Beit Hanina from the adjacent neighborhood of Pisgat Ze'ev. Sometimes the cousins played soccer, but Hassan and Ahmed particularly enjoyed training for parkour—the gymnastic running discipline that uses urban space as an obstacle course. The concrete pylons and grassy embankments under the highway were ideal for practicing vaults and tumbles.

The highway divides two East Jerusalem neighborhoods—the House of Hanina and the Peak of Ze'ev—that face each other across a shallow valley. Both are long-settled places. Beit Hanina was home to a few farming families as early as Canaanite times; in Pisgat Ze'ev, excavations have uncovered ritual baths from the Second Temple period.

Both neighborhoods have seen explosive population growth since 1967, when Israel captured this territory from Jordan in the Six-Day War. In the years since, their built-up areas have reached out to each other across land that once supported only olive groves and vineyards. Now the busy highway is all that marks the division between the Palestinian neighborhood and the Jewish one. Pisgat Ze'ev is the last stop on the Jerusalem tramline, Beit Hanina the second-to-last. Residents of the two neighborhoods live cheek by jowl, yet they inhabit two different worlds.

Pisgat Ze'ev, named for the Revisionist Zionist Ze'ev Jabotinsky, was one of the new settlements rapidly built on land annexed by Israel after the war, intended to connect and thicken the Jewish areas of East Jerusalem. Although the annexation remains illegal under international law (the United States, for one, does not recognize it), Pisgat Ze'ev is now one of Jerusalem's largest neighborhoods, with some forty-two thousand residents, around five hundred of them Palestinians. Shady trees have grown up, softening the lines of its medium-rise, stone-clad apartment blocks and humming commercial areas.

Beit Hanina has grown organically over time from its village origins, and it contains a range of old and new homes. Some thirty-five thousand Palestinians live there, on land Israel has annexed. Another thousand have been severed from their neighbors by the building of the separation barrier a decade ago, after the wave of suicide bombings that characterized the uprising known as the second intifada. The looming concrete wall, which mostly divides annexed land claimed by Israel from occupied land administered by the Israeli military, has huge implications. Those on the Palestinian side may not cross into annexed East Jerusalem—to go to work or school, to visit family, to buy groceries—without a temporary pass issued at the discretion of the Israeli authorities.

On the other side of the barrier, Palestinians have free movement but often face hostility from Jewish hard-liners, whose numbers have grown with Israel's tilt to the right in recent years. Residents of Beit Hanina sometimes awake to graffiti messages such as "Death to Arabs" and "Jerusalem for Jews" spray-painted on their homes. Cars have been vandalized and burned, tires slashed. Palestinians put the blame on militants from Pisgat Ze'ev. Pisgat Ze'ev residents can be just as quick to blame Palestinians for crimes in their neighborhood.

Not long ago, a Jewish woman accosted the Manasra boys as they practiced parkour under the highway. She accused them of stealing her son's gloves. The boys' uncle, also named Ahmed, who was home at the time, was called to the scene. "When I got down there, the boys were looking like scared rabbits, surrounded by settlers and police," he says. Because of the wave of vandalism, he and his brothers had installed a security camera on the outside of their compound. He suggested the police review the film to see if the boys had left the play area to go and steal in the Israeli neighborhood. The footage proved they'd been playing innocently under the bridge at the time of the alleged theft. The police, he said, accepted the evidence, but the woman continued to accuse and berate the boys. Ahmed Manasra has thought about that incident, and whether the fear it engendered may have been a kind of tipping point for his nephews. "Our children don't have normal childhoods," he says. "From the minute they open their eyes they wake into a reality of checkpoints, soldiers, settlers insulting their mom. They see the news from Gaza, children like them, bombed and homeless. They hear about a boy their age, burned alive by Israelis. They are sad and afraid. It's not a healthy environment." Even so, he says, he still can't bring himself to believe that his nephews were capable of doing what they did on an ordinary afternoon in 2015.

It was a Monday, and Hassan came home as usual from his tenth-grade class at Ibn Khaldoun School, where he excelled at his studies and was known for good behavior. Ahmed, who struggled academically and was considered rather young for his age, returned from the nearby New Generation Primary School. Hassan told his mother he was going out to buy a video game for his PlayStation. He asked what she was making for dinner. He was hungry, he told her, and he wouldn't be gone long. It was about three o'clock in the afternoon.

In CCTV footage captured soon after, Ahmed and Hassan are seen strolling together towards the shopping district of Pisgat Ze'ev, an easy walk from their home once you get across the busy highway. They appear relaxed and unremarkable—two kids out for a walk after school. They amble out of the shot. Then, suddenly, the camera captures a very different image. A young man, wearing the white shirt and black trousers of the Orthodox, runs past the camera, desperately glancing behind him as the two boys, long knives now unsheathed, chase after him. Although Hassan had already stabbed the man, Yosef Ben Shalom, age twenty-one, in the upper body, he managed to outrun them. The boys turned then, and ran on towards the shops on Sisha Asar Street.

Just minutes later, a few blocks away in her top-floor apartment, Ruti Ben Ezra heard three quick pops. A sinewy woman with jet-black hair and cobalt-blue eyes, she came to Israel in 1977 from Argentina when she was eight years old. Ten years later, she served in the army in Gaza during the first intifada, so she had no doubt that what she heard were gunshots. As she rushed down the stairs to see what had happened, she did a mental accounting of the whereabouts of her five children. Two were still at school, two had gone to play football, and one, Ofek, had just left to visit his grandmother. It was Ofek who came barreling back towards the apartment, screaming. "Mum! Mum! Orlev, Na'or . . . Terrorist!"

"Go upstairs! Close the door!" she told him, and ran out into the road towards the shopping area. A terrified Orlev ran to her. She grasped his hand as he pulled her to the candy store where his older brother Na'or, thirteen, lay sprawled on the sidewalk. Ruti threw herself down beside her son and called his name, begging him to open his eyes. Within minutes, paramedics were at her shoulder, yelling at her to move.

"No!" she said. "I'm his mother!"

"Do you want us to save him? Then get out of the way."

She stood back as they worked on her unconscious son. Pulse: weak. Blood pressure: plunging. What was evident to the paramedics was that Na'or had been knifed three times, from behind his shoulder. But the amount of blood on the sidewalk didn't account for his plummeting vital signs. What was not evident: the deadliest of the wounds had punctured his jugular. Internally, invisibly, he was bleeding to death.

A few blocks away, Hassan Manasra was already dead, shot at close range by police officers as he'd rushed at them with his knife. Farther down the tram tracks, his cousin Ahmed lay where a car had struck him. The impact had sent him sprawling, his lower legs twisted up on either side of his body in a grotesque and unnatural shape, like an action figure cast aside by a careless child. Blood pooled around his skull, fractured by the blow from a club wielded by a storekeeper who'd chased him down.

Despite his head injury, he had not lost consciousness. A cell phone video showed his face, contorted, as a mob gathered around him. A voice yelled: "Die, you son of a whore!"

Within hours, that cell phone footage went viral and Ahmed Manasra became a Rorschach blot; a scrim onto which each side of the conflict could project its own narrative.

The Palestinian leader Mahmoud Abbas was the first to use the boy, erroneously claiming in a televised address that Israelis had summarily executed him. In answer, the Israeli prime minister Bibi Netanyahu released footage of Ahmed in Hadassah Medical Center, head bandaged, being fed pureed food. Palestinians were quick to point out that it was not Israelis offering this succor, but the boy's Palestinian lawyer, who had noticed the untouched food and realized that

Ahmed might not manage to eat it, since his hand was shackled to the bed. On the video, Ahmed is seen raising his free hand, perhaps to shoo the videographer away. An Israeli commentator described the gesture as "an ISIS salute." Meanwhile, Physicians for Human Rights released a statement decrying the release of the footage as an illegal exposure of the identity of a minor and an unethical violation of patient privacy.

But in this explosive case, privacy didn't seem respected by either side. A few weeks later, Palestinian television screened a lengthy video of Ahmed's interrogation. It remains unclear who leaked it. Ahmed sat hunched at a corner of a desk in what appeared to be an Israeli police station, surrounded by three plainclothes officers. The lead interrogator, a brawny man with sunglasses pushed back on top of his knitted *kippa*, attempted to extract a confession to two counts of attempted murder.

At first, as the interrogator screamed in Arabic and waved his finger in Ahmed's face, the boy repeatedly hit his injured head.

"I swear by God I can't remember," he whimpered.

"You swear by God? Who is this shit God?" Looming over the boy, the interrogator demanded to know why he helped his cousin.

"I don't know," Ahmed cried, once again hitting at his head. "Take me to the doctor."

"Shut up!" yelled the interrogator. "Sit up straight. Put your hands down!"

The film as aired had been edited, so it is impossible to know how long all this went on. But in the end, the boy was sobbing convulsively. "Everything you say is true!" he wailed. "Just stop!"

Since the Manasras live on the Israeli side of the separation barrier, Ahmed Manasra was tried in a civil court rather than under the military justice system, where the conviction rate is 99.74 percent. In Israeli courts, no minor under the age of fourteen at the time of conviction may be sent to prison.

But it was evident from the outset that Ahmed's case would strain public opinion regarding the protections extended to him. Minors are required to have a parent or an attorney present during questioning. But Ahmed did not. In fact, his parents had difficulty even finding an attorney both qualified and prepared to take his case to trial. One lawyer agreed, and then called the next day to apologize, saying he'd been warned that the case would be a career ender for him. The family finally chose Leah Tsemel, a veteran civil rights attorney who has practiced in Israel's civil and military courts for over forty-five years.

Tsemel is an Israeli-born Jew whose parents migrated to Israel from Russia and Poland in the 1930s. Raised in Haifa, she served in the army and was studying at university when the Six-Day War broke out, threatening Israel's survival. During intense fighting in East Jerusalem, she volunteered with the army, evacuating Jewish civilians from the most threatened neighborhoods. When combat was over, the soldiers took her to the newly occupied territory of the West Bank, the biblical lands of Judea and Samaria that had been off limits to Jews during the years of Jordanian rule. The trip was supposed to be a reward, a treat. But the sight of columns of Palestinian refugees trudging down the roadside sickened her, evoking her parents' stories of European persecutions and the resonance of the homeless, wandering Jew. She was, she said, "naive and apolitical" at that time. "I thought it was a war for peace, that we would use the victory to make peace with our neighbors." Instead, she soon realized that what she had witnessed was the beginning of occupation, and that even key leaders in the Labor Party had no intention of giving back the land. So, she embraced the far left, and when she graduated from law school went to work in defense of Palestinians. "What I am doing is in Israel's interest," she asserts, "even if Israelis don't realize it."

Na'or's mother, Ruti Ben Ezra, is one such Israeli. "Some people will do anything for money, even sell their soul to the devil," she says. "I hope her own children will be injured or killed by a terrorist."

Even though Na'or has recovered physically, his parents say his mental scars are far from healed. "The street is his worst enemy," says his father, Shai, a forty-six-year-old electrician. He says Na'or can't concentrate at school. His temper has become explosive. "Everything bothers him. He and his brother fight much more than they used to. Orlev feels guilty he ran away and didn't help his brother."

Shai has had to give up his job because he needs to be with Na'or night and day. He opens his hands in a gesture of helplessness. "We are crushed," he says.

Ruti, a kindergarten assistant, also has stopped working, afraid to leave her children alone. Two days after the attack on Na'or, her youngest child, age seven, took a knife to school. "The teacher called to tell me," recalls Ruti. "I didn't see. I didn't see that he'd taken it. A seven-year-old shouldn't have to be so afraid." And she, too, lives with fear. "Every time I hear a siren, I think, 'Where are my children?' In this, they succeeded," she says. "They want us to be afraid. I'm afraid."

And that, Ahmed Manasra told his lawyer, Leah Tsemel, when he was finally allowed to see her, was indeed what he had intended. "His cousin said, 'Let's go scare them, as they scare us.' The maximum they intended was to wound. That was the scenario, as they saw it." Tacitly acknowledging how implausible this version will seem, she shrugs. "They are children," she says. "But what they did understand, even as children: lifting a knife, they'd probably be killed."

Ahmed told Tsemel that Hassan had proclaimed he was ready to die, to join the so-called martyrs whose tattered portraits peel off the walls of many Palestinian buildings. But Ahmed says he didn't feel that way at all. He can't say why he went along with his older cousin, but once he saw the blood of the first victim, he was terrified. As that man outran them, he saw Hassan glance towards a woman with children. He told Tsemel that he cried out: "Don't even look at her!" Then Hassan spotted Na'or coming out of the candy store on his bicycle and moved in on him. Ahmed told Tsemel that he cried out "*Haram!*"—the Arabic word for something unholy, forbidden—"We decided not to!" But Hassan stabbed the boy anyway. Bystanders and storekeepers rushed them, and within a minute or two Hassan was shot dead and Ahmed was bleeding on the tram tracks.

Before Ahmed first appeared in court, he faced a difficult choice. Since he was below the age of criminal responsibility, if he pled guilty to attempted murder at his first hearing, the case would be closed and he could not be sent to prison. But had this happened, Tsemel believed, the Israeli outcry would have been such that the law would have been changed. "They would have found a way to detain him," she asserts. In any case, Ahmed's family would not allow a guilty plea. He had not touched either of the victims in the attacks. Forensics confirmed that his knife had not been used, and he maintained that he never had intent to kill. So Tsemel took the case to trial, knowing that on January 20, 2016, Ahmed's fourteenth birthday, his protections as a minor would expire. He would be sentenced as an adult and face up to twenty years in prison. As Ahmed was brought, handcuffed, into the courthouse for the first day of his trial, two other Palestinian cousins, aged fourteen and twelve, from Beit Hanina and the nearby Shuafat refugee camp, stabbed and wounded an Israeli security guard. Media reports began to refer to the wave of violence as "the children's intifada."

"The children are doing it because the older ones don't do it. That's the feeling," says Tsemel. "If the adults acted—if only there was some political movement—they would not feel this way."

During the trial, Tsemel argued that no Jewish boy in the same circumstances would be charged with attempted murder for attacking Arabs on nationalistic grounds. "They will always face a lesser charge—manslaughter, grievous bodily harm," she said. Settlers who injure Palestinians often are released from custody on payment of a small fine.

On April 18, 2016, the day Ahmed's verdict was expected, his family gathered nervously at Jerusalem's Central Court. His thirty-two-year-old mother, Maysoon, sat rigidly on a bench, meticulously dressed in a gray headscarf, a long navy skirt, and a turmeric-yellow jacket. As she waited for the guards to bring her son, she said she was still in a state of disbelief that Ahmed could have been involved in the stabbings. "I didn't believe it then and I don't believe it now," she says, shaking her head. "I can't. I can't. The first video, it shocked me. He's a small, small kid. Shy. Always with me in the kitchen, or playing with his pet doves." She gave a wan smile. "He always wanted to bring them inside, to fly around the house. I would complain to him, 'They make a mess!' but he would just smile and say, 'Mama, you know I always clean it up.'" She inclined her head to a nearby bench where Ahmed's cousins waited to catch a word with him on his way into the courtroom, since they were not allowed to visit him in detention. "They want to tell him that they are taking care of his birds," his mother says. "They know how much he cares about them."

Ahmed, small and delicately built, arrived flanked by two juvenile justice counselors. He looked overwhelmed and near tears when he saw his family. He tugged nervously at his green hoodie as his mother embraced him, and managed a brief grin for his cousins. Tsemel, her black attorney's gown slipping casually off one shoulder, ruffled his hair. "How are you, kid?" she asked in Arabic, before his counselors ushered him away, into the courtroom.

Inside, the three judges who had heard the case confirmed a postponement in their verdict and ordered Ahmed returned to the juvenile facility while they deliberated further. Tsemel emerged from the closed hearing taking some small measure of optimism from the delay. "I hope they have debates. I hope they have doubts. I hope we had a strong enough argument to make them hesitate." On the other hand, she said, Israeli public opinion remained overwhelmingly against any hint of leniency. Newspaper reports referred to Ahmed "the terrorist" and "the stabber" even though he had not used his knife. "At the trial, the cross-examination and the witnesses were very hostile." The prosecution had asked for the maximum twenty-year sentence.

But Ahmed's family was relieved that he would remain at the juvenile facility, where he could attend class and have regular visits with his parents, for at least a few more weeks. They said good-bye in the courthouse hallway as the counselors escorted him away.

At the Manasra compound, the family still struggles to understand how the two cousins became so radicalized. Because he is now a law student at al-Quds University, the boys' uncle Ahmed has become the family's spokesman during his nephew's court proceedings. But very often, he admits, he is at a loss for words. "They did normal things kids do," he says. "Of course, we don't know what they see on the computer, what they read on the Internet."

His brothers, he says, are no more or less radical than most Palestinians of their generation: "Every family has an activist." As a young man, he took part in demonstrations and was jailed for seven years for throwing a Molotov cocktail at soldiers. Two others among the fourteen Manasra brothers also were jailed for throwing stones during the first intifada in 1987. "But we were men when we did these things," he said. "It's painful that we've reached this point— that children are involved. This is not the business of children. Not one Palestinian parent wants this. Not one. The only people who benefit are the greedy, rotten politicians who want to stay in their chairs. Calm isn't in their interest."

He gazes through the fluttering curtains at the view of his divided city and recalls a time when Jerusalem's children did not encounter one another as enemies. "There was a park in West Jerusalem—the Bell Garden," he says. "At Ahmed's age, I would go there all the time, to play with my Israeli friends."

Now that is impossible. Even as an adult, he feels insecure in Jewish neighborhoods. "Before, if an extremist tried to assault you, other Israelis would step in and break it up. Now, if something happens—a car accident, anything—it will be misunderstood. Everyone will attack you, because you are an Arab."

He says every child in the family has been traumatized. Hassan's seventeen-year-old brother Ibrahim was beaten and arrested the day of the stabbing, when heavily armed police swarmed the compound. A policeman claimed Ibrahim tried to grab his weapon. Since the police shattered the security camera that would have shown what occurred, Ibrahim had no way to prove his assertion that he had not. He was struck repeatedly with the butt of a rifle and suffered broken ribs and facial contusions and returned home only after almost five months in prison. Though he has returned to classes at his technical school, he can't concentrate. His younger sister, who is ten, witnessed the beating and did not speak for weeks after. Another of the cousins, age five, didn't leave the house for more than four months.

It was three weeks, Ahmed said, since Israeli authorities had finally offered to return Hassan's body to his family. Both Jewish and Islamic custom demands the swift burial of the dead, but the Israeli police have recently made a practice of retaining the corpses of Palestinians killed while committing terror attacks. They had retained Hassan's corpse for four months before offering the return of the body under stringent conditions: a night burial with only uncles and cemetery staff present; everyone to submit to a thorough security check beforehand. Hassan's family accepted. But they asked that, since the Muslim custom is to carry the body from the home to the grave wrapped only in a shroud and often with the face visible, Hassan's body not be brought home frozen.

On the appointed date, the Israeli authorities arrived with the body at midnight. "When he arrived, he was stiff as that table," said his uncle, tapping the mahogany surface in front of him. "His face was blue. How do you say good-bye to an ice cube?" The family refused to accept Hassan in that condition. The police took his body back to the freezer.

"Hassan's soul rests in peace, and may God forgive him," Ahmed said. "A body is a body. At the end of the day, what's left is the pain of those around him."

ENDNOTE

On December 17, 2015, at Jerusalem's Kotel, Na'or Ben Ezra was called to the Torah as a bar mitzvah.

On May 10, 2016, Ahmed Manasra was found guilty of two counts of attempted murder. He was sentenced to twelve years in prison and fined 180,000 shekels to be paid directly to the victim.

Hassan Manasra's thawed body was finally returned to his family for burial seven months after his death.

ONE'S OWN PEOPLE

JACQUELINE WOODSON

IN AMERICA, BROWN BODIES WERE FALLING SO HARD AND SO FAST IT was hard to look away. The faces of young brown men popping up on social media platforms, beautiful brown women sending selfies into the universe long after they had been taken from it at the hands of those badged to protect them, little brown boys looking innocently at us from middle school photos. In the heat and energy of this, I boarded a plane. For Israel-Palestine.

For many weeks before I was to travel, I came to tears often. I was afraid not only because of the daily horrors moving across my computer screen, but because my partner, a physician, had visited Hebron four years before and I had been terrified that she wouldn't return to us, that I would be left not only with two young children but having to live a life without her. That I would be left raising a beautiful brown boy in a country that hated its brown boys. A brown girl in a world that didn't see her. I cried because years after my partner's journey, we would be traveling to Palestine together, our children at a summer camp in New Hampshire, miles away from family, and, I would come to understand, a world away from anything they could even begin to comprehend at this point in their lives. Because even while we caution our brown boy about his behavior when addressing cops (eyes up, hands visible, never run), and our brown girl about how to walk into a room with her brown body (cover it, please!),

I know now that there are mothers in Hebron who are waiting for their children to come home. I was *in* Hebron and watched soldiers close all checkpoints as two small boys sharing a bicycle stood outside, crying that their mothers didn't know where they were. *Please let us go home*, they said again and again, their words falling into the dust. I was with a Palestinian activist named Issa Amro and my partner, Juliet. The soldiers, no more than young people themselves, their guns slung across their torsos, looked on or away, their young faces set into the work they were drafted to do for three years. The children, still holding tight to their bicycle, continued to beg. There was nothing we could do.

That evening, my partner and I went back to our hotel room, turned on our computer, and exhaled to dispatches from the New Hampshire camp. Our children were safe. Our children were happy. But we were different now. With us, we carried those crying boys.

IN THE WEEKS BEFORE LEAVING, OUR FAMILY SAT DOWN TO DINNER EACH evening, inside our brownstone built in 1878, around a table that we had owned for four years, passing dishes that we could easily replace at Ikea should they become chipped or broken. We moved inside our bubble of comfort easily, save me, with my head halfway in a place that was as foreign and frightening as ignorance. As palpable as the daily news.

What I "knew" about Israel-Palestine was that it was a dangerous place, a place where buses full of people exploded at midday and small boys ran through the streets aiming semiautomatic weapons at innocent passersby. The Israel-Palestine I thought I knew was not a place nice Jewish women (my partner) step into and out of unharmed. I knew the Palestine-Israel of newspaper articles and television journalism. This Palestine-Israel was as foreign to me as Yemen, a place somewhere out there where people who had no connection to me fought among themselves—and killed others. People who were not 100 percent people . . . how could they be? They were outside my very comfortable America. Outside anything I could—or needed to—imagine. Daily reports of the devastation of the occupation fell on ears attuned more to domestic tragedies—the overshadowing of police brutality, my own people dying. If I couldn't change this, what could I change? The reports again and again of Jews and Palestinians dying arrived to me in murky shadow. Bloodless. Boneless. These were not schoolchildren who begged for an extra sweet, not mothers lifting a breast to a newborn's mouth. Not that same newborn instinctively lifting her head to meet it. No boys outside a checkpoint, gates locked, soldiers walking away. *When will it open again?* I asked the people with me. *It could be hours. The soldiers decide.* No. If I couldn't save my own people, why even begin to imagine the murky shadows as fully human?

My own people dying.

What I know now is that there is no longer such a thing as *one's own people.*

In Umm al-Khair, a Bedouin village in the South Hebron Hills, an artist named Eid Hthaleen served us sage tea in tiny, beautiful glasses. We sat on rugs underneath a large canopy, our shoes left just outside. In the hills beyond the tent, we could see his thin goats moving over the land. We could see the makeshift homes, built from tin and plastic and tarps. Beyond that, the piles of metal where soldiers had come in with orders to destroy the homes. Small children looked at me wide eyed. A dark man, nearly toothless, chain-smoked, his fingertips yellow. During a silence, he turned to me and asked through a translator, *What is going on in your America? Why are they killing all the black people?*

I couldn't answer.

I do not know. Later, Eid took us to his studio, a tiny lean-to outside a small stone two-room home. He showed us the amazing trucks he had made—tiny renditions of the bulldozers and eighteen-wheelers that had come to destroy past homes, built from the materials and leftover metals of that destruction. This home, he said, was also under orders to be destroyed. All the structures were. He didn't know where he'd go with his family from here. He didn't know where the other families would go. They had been living on this land for over half a century. *It's land*, Eid said. *It will be here long after we've all stopped fighting over it.*

SOME MORNINGS, WHEN I'M FEELING BRAVE, I PULL MY BLACK IS BEAUTIFUL T-shirt over my head—black shirt with white lettering; the people I pass either smile or glare or look surprised. My pro-Blackness is not antiwhite. This shirt isn't my own middle finger thrown up into the air but rather an expression of my belief that love can exist for the self without annihilating others. Why is it I wear the shirt only when I'm feeling strong enough?

In Israel-Palestine, I meet both Israeli and Palestinian activists working hard toward creating a safer, freer, fairer nation. I take a bus to the Qalandiya checkpoint and watch the Palestinians moving slowly through it on their way to work. The checkpoint is a high structure of razor wire, iron bars, and metal detectors. IDs must be shown, and sometimes, for reasons no one can explain, people are not allowed to go through, losing days, sometimes weeks of work. A small white-haired Israeli woman, Hanna Barag, arrives early in the morning, to bear witness, to fight for the rights of the Palestinians, to help people move through their days, live their lives, feed their families. I watch her, see the hope in her actions, see the hope in the faces of the Palestinians who know who she is and why she's there. The checkpoint reminds me of Comstock, Coxsackie, Elmira—the many prisons I saw as a child visiting my incarcerated uncle. In the heat of the early morning, I watch the people move slowly through, their heads bowed, their IDs held out hopefully—and I wonder what crime brought them to this moment. And I know, it is simply the crime of the accident of their birth. And the crime of a nation, of many nations, refusing to see people . . . as people.

In Hebron, a small red-haired Palestinian boy points to my hair and says *It's not real. Your hair isn't real!* I let him touch it and he yanks it hard. I do what any mother does. I yank his hair back. He is surprised. And then he laughs. I am as surprised by a red-haired Palestinian as he is by a brown-skinned Afroed woman. And then we aren't surprised. We are just who we are.

I am one of three Black people on the plane to Israel-Palestine. A dark man with a yarmulke waves to me. Do you know him, the flight attendant wants to know. I smile at her, silent as bone, my back and voice tense for the journey. I am a mother. A partner. A writer. In Brooklyn, I have a life filled with people whom we share Sunday dinners with and have done so, with only a few misses, for fourteen years. We are well versed in Bordeaux and politics. We laugh a lot and comment on our children's pituitary glands—how did this come to pass so quickly, that this one is taller than I am now and that one is about to graduate from high school, college, a master's program? A voice comes over the intercom in Hebrew. My partner takes my hand, tells me again that her own parents used to fly in separate planes lest something happened and their three children were left parentless. And beyond the plane, I want to ask. What then?

The camp in New Hampshire has every auntie's phone number from New York to Vermont to California. I remember again that we still haven't gotten to our will. My sister will know what to do. Or maybe she won't.

Memory is strange. As I write this months later, what I know is that my fear of Israel-Palestine, like so many fears, was one of ignorance, the unknown, the backstory of others brought into my own present. There is a quiet loveliness to the people of Palestine. Before you can remove your sandals and step into their homes, there is the offering of tea, the shy bowed heads of both the women and men, followed by the warm smiles often reflecting the tortured teeth of poverty. There is the deep heat of a moral core moving through the bodies of Israeli activists—a true belief in justice and equality for all people, a not-looking-away-ness from the pain that is this moment in Palestine-Israel. For many years, I stood outside these worlds. And then I stood inside my fear. Slowly, a bit reluctantly, I stepped inside, opened my eyes, touched, tasted, smelled, and pulled at the hair of a world I had tried to not see, to not know.

It's not real, the boy said, pulling my hair. But like thirteen-year-old Ahmad Abdullah Sharaka, and twelve-year-old Tamir Rice, and eleven-year-old Abdul-Rahman Obeidallah and seventeen-year-old Dania Jihad Irshaid and eighty-four-year-old Marilyn May Bettencourt and the hundreds of Palestinians and African Americans killed between 2015 and 2016, my hair is as real as their bodies, as thick as their family's grief, as dark as the blood that flows and continues to flow—from the United States to Israel-Palestine.

BLOATED TIME AND THE DEATH OF MEANING

ALA HLEHEL

THE OCCUPATION DEPRIVES YOU OF YOUR HUMANITY BY DEPRIVING you of the ability to control time.

A free human being controls his time: he gets up when he wants and goes to bed when he wants; he goes to work according to a simple daily routine; she visits her relatives and her fiancé; he goes to the movies; she goes for a walk amid nature around her home any time she wishes. A human being is human because he makes his own decisions, because he has the ability to plan for tomorrow and the day after tomorrow, for next week and for the next ten years. A human being pursues her freedom through her ability to control her time. Freedom guarantees that simple, extraordinary, and sometimes hard-to-define thing: dignity.

The occupation is a machine: a complex, octopus-like regime that functions to exhaust those who are subject to it. It is a regime based on repression under the cover of administrative legitimacy, the courts, and legal authority. At first glance, everything is legal, and human rights are vouched for. A boy accused of throwing stones will enjoy legal representation in the military court, and an interpreter, and his mother's right to weep yearningly in front of him for the four minutes the expeditious deliberation lasts in the reinforced plastic trailer. Tables, chairs, computers, soldiers male and female, secretaries, the national emblem, its flag, smart security cameras, a metal frame around the place where the accused are seated, a brown wooden podium behind which stands the defense attorney, white shirts with black neckties, an impatient military judge, and three young men in the prime of life who threw stones at a military jeep during a demonstration. Everything but justice.

The machine resembles an old clock with its cogwheels: each wheel turns and pushes the wheel interlocked with it to turn as well. Cogwheel turns cogwheel turns cogwheel, and so on. And so the occupation machine is so tightly wound, integrated, and coherent that it is hard to distinguish its beginning from its end. Who drives whom? Do the settlements drive the government, or vice versa? Do financial resources drive the ideology, or is it the other way around? Does the army drive the security justifications, or is it the other way around? Do the bypass roads drive settlement population growth, or is it the other way around?

Why do Palestinians throw stones at the soldiers' and settlers' vehicles? Because they are jealous of their wheels' ability to turn endlessly in search of five-star bypass roads. It is a simple and human jealousy; the jealousy of those abandoned behind an illusory, unwritten line, watching life pass by at an insane pace. How does a Palestinian know life is passing by? By the endless red tile roofs, which stand out, stand out and increase, amid the verdancy of his confiscated land. The red tiles are in service to the occupation. They are the truest indicator of time, over fifty years of killing time. In a public square in a European town, a clever way of marking the passing of the daylight hours was invented: from within a huge clock emerged a metal soldier carrying a tiny pistol; he would mechanically raise his metal arm and fire one shot into the air as each hour struck, and then return into the clock. A creative idea to embody the concept of killing time. A clear and direct borrowing, which yet remains baffling in its power and the coldness of its metal; the occupation is a cold metal that kills with savage cruelty the most important thing life affords us: the finite seconds we are given once and once alone. The seconds which provide a direct, clear, and profound sense of our humanity.

In the writers' tour I took part in, time was a decisive factor: when we left the hotel, when we would arrive, when we would rest, when we would drink coffee, when we would get out of the car, when we'd come back to it. A free man divides his time into definable units. That is what differentiates him from a prisoner languishing in a huge prison: the manacled prisoner does not divide his time into definable units. Time, to him, is waking and sleep. When sleeping, he sleeps, and when he is awake, he waits for sleep. And so time loses its meaning, but the greater tragedy isn't that; it is that time's losing its meaning becomes part of the routine, a routine that he even starts to accept. The occupation does not kill you with bullets, most of the time, but with the pistol of time. Military jeeps arrive at the entrance to the village and unholster the pistol of time, and fire a bullet at it every hour on the hour. That is how the occupation kills you.

The occupation kills time and deprives a Palestinian of his basic dignity as a human being. There is a crushing, fatal sadness in this. God alone (according to Jewish exegesis) exists outside time. "In the beginning" means before time was created. It is the moment when God created time as a vessel to contain existence. God was before the creation of this verse and will continue to exist after it. The settlers believe that they were here before the creation of the era of the occupation and will remain here after it. Maimonides taught that this verse's meaning was that time becomes manifest to us through the movement of palpable substances, and if these substances had not begun moving, time would disappear.

Time here proceeds in a circular movement, and so it does not move, it does not advance. Man turns in vicious circles of circular time, and so he is like a rodent on a hamster wheel: he runs, standing in place. Palestinians, abandoned to the occupation, search for fresh ways of killing the time that does not pass. Time weighs heavily on you, becoming as heavy as a dark winter cloudbank. Time needs to be managed, maneuvered, and directed. A Palestinian in the West Bank faces time more often than he ever faces a tank or a rifle. We smoke outside the car and try to do the impossible that every smoker understands: holding the cigarette in your hand and keeping it lit at the same time. In these moments, in which three minutes are stolen to take refuge in your fleeting pleasure in the claws of fatal despair, we realize that a man can endure anything, if he holds to his little habits. They are the last indicators of his humanity. "We cultivate hope," is what Mahmoud Darwish said about those subjected to the blockade.

OVER THE PAST FEW DECADES, SETTLERS TOOK OVER TWO BUILDINGS IN Silwan in East Jerusalem, and that was the first spark in the great and manifold settlement operation, which we see today in more than ten buildings in Silwan and in the "City of David," which was set up there as a site for ideological and religious tourism embodying quite simply the whole complex Zionist idea: a settler ideology with prominent colonial features under the cover of the Torah narrative. One of the settlers took revenge against his Palestinian neighbor by routing his sewer pipe by his house. "Living in the shit" went from slang to a highly pungent reality. The Palestinian homeowner took us into a small room in his house overflowing with sewage. The smell was hideous, but the truly sad and painful thing was the silent sorrow in his wide eyes as he told us with such spirit what the settlers had done to him. To whom should he complain, whom should he beseech?

An armored minibus moves into the neighborhood, escorted by border police officers bristling with weapons. A settlement barracks outside time and context. Life in the alley comes to a halt while the sons of the settlers returning from school climb out and go into the building, Yonatan's Building, built there as tall as a middle finger aimed at them all. Suddenly you understand the meaning of "the right of self-determination," which the Palestinians demand. It is simply the right to walk down the street by your house whenever you want, without being searched or pursued by security. The borders, the capital, the security arrangements, the control over resources, all of these abridge your ability to walk down the street by your house without being insulted or besieged or interrogated, and, most important, without giving up this simple right, the right to walk down the street without fear. The occupation drains your desire to live, to take chances, to walk at random down the street without a defined direction or plan specific enough to satisfy a soldier's curiosity.

The occupation turns your joy in walking barefoot on the sandy beach into a luxury that a member of a struggling people cannot allow himself. The occupation reduces your joys and desires to the lowest point. That is how they triumph over you without firing a shot.

The soldiers ask you about everything. You must be convincing to get past the barrier or cross the checkpoint. There is no such thing as normal under the occupation. Everything must be exceptional, out of the ordinary, worthy of the soldier's bothering to read your permit or search your luggage. The occupation turns your life into a series of exceptional moments between which stretch dead, passionless periods of time, filled with indolence, inactivity, and lack of desire.

OFRA: AMONG THE FIRST SETTLEMENTS ESTABLISHED BY THE GUSH EMU-nim movement, in collusion with that dove of peace Shimon Peres. In 1977, the Likud Party came to power, and Ariel Sharon as a cabinet minister undertook to pursue the "swiss cheese" principle of settlements: a hole here and a hole there. With time, these holes cohered into a body, as the Palestinian body turned into holes. Palestinians became holes in the settlement body, an irritating thorn in the settlers' ass, to borrow from a metaphor used by Education Minister Naftali Bennett. This game is fixed: he who possesses the power, control, and rule will become a body, and you, who lack these, will become a black hole. The Palestinian black hole has no element of time; as with any black hole, it obliterates, it hides you in your segregated streets and the segregated legal system and the segregated security measures.

With the ratification of the Oslo accords in 1993, the swiss cheese course further intensified: bypass roads, "legal and agreed upon," were established to legitimize the settlements permanently, transforming these distant, remote places in frightful locations (holes) into suburbs convenient to Jerusalem and Tel Aviv from which one might come and go using roads restricted to Jews, modern streets (as in Europe or America), unlike the Palestinians' streets (as in the Middle East), which increased the popularity of living there (in the body of the cheese). For that, you must guarantee freedom of movement for the new Jewish residents in the luxurious suburbs, and limit this freedom for the other side, so that the new residents of the suburbs feel safe and secure. How? By a number of basic means, including limiting the exits and entrances to and from the Palestinians' towns and villages to only two for each town; and directing the Palestinian traffic toward the "must-use roads." In this way the mouse can be kept inside the holes. He can go out only on orders and can come back only on orders. This was a win-win: control over these bothersome, overly possessive Palestinians, and a comfortable and economically beneficial suburban life for the new owners of the place.

THE SHEPHERD ABU ALI STROLLS ALONGSIDE THE LANDS OF THE PALES-tinian village of Susiya in the Hebron Hills and tries to maintain the status quo: it is forbidden to graze in the hills in that direction, because that is a closed military zone, and it is forbidden to graze in the hills opposite, because they belong to the settlers, so he must be careful that none of the dozens of sheep he is tending violate these restrictions. We stand with him in the bitter cold, talking and smoking. I am surprised by how he is able to stand there with us without gloves or a heavy coat. A stubborn, cold, painful question occupies me: What have they done to us, Palestinian shepherd? Why are you this foreign to me; do you know how we can break the ice (literal and figurative) between us? What does Abu Ali want from life? To be allowed to graze his sheep on the forbidden hill opposite, where there is ample pasturage. How is it possible for this wish to be so hard? It is nothing but a wish to save time: if he grazes his sheep on the hill, the sheep will satisfy their appetites quickly, and he will go back to his cave or hut quickly to sit next to the warm stove with his wife and children. All he wants is to shorten this bitter, cold time.

But this wish runs into "official" complications: the settlers have planted trees in tubs in order to assert that they are growing. The Ottoman law that is still in force here states that whoever cultivates the land for several years obtains the right to possess it; the law does not clarify the meaning, size, or extent of "cultivation." To work around the law, the settlers plant the trees in tubs and spread them over vast areas in order for the land to become "theirs." One and a half percent of the land in the West Bank is cultivated by settlers, some of it in this way. It is an invented method of cultivating the land that does not concern itself with time, or time passing: you don't need decades of tilling the earth, tending it, watering it, sleeping under its trees, learning its language and listening to its stories, for it to become yours. These Palestinians are traditional in their farming, and slow; whereas high-tech farming in tubs is very fast. Another Israeli "exit."

In Susiya, they are searching for water and wells. They dig wells and the army floods them. There is no life without water, and there is no water without a permit, and there is no permit unless you are part of the controlling settler body. It does not count that you were here before the occupation and even before the establishment of Israel; what counts is that you have become outside the context. And the context is that the hole has become the body. You have become a bothersome hole. Susiya is not bothersome for this reason alone, but also because it was originally built on a highly "significant" archaeological site. And so they expelled its residents, and in a grand paradox, brought in Jewish settlers to replace them. For this is a known fact: Jews are better than Palestinians at living in ruins. The whole country was established to rebuild ruins, so who are these shepherds from Susiya to demand back a place that is reserved for Jews only?

THE WALL ROBS YOU OF TIME AND YOUR RIGHT TO KILL IT AS YOU LIKE. Walking through the fields or strolling on the dirt roads is no longer a given. The walls tear your existence into little unconnected bits of approved areas and forbidden areas, so you become an acrobat who must leap, skip, bend, and crawl according to the type of permit, the wish of the area commander, or the considerations of the sullen soldier at the checkpoint. The wall is a memorial to the past; it was raised upright between everything you have experienced before and everything you will experience after. Distant kilometers of barbed wire and tall cement slabs stand between you and your ability to extend your gaze and imagination toward the sea, for example, or toward a nearby brook, or the fast road that carries people from the sea to the brook that was once yours.

Nabi Saleh: the stubborn, peaceful demonstration against the settlements in general, and against the nearby settlement of Halamish's takeover of Nabi Saleh's spring in particular. Tear gas and metal bullets covered with rubber. Amid the ferocity of the confrontations and the suffocation in the houses, a mother drops her little daughter from a second-story window to her husband in the street to save her from suffocating. It is both a courageous and a rational deed. Feelings mixed, between admiration for the willingness of this mother to do anything to save her child, and astonishment at her willingness to drop her from the window. But this child does not yet know the meaning of paradox: afterwards she refused to go near her mother for two whole months! If you ask me for a one-sentence definition of the meaning of the occupation, I will tell you with great confidence: a mother dropping her daughter from a window to save her life.

But time is liable to ease any paradox and dispel any admiration. The occupation resembles the *Thousand and One Nights*. Every day brings a new story, a new adventure that makes you forget what came before and prepare for what comes after. The complex bureaucratic machine is the Scheherazade of our era. From among its shirtfronts policies emerge, and by way of its tent flaps stories are generated: in the line of cars at the checkpoint; in the ambulance that carries a patient who will die of waiting (I almost wrote *of boredom*, but that metaphor would be excessive here); in a demonstration overrun with conquering military jeeps; in the liaison office that refuses, in bulk, entry permits to Israel for medical care, except for those willing to collaborate with the machine; in the drinking water that "takes its time" in coming and going; in the waste of two hours of your life at the impromptu checkpoint, which you later find out was arbitrary and no longer meant anything to anyone. What a humiliation, to be held up at an arbitrary checkpoint!

We arrive at Khirbet Umm al-Khair in the Hebron Hills and

see what remains of the temporary residential buildings after their demolition by the Israeli Civil Administration's bulldozers a few days before. The elderly father of the family is shouting nonstop. *I am an Arab, son of this land.* I can scarcely understand his screaming. He jumps from one delegation member to another, shouting out his pain and his story. He longs to tell his tale. *They came . . . they demolished . . . they came . . . they demolished . . . look at the children . . . look at the settlers' houses around us.* But he does not weep or break down. He shouts with rage, with ferocity. He wants the world to see and hear. I take him aside and start filming a video of him so that we can allow the rest of the delegation to walk around and get the clear details from the other family members who speak English or Hebrew. I hold the camera in front of him for more than twenty minutes as he recites his rapid monologue, frenziedly, without pausing for a moment. My arm is getting tired, my eye is getting tired of looking through the lens, then I realize I am a little bored. This discovery kills me. Is it possible for one to feel boredom from hearing the story of a man in his seventies whose home was demolished just days ago, for the . . . no one knows, how many times? Then I am struck by this sad, futile situation: one Palestinian shouting into the camera of another Palestinian what we must shout to the whole world. Once again, we leap into a small site and speak among ourselves. Our language is not understood, our body language is not loved, our shouting is uncivilized. And suddenly my eyes fill with tears and I feel sorrow, shame, and bitterness. Despite my endless promises to the family members to post their father's oration on my Facebook page, I have not done it. It would provoke laughter, no question. No one would understand half his words or his sentences, and no neutral or distant viewer could endure his tense body movements and his fierce jumping up and down. Forgive me, old man, I don't know which is harder on you: people seeing you and laughing at you, or me hiding you from them, not giving even a single one of them the opportunity to understand you.

The occupation bloats time.

The occupation is the death of meaning.

(TRANSLATED FROM THE ARABIC BY PETER THEROUX)

GIANT IN A CAGE

MICHAEL CHABON

1.

The tallest man in Ramallah offered to give us a tour of his cage. We would not even have to leave our table at Rukab's Ice Cream, on Rukab Street; all he needed to do was reach into his pocket. At nearly two meters—six feet four—Sam Bahour might well have been the tallest man in the whole West Bank, but his cage was constructed so ingeniously that it could fit into a leather billfold.

"Now, what do I mean, 'my cage'?" He spoke with emphatic patience, like a remedial math instructor, a man well practiced in keeping his cool. With his large, dignified head, hairless on top and heavy at the jawline, with his deep-set dark eyes and the note of restraint that often crept into his voice, Sam had something that reminded me of Edgar Kennedy in the old Hal Roach comedies, the master of the slow burn. "Sam," he said, pretending to be us, his visitors, we innocents abroad, "what is this cage you're talking about? We saw the checkpoints. We saw the separation barrier. Is that what you mean by cage?"

Some of us laughed; he had us down. What did we know about cages? When we finished our ice cream—a gaudy, sticky business in Ramallah, where the recipe is an Ottoman vestige, intensely colored and thickened with tree gum—we would pile back into our hired bus and return to the liberty we had not earned and were free to squander.

"Yes, that's part of what I mean," he said, answering the question he had posed on our behalf. "But there is more than that."

Sam Bahour took the leather billfold out of the pocket of his dark blue warm-up jacket and held it up for our inspection. It bulged like a paperback that had fallen into a bathtub. When he dropped it onto the tabletop it landed with a law book thump. It was a book of evidence, proof that the cage he lived in was neither a metaphor nor simply a matter of four hundred miles of concrete and razor wire.

"In 1994, after Oslo," Sam said, "my wife and I decided to move back here." They had been married for a year, at that point, and decided to apply to the Israeli government for residency in Palestine "under a policy they called family reunification." He flipped open the billfold and took out a passport with a familiar dark blue cover. "As an American citizen, I entered as a tourist, on a three-month visa."

Sam Bahour was born in Youngstown, in 1964. His mother is a second-generation Ohioan of Lebanese Christian descent; his father emigrated to the United States from the town of al-Bireh, then under Jordanian control, in 1957. After spending a few unhappy years working for relatives as a traveling salesman in the rural South ("Basically a peddler," in Sam's words, "selling cheap goods to poor people at like a two hundred percent markup; it really bothered him"), Sam's father settled in Youngstown, with its sizable Arab population. He bought the first of a series of independent grocery stores he would own and operate over the course of his career, got married, became a citizen, had a couple of kids, worked hard, made good.

A few things Sam said about his father seemed to suggest that though the elder Bahour settled and prospered in Ohio, he did not entirely lose himself in the embrace of his adopted country. When Sam was born his father had named him Bilal, after the most loyal of the Prophet's companions. But when non-Muslim neighbors in Youngstown shortened Bilal to "Billy," Sam's father—whose name was the American-sounding but authentically Arabic Sami—had his young son's name legally changed to match his own. The freedom to return home that an American passport would afford, if only for three months at a time, had been among his motivations for marrying Sam's mother and becoming a naturalized citizen. Some key part of the man—words like *heart, mind,* and *spirit* are only idioms, approximations—never left the house on Ma'arif Street where he had been born and raised, in the al-Bireh neighborhood of al-Sharafa, which belonged not to the Ottomans, the British, the Hashemites, or the Israelis but only to the people who lived in it.

"I was brought up in a household that lived and ate and slept Palestine," Sam would tell me, a couple of days after our first meeting over ice cream at Rakub's. "I lived in Youngstown, where I didn't know most of my neighbors, but I could tell you everybody in my neighborhood here in Ramallah. That's an odd kind of way to grow up."

That enchanted blue American passport, part skeleton key, part protective force field, could work powerful three-month spells, both for Sam's father and for Sam, once he and his Jerusalem-born wife, Abeer Barghouty, decided to try to make a life in al-Bireh. For thirteen years after his application for a residency card under the Israeli-controlled family reunification policy, Sam raised his daughters, built a number of businesses (telecommunications, retail development, consulting), worked for himself and his partners, for his clients and for the future of his half-born country, and lived a Palestinian life, all in tourist-visa tablespoonfuls, ninety days at a time. But in 2006, for reasons that remain mysterious, the magic embedded in his US passport abruptly ran out. Returning to the West Bank from a visa-renewing trip to Jordan, Sam handed over his passport to an Israeli border officer, expecting the routine ninety-day rubber stamp. But when the passport was returned to him Sam saw that alongside the stamp, in Arabic, Hebrew, and English, the officer had handwritten the words *last permit.* Once this final allotment of ninety days ran out, Sam would no longer have permission to stay in the West Bank or Israel, and when he left—left his home, his family, his business, his community, and everything he had worked to build over the past thirteen years—he would not be permitted to return.

"So I lobbied at very significant levels," he explained, flipping to the passport's back pages, "but they were only able to get me renewals—somebody got me two months, somebody got me one month. Very troubling. And then out of the blue I got a call . . . and they say, 'Your residency card has been issued.' I applied in 1993, the call came in 2009. I said, 'Oh, yeah, I did apply, I remember.'"

He rolled his eyes upward in a pantomime of searching for a dim and ancient recollection, reenacting the moment. He waited, inviting us to find comedy in this epic feat of bureaucratic sluggishness, showing us that he maintained a sense of humor about his predicament, the way you might maintain a vintage car or a gravel road. It required diligence, effort, and will.

"So they say, it's been issued, come down to the office and pick it up. And bring your passport. And I hung up the phone and I told my wife, 'This is problematic. What do they want with my passport?' Because like you, I travel a lot, and I actually read the fine print." He turned to the fifth page in his passport, where the bearer was reminded that his passport was the property of the US government. "This isn't ours. This is the State Department's. So it's not mine to give to anybody. But I took a chance. I took my passport, I drove my yellow-plated car to this office."

One of the first things a visitor to the West Bank learns to notice is the color-coding of vehicle license plates. On cars owned by Palestinians they are white; the plates of Israelis (or licensed tourists) are yellow. Yellow gives drivers access, in their brand-new Hyundais or Skodas, to a system of excellent highways that bypass and isolate the towns and villages of the occupied, with their white plates, and their older cars, and their pitted blacktops thwarted by checkpoints and roadblocks. For the sixteen years of his life as an American tourist in the West Bank, Sam drove a car with yellow plates.

"So I give the lady my passport." He flipped through the pages till he reached a stamped and printed label some clerical hand had pasted in at the back. "It took two seconds. They stamp it, and they say, 'Congratulations, here's your ID.' First, I look, I say, '*What the fuck did they just do to my passport?*'" He turned to one of the Israelis in our party. "You read Hebrew, I don't, but I know it says, 'The holder of this passport has been issued a West Bank residency card.'

And they take the number of my residency card, and they place it here, in my American passport. Let me tell you what that means. It means that for all intents and purposes, this lady with her stamp has just invalidated my American status here. Because say I get in the bus with you now, and go back to Jerusalem, and a soldier finds this stamp? He's not going to find a visa anymore. He's going to say, 'Wait a minute. You've been identified as a Palestinian in our eyes. Where's your ID?'

"At this point I have three options. One, play stupid American, I don't know what you're talking about. What do you mean, ID? Not too smart, they take my passport, look at the ID number here, enter it on the computer, turn the screen around, and say, 'Does that person look familiar?'

"The second option: 'I'm sorry, Officer, I forgot my ID at home.' Not smart. Anybody that's been issued an ID, especially if you are a male, has to have it with him at all times. Without an ID, I can be administratively detained for six months."

Administrative detention—imprisonment without charge or finite term—is among the most feared of the specters stalking everyday Palestinian life. The Fourth Geneva Convention, the finest flower of the Nazi defeat, strictly and explicitly forbids it, except under the most extraordinary circumstances. One may safely assume that in the view of the convention's drafters, having left one's ID in one's other pants would likely not merit the suspension of habeas corpus.

"So, third option, let's say I show this officer my ID." From the billfold he now took out a bifold plastic case, dark green, and unfolded it to reveal his identity card behind its clear plastic window. It looked like a typical driver's license or photo ID, thumbnail headshot of Sam, text printed Hebrew and Arabic characters, moiré of anti-counterfeit security printing. "He opens the ID, what does he find? Arabic so we can understand, Hebrew so the issuer can understand. It has my place of birth, my date of birth, my religion—for some reason—and: what's my cage."

Most of us understood that he was joking, but it seemed like an angry joke. After a pause, there was a chuckle or two around the table.

"Actually it doesn't say *cage*, it says *place of residence*. But there is no part of area A"—Sam was referring to the archipelago of major Palestinian population centers that has been strewn by Oslo II across the sea of occupation—"which is not an open-air cage, surrounded by fences, walls, checkpoints, military installations, et cetera. So I'm from the cage of Ramallah, actually it says the cage of al-Bireh, very precise. It means I can't be in the cage of Gaza, but Gaza is just as occupied. I can't be in the cage of East Jerusalem, but East Jerusalem is just as occupied. I can't even be in forty percent of the Jordan Valley, which is off limits to anyone who doesn't live in the Jordan Valley.

"So there I am, in the office, with this new little stamp in my American passport. I can't use the airport, I can't go to Tel Aviv University, where I used to be a graduate student, even though as a US citizen, getting my MBA there, I had no problem going and coming. I went back to my car, and I thought, Do I take my car home? Or do I take a taxi? Why would I say that, right? It's my car. It belongs to me, I paid for it with my money. Why? Because anyone that has one of these"—he pointed to the stamp again—"is not allowed to drive a yellow-plated car.

"And now, all of a sudden, I start to feel what it's like to be a full-scale Palestinian."

2.

Two days later I met Sam at his house, in al-Bireh. In its present form it was a high, flat-topped box of pale gray stone, three stories tall, with nine arched windows—three per floor—stacked in a tic-tac-toe grid. It was the house that Sami Bahour, Sam's father, had been born and grown up in, enlarged by the addition of the third story to accommodate the elder Bahours during their regular visits; the ground-floor tenants were Sam's in-laws. I knew that traditional Arab houses, even those of wealthy families, often show a deliberately plain face to the world. Entering the home of a man who had been successful for a long time in a number of business ventures, I wondered if I were in for Levantine extravagance, or American-style glitz. But the interior of Sam's home was no fancier than the exterior and not very different from the kind of thing I had seen in the homes of much less prosperous families in other parts of the West Bank: sparse stucco walls, rugs scattered on the tile floors, somber furniture, the surprising cool and shadow of vernacular houses in hot countries. I wondered if I ought to ascribe this relative austerity to local custom, personal modesty, or simply the relative nature of wealth in a culture of enforced scarcity where the readiest treasure is stored not in banks, but in black PVC cisterns on the roof.

While we sat in a small enclosed porch overlooking the street, and I drank the coffee that seemed to serve as emblem, vehicle, and baseline of hospitality in every Palestinian home, Sam presented the day's schedule. We would be driving to Nablus, where he had an appointment to meet the owner of a soap factory, and along the way would be paying a visit to a newly opened Bravo supermarket there. Sam apologized; he was afraid it didn't sound like a very exciting day. I assured him, truthfully, that the most fascinating places to visit in foreign countries were often the ones, like supermarkets, that were superficially most similar to places at home, and that it was always interesting to see how common household objects were manufactured; but there was more to it than that. I was now sitting in a house, and soon I would be driving in a car, and then I would be standing in a supermarket, and after that touring a soap factory, in a country that was living under military occupation. Anything that we did today would partake of the novelty—to me—of that circumstance.

Flushing a toilet, for example. Before we set off for what might, depending on the whim of IDF roadblocks, turn out to be a long drive, I thought I had better use the Bahours' bathroom. When I pulled the handle I heard the water flowing down through the pipe from one of the cisterns on the roof. I considered the vulnerability and irregularity of the water supply in Palestine, and the disproportionate splurging of my fellow Jews, running their dishwashers and washing machines and lawn sprinklers, over in the hilltop settlement, amply furnished with water from confiscated wells and expropriated aquifers, that the Bahours were obliged to contemplate every time they looked out their back windows. We went downstairs and climbed into Sam's car, a maroon 2008 Mazda, with its white plates.

"We'll see what happens," Sam said. "Nablus is always an adventure. It could be almost a straight shot, it could be a lot of checkpoints, you never know. When I first relocated here, the telecommunications company I worked for was based in Nablus." Sam had studied computer technology at Youngstown State University, and had been tempted to make the leap, in 1993, by provisions in the Oslo accords for some degree of Palestinian control over telecommunication operations. "That's where the owners were, so that's where we built the company. I made the drive every day, morning and night. So for me, Nablus is forty minutes away. It's supposed to be a straight shot, this road we're driving on is actually called the Nablus Road, it goes from here to Nablus. Only now it doesn't, not directly. We have to make a detour to the east . . . passing through checkpoints. And it's going to take longer than forty minutes. Or it might not. You never know."

I checked the time on my phone and saw that, thanks to the cellular tower in the settlement on the hilltop behind the Bahours' house, I had a strong 4G signal through Cellcom, an Israeli carrier whose SIM card I had purchased on landing at Ben Gurion Airport. If I had been a law-abiding Palestinian I would have had only an Edge, or 2G, connection, since Israel would not allocate the electromagnetic spectrum necessary for Palestinian carriers to provide 4G or even 3G service.

"They say what they always say," Sam told me when I asked about Israeli restrictions on Palestinian bandwidth. "'Security.'" If part of the business of tyranny is to bankrupt certain words of meaning, then in Israel and Palestine under occupation the most destitute word is probably *security*. Sam's voice took on that Edgar Kennedy note of effortful forbearance. "Of course, any Palestinian can go to the store, buy an Israeli SIM card, plug it in, get a signal from a settlement. We have 3G, so what exactly is the security concern?"

Sam explained that American presidents, envoys, and secretaries of state, from both parties, going back as far as Condoleezza Rice, had seen the absurdity of the argument against licensing the 3G spectrum because of "security" and had, one after the other—"Rice,

Bush, Obama, Kerry, Mitchell, the whole nine yards"—waded into the weeds of the issue, to no effect. "Meanwhile, the rest of the world is moving on to 5G now, here we are, still begging the Israeli side for 3G service. It's almost embarrassing."

I wondered if the "security" at issue in this instance might not be the security of revenue flowing from Palestinian pockets to Israeli cellular providers, whose advantage in bandwidth, at least, was being protected by the Israeli government. Sam conceded that might be part of it. There is no question that the near-total dominance over Palestinian markets enjoyed by Israeli companies, like Israel's control over the exploitation of Palestinian land, water, and mineral resources, is an important source of revenue for Israel. The occupation of the West Bank and Gaza has been so incredibly expensive—in 2010, *Newsweek* magazine estimated the total cost since 1967 to be in the neighborhood of ninety billion dollars—that one could hardly blame the Israeli government, Sam observed dryly, for trying to make a little money off it. But his next words made me think that from his point of view my cynicism came a little too easily, that it might, in its way, be as unearned as my liberty.

"The politicians who are supposed to be solving the greater conflict have all, over time, been dragged into this, really, it's a side discussion, with Israel," he said. "'Let the Palestinians have their 3G frequency.' The Israelis, in their excellent strategizing, pulled the politicians away from the main topic, into something which is minor. Instead of . . . solving the conflict."

Despite the restrictions imposed on Palestinian providers and the unfair competitive advantage of unfettered Israeli companies, PALTEL, the telecom company that Sam set up after his arrival in Palestine, managed to grow and to thrive, becoming Palestine's largest private-sector employer. "It became overly successful," Sam said, and its success was actually one of the reasons for Sam's decision, in 1997, to move on and try something new. He was as uncomfortable "making excessive profit on a people who are occupied" as his father had been forty years earlier, working Southern backroads and Appalachian hollers for the family business, getting twenty-five, thirty, or even forty dollars, on a good day, for a five-dollar Japanese wristwatch. "I didn't

come here to make a million dollars," Sam told me. "Not every busi-
nessman or investor has that kind of mind-set."

3.

The next stop on Sam Bahour's pocket tour of his cage, after the
Palestinian identity card and the stamp in his US passport that had
put an end to his entering and leaving the occupied territories as an
American citizen, turned out to be a slip of printed paper, heavily
watermarked and intricately Spirographed, somewhere between an
employee ID badge and a modern banknote.

"I'm a business consultant, right?" he said, signaling to the young
man working the counter at Rukab's. We had finished our strangely
malleable, taffy-like ice cream, all those colorful little scoops dyed in
a mad Muppets palette. It was time for coffee. "I travel. For the work
I do, I have a lot of business in Jerusalem. Obviously, I'm going to
want to go to Jerusalem. But now I'm a full-scale Palestinian, right?
I have to stay in my Ramallah cage, I'm not allowed to go into the
Jerusalem cage. So what do I do?"

The counterman approached, a certain deference unmistakable in
his manner toward Sam. He leaned in with a soft Arabic word of in-
quiry and Sam softly ordered coffee around the table. Speaking English
to his visitors—most of us Americans like him—Sam seemed entirely
a businessman from Youngstown, Ohio, a perfect Rotarian, genial,
expansive, eloquent, an unexpected touch of the professor about him.
But ordering coffee in his soft-spoken Arabic, or striding on his long
stems through the center of Ramallah, at least a head taller than all the
men around him, many of whom had seemed to show him the same
gentle deference as the counterman at Rukab's, there was something
princely about Sam Bahour. A prince in exile, I thought, then, No,
that's wrong, of course; he's home, he's not in exile. Yet somehow the
word seemed to accord with his demeanor. He had left Youngstown
behind him—the city of his birth and education, where he had first
met his wife, where his parents and his sister still lived—to come and
live in the house of his forefathers, in the neighborhood that had been

the home of his imagination as a child. But did he really feel that he belonged in al-Bireh? More important, did he feel—could any "full-scale Palestinian" feel—that al-Bireh, ringed by Israeli settlements and checkpoints, belonged to him?

"So I look around the Ramallah business community," he told us, resuming the tour, "and look, I see people going to Jerusalem. I'm like, 'How do you do that? I was told I could not go to Jerusalem.' And they said, 'No, Sam, there's something called the permit system.' What's the permit system? You bring an invitation letter from someone in Jerusalem or Israel, fill out a stupid one-page application, go to the Israeli military, take your ID with you, and you apply, and either you get a permit, or you don't."

He reached into the billfold again and took out a second note of the strange tender of his captivity. He took out another, and then a third. He dug around with his fingers and came out with a whole little pile of them, a jackpot of winning tickets in a bitter lottery, all of them expired.

"These are all permits," he said. "I have many more tens of them at home. I've promised my kids that I would wallpaper my office with permits." It was a laugh line—probably an old one—but he didn't sound like he really thought it was funny. We laughed at it nevertheless. "A permit is a single piece of paper issued by the same people that issued this." He held up the green sleeve that held his identity card. "But a permit, usually, is only good for one day, from five o'clock in the morning until seven o'clock at night. I can use it to travel to Jerusalem, as long as I'm back by seven. If I don't come back at seven p.m., they could arrest me. If I got caught coming in late, and the soldier who caught me wanted to arrest me, I would never get a permit again."

The counterman returned with a tray crowded with coffee in tiny cups. Sam watched approvingly as the counterman distributed them to everyone who had wanted coffee.

"So I start getting permits. It's a headache, and it takes a lot of time—the control of time is one of the biggest weapons of the occupation. It takes a day to apply, a day to get the answer. Imagine how hard it is to make an appointment for a business meeting when it takes two days to get the permit—and they might say no. And then a whole day for the trip to Jerusalem, because you have to go on foot. So I can never make an appointment for an exact time, I can't make a two p.m. meeting. I have to say, 'I'll meet you between twelve and three.'

"But it's not like I go to Jerusalem often. I have diabetes, you know what that means, right? It means, guaranteed, you have to use the restroom! If I get stuck at the checkpoint and there's fifty people behind me, and fifty people in front of me, I get frustrated, because when I have to use the restroom, I can't go back the way I came, and of course I can't go forward. You're in an area that is as wide as this." He held up his hands separated by a gap the width of his shoulders. "There's a gate in front of you, a gate behind you. A fence all around you. You don't turn around when you have fifty people behind you, waiting, one by one, and start pushing, saying, 'Please, back up, I need to use the restroom.' It doesn't work like that. These are people who have to cross every day. I think I'm frustrated? They are frustrated to the *n*th degree.

"So, I don't go very often." He slid the pile of expired permits back into the billfold. "I stay in my Ramallah cage, right? The way I'm supposed to."

If Youngstown, Ohio, had not felt like home because it was not al-Bireh, Palestine, al-Bireh could never feel like home as long as it was under occupation. Sam Bahour was an imposing man with a quietly arresting presence who towered over the people around him, but he was not a prince in exile. He was a giant in a cage.

4.

Not long after leaving PALTEL, Sam was approached by some investors who had purchased land in Ramallah and were looking to build a Western-style supermarket. It would be the first of its kind in Palestine. They wanted Sam's help putting the project together.

"The first thing I asked was, 'Why me?' They said, 'We happen to have looked at your CV; the last thing on your CV before you came here is that you worked for ten years for your dad, and your dad is a grocer.' I said, 'Yeah, you're right.'" In his recounting of the moment the admission sounded reluctant. "That's a good lesson," he told me, in a rueful aside, "always delete the last thing on your CV." I laughed and Sam, just barely, smiled. "They said, 'It's a year-and-a-half commitment, put it together, just be project manager for us.'"

The property they had in mind was in al-Bireh. It was in a part of town called al-Balou that the municipality had slated for development as a commercial district. Land there was expensive. Sam realized that, given real estate costs, a supermarket alone could never be profitable. Palestinians bought their food in street markets and specialty shops, from butchers and bakers and fruiterers; one-stop shopping at a supermarket might take time to catch on. So he persuaded the investors to imagine something even more unprecedented: a shopping plaza, a minimall that would incorporate a number of separate retail outlets and restaurants of various kinds—a Cineplex, a consumer electronics shop, a Domino's Pizza—anchored by the proposed new supermarket. There would be an indoor play area, a themed "fun zone" with climbing tubes and ball pits, where parents could amuse their children or safely park them while they shopped. In Sam's vision, as he laid it out for the investors, this would be only the first of a half-dozen or more Plazas they might, in time, put up across the nation that seemed, after the intifada, to be imminent. As he re-created it for me so many years later, it was still possible, despite all the ensuing compromises, conflicts, heartbreaks, and disillusionments, to catch an echo of the audacity, the thrilling scope, the sheer hopefulness, inherent in Sam's pitch to the investors.

"We decided to call the supermarket 'Bravo,'" Sam told me, his smile less weary now, more sly. "Because with what we went through to build it, we deserved some congratulations."

The architects' original plan for the first proposed Plaza showed a U-shaped structure, but as the second intifada broke out and costs escalated—every nail and plank and length of rebar had to be imported from Israel, finessed through the labyrinth of checkpoints and regulations, with deliveries constantly subject to delay, diversion, cancellation—Sam was obliged to amputate one of the U's legs, and settle for an L. Then there turned out not to be enough money to engineer the structure adequately to include the Cineplex; the Cineplex was dropped from the plan. The architects' design called for the Plaza, like any self-respecting building in Ramallah, to be clad in the locally quarried limestone known as Jerusalem stone, but it was going to take a lot of limestone to cover so large a building (even after it had lost a leg)—more limestone, unfortunately, than the project could afford.

The building site lay between two streets that had been laid out but not yet rezoned as commercial; one was set to be a main drag and the other a service road. Sam shocked the investors by suggesting that only the side of the Plaza facing the main thoroughfare needed to be stone-clad; nobody but teamsters and store employees was ever going to see the place from the back. After the investors had recovered from their shock, Sam went to the municipality to confirm which of the as-yet-unbuilt streets would be the principal thoroughfare. He oriented the unclad, plain-stucco rear of the structure accordingly. No sooner was the Plaza completed than, all along the alleged "service road," glittery new office buildings and commercial spaces started to crop up. The municipality, it turned out, had misinformed Sam, or changed its mind; and so the first supermarket-anchored shopping plaza ever built in Palestine shows its naked backside to the world.

It wasn't just artificially inflated building costs and the contortions of a stunted and questionable bureaucracy; every aspect of getting the first Bravo store up and running was made harder by the occupation. A properly modern supermarket must have a modern point-of-sale system, and while internationally there were many vendors to choose among, none was willing to take on the challenge of providing long-distance after-sale support to the occupied territory, not in the thick of an armed uprising. Through his solid business contacts—he holds an MBA from Tel Aviv University—Sam found a "local" firm, Retalix, based in Ra'anana, Israel, that was prepared to commit to Bravo. When the time came to install the software, however, none of Retalix's Israeli IT staff was permitted to travel to al-Bireh to perform the installation.

"So, being an IT person, even though the GM of the company

shouldn't be doing this, I became the liaison by phone, by fax, by e-mail, between the supplier over there, and the technical people on my side. And we did it, it was the first retail bar code system in Palestine. The head of their company, a company with customers all around the world, he was so amazed that we could do something like that, in the middle of an armed uprising, they put it in their annual report; it said, 'We have entered the Middle East.'"

The memory tickled Sam, though he said that if he were to do it today, he would not use Israeli suppliers, as he also did for the store's refrigeration systems. "Today I would go to NCR, in Texas. Because today I have a choice, given that intifada conditions have waned, and I understand what it means to be dependent on Israel. That's a political decision. If you go with the business decision, by design of Israeli strategy, it will take you to their market, because they've created all these obstacles to going outside their market. And I actually think that's part of the reason, for them, for continuing the occupation. Somebody's benefiting from it, to the tune of five billion dollars a year."

As for the merchandise that was to be scanned and inventoried by the Retalix software, the same labyrinth of barriers—legal, military, and physical—that had driven up the price of construction also caused constant headaches with inventory. Shipments of goods from Israel or Israeli ports arrived late, spoiled, or not at all. Even when they showed up whole and on time they still arrived freighted with politics and tainted by the bitter flavor of occupation. Sometime before the first Ramallah Bravo opened for business, Sam was approached by "local activists in town" who wanted him to guarantee that the store would not carry any Israeli products.

Sam—an activist himself, arrested for the first time in 1988, along with protesters who chained themselves to a fence outside the Saltsburg, Pennsylvania, headquarters of Federal Laboratories, which manufactured and sold the tear gas used by the Israeli army against Palestinian civilians—had been expecting a visit of this sort. Refraining from pointing out that, given the state of the Palestinian food industry, it would be impossible to stock a modern supermarket with only produce and foodstuffs manufactured in Palestine, Sam—

who was the project manager, not the owner or operator—framed the matter to the activists as one of official Palestinian policy. He offered to accompany the activists to meet with the Palestinian Authority. Together, he suggested, perhaps they might persuade the PA to set a bold new policy prohibiting the sale by any Palestinian retailer of any Israeli products. They should in no way be discouraged, he further suggested, by the undeniable fact, in the unlikely event the PA were willing to take such a step, that it would be impossible to enforce.

While his fellow activists chewed over this mildly disingenuous invitation, Sam said he could assure them, on behalf of the investors, that unlike other grocers throughout the occupied territories, Bravo would refuse to carry any goods grown or manufactured in the settlements. He also came up with an idea he thought might appeal to them: Bravo would strive, whenever possible, to offer a local Palestinian alternative to every Israeli or foreign item, and would highlight these local products by means of end-cap displays and signage, in particular the small, detachable "shelf talkers" that his father's Youngstown grocery stores had used to draw shoppers' attention to specials, new items, and the like.

The activists went away reasonably satisfied, and the political pressure eased; construction proceeded. Costs were cut, frills discarded, workarounds found. The U became an L, the Plaza was left half-naked. Slowly, fitfully, the concrete-and-glass contours of Sam Bahour's vision began to be discernible, a gleaming, air-conditioned foretaste of what the modern nation of Palestine might by and by become.

Then Sharon went to the Temple Mount, and the second intifada erupted, vastly more brutal, more violent, more destabilizing, than the first.

"That's when it became not work, but a challenge," Sam said. Given everything Sam had already told me about the reversals, obstacles, and difficulties he had faced on the Plaza project, this struck me as setting the bar awfully high for deeming something a *challenge*. The word must mean something different for him, I thought, at least in this context. It must have some more profound, or more personal, connotation. "So that's when I told the owners, I will not leave this project until it's up and running. And that took five years to do."

He paused, as if allowing himself to dwell again, for a moment, in that challenging time.

"At one point," he resumed, "the owners came to me and said, 'Sam, we love you, but you're ordering a glass facade for your mall, and if you haven't noticed, there are F-16s bombing outside.' So I made a deal with them, and I said, 'I will not ask you for any more money. Let me take the investment you've made and try to make something out of it. You're going to lose it, anyway.'"

I wondered if Sam had actually offered such an openly pessimistic assessment to the investors, or if he were paraphrasing what he had felt, what they had all felt but were perhaps afraid to express, about the probable fate of the Plaza project, and the investors' money, in that dark and violent hour. *You're going to lose it, anyway*: I wondered if any project manager in the history of real estate development had ever provided his investors with a more bleak, even nihilistic argument in the hope of keeping his job and ensuring that his budget not be cut any further. It went beyond nihilism, I thought; it summed up, with perfect succinctness, the existential quest on which, because he'd never deleted that line in his CV, Sam Bahour had embarked. He wasn't just trying to build a supermarket in what had become a war zone. He was making it out of glass. It made me think of Klaus Kinski's character in *Fitzcarraldo*, dragging a steamboat over a mountain in order to bring opera to the Amazon jungle.

"I think the investors just said to themselves, 'Look, clearly he's just a little off balance. Let him work.' And yes, I cut corners in the project, big time. But the project opened. And they were shocked. The place we're going to see today, in Nablus, I didn't do that one, but I think it's the ninth or tenth in the chain. To see it expand that way . . . there is a lot of pride in that."

It seemed a funny way to put it—the pride lay unclaimed in the middle of the sentence like property forgotten in a locker. He said it quietly, with a hint of something that sounded like doubt, or maybe it was wistfulness.

After an hour and a half—slowing down for a few checkpoints, getting lost a few times—we came to the new Nablus Bravo. Built very much on the pattern of Sam's innovations in Ramallah—minus the minimall; apart from the "fun zone" for kids, that part of the vision was never afterward repeated—it had been open only a week. In the middle of a Thursday afternoon it was almost completely deserted. The staff of the new store made a fuss over Sam, who towered over all of them. The store manager seemed to be in awe, and confessed that several years ago he had attended a presentation for young people that "Mister Sam" had given, aimed at energizing and inspiring future business leaders of Palestine. He said that he had been energized, and inspired. Everyone agreed that the new location was off to a fine start. The grand opening had been jammed, and the store got extremely busy three times a day: first thing in the morning, at the end of the workday right before dinnertime, and in the evenings, when entire families came down from the surrounding neighborhood, on the booming outskirts of Nablus, just to hang, to see and be seen.

At the moment, however, Sam and I were almost the only non-employees in the store. Sam showed me how to distinguish among Israel-, Palestine-, and foreign-sourced products, and he pointed out the shelf talkers all over the store drawing shoppers' attention to locally made fare. The decor was Euro-minimalist, white paint and exposed air ducts, big primary-colored signage in simple geometric shapes, sans serif type. The merchandise on offer—cold cereal, packaged rice, processed meats, snacks and baked goods, yogurt and canned soups—was all but indistinguishable from what you would have seen in a supermarket in France or Italy. The air-conditioning was first-rate and it was beautifully cool. Arabic-language pop music drifted from speakers all over the store. It was, convincingly and indisputably, a modern, state-of-the-art supermarket.

"Nice," I told Sam.

"Yeah," he said, and I thought I heard that uncertain, wistful tone again. "Very nice."

Maybe he was just thinking about how long it had been, how distant the vision he had initially pitched to the investors in that time of relative peace and progress between intifadas. Maybe he was thinking about the darkest moment in the history of the project, in the first year of the second intifada, when the IDF, making a sweep, commandeered the construction site, confined Sam and his staff to the basement offices, and for three or four hours used the still-roofless, bare-concrete upper floor of the supermarket building to interrogate Palestinian detainees. Maybe he was reflecting on how he had devoted five years of his life, five years of near-constant struggle, negotiation, improvisation, and compromise in order to bring the convenience of one-stop-shopping and microwaveable suppers to Palestine. But, unlike Werner Herzog's demented Fitzcarraldo, Sam had pulled the job off, without losing his sanity. He had kept his promise to the investors, to the people of the West Bank, to himself; there was a lot of pride in it. Or maybe Sam Bahour was thinking about how, after that first Bravo store with its Palestinian-pride shelf talkers and Israeli-made refrigerators had opened for business in 2003—finally, miraculously—he had gotten out of the supermarket-construction-and-management business, and had never gone back.

"Okay," Sam said. "Soap factory."

5.

"I love soap," said Mr. Tbeleh. We were sitting in his office, up a flight of stairs in the main building of the Nablus Soap Company's headquarters and manufacturing plant. "Really, this is the truth."

He said it very gravely, almost helplessly, like a uxorious man talking about his wife. He was a handsome guy in his mid-sixties, with Mastroianni cheekbones, a brush moustache, and a good head of dark hair. He had in general a sober and unsmiling demeanor, and yet he struck me as the happiest, or at least the most contented person, I had met over the course of a week in East Jerusalem and the West Bank. He was proud of his factory, a tidy compound of corrugated steel and cinder block structures behind a cinder block wall in Beit Furik, outside Nablus. He was proud of the machinery on his soap production line, the most advanced in all of Nablus, a town known since the early Middle Ages for the excellence of its soap. Most of all, he was proud of his soap. It was made, like all "nabulsi" soap, from three main ingredients: olive oil, water, and caustic soda (a mixture of lime and the refined ashes of the saltwort plant). Mr. Tbeleh's oil, according to Mr. Tbeleh, was of the first quality, however, and organic, and his other ingredients were costly and pure. Traditional nabulsi soap, nearly odorless, is cut into small blocks, stamped with the soap makers' trademarks on one side, and wrapped in crinkly paper, but Mr. Tbeleh had introduced fragrances and special ingredients into the recipe—mint, cumin, Dead Sea mud—and his product shipped in a bewildering variety of shapes and packages aimed at various markets around the world: Italy, Japan, France, the Netherlands, the United Kingdom.

For the benefit of Sam Bahour, whose Palestinian American trade organization was considering whether it wanted to help fulfill Mr. Tbeleh's dream of cracking the US market, Mr. Tbeleh went enthusiastically into considerable detail about his soap and its sale and manufacture, but I got the feeling he would have done the same if we had simply happened by. He really did seem to love soap, which was probably a good thing, I reflected, since he seemed to have had relatively little choice in the matter. His family has been in the soap business since 1611. They have been at it for so long that in Nablus, in the trade, a cutter—the man whose job it is to score and break the giant floor-sized slabs of poured and hardened soap into bars—is known as a *tbeleh*. Mr. Tbeleh's destiny seemed to have perfectly converged with his predilection, which was probably the recipe for contentment, I thought—with or without Dead Sea mud. It made me happy just to sit sipping coffee with Mr. Tbeleh, in one of the leather-covered chairs in his dark-paneled office, listening to him go on, in rough but fluent English, about soap. Even when he and Sam got down to business in Arabic I enjoyed the contented rumble of their discussion, though I couldn't follow a word. I had met a lot of brutalized people and heard a lot of awful stories over the course of the week. What they did was overshadowed, what they needed was denied, what they carried was encumbered by the occupation, and what they owned had been broken, diminished, or taken. All the everyday hardships and obstacles they faced were as much the fruit of the occupation as the extraordinary and terrible ones. But the obstacles Mr. Tbeleh complained about were mostly the kind of thing that any small manufacturer anywhere might face: quality control, competition, access to markets, espionage of the purely industrial variety (apparently there were soap Slugworths out to steal his recipes).

Nothing seemed to have ever discouraged him or weakened his resolve, not even—especially not—the occupation. When, in the early days of his modernization plans, he could not obtain the machinery he needed, he designed and built his own. When settlers in nearby settlements seized wells and springs and cut off Mr. Tbeleh's access to water—it takes a lot of water to make soap—he found new sources. He had a favorite English phrase, a kind of signature that he interjected liberally into conversation: *Of course!* Had he designed and built a soap-stamping machine himself, with his own two hands? *Of course!* Did the Israelis interfere with his supply chain, and his access to water? *Of course!* Didn't it take a lot of water to make soap? *Of course!* Would they really pay thirty dollars in Japan for a bar of premium nabulsi soap in premium packaging? *Of course!* Everything, to Mr. Tbeleh, seemed to fall into its proper place—however disruptive or aggravating—in the course of things.

As I listened to Mr. Tbeleh talk, and toured the factory floor, where thousands of soap bars stood not in the traditional stacked cones but on special racks, for the months of drying required, I found myself thinking the same thing I had thought while touring East Jerusalem, where well-financed settlers were attempting to drive out the residents of Silwan; or in Hebron, where the local Arab residents had been banned from their own shops and main street; or in Susiya, where the people were forced into makeshift tents after their entire village was seized: These people aren't going anywhere. Was the occupation a grievous injustice on a colossal scale, so brutal and unremitting that it would lead anyone to consider the appealing alternative of fleeing and never coming back? Of course! And yet here they still were, after fifty years of violence and deliberate degradation, listening to reggae music, shopping in their marketplaces, eating their sticky ice cream, and sending their children out to play. Of course.

6.

I had heard that Nablus, in addition to its soap, was known for its excellent *kanafe*. This is a traditional Ottoman pastry, similar to baklava but filled with cheese and wrapped in honey-soaked shredded wheat instead of phyllo. Before Sam and I returned to Ramallah, he said, he would take me to get some kanafe; he knew a good place. But before he could make the correct turn on the road coming back from the soap factory, we came upon a checkpoint that Sam had not been expecting.

A couple of IDF soldiers stood at a fork in the road, squinting in the bright sun, pallid young men with Tavor assault rifles slung over their shoulders looking, like so many Israeli soldiers, as if they had gotten dressed in a dark room and put on someone else's uniform by mistake. I had seen bored young men before—I had been a bored young man—but these guys took the gold. I was reasonably sure they were not going to shoot me or Sam, but if they did at least it would keep them awake. To get me to the promised kanafe, Sam wanted to take the right-hand fork; one of the soldiers—he looked to be about twenty, and the elder of the pair—told Sam, in Arabic, that he would have to take the left. The soldier's tone was curt but not hostile. It bordered on rudeness but he was too bored, for the moment, at least, to step across that border.

"I have a foreigner with me," Sam said, in Youngstown-accented English. "Why can't we go to the right?"

I was oddly relieved that Sam didn't mention the kanafe. Pastry did not seem like an adequate reason to irritate a heavily armed man. The soldier repeated, in Arabic, that Sam would have to go to the left and, in a more helpful tone of voice, he added something in Hebrew. After that he repeated the original dull formula, in Arabic: we would have to go to the left. Meanwhile a car with white plates was coming along the forbidden road from the other side of the checkpoint. The soldiers waved it and its Palestinian driver through without any show of interest, or even attention. That was when Sam did something that seemed to catch the older of the two soldiers by surprise: he asked why.

"Why can't we go to the right?" Sam said. "What is the reason?"

The soldier roused himself from his torpor long enough to shrug one shoulder elaborately and give Sam Bahour a look in which were mingled contempt, incredulity, and suspicion about the state of Sam's sanity. It appeared to have been the stupidest, most pointless, least answerable question anyone had ever asked the soldier. *What kind of dumbass question is that, Shit-for-brains?*, the look seemed to say. "Why?" *How the fuck should I know?*

The soldier had no idea why he had been ordered to come stand with his gun and his somnolent young comrade at this particular fork in this particular road on this particular afternoon, and if he did, the last person with whom he would have shared this explanation was Sam. That was what the look said, in the instant before it vanished and the proper boredom was restored. We went left.

"What did he say, in Hebrew?" I asked Sam, after we had been driving away from the checkpoint, in silence, for almost a minute. The silence on Sam's side of the car endured for another few seconds after I ended mine. When Sam finally spoke, the strangulated Edgar Kennedy tone of restraint in his voice was more pronounced than ever.

"He told me—such a helpful guy—that this road would take us to the very same place as the other way, to the road back to Ramallah. Which is true, except we'll hit it much farther along, and we won't go past where we can get you your kanafe."

I reassured Sam that I could live without kanafe. I tried to make a joke of it—my jones for kanafe, another victim of an unjust system—but Sam didn't seem to be listening, or in the mood for laughing, just then. I had a sudden realization.

"Wait," I said, "is the other road blocked at the far end, too?"

"Of course not," Sam said. "You saw the car? They're letting people through from that end."

"So we could, hold on, we could just take this road to the Ramallah road, then backtrack to that other road a little way, and then come back to where the kanafe is from that end?"

"We could drive all the way back to the checkpoint on that road, and come up right behind those two guys, and then we could beep the horn, and say, 'Look, here we are!' And then turn around and go back. And it would be just like they had let us through the checkpoint. Except that it took forty-five minutes instead of ten." He laughed. It was an irritated-sounding chuckle, and it was followed by another silence. The checkpoint and the soldiers had definitely spoiled Sam's mood.

There had been times, Sam said, at the end of the long pause, at other checkpoints, when he had actually enacted the above-mentioned scenario of circumvention, including the defiant beep, just to point out to soldiers manning a roadblock how useless, pointless, and arbitrary their service was. I wondered how much more irritated he had been on those days than he was right now. Irritated enough to give in, at that level, to futility.

Because of course, I thought, pointlessness was the point of the roadblocks that forced you to make a stop at Z on your way from A to B. Pointlessness was the point of the regulations forbidding access to cellular bandwidth that everybody had access to, of the Byzantine application process to get a permit for a ten-mile journey that would take all day, even though everyone knew that the permit would automatically be granted, except on those days when, for no reason, it was denied. We tend to think of violence as the most naked expression of power but—*of course!*—at its purest, power is fundamentally arbitrary. It obliges you to confront the absurdity of your existence. Violence is just another way of doing that.

I tried to return our conversation and the remainder of our time together to an earlier, less infuriating and humiliating portion of that time. I told Sam how much I had enjoyed meeting Mr. Tbeleh, how encouraging it was to see that a single-minded and determined individual could, through hard work and a touch of obsessiveness, overcome all the difficulties and indignities of the occupation, and find a way to thrive. I was talking about Mr. Tbeleh, but I was probably thinking of Sam, too. I shared with him the sense that had occurred to me, over and over again in East Jerusalem and the West Bank, that the Palestinians were not going anywhere. Listening to

Mr. Tbeleh, I said, had aroused the same certainty in my mind. He and his soap factory were proof of and testimony to the resilience of the Palestinian people.

"Yes," Sam said gravely. "That's our problem. We're too resilient. We can adjust to anything. You put up a roadblock for a while, everybody complains, but then they get used to it. And then when you take it away, they say, 'Ah! Progress!' When all it is, they just got back what they always had a right to, and nobody should have ever been able to take it away from them. That isn't progress at all."

I thought about that, about how much reassurance I had found in the soap factory and in Mr. Tbeleh. Obviously a Palestinian could find reassurance there, too. *Look*, the soap factory says, *it's bad, it's even very bad, but it's not all about administrative detention and collective punishment and bulldozed olive orchards and helpless, wounded men shot dead in the street.* The soap factory said that if you just kept your head down and focused on soap, if you loved soap, you could just make soap; and it would be excellent soap. You would be able to sell it to the Italians and the Japanese. Maybe one day you might sell it at Whole Foods, the way Canaan Fair Trade, a firm in the city of Jenin, does with its olive oil. You could have 3G, or 4G, or 5G. You could have a nice place to drop your kids while you shopped for yogurt from Israel, Nablus, or Greece. You could get from point A to point B, as long as you were willing to go through point Z, forty-five minutes out of your way, for no reason other than it served Israel's purpose to force you to accept a pointless forty-five-minute detour. As long as you were willing to accept, consciously and unconsciously, the arbitrariness that governed every aspect of your life, you could actually get something done.

Suddenly I felt that I understood something that had puzzled me, so far, about the career of Sam Bahour. In objective terms, Sam had prospered at every business he had undertaken, and at every project he had put his hand to since coming to Palestine in 1993. And yet at key moments, it seemed, at the peak of success, at the moment of accomplishment, he had parted ways with his partners or investors. He had set the cup of triumph aside, stood up, and left the table. I had wondered about this all afternoon, but as we drove away from the pointless checkpoint, I thought I understood. In a Palestinian life there were checkpoints everywhere—crossroads, real and figurative, where you were obliged to confront the fundamental futility, under occupation, of any accomplishment, no matter how humble or how splendid, from opening a multimillion-dollar glass shopping plaza in the midst of a violent uprising to restoring your village's access to its ancestral water to keeping your child alive long enough to graduate from Birzeit University.

When Sam said that Palestinians' problem was being too resilient, I saw that accomplishments of this nature—accomplishments like Sam's—were not merely futile; secretly they served Israel's strategic goals. They lent the color of "normal life" to an existence that every day deliberately confronted four and a half million people with the absurdity of their existence, which was determined and defined by the greatest sustained exercise of utterly arbitrary authority the world had ever seen. Under occupation, every success was really a failure, every victory was a defeat, every apparent triumph of the ordinary was really a gesture empty of any significance apart from reinforcing the unlimited power of Israel to make it. That, more than any road-block, checkpoint, border fence, or paper labyrinth of permits and identity cards, was the cage that Sam Bahour lived in. It was the limit of every reach, and the ceiling that he bumped against every time he tried to stretch himself to his full height.

"He does love soap, though," Sam Bahour conceded, thinking back to our meeting with Mr. Tbeleh, in his tidy little kingdom of olive oil and ashes. "He really, really does."

THE LAND IN WINTER

MADELEINE THIEN

If I tell you that the city towards which my journey tends is discontinuous in space and time, now scattered, now more condensed, you must not believe the search for it can stop.
—ITALO CALVINO, *Invisible Cities*

CITIES AND SIGNS

From a hilltop just beyond the checkpoint, I can see the southern boundary between Israel and Palestine. But, eyes moving between map and world, I can find no border, wall, checkpoint, or cut in the earth to mark the Green Line, the pre-1967 boundary. In the aftermath of the Six-Day War, the UN Security Council and the international community reaffirmed this line, which in 1948 had moved 78.5 percent of historic Palestine into Israeli possession, as the border to be maintained "for a just and lasting peace in the Middle East in which every State in the area can live in security."*

---

* United Nations Security Council Resolution 242, adopted unanimously on November 22, 1967. The preamble asserts the "inadmissibility of the acquisition of territory by war and the need to work for a just and lasting peace in the Middle East in which every State in the area can live in security." The first clause of Operative

There is nothing to be seen of it now, and certainly no sign of it here in the South Hebron Hills, where an Israeli traveler would never know he or she had passed the boundary into Palestine.

A little more than an hour from the deep valleys and soaring hills of Jerusalem, this rocky, barren landscape seems to inhabit another time. Even the sky is austere, a pale blue cloth made entirely of heat.

Days after my visit, as I thought aloud about the emotional pull of the South Hebron Hills, the Palestinian writer Raja Shehadeh reminded me, "Don't forget, you're seeing the land in summer. It will look completely different in the winter." I was startled to realize that all I could see was one aspect of a harsh, inhospitable season. Raja could see this alongside its opposite: a floating green, both the withering and the generation of possibilities.

SATURDAY, AND THE SOUTH HEBRON HILLS FLOWED OUT LIKE DEEP waves on the sea, dipped in the colours of straw and dust. A shepherd was being detained, his flock alleged to have crossed into a military buffer zone. Six bulky soldiers stood with their hands draped over their rifles. The border of the closed military zone was a dirt path along the ridge; surrounded by hills, it appeared innocuous as a line of string. An Israeli settlement, Mitzpeh Avigayil, stood on the opposite hilltop, too distant to be clearly seen. The land, just rocks and slope and wind, seemingly bereft of everything but its longevity, made me feel at once insignificant and alive and ancient.

The shepherd, Nael Abu Aram, a Palestinian, was thirty years old, of slender build, with close-cropped hair and a look of quiet containment. Under the blistering sun, we stood together, waiting to see what the soldiers and the police would do. The pages of our notebooks clapped in the wind, pens fell in the dust. Children, who had run up from a neighbouring village, spun around us.

Nael described his life as a quiet and unremarkable one, which changed dramatically in 1998. Since then, the number of times he

---

Paragraph One is, "Withdrawal of Israeli armed forces from territories occupied in recent conflict."

had been detained, arrested, and imprisoned was lost to him. Settlers had attacked his sheep with metal pipes. They shook bottles filled with rocks, which frightened the flock and caused them to disperse. He had been beaten by Israeli Defense Force (IDF) soldiers, border police, and settlers, had his mouth and skin burned by cigarettes, and his skin cut with knives. After one arrest, he was blindfolded and then released, disoriented, on the wrong side of a checkpoint in the middle of the night. Of this encounter, the Israeli newspaper *Haaretz* published video footage of an army commander telling him, "You're not allowed to be here, because this is Mitzpeh Avigayil. You're not allowed to be here. There's a Jewish community here, and you're not allowed near it."* He had been fined numerous times. In 2014, settlers cut down thirty mature olive trees belonging to his family. Last year, his family's crops were burned. Citing security risks to the settlers, he had been warned against coming too close to the military buffer zone, which is not only adjacent to his land, but on land that once belonged to him.

We watched the police officers drive away to their station, inside the settler outpost. The soldiers and the incessant sun remained. More time passed. Finally, having never been charged, Nael was free to go. "Please excuse me," he said. "I'm very tired." He counted the flock and set off, cutting a quick pace across the hills. We followed at a distance. A kilometer later, the sheep made riotous, guttural shouts as they arrived home to water and shade. They leaped comically high, like bouncing balls. It was midday now, the height of summer.

IN ITALO CALVINO'S *INVISIBLE CITIES*, PLACES ARE FOLDED INSIDE OTHER places. Cities are not only what they appear to be, but also what they

---

* Mitzpeh Avigayil is an Israeli settler outpost, illegal under Israeli law. The High Court of Justice ordered a freeze on its development, and in 2003 the outpost was slated for demolition by the Israeli government. The demolition was never carried out; rather, the settlement grew. In 2014, the Israeli government announced procedures to legalize the outpost. Mitzpeh Avigayil borders Nael Abu Aram's land, his property rights to which were recognized by the Israeli courts, but a portion of which was seized by Israel as a "closed military zone."

are subjected to: memory, history, desire, forgetfulness, dreams. The buildings, storehouses of emotion, are far more than mere edifices; they are the visible structures of the human condition. In Israel and Palestine, I thought often of Calvino's seen and unseen places, where the horizontal and vertical axes of history and place bend into the space-time of memory and desire. Of cities, Calvino writes, "Everything imaginable can be dreamed, but even the most unexpected dream is a rebus that conceals a desire or, its reverse, a fear."

Those words were on my mind when I came to Wadi a-Jheish ("Valley of the Little Donkey"), where the concrete rubble was a glaring white. Two weeks earlier, on June 19, 2016, the Israeli army had arrived in the afternoon and bulldozed two buildings. I was surprised to see that the home had not simply been pushed over; it had been carefully, even cleanly, buried under its own rubble. A boy was standing balanced on the loose stones, reminiscent of the Little Prince perched on a moonscape.

Amir, eight years old, had lived here. When I asked him what had happened, he pointed to the rocks. "I lost my clothes. I lost my shoes and we lost our food." The army had not let them retrieve their possessions, and along with their plates, cooking utensils, and personal objects, had buried the family's flour, sugar, and rice underneath the rubble. The two structures had been home to twenty-one people, including fourteen children and teenagers. Bits of Tupperware and a torn, very small pair of pants were visible in the debris.

Amir's smile was troubled. He nonetheless offered up his memory of that day to me like a piece of bread on a plate, like a possession. He took me to see the family's sheep. His three sisters were sitting underneath a truck, inside a slip of shade; the oldest, Wouroud ("Bouquet of Roses"), sixteen years old, joined us. With a video camera borrowed from an uncle, she had filmed the demolition. When I asked if she had been scared, she answered patiently, "Of course."

We talked about school and marriage and life while, beside us, the family's twenty sheep swayed restlessly. I asked Amir what he liked best. "I like to graze," he said. "I like to be with the flock because that's how we make the milk and butter and cheese. I like them." But when he grew up, he wanted to leave and go far away.

"To live somewhere else," I said, assuming that I understood.

"To bring money for my family."

When I asked Wouroud what she liked best, she looked me straight in the eyes. "I just want to live," she replied, shrugging.

I asked what her mother had said to them, after the demolition.

"She said we only had one house, we didn't have an alternative. She was very sad. She said to us, we need help. We were in the sun since this moment, and it was Ramadan."

I was reminded of another Palestinian home I recently saw. Half concrete wall, half tent, yet the makeshift kitchen somehow pristine, under the strict care of two women who cooked the family's meals while children leaped about their skirts. As the temperature soared, women and children lay down on the cool concrete. Tucked away were the bedding, wash buckets, soap, pots and implements, cups and dishes, jars of flour, barley, and sugar, a coffee pot—the necessities for basic family life. It struck me that every demolition carried out by men with bulldozers and guns was a demolition of the world of women, whose lives, already precarious, already exhausting, were destroyed anew.

"In three years, when I get married, I'll need a home for my family," Wouroud said. "What do they want from us? We have to live. We have to exist."

Their village, Wadi a-Jheish, is in Area C of the West Bank. According to the terms of the 1993 Oslo accords, Palestinian residents of Area C are under full Israeli control for security, zoning, and planning. Area C, containing most of the West Bank's natural resources and open spaces, best exemplifies the policy known as "maximum land, minimum Arabs."* Although the number of Israeli settlers in the West Bank has grown by 340,000 in the last forty years, and settlers have been provided with police and military protection as

---

* According to a map from the United Nations Office for the Coordination of Humanitarian Affairs, Occupied Palestinian Territory (OCHA oPt), "Restricting Space in the OPT Area C Map, December 2011," 99 percent of Area C is heavily restricted or off limits to Palestinian development, with 68 percent reserved for Israeli settlements, approximately 21 percent for closed military zones, and 9 percent for nature reserves.

well as connected to Israel's water, electricity, and sanitation services, Palestinian construction—even on land the Israeli courts have recognized as registered to Palestinians—has been curtailed. Area C comprises 60 percent of the land in the West Bank and is home to 300,000 Palestinians. In 2014 only one Palestinian building permit was approved; in 2015, the number was zero. A 2013 World Bank report found that potential revenue for Palestinians in Area C alone, of which 99 percent is currently off limits to Palestinian development, would be a staggering USD 3.4 billion, over a billion dollars more than Palestine's entire current revenue.*

My eyes saw what was before me, but it was so confounding, my mind resisted its credibility.

The question that solidified in my mind was this one: Are the Palestinian people fated to disappear, and does Israel's interaction with this land inevitably rely on the physical control and consequent disappearance of the Palestinians? Is it true that the state of Israel cannot exist if the state of Palestine does? What does it mean, in our contemporary world, to have a promised land?

Yigal Bronner, a professor at the Hebrew University of Jerusalem, answered it this way: "Susiya against Susya, this is the whole story."

CITIES AND NAMES (1)

The Palestinian village of Susiya, located on a rocky escarpment in the South Hebron Hills, does not look like much. Constructed of light metal, the occasional concrete wall, tarps, and canvas, the village is a ragged collection of homes, sheep pens, water filters and cisterns, and a medical clinic. Sustenance comes from the basic storehouse of what the land makes possible: olives, wheat, barley, cucum-

---

* A World Bank report found that potential revenue from Area C for Palestinians would be at least USD 2.2 billion per year, or 23 percent of the Palestinian GDP; the total potential value added would be USD 3.4 billion, or 35 percent of the GDP. See "West Bank and Gaza—Area C and the Future of the Palestinian Economy," World Bank, 2 October 2013.

bers, tobacco, thyme, tomatoes, and grazing land for herds. Given the harshness of its summer and the desertification of its climate, the South Hebron Hills are emblematic of things perpetually at odds yet bound in coexistence: summer and winter, drought and rain, people and land.

Nasser Najawa's grandfather was born in the village of Qary-atayn, a few kilometres on the other side of the Green Line. Unable to return to his home after the founding of Israel, his grandfather took the family to Susiya al-Qadim ("Old Susiya," or Khirbet Su-siya), where he continued a life of herding and agriculture. People relied on rainwater caught from the sky via a network of ancient and modern cisterns. They lived below ground, in caverns hollowed out beneath the rocks. These caves stayed remarkably cool in the summer and dry in the winter, and in the harsher months, the herd stayed underground as well.

In 1986, the Israeli government expropriated the land of Susiya al-Qadim, expelling the twenty-five families and demolishing most of the caverns, citing the presence of the ruins of a synagogue, dating from between AD 400 to 700. The government asserted, "There was no historic Palestinian village at the archaeological site there; that the village consists of only a few seasonal residences for a few families; and the land is necessary for the continuation of the archae-ological work." Yet only four years earlier, Plia Albeck, a key Israeli settlement planner who referred to the settlements as "my children," had surveyed the area and concluded, "There is a formal registration on the land of Khirbet Susiya with the Land Registry, according to which this land, amounting to approximately 3,000 dunam [741 acres] is privately held by many Arab owners. Therefore the area proximal to the synagogue is in all regards privately owned."

Asked if he believed that the archaeologists were telling the truth, Nasser said, "I am not an expert but yes, I believe it." He did not mention other discoveries as well: the ruins of an AD 900 mosque and an AD 1100 Byzantine church. These details I learned only later.

Three years before the excavation, in 1983, the Israeli govern-ment had given the green light to the settlement of Susya, part of three new settlements in the region. The government pledged 20 million shekels to support fifty to sixty Jewish families. In three months in 1990 alone, Israel restricted Palestinian access to 32,545 acres of land in the West Bank by declaring it *miri* ("state land") or part of closed military zones.* (Kiryat Arba, now home to almost eight thousand Jewish settlers, began on land that was confiscated from Palestinians for military use.) In 1991, a Jewish settler shot twelve sheep before turning his M16 on a Palestinian shepherd, Mahmoud al-Nawaja, killing him. Al-Nawaja's son told a journalist, "The settlement has no border. Every year it spreads, each year it is larger than before." Two years later, Musa Suliman Abu Sabha, who, according to conflicting reports may or may not have been carrying a grenade, but whom the Israeli army confirmed was "bound hand and foot" at the time of his death, was shot eight times at close range by a settler, Yoram Skolnick.

In 1986, with the arrival of the archaeological park in Susiya, the villagers relocated to their grazing lands. Four years later, in 1990, a second expulsion took place. David Shulman, a professor at the Hebrew University of Jerusalem, and the recipient of a MacArthur fellowship and the Israel Prize, reported that the villagers were loaded onto trucks by the IDF and deposited fifteen kilometres south, at the edge of the desert. Of the villagers, Shulman wrote, "They have hurt nobody. . . . They led peaceful, if somewhat impoverished lives until the settlers came. Since then, there has been no peace. They are tormented, terrified, incredulous. As am I." Amnesty International reported that 113 tents in Palestinian Susiya were demolished in 1993; and, in 1996, ten inhabited caves were blown up by the IDF.

Nasser grew up in this precarious Susiya. He walked many kilometres, depending on road closures or restricted paths, to attend school each day in the town of Yatta. "I hoped to be like other children," he recalled, "to have a home and go to school easily."

After each removal, the villagers of Susiya rebuilt. Their stubbornness must have driven the settlers mad. But the villagers believed they were on the side of right. What did they possess but their own intimacy with the hills in summer and winter, and those

---

* "State land," a term taken from the Ottoman land-tenure system.

seemingly crucial Ottoman land deeds? Those who have precious little will hold fast to what little they have. Israel did not dispute their ownership; rather, the government argued that building on this land, registered for grazing, required permits. That the Palestinians of Susiya had been evicted from their village without compensation, and were in need of shelter, was immaterial.

On the night of July 2, 2001, Yair Har-Sinai, a Jewish guard, described both as a "pacifist" and as a man who "terrorized the Palestinians" was killed in a fight. The killer did not come from Susiya, but the Israeli military carried out a retaliatory action. That night, forty-five or more people from the area, including Nasser, were rounded up. He was a teenager at the time, utterly terrified. After being interrogated all night, he was released in the morning and walked home.

"I could not see anything," he says. "Everything was demolished. All of my home. Everything. To the ground. The caves. Water cisterns. Everything." With only women and children present, the men having been detained, bulldozers had drilled through the roofs of the caverns and filled them with rubble; cisterns and wells, livestock pens, and tents were gone.

The loss was unbearable, so too the ensuing anger.

THE PATH NASSER CHOSE WOULD HAVE A LASTING IMPACT ON THE FUTURE of Susiya. After the demolitions of 2001, he decided to work with Israeli activists.

CITIES AND NAMES (2)

In 1983, Susya, the Israeli settlement, was established next door to the Palestinian village of Susiya. Under international law, the settlement is in violation of the Fourth Geneva Convention, in which an occupying power cannot transfer civilian population to an occupied territory, and is considered illegal. The Israeli government is the only government in the world that disputes this illegality, despite a ruling of the International Court of Justice. In a 2015 report submitted to the Netanyahu government, the settlers' NGO, Regavim ("Patches of Soil"), a right-wing organization whose stated mission is to "preserve Israel's national lands," calculated that Jewish settlers had built 2,026 structures on private Palestinian property. Back in February 2012, Regavim had petitioned the Israeli Supreme Court to expedite the demolition of Palestinian Susiya, claiming that it was an illegal outpost, a petition that is, as of this writing, very much ongoing.

The Israeli government contends that all structures in Palestinian Susiya have been built without permits and are therefore illegal and subject to demolition. The settlers believe that the South Hebron Hills are part of the biblical heartland of Judea and Samaria, a currently "empty area" that belongs to the Jewish state. Yochai Damri, the chairman of the Har Hevron Regional Council, told the UK *Independent* that it was not the settlers who were newcomers; rather the villagers of Palestinian Susiya had arrived only fifteen years ago. He concluded, "These are criminals who invaded an area that doesn't belong to them." The surrounding land allocated to Israeli Susya by the government is now ten times the size of the settlement itself.

Driving in the West Bank, along a Route 60 altered to provide a highly modern and convenient highway between the settlements, and along which, for long stretches, Palestinians were once forbidden to travel (funneled instead to a network of narrow roads slowed by detours, checkpoints, and barriers, a system the Israeli government named "the fabric of life"), I find it frankly impossible to remember that I'm in Palestine. When we visited the settlement of Kiryat Arba and were confronted by hostile settlers, a man, who proudly told us he had relocated from France five years ago, cried out to his companion, "Ask her where she thinks she's standing! Is she in Israel or Palestine? Then you'll know whose side she's on." I did feel then that perhaps I shouldn't be standing in his park, which contained a memorial celebrating Baruch Goldstein, who in 1994 walked into a place sacred to both Judaism and Islam, the Cave of the Patriarchs (Hebrew), also known as the Sanctuary of Abraham (Arabic), and opened fire in a room that was being used as a mosque, killing 29 Palestinians and wounding 125. I was relieved to depart. The police station here in the settlement of Kiryat Arba is where a Palestinian from the South Hebron Hills must come if she or he wishes to report a crime.

From Route 60, there are two signs, one for Susiya, the archaeological park; and one for Susya, the settlement. There are almost no road signs for the Palestinian villages. Israeli Susya should feel optimistic about its future prospects. The government has offered Palestinian Susiya a piece of land near the boundaries of Yatta (population sixty-four thousand), which would effectively move them into Area A, where more than 90 percent of Palestinians live. I have written earlier about the difficulty of aligning what one reads on a map and what one observes on the land and roads themselves, but there is one important detail in which both suddenly cohere: the highly populated Areas A and B are the cramped spaces of Palestinian life. Home to more than two-and-a-half million Palestinians, and including the cities of Ramallah, Hebron, Bethlehem, Nablus, Yatta, and others, it has been subdivided into 166 separate units that have no territorial contiguity. In other words, they are like shattered glass. Encircling each shard are long lines of Israeli settlements. Where the shape of Palestine, according to the Green Line, once appeared like a broad river, now it is a handful of pools, cut off from one another, slowly evaporating. Palestinian Susiya is a droplet being diverted into the nearest pool.

I spent a night in Palestinian Susiya, gazing up at Israeli Susya. I had some childish idea that, from this holy and beautiful landscape, I would see the immensity of the sky and the blanket of stars. As night fell, I sat on the rocky escarpment with Nasser's son, Ahmed, who attempted to teach me to count to ten in Arabic. His father scrolled idly on his phone. The two places, Susya and Susiya, are literally one above the other. I could walk uphill and be in Israeli Susya within five minutes. Around us, dogs barked. The voices of women came and went. The evening sun diminished and was gone.

All night, Israeli Susya glowed. Its houses, perimeter roads, and guard stations, connected to the electricity grid, were powerfully, warmly lit. Palestinian Susiya, meanwhile, deemed illegal, was barred from connecting to the power supply. Its electricity came from solar panels donated by a German NGO and installed by an Israeli NGO, its water filters from Ireland, also installed by an Israeli NGO, its medical clinic from Australia, and its school from Spain, resulting in an unlikely cosmopolitanism. Prior to the solar panels, villagers would go to the town of Yatta to charge their phones. The visual contrast was crushing: light above, dark below. The future, the past. Safety, the wild. I couldn't make out the stars. The sky was too well lit, as if we were on the outskirts of a bustling American town.

I fell asleep reading Calvino by the light of my phone—"It is the desperate moment when we discover that this empire, which had seemed to us the sum of all wonders, is an endless, formless ruin"—and his description of the city of Berenice, whose just and unjust cities germinate secretly, ad infinitum, inside one another: "all the future Berenices are already present in this instant, wrapped one within the other."

Earlier in the day, when I asked Nasser's father what he hoped for, the elderly man had answered, "I wish not to be woken in the night to have my home demolished." Unsurprisingly, I slept fitfully. I curled up as small as I could on my mat, in the room I shared with the elderly man and Nasser's two small sons. All night, the dogs of Palestinian Susiya howled and barked, as if to warn something off, or as if perplexed by their own existence. My dreams clung to this broken sound. I opened my eyes, exhausted, to the sound of Nasser's wife, Hiam, going out to tend the chickens and the sheep, and to bake the daily bread in the communal *taboon*, the earth oven.

I got up. On our knees, we mixed feed for the sheep. My notebook fell into the dirt, fluttering stupidly, and my pen rolled away. My grandparents, too, had been villagers. They fled war and poverty, but my grandfather could not escape, and was executed by Japanese soldiers during the Second World War. My father had been five years old, but he survived this devastation that claimed thirty-six million lives in Asia alone. The things I tried to see here seemed cloaked from my eyes, as if I walked in a hall of mirrors, surrounded by conjoined cities with the same destiny. As the morning wore on, Nasser's son led me through the chores, including the milking. Ahmed was so full of goodwill and curiosity it broke my heart. *Here*, he would say, using every bit of English he possessed. *Come here*. He smiled as

I photographed him holding fast to a sheep. *Eat*, he said to me. He brought me bread, sheep's milk, a little hummus, an egg. I learned another word, *baladi*. The taste of the village and the earth.

Above us, the high-wattage security lights of Israeli Susya were dimming. Here, in the other Susiya, the solar panels were not functioning, and there would be no electricity this morning, but in the crisp morning light, everything could be seen. All the invisibilities were laid bare.

CITIES AND DESIRE

In 2001, as he stood at the crossroads of his life, Nasser met a small group of Jewish activists who offered solidarity to Susiya. It was confounding: Jewish soldiers were demolishing his home and protecting the settlers, and Jewish individuals were volunteering to work beside him, but Nasser wanted to be neither the target of violence nor the recipient of charity. The questions he asked himself were philosophical: How to exist freely in a place where he was not free? Violent resistance showed him how to die, but what if nonviolence led only to the slow death of capitulation? How could he change his conditions? I thought of sixteen-year-old Wouroud and her searching smile. "I just want to live." For Nasser, the histories of civil rights movements allowed him to glimpse a possible future.

"I think nonviolent action is the way to change," he said, as we looked out at his family's small orchard. "This is the only way." Injustice persisted, he reasoned, because the world did not know, therefore he would make visible what was happening to them.

The ensuing years of activism led to cooperation with B'Tselem and coordination with other activist groups, including Ta'ayush.* Nasser learned fluent Hebrew and later English. Solidarity work in Susiya became organized, flexible, and creative. Israeli and Palestinian activists

---

* B'Tselem is the Israeli Information Centre for Human Rights in the Occupied Territories; Ta'ayush is the Arab-Jewish Partnership, Israelis and Palestinians striving together to end the Israeli occupation and to achieve full civil equality through daily nonviolent direct action.

are treated unequally before the law, which makes their cooperation all the more potent: Israeli citizens, protected by Israel's Basic Laws, have civil rights, including freedom of assembly. Israeli citizens can move through all parts of Area C without any restrictions whatsoever; Palestinians are barred from entering vast areas surrounding settlements without prior coordination with the Israeli Civil Administration, even to cultivate their own land.

Volunteers from Ta'ayush began escorting shepherds to their grazing lands. During planting and harvesting windows, they came singly and sometimes en masse. A small but dedicated group of volunteers hoped their presence would forestall settler attacks, but when it didn't, they documented the encounters and, most important, put their bodies in the way. The video evidence of violent attacks on shepherds, activists, and Palestinian schoolchildren is horrifying and disturbing—but even video proof did not convince the police to apply the law. Meanwhile, Susiya was mired in a desperate legal battle to save its homes from demolition. Year by year, Nasser's day-to-day work—with lawyers, activists, and peacemakers—not only strengthened but humanized the ties of Palestinian and Israeli civil society: acts of solidarity became acts of friendship. By 2015, the relentless paper and video documentation by Jewish and Palestinian activists would culminate in stunning international diplomatic and media attention on Susiya, as the village became emblematic of Israel's policies of land seizure. In June 2015, Israel's Supreme Court ruled that the Civil Administration had the right to demolish the village. A month later, the Israeli Defense Ministry concluded that Susiya sat on private Palestinian land and that local people had the 1881 Ottoman documents to prove it. Diplomats from twenty-eight European member states traveled to Susiya to protest Israel's decision, and the US State Department spoke up in Susiya's defense.*

---

* A sampling of the July 2015 international media: Diaa Hadid, "How a Palestinian Hamlet of 340 Drew Global Attention," *New York Times*, 23 July 2015; Erin McLaughlin, Kareem Khadder, and Bryony Jones, "Life in Susiya, the Palestinian Village Under Threat from Israeli Bulldozers," CNN, 24 July 2015, www.cnn.com/2015/07/24/middleeast/susiya-palestinian-village-under-threat/; Peter Beaumont, "EU Protests against Israeli Plans to Demolish Palestinian Village," *The Guardian*, 21 July 2015.

The conceptual, legal, and physical infrastructure of occupation aims to entrench separation, disaffiliation, and, most profoundly, estrangement. Muslim, Christian, and Jewish descendants of Israel-Palestine, if they come from the same land, will inevitably carry shared physical attributes and cultural norms. Physical separation is key if one population is deemed to have a different destiny than another. Something as innocuous as friendship, therefore, goes against the totality of the barriers, the checkpoints, outposts, ID cards, sterile streets, the "fabric of life," and the separation wall. Friendship, such a seemingly flimsy thing, seemed almost a joke in a world of continuous violence.

IN JANUARY 2016, AFTER THE REMARKABLE SUCCESS OF SUSIYA'S INTERnational appeal, thirty riot police forced their way into Nasser's home in the dead of night. M16s at the ready, they surrounded his elderly father, his wife, and three small children, forced Nasser to the floor, and shackled his hands together as his family watched in terror. This moment is seared into him: his own humiliation, the sick fear and shock, and the mirrored expressions on his children's faces. They were punishing not just him, he understood, but his family.

Nasser, who through all the years as a community leader and field worker for B'Tselem was well known to Israeli police and military, disappeared into the police's interrogation rooms.

"The interrogation is very tough," he conceded. He did not divulge the following easily. "The pressure starts the second they arrest you, they are shouting, pulling you from one place to another. You sit in a room with two or three of them, they ask different questions in parallel, you get disoriented and confused, you don't know who to answer. You sit on a chair facing the wall, you are not allowed to look up or down, your legs and hands are cuffed." When he said this, he kept his hands, open and face down, on his knees. "When you're not in interrogation, you are in a small room two metres by two metres, all you have is a metal table, and they keep the air conditioning on extremely cold. They put me in solitary confinement underground, a room without light." His next words, spoken quietly, were followed by silence. "It was a difficult period. They said things about the [Jewish] activists in Ta'ayush, my Israeli friends."

The legal case that was later brought against Ta'ayush activists—and eventually nullified by the Jerusalem High Court—is complex, sensationalist and heartbreaking, and received wall to wall coverage in the Israeli media. Out of respect for the privacy and health of those involved, I have elected not to detail it here.

THE CHOICE, BY BOTH PALESTINIANS AND ISRAELI JEWS, TO TRUST ONE another is perilous. Day after day, the mechanisms of life under occupation succeed in their aim: to disavow the possibility of commonality and coexistence. There is a profound loneliness to the Palestinian experience, a heavy irony given that the conflict has been a staple of international news for almost seventy years. Despite worldwide consensus that the Israeli settlement of the West Bank is a clear violation of international law, Palestinians are widely viewed, in North America at least, as the instigators and perpetrators of violence; indeed, as violence itself. Palestinian crimes of hijackings, knifings, suicide bombings, and murders have become, for many, the entirety of the Israeli-Palestinian conflict and the only tragedies to be mourned. At the same time, Palestinian suffering—more than 10,000 dead since the year 2000, including 1,977 children—is to some an acceptable form of collateral damage.

I wondered if Nasser's story served as both a microcosm and a warning, exposing the danger of collaboration between Israelis and Palestinians. Historical legacies—not only national but deeply, catastrophically personal—could shatter trust and friendships in an instant.

To my surprise, Nasser disagreed. For him, the old question of how to exist endured. He was committed to the life he had chosen.

But surely his arrest, I said, had changed something in him.

He answered without hesitation. "I think this has given me more power to be active and nonviolent. If Israel wants to separate Palestinian and Israeli activists, my arrest is a sign that what we are doing is working in South Hebron."

CITIES AND THE LIVING

*[The inferno of the living] is what is already here. . . . There are
two ways to escape suffering it. The first is easy for many: accept the
inferno and become such a part of it that you can no longer see it. The
second is risky and demands constant vigilance and apprehension:
seek and learn to recognize who and what, in the midst of the inferno,
are not the inferno, then make them endure, give them space.*
—ITALO CALVINO, *Invisible Cities*

Before leaving Palestine and Israel in mid-July 2016, I made my
way to Palestinian friends in Bethlehem, to a Jewish Israeli friend in
Akko, and to Tel Aviv for a gathering of former IDF soldiers who
had given testimony on the policies and practices of the army. As I
climbed the staircases and walked the chambers of both the visible
and invisible worlds, I refused to feel estranged from either the hu-
manity or the despair around me.

Earlier, I had asked Nasser if having children had given him hope
or made him more fearful. He had laughed and shaken his head. "Yes,
things changed. But I don't know how to tell you this in English."

When I pushed him, he said, "My children live in this situation."
The smallness of the word *situation* and the sorrow of the word *chil-
dren* struck me with a terrible force. "I tell them about my Jewish
friends," he continued. "I try to bring in my friends, like Yehuda. He
wears a *kippa* and the children think he's a settler, and I try to teach
them no, he's not a settler. *Inshallah* one day I will visit Yehuda in his
country and he in my country."

Shulman writes, "To watch the destruction-self-destruction of an
entire world, you need only ordinary eyes and the gift of not looking
away." I try to hold the invisible within the real. The occupation
began before I was born, but this numbing of our souls and our re-
liance on the word *intractable*: surely this cannot be our apology and
our answer.

IN THE OPENING PAGES OF *THE UNBEARABLE LIGHTNESS OF BEING*, MILAN Kundera considers the idea of eternal return. Would a horrific and bloody war, he wonders, if it recurred in the same way over and over again, be altered in any way? "It will: it will become a solid mass," Kundera concludes, "permanently protuberant, its inanity irreparable." But the world as we perceive it, where atrocities or violence occur and are then rinsed from our memories, has also led to its own "profound moral perversity . . . for in this world everything is pardoned in advance, and everything is cynically permitted." This cynical relationship with history is one we embrace at our peril.

On one of my last nights in the territory, I watched a group of seventy Jewish diaspora volunteers, Israeli activists, and Issa Amro and Youth Against Settlements, work side by side, attempting to clean up a disused Palestinian-owned warehouse in Hebron. Their aim was to lay the ground for what would be the only cinema for Hebron's 150,000 Palestinians.

Settlers and police instantly appeared, followed by soldiers, who would momentarily begin arresting the activists for disturbing the peace. Watching the scene unfold, which included the activists' elated singing of African American spirituals and Hebrew traditional songs, the children of the settlers frowned. They asked aloud, again and again, *They're Jews?* Through a translator, I spoke to them, wondering about their names and thoughts. A boy, no older than ten, looked me in the eyes and said, "Fuck you." But behind him, others watched in consternation, with a pensive fascination. An older woman reminded them, "There were Jews who helped Hitler, too." "Thank you for building Jewish property," another called out.

"What do their T-shirts say?" a boy asked.

The words were OCCUPATION IS NOT MY JUDAISM.

One of the activists said to him, "Do you think that occupation can really continue like this?"

The boy looked at us through the fence, his face open in surprise. His confusion was real and profound. "What occupation?"

The very earth we stood on momentarily vanished, rendered invisible.

MR. NICE GUY

RACHEL KUSHNER

STANDING AT AN INTERSECTION IN SHUAFAT REFUGEE CAMP, IN East Jerusalem, I watched as a small boy, sunk down behind the steering wheel of a beat-up sedan, zoomed through an intersection with his arm out the driver's side window, signaling like a NASCAR driver pulling in for a pit stop. I was amazed. He looked about twelve years old.

"No one cares here," my host, Baha Nababta, said, laughing at my astonishment. "Anyone can do anything they want."

As Baha and I walked around the refugee camp this past spring, teenagers fell in behind us, forming a kind of retinue. Among them were cool kids who looked like cool kids the world over, tuned in to that teen frequency, a dog whistle, with global reach. I did notice that white was a popular color, and that might have been regional, local to Shuafat camp. White slouchy but pegged jeans, and white polo shirts, white high-tops. Maybe white has extra status in a place where roads are unpaved and turn to mud, where garbage is everywhere, literally, and where water shortages make it exceedingly difficult to keep people and clothing clean.

So few nonresidents enter Shuafat camp that my appearance there seemed like a highly unusual event, met with warm greetings verging on hysteria, crowds of kids following along. "Hello, America!" they called excitedly. I was a novelty, but also I was with Baha Nababta, a twenty-nine-year-old Palestinian community organizer beloved by the kids of Shuafat. Those who followed us wanted not just my attention, but his. Baha had a rare kind of charisma. Camp counselor charisma, you might call it. He was a natural leader of boys. Every kid we passed knew him, and either waved or stopped to speak to him. Baha had founded a community center so that older children would have a place to hang out, since there is no open space in Shuafat Refugee Camp, no park, not a single playground, nowhere for kids to go, not even a street, really, where they can play, since there is no place to stand, most of the narrow and unpaved roads barely fitting the cars that ramble down them. Littler kids tapped me on the arms and wanted to show me the mural they'd painted with Baha. The road they had helped pave with Baha, who had supervised its completion. The plants they'd planted with Baha along a narrow strip. Baha, Baha, Baha. It was like that with the adults too. They all wanted his attention. His phone was blowing up in his pocket as we walked. He finally answered. There was a dispute between a man whose baby had died at the clinic in the camp, and the doctor who had treated the baby. The man whose baby had died had tried to burn the doctor alive, and now the doctor was in critical condition, in a hospital in Jerusalem. Throughout the two days I spent with Baha, I heard stories like this that he was asked to help resolve. People relied on him. He had a vision for the Shuafat camp, where he was born and raised, that went beyond what could be imagined from within the very limited confines of the place.

In an area of high-rise apartment buildings clustered around a mosque with spindly, futuristic minarets, a pudgy boy of ten or eleven called over to us. "My dad is trying to reach you," he said to Baha. Baha told me the buildings in that part of the camp had no water, and that everyone was contacting him about it. He had not been answering his phone, he confessed, because he didn't have any good news yet for the residents. I got the impression Baha was something like an informal mayor, a community leader on whom people depended to resolve disputes, build roads, put together volunteer committees, and attempt to make Shuafat camp safe for children. The building next to us was twelve stories. Next to it was another twelve-story building.

High-rise apartments in the camp are built so close together that if a fire should happen, the result would be devastating. There would be no way to put it out. The buildings here were all built of stone blocks that featured, between blocks, wooden wedges that stuck out intermittently, as if the builders never returned to fill the gaps with mortar. I gazed up at a towering facade, the strange wooden wedges, which made the building look like a model of a structure, except that it was occupied. The pudgy boy turned to me as I craned my neck, looking up at the facade. "This building is stupidly built," he said. "It's junk."

"Do you live here?" I asked him, and he said yes.

SHUAFAT REFUGEE CAMP IS INSIDE JERUSALEM PROPER, ACCORDING TO the municipal boundaries that Israel declared after the Six-Day War, in 1967. The Palestinian Authority has no jurisdiction there: the camp is, according to Israeli law, inside Israel, and the people who live there are Jerusalem residents, but they are refugees in their own city. Camp residents pay taxes to Israel, but the camp is not serviced. There is very little legally supplied water, a barely functioning sewage system, essentially no garbage pickup, no road building, no mail service (the streets don't even have names, much less addresses), virtually no infrastructure of any kind. There is no adequate school system. Israeli emergency fire and medical services never enter the camp. Israeli police only enter to make arrests, but provide no security for camp residents. There is chaotic land registration. While no one knows how many people really live in the Shuafat camp and its surrounding areas, which is roughly one square kilometer, it's estimated that the population is between eighty and eighty-five thousand people. They live surrounded by a twenty-five-foot concrete wall, a wall interspersed by guard towers and trap doors that swing open when Israeli forces raid the camp, with reinforcements in the hundreds, or even, as in December 2015, over a thousand troops.

Effectively, there are no laws in the Shuafat Refugee Camp, despite its geographical location inside Jerusalem. The Shuafat camp's original citizens were moved from the Old City, where they had sought asylum in 1948, during the Arab-Israeli War, to the camp's boundaries starting in 1965, with more arriving, in need of asylum, at the beginning of the war in 1967, when the camp was under the control of the Jordanian government. Now, fifty years after Israel's new 1967 boundaries were drawn, even Israeli security experts don't quite know why the Shuafat Refugee Camp was placed inside the Jerusalem municipal boundaries. The population was then much smaller, and surrounded by beautiful green open forestland, which stretched to land on which the Jewish settlement of Pisgat Ze'ev was later built (the forestland is still there, visible beyond the separation wall, but inaccessible to camp residents, on account of the wall). Perhaps the Israelis were hoping the camp's residents could be relocated, since they numbered in the mere hundreds. Instead, the population of the camp exploded in the following decades into the tens of thousands. In 1980, Israel declared Jerusalem the "complete and united" capital of Israel. In 2004, the concrete wall was erected around the camp, cutting inside Israel's own declared boundaries, as if to stanch and cauterize the camp from "united" Jerusalem.

IF HIGH-RISE BUILDINGS ARE NOT TYPICALLY CONJURED BY THE TERM REF-ugee camp, a person may neither imagine an indoor shopping mall, but there is one in the Shuafat camp—two floors, and a third under construction, an escalator up, and down, and a store called "Fendi" that sells inexpensive women's clothes. The mall owner greeted us with exuberance, and pulled Baha aside for advice of some kind. A kid who worked at a mall ice cream parlor, a hipster in lenseless eyeglasses and a hoodie, did a world class beatbox for me and Moriel Rothman-Zecher, a writer and organizer who had walked me into the camp in order to make introductions between me and Baha, and to serve as interpreter. Moriel and the kid from the ice cream shop took turns. Moriel's own beatbox was good but not quite up to the Shuafat Refugee Camp beatbox standard. We met an accountant named Fahed who had just opened his shop in the mall, to prepare taxes for residents. He was stunned to hear English being spoken and eager to use his own. The tax forms are in Hebrew, he explained, so most people in the camp must hire a bilingual accountant to complete them.

Before the separation wall was constructed, the mall was bulldozed twice by the Israeli authorities, but the owner rebuilt both times. Since the wall has gone up, the Israelis have not attempted to demolish any large buildings in Shufat, though they have destroyed individual homes. Meanwhile, the population has exploded. The Israelis could come in and raze the entire place at any time. Armed Palestinian gangsters could take away someone's land or apartment. A fire or earthquake would be catastrophic. There are multiple risks to buying property in the Shuafat camp, but the cost of an apartment there is less than one-tenth of what an apartment would cost on the other side of the separation wall, in East Jerusalem. And living in the Shuafat camp is a way to try to hold on to Jerusalem residency status. Jerusalem residents have a coveted blue ID card, meaning they can enter Israel in order to work, and support their families, without going through the military checkpoint at Qalandiya, which is for Palestinians with green, or West Bank, ID cards, who must wait in hours-long predawn lines with many supporting documents, in order to enter Israel. Jerusalem residency is, quite simply, a lifeline to employment, a matter of survival. There are also non-Jerusalemites in the Shuafat camp. Since the wall went up, it became a sanctuary, a haven. I met people from Gaza, who cannot leave the square kilometer of the camp or they will be arrested, since the military occupation and its limits on freedom of movement have made it illegal for Gazans to enter Israel or the West Bank except with Israeli permission, which is almost never granted. I met a family of Brazilian Palestinians with long-expired passports who also cannot leave the camp, because they do not have West Bank green IDs, nor Jerusalem blue IDs.

SHUAFAT CAMP IS OFTEN DEPICTED IN THE INTERNATIONAL MEDIA AS THE most dangerous place in Jerusalem, a crucible of crime, jihad, and trash fires. On the day that I arrived, garbage was indeed smoldering in great heaps just inside the checkpoint entrance, against the concrete separation wall, flames jumping thinly in the strong morning sun. I had been to countries before that burn their trash; it is a smell you get used to. My main concern, over the weekend I spent in the camp, was not getting my foot run over by a car. If you get seriously hurt in the camp, there isn't much help. Ill or injured people are carried through the checkpoint, on foot or by car, and put in ambulances on the other side of the wall. According to residents of the camp, several people have unnecessarily died in this manner. As we walked, I began to understand how to face the traffic without flinching, to expect that drivers are experienced at navigating such incredible human density. I asked Baha if people are ever run over by cars, assuming he'd say no.

"Yes, all the time," he said. "A child was just killed this way," he added. I hugged the walls of the apartment buildings as we strolled. Later that evening, I watched as a tiny boy riding a grown man's bicycle was bumped by a car. He crashed in the road. I ran to help him. He was crying, holding out his abraded hands. I remembered how painful it is to scrape your palms, how many nerve endings there are in an open hand. A Palestinian man told the little boy he was okay and ruffled his hair.

When I asked Baha if garbage was burned by the separation wall because it was safer—a way to contain a fire, like a giant fireplace—he shook his head. "It's, ah, symbolic." In other words, garbage is burned by the wall because the wall is Israeli. Drugs are sold along the wall by the Israeli checkpoint, not for symbolic reasons. The camp organizers, like Baha, cannot control the drug trade in a zone patrolled by the Israeli police and monitored by security cameras. Dealers are safe there from the means of popular justice exacted inside the camp. The most heavily militarized area of the camp is thus its most lawless.

The popular drug the dealers sell is called Mr. Nice Guy, which is sometimes categorized as a "synthetic cannabinoid"—a meaningless nomenclature. It is highly toxic, and its effects are nothing like cannabis. It damages brains and ruins lives. Mr. Nice Guy is popular with kids as young as age eight, and it can bring on psychosis. Empty packets of it sifted around our feet as we crossed the large parking lot where buses pick up six thousand children daily and transport them through the checkpoint, into East Jerusalem for school, since the camp has only a few public schools, for elementary students. Every afternoon, children stream back into camp, passing the dealers and users who cluster near the checkpoint.

I didn't see the dealers, but I doubt Baha would have pointed them out. What I mostly noticed were kids working, being industrious, trying to find productive ways to live in a miserable environment, and to survive. Across from Baha's house, a group of kids ran a car wash. We waved to them from Baha's roof. Baha introduced me to a group of teenage boys who own their own moped- and scooter-repair service. He took me to a barber shop, where kids in flawless outfits with high-side fades were hanging out, listening to music, while a boy of about thirteen gave a haircut to a boy of about five. A young teen in a pristine white polo shirt and delicate gold neck chain flexed his baby potato of a biceps and announced his family name, "Alqam!" The kids in the barbershop were all Alqam. They ran the shop. They were ecstatic to see Baha. We were all ecstatic. The language barrier between me and the boys only thickened our collective joy, as my interpreter Moriel was whisked into a barber chair for a playfully coerced beard trim, on the house. The boys and I shouldered up for selfies, put on our sunglasses, and posed. I sensed with them, and, especially after Moriel left that afternoon, and I was the lone visitor for the weekend, that whenever men shook my hand after Baha introduced me, that men and boys would not get so physically close to a Palestinian woman who was a stranger. I was an American female, and I was with Baha, which made me something like an honorary man.

Later I told myself and everyone else how wonderful it was in the Shuafat camp. How safe I felt. How positive Baha was. All that still feels true to me. But I also insisted, to myself and everyone else, that Baha never expressed any fears for his own safety. In looking at my notes, I see now that my insistence on this point was sheer will. A fiction. It's right there in the notes. He said he was nervous. He said he'd been threatened.

Also in the notes, this:

Baha says, two types

1. THOSE WHO WANT TO HELP MAKE A BETTER LIFE
2. THOSE WHO WANT TO DESTROY EVERYTHING

And in parentheses: *Arms trade. Drugs trade. Construction profits. No oversight wanted.*

"I wanted you to meet the boys because they are nice people," Baha said, after we left the barber shop. "But they do all carry guns." It was only after I returned home to the US that I learned in the banal and cowardly way, with a few taps on my computer, that two Alqam boys, cousins who were eleven and fourteen, had been accused of stabbing, with a knife and scissors, a security guard on a tram in East Jerusalem. I still don't know whether they were related to the boys in the barbershop. Several of the young assailants in what's been called the Knives Intifada, if it is an intifada, have been from the Shuafat camp, which has also been the site of huge and violent protests, in which Palestinians have been killed by Israeli forces. In 2015, three children from the Shuafat Refugee Camp lost eyes from sponge bullets shot by Israeli forces.

The other thing I suppressed, besides Baha's admissions of fear, was his desire for police. I didn't write that down. It wasn't part of my hero narrative, because police are not part of my hero narrative. "Even if they have to bring them from India," he said several times, "we need police here. We cannot handle the disputes on our own. People take revenge. They murder."

A MIDDLE EAST CORRESPONDENT I'D MET IN THE WEST BANK, HEARING that I was going to spend the weekend in the Shuafat camp, had asked me if I planned to visit Shit Lake while there. Apparently that was his single image of the place. I assumed he was referring to a sewage dump, but Baha never mentioned it, and after seeing Baha's pleasure in showing me the community center, the roads his committee had built, the mall, which was the only open gathering space, all things that, for him, were hopeful, I wasn't going to ask him for Shit Lake.

That correspondent had never stepped foot in the Shuafat camp. From my own time there, the sustaining image is shimmering white. The kids, dressed in white. The buildings, a baked tone of dusty, smoke-stained white. The minarets, all white. And there was the

1972 Volkswagen beetle in gleaming white, meticulously restored. It was on the shop floor of a garage run by Baha's friend Adel. A classic car enthusiast and owner myself, I wanted to talk to Adel about the car. He showed me his garage, his compressor, his lift. Like the escalator in the mall, these were things you would never expect to find in a place without services.

We sat, and Adel made coffee. He and Baha told me about the troubles with the drug Mr. Nice Guy. They said every family has an addict among its children, and sometimes the older people as well. A third of the population of the camp is strung out on it, they said. It makes people crazy, Adel and Baha agreed. Is there a link, I asked, between Mr. Nice Guy, and the kids who decide, essentially, to end it all, by running at a soldier with a knife? They both concurred that there was. Two years earlier, Baha said, by way of contrast, there had been a man from the Shuafat camp who did a ramming operation. The Israelis came and blew up his house. He was older, Baha said, he was out of work, and he decided that he was finally ready to lose everything. With the kids, Baha said, it's different. It's an act of impulsive courage. The drug helps enormously with that.

Adel kept making references to his nine-year-old daughter, who is physically disabled and cannot attend school. Perhaps I asked to meet her, or Adel asked if I wanted to meet her. Either way, we ended up in Adel's large apartment, and his daughter Mira was wheeled out to the living room. Mira was burned over most of her body and is missing one arm and a kneecap. Her face and scalp are disfigured. A school bus filled with children from the Shuafat camp was on a trip to Ramallah when it collided with a truck on a wet, rainy road. The bus overturned and burst into flames. Five children and a teacher burned to death. Dozens were injured. Emergency services were delayed by confusion over who had jurisdiction. As a result, Mira and other children had to be taken in the cars of bystanders to the closest hospital. The accident took place between the Adam settlement and Qalandiya checkpoints, in what is called Area C of the West Bank, which is entirely under Israeli control. The likelihood of something like this occurring was well known. Later, a report from Ir Amim, an Israeli human rights NGO, established that the tragedy resulted from the multiple challenges of living beyond the separation barrier. Roads were substandard. The bus was unsafe, there were too many children on the bus, the children had no access to education in their own communities, and there was no oversight.

"When the accident happened, we didn't know how to cope with it," Baha told me. Someone got up on a loading dock in the camp and called out the names of the dead. Afterward, Baha and Adel both cried all the time. They felt that the lives of Shuafat's children were disposable. They decided to start their own volunteer emergency team, through WhatsApp, and it now has eighty members, who are trained in first aid, each with special skills they are ready to employ at a moment's notice. They are saving up to purchase their own Shuafat camp ambulance, whose volunteer drivers will be trained medical professionals, like Baha's wife, Hiba, who is a nurse.

Baha, I noticed, seemed more optimistic about the emergency team, and about the future, than Adel did. At one point, Adel, who has a shattered and frantic, but loving, warm energy, turned to me and said, "We are orphans here."

Adel's daughter Mira, who had been transferred from her wheel-chair to the couch, sat and fidgeted. She understood no English but was forced to quietly pretend she was listening. I kept smiling at her, and she smiled back. I was desperate to give her something, to prom-ise something. It's very difficult to see a child who has suffered so tre-mendously. It's basically unbearable. I should give her the ring I was wearing, I thought. But then I saw that it would never fit her fingers, which were very swollen and large, despite her young age; her de-velopment, after the fire, was thwarted because her bones could not properly grow. I'll give her my earrings, was my next idea, and then I realized that her ears had been burned off in the fire. I felt obscene. I sat and smiled as if my oversize teeth could beam a protective fiction over this poor child, blind us both to the truth, that no shallow ges-ture or petty generosity would make any lasting difference.

THE TRAVEL AGENCY IN THE SHUAFAT REFUGEE CAMP MALL IS CALLED Hope. There is a toy store in the mall called The Happy Child. The children I met were all Baha's kids, part of his group, on his team, drafting off his energy, which was relentlessly upbeat.

I have to recreate with all the precision I can manage, to remember what I am able to about Baha. I see Baha in his pink polo shirt, tall and handsome, but with a soft belly that somehow reinforces his integrity, makes him imperfectly, perfectly human. Baha singing "Bella Ciao" in well-keyed Italian, a language he'd learned at age nineteen, on the trip that changed his life, working with Vento di Terra, a community development and human rights NGO based in Italy. Later, I sent a video of Baha singing to various Italian friends, leftists who were thrilled that a guy in a Palestinian refugee camp knew the words to "Bella Ciao."

Baha's friends and relatives all hugging me and cheek-kissing me, the women bringing out boxes that contained their hand-embroidered wedding dresses, insisting I try on each dress, whose colors and designs specified where they were from—one black with white stitching, from Ramallah. Cream with red, Jerusalem. In each case we took a photo, laughing, me in each dress, with the woman it belonged to on my arm.

Everyone imploring me to come back, and to bring Remy, my eight-year-old, and I was sure that I would come back, and bring Remy, because I had fallen in love with these people.

And in the background of the hugs and kisses, in almost every home where we spent time, the TV playing the Islamic channel, Palestine-Al-Yawm, a relentless montage of blood, smoke, fire, and keffiyeh-wrapped fighters with M16s.

The constant hospitality. Coffee, tea, mint lemonade, ice water, all the drinks I politely accepted. Drank and then sloshed along, past faded wheatpastes of jihad martyrs.

Come back. Bring Remy. I will, I told them, and I meant it.

Late at night, Baha and his wife, Hiba, decided to show me their digital wedding photobook. It was midnight, their two young daughters asleep on couches around us. Hiba propped her iPad on her belly—she was five months' pregnant, expecting her third child, a boy—and we looked at every last image, hundreds of images, of her and Baha in highly curated poses and stiff wedding clothes, her fake pearl and rhinestone tiara, her beautiful face neutralized by heavy makeup, but the makeup part of the ritual, and the ritual part of the glory. The two of them in a lush park in West Jerusalem. Every picture we looked at was, for them watching me see the images, a new delight: there were more and more and more. For me, they all started to run together, it was now one in the morning, I was exhausted, but I made myself regard each photograph as something unique, a vital integer in the stream of these people's refusal to be reduced.

I slept in what they called their Arabic room, on low cushions, a barred window above me issuing a cool breeze. I listened to roosters crow, and the semiautomatic weapons being fired at a nearby wedding celebration, and eventually I drifted into the calmest, heaviest sleep I'd had in months.

The next day, Baha had meetings to attend to try to solve the water problem. I spoke to Hiba about their kids. She asked me at what age Remy had started his piano lessons. "I want music lessons for the girls," she said, "I think it's very good for their development." As she said it, more machine gun fire erupted from the roof of a nearby building. "I want them to know the feel, the smells, of a different environment. To be able to imagine other lives."

When I think of Hiba Nababta wanting what I want for my child, her rightful desire that her kids should have an equal chance, everything feels hopeless, and more obscene, even, than my wanting to give earrings to a child without ears.

I went with Hiba that morning to her mother's house, where Hiba's mother and her sisters were preparing an exquisite meal of stuffed grape leaves and stuffed squashes, the grape leaves and vegetables grown on her mother's patio in the camp. We were all women, eating together in relaxed company. A sister-in-law came downstairs to join us, sleepy, beautiful, thin, with long red nails and hair dyed honey blond, in her pajamas and slippers. She said that she was leaving for New Jersey, in just a few days, with her husband, Hiba's brother, and their new baby. Relatives had arranged for them to immigrate. She would learn English and go to school.

When it was time to say goodbye, a younger sister was appointed to walk me to the checkpoint. Halfway there, I assured her I could walk alone.

On the main road, shopkeepers came out to wave and smile. Everyone seemed to know who I was, the American who had come to meet with Baha.

At the checkpoint, the Palestinian boy in front of me was detained. I was next, and the soldiers were shocked to see an American, as they would have been shocked to see any non-Palestinian. There was much consternation in the reinforced checkpoint station. My passport went from hand to hand. Finally, the commander approached the scratched window. "You're a Jew, right?" he blurted into the microphone. For the context in which he asked, for its reasoning, I said no. But in fact, I'm ethnically half-Jewish, on my father's side, although I was not raised with any religious or even a cultural connection to Judaism. My mother is a white protestant from Tennessee. I might have said "yes, partly," but I found the question unanswerable, on account of its conflation of Zionism and Jewish identity. My Yiddish-speaking Odessan great-grandfather was a clothing merchant on Orchard Street. My grandfather worked in his shop as a boy. That is classically Jewish, but my sense of self, of what it might mean to inherit some trace of that lineage, was not the kind of patrimony the soldier was asking after. I was eventually waved along.

The day I left Shuafat camp was April 17. Fifteen days later, on May 2, Baha Nababta was murdered in the camp. An unknown person approached on a motorcycle as Baha worked with roughly a hundred fellow camp residents to pave a road. In front of this very large crowd of people, working together, the person on the motorcycle shot at Baha ten times and fled. Seven bullets hit him.

It is now November. Baha's wife, Hiba, has given birth to their son. His father is gone. His mother is widowed. But a baby—a baby can thrive no matter. A baby won't even know, until it is told, that someone is missing.

SAMI

RAJA SHEHADEH

EVERY CONFLICT HAS ITS UNSUNG HEROES. IN PALESTINE THEY'RE the taxi drivers. After living for half a century under occupation, my nerves are strained. I can no longer endure the anxiety of what might appear on the road, whether it is angry drivers converging into long bottlenecks as they jostle to get in place at the more than five hundred checkpoints scattered in the small area of the West Bank, or the pathetic boys who throw themselves at your car pretending to clean the windshield, asking for money. Every time I see a scrawny kid clinging to the car, I am torn between giving him a few coins and encouraging begging, or driving on and possibly injuring him. The plight of these boys invariably makes me hate myself, forcing me to confront the extent to which my society has failed.

Then there is the indignity of having to wait on the whim of a teenage soldier to motion me to pass or to prevent me from passing and ordering me to "get out of your car, leave the keys in, and stand against the wall," or whatever other insult pops into his or her head.

But perhaps the main reason why I stopped driving out of Ramallah is that the roads Israel built to link the Jewish settlements with Israel have replaced the familiar old roads, making the whole network so complicated and confusing that I often get lost. And this is the greatest indignity of all, getting lost in your own country.

This is why I began asking Sami to drive me in his taxi. Patient, considerate, well tempered and kind, he also possesses the other signal virtue of punctuality. I'm just amazed at how he manages always to arrive on time when there are so many imponderables. Short, well built with cropped hair, he looks sturdy but unthreatening, with a pleasant smile that rarely leaves his face. I never cease to wonder how he can remain so even tempered despite the tragedies his family has endured and the difficulties he experiences on the road. Besides, gentle Sami, with his slight lisp, is such a good storyteller.

I realized how truly outstanding he is when he sent a colleague of his, Abed, in his stead. That day Sami could not drive me, because his wife was going to see an Israeli doctor and he needed to be with her to act as an interpreter. I could immediately see how different Sami with his calm manner was from Abed, who, perturbed and anxious, kept thanking God every time we passed through a checkpoint. Abed managed to arrive at my house on time, but he immediately announced that he had had a hard time getting from Jerusalem to Ramallah.

"It's easier to go to Tel Aviv than to come to Ramallah," he said in an aggrieved fashion. "I went to Qalandiya and it was totally clogged so I risked going to al-Jeeb. Yesterday a friend of mine used that checkpoint. After he went through he found that the soldiers had placed another barrier some distance away. So he was stuck. He could neither go forward into Ramallah nor back to Jerusalem. But today, thank God, it was open and I made it on time.

"Which road should I take now?" Abed asked me forlornly.

"No idea," I said. "It's up to you."

Abed breathed deeply. "I'll try Qalandiya. It's Monday, you know. That's the worst day. Schools are open and everyone's at work. Then we have to pass through the bridge at Sheikh Jarrah and this tends to be clogged. I don't know how long it will take me to get to Jerusalem."

Fortunately, last Thursday, it was Sami and not Abed who had driven me to the airport.

I was going to London for only a week and my flight was at five in the afternoon. The drive from Ramallah to the airport used to take fifty minutes. With so many checkpoints on the way, I left the house at noon, five hours before the flight.

I held my breath when we passed the first checkpoint. Sami does not lie: not only is he kind and considerate, but he is also honest, perhaps far too honest for our situation. Unlike other drivers I've used to get to the airport, Sami's honesty extends to telling the truth even to soldiers. Though he's fluent in Hebrew and could easily pass for a Jew, he never lies and says he lives in one of the East Jerusalem neighborhoods that are really Jewish settlements. Nor does he ever place a Hebrew newspaper on the dashboard or play Israeli music so that the soldiers will wave him through, thinking he's one of them.

The spring weather was pleasant and refreshing as we drove through the Palestinian village of Ayn Arik, which sits in a valley famed for its pomegranate trees. The village has a mixed Christian and Muslim population. The hills on both sides of the road were covered with olive trees. In the course of his long experience of driving in the country, Sami had witnessed the extensive transformation of the landscape and was often able to correct my misconceptions about the basis of Israeli planning. We were heading to Bethlehem, driving through the beautiful hills south of Jerusalem. It was not possible to use the road that connects the two cities, which are only seven kilometers apart, because Israel does not allow taxis through the Bethlehem checkpoint. We had to circle around, go through the tunnels to Beit Jala and from there to Bethlehem.

My eyes wandered from the Palestinian villages spread out on the hills to the fortresslike Jewish settlements on top. I noticed that there was no separation wall here. It seemed to me anyone could cross over by walking down the hill. But when I suggested this to Sami, he said the guards at the settlement on top of the hill would immediately spot someone. He was right, of course. I could see they plan the settlements to act as buffers that allow for the surveillance of the entire valley.

As we drove through Jerusalem, we had to stop for the recently built light rail to pass. Sami said: "If Israel had built a line connecting Ramallah to Jerusalem, how different it would have been between us."

From the valley of the pomegranate trees we drove up a steep and dangerous road, passing through the village of Deir Ibzi, then descended again into another valley only to climb up another hill. It was like riding the waves of a turbulent sea. Or was it my troubled mind that made me think of this image for these familiar hills?

On one solitary hill stood the Jewish settlement of Dolev, a mere nine kilometers away from where I live in Ramallah. But the road from Ramallah to Dolev has long been closed to Palestinian traffic. Our detour took about forty-five minutes. We continued driving down a winding, single-lane road to get to the motorway linking the settlements together. But as soon as we got to the crossroads we found that the Israeli army had placed concrete barrier blocks there, preventing Palestinian access to this road. Israel planned this new road network three decades ago, to enable the military to block Palestinian traffic on a whim, without affecting Israeli settlement traffic.

As we stood there wondering what to do, we could see the settlers' cars and buses zooming by along the double-lane, well-designed road, unaware of our miserable fate. Sami muttered: "Just when we find a possible road to the airport, the army closes it." He then picked up his mobile phone and began calling a colleague to find out how it was at the Qalandiya crossing, at least an hour away.

"It's very bad," he was told. His friend said he had been held up for two hours. "Don't come here. It's a trap," the friend said. Sami was also informed that the checkpoint we were heading to, near the village of Ni'leen, had also been closed to nonsettler traffic.

He now turned to me with a look of desperation and said: "We have no other choice but to try going through the Rantis checkpoint." The only problem is that only Israeli citizens are allowed through and neither Sami nor I is an Israeli citizen. "If we're stopped I could get in trouble for attempting to smuggle you through, and you might end up being detained. Or, if they want to be kind, they might simply send us back. But then there would be no possibility that you'll make it in time for your flight. What do you say? Shall we risk it?"

"Not much choice," I said calmly and with as much confidence as I could muster, though I was feeling utterly nervous and uncertain. "We've already spent forty-five minutes and I must be at the airport three hours before my flight or they will not let me fly."

"I know," said Sami, "I'll do what I can to get you there in time."

"Let's risk it." I said this knowing that I was not only taking an individual risk but also one on behalf of Sami, because both of us are not Israeli citizens, and a driver trying to smuggle someone who doesn't qualify would also be guilty of an offence.

Now we had to figure out how to find a different access point to get on the main road. Sami began dialing to find another driver who might have an idea where we could find this when a taxi drove by. He saw that the road was closed and began turning back. Sami flashed his lights. The taxi stopped.

The two drivers consulted, and Sami learned that the other driver knew another way we could take to get to the settlers' road. We proceeded to follow him. I have always admired the camaraderie among taxi drivers, who look after each other and try their best to help one another endure these tiresome and frustrating times.

We drove through narrow roads, passing many more Palestinian villages along the way. They all seemed crammed in contrast to the settlements, which were spread out, with lots of green areas between the rows of mostly red-tile-roofed houses. A wall or a barbed wire fence surrounded each settlement, and the entry was through a well-guarded gate. I thanked my lucky stars that I wasn't driving. I would not have been able to find my way. I confessed to Sami that I was totally lost.

Kind Sami said: "You're not the only one who gets confused by the new roads and changes to the land. During the last al-Adha feast I was driving a man who finally got a permit to visit Jerusalem. It was the first time after an absence of many years that he was allowed into the city, though he lives just fifteen kilometers away. When he saw the new road grid and the settlements surrounding East Jerusalem he turned to me and confessed that 'except for the white sculpture [which the Israelis erected as a symbol for peace] I would not have realized we were in the Jerusalem I thought I knew.'"

We continued driving for another forty-five minutes, wandering from one Palestinian village to another. We finally found an opening on the side of the road that had not been blocked by the army. It was not a proper entry to the main road, which meant that we had to drive over unpaved ground, then risk being hit by speeding cars coming the other way.

How I wish I were fatalistic, someone who tells himself *I did all I could, and now will leave my destiny to fate*. But I'm not like that. I start eating myself up, even blaming myself for the occupation and the bad behavior of its soldiers. I tried to assure myself that it wouldn't be the end of the world if I didn't get on the flight. I was only going on a short trip to London to do a series of talks on human rights. Was it worth it to go through all this for just one week? Perhaps I should not have accepted this invitation. Perhaps I should stay put in my house and give up on traveling altogether, rather than subject myself to this agony. But though of short duration, my schedule at my destination was utterly packed. Every single day—almost every hour—was filled with meetings and events at which I was speaking. So much had gone into the planning of this week, so many people were involved. I had to do my very best and take every risk in order not to disappoint my hosts by failing to arrive at the airport on time. The more I thought in these terms, the more anxious and fretful I became. Would they understand if I didn't make it? I would assure them that I had allowed enough time for getting to the airport. But would they appreciate the complications of our life under occupation? I know it is not easy for those who are used to roads being accessible to appreciate that passage on the roads of my country is a privilege that is not afforded to everyone. I hate to have to keep excusing myself because of the occupation, and yet this is the reality I live under and that I've had to endure now for half a century.

Pondering the possibility of having to go back home in defeat and emptying the bag that I had so carefully packed made me realize how the occupation has rid me of the most simple joys. There were times when I felt excitement about traveling abroad. Now all the fun is gone. I no longer find pleasure in driving through our lovely hills, not even in springtime when they look their best.

The occupation has been like a dark, heavy cloud hovering over the land, a lump in the throat. Sometimes it descends and threatens to completely asphyxiate. Then it lifts temporarily but never entirely. No one living under its shadow ever forgets the oppressive occupation.

Once, when we were stopped for hours waiting at a checkpoint to be allowed through, I heard Sami say: "Sometimes I cannot endure it, but I have a family to feed. If I stop, who will take care of them? This is the only thing that keeps me going."

The closer we got to Rantis, the more anxious I felt. Much as I tried to relax, it was no use. I know myself and know that I cannot help fretting over passing through checkpoints. Fretting, in turn, makes me look guilty, as though I were smuggling a bomb or going on a violent mission. Just thinking of how I look when I fret made me more anxious and more likely to be stopped.

I kept on telling myself I had to try to relax: otherwise, by the time we got to Rantis, I would be in such a state that would alarm the soldiers at the checkpoint, then we would surely be stopped and I'd be found out as someone crossing at a checkpoint reserved only for Israeli citizens. Yet how could I relax? The next half hour or so, I knew, was going to be a real challenge.

After having driven me for so long, Sami knew me well. He could read my mood. He could see how tense I was. But he was too polite to refer to my agitated state and tell me to take it easy. Instead, as he drove, he tried to distract me and help me pass the time by telling me one story after another. He was a good raconteur; still, most of the stories he told me were about checkpoints, a Palestinian vein of narrative that is almost inescapable. The more I heard from him, the more anxious I became.

Usually when Sami drives me, we talk for a bit and then drive on in silence. He knows how much I like silence, how I try to enjoy looking around at the landscape and dreaming. Most often I think about how much I'd rather be walking in the hills we are passing than driving by them. But this time Sami was going from one story to another, hardly stopping. Could he also be tense, I wondered? Sami was and is the calmest man I know.

"Imagine this," he said. "Once, I was going to the Allenby Bridge. It was very hot and there was a long wait at a checkpoint. When my turn finally came, an Israeli soldier came over and asked whether I often came this way. I answered that I did.

"'Will you be coming back this way?' he asked.

"I said I would.

"'Don't stand in line. Come straight through, because I want to speak to you.'

"'On the way back I didn't jump the long queue as he had told me to do. When I got to where he was standing he asked me, 'Why didn't you do as I told you?' I said I always wait in line. He then asked for my telephone number, saying he wanted to talk to me. I gave him a number. He called it immediately and heard no ring tone. 'You gave me a wrong number,' he said. I explained that I have two numbers, one for work and one for use on Fridays, my day off. 'Then give me your work number,' he demanded. I had to give it to him. He tried it, and it rang. Satisfied, he said: 'I'll call you later.'

"And indeed, when I got home he called and proposed that I meet with him. I knew what he wanted and told him I was not that sort of man. He said he could help me so I wouldn't have to wait in line anymore, but would be able to go straight through. In return, he wanted me to tell him who the troublemakers were in the Jerusalem neighborhood where I live, and he'd reward me. I told him I didn't need his help and hung up."

Sami's storytelling was often interrupted by phone calls from his customers, which he promptly answered. What a huge difference the mobile phone has made for drivers like him. For many years, Israel would not allow car phones. Now the phone made it possible for drivers to check on the state of the roads and checkpoints. There is even a special app that updates drivers about the roads and congestion at the checkpoints. Sami's car was like his office. He handled his schedule so competently.

I had always wondered why intelligent Sami had not pursued his studies. Once, when I asked him, he told me that in school, he was good at science and his teacher had great hopes for him. He applied and was accepted to a university in Jordan and was preparing to go to start his studies when his older brother Majid was killed by an American settler. Posing as a passenger, the settler asked to be driven to the Holy Land Hotel. Before they arrived, he put a bullet in Majid's head, left him to die in the car, and escaped.

Sami's father urged him to leave for university anyway, but Sami would not. He said, "I could see how distressed my father was, and I did not want to leave him. I decided to stay and become a full-time driver."

For twelve years, the police failed to investigate the murder. Worse, they insinuated that it was Sami who had killed his brother. I was with Sami in the car when he finally got the news that he'd been waiting a decade for: they had found the culprit. I was impressed at how restrained Sami was. He did not even flinch, just kept on driving. Most Palestinians have learned to keep their anger down, to control their emotions, to spare themselves for the long haul, a lifetime of hardship and difficulties of life at the top of a volcano ready to erupt at any moment. How I wished I were like that.

Now, in the car, Sami began another story. He told me how once he was driving a young disabled woman through the Jordan Valley and they were stopped at a checkpoint. The guards there gave this young woman a very hard time. They wanted Sami to take her heavy wheelchair out of the trunk. But Sami, who is no wimp, told them that his job was to drive, and if they wanted to search the chair they could take it out themselves. "We Arabs are forgiving," he commented. "We are willing so quickly to forget and forgive. But they are different."

Every time Sami dropped me off at home, I would think about how for me, my anxiety was over, while Sami still had to pass through the Qalandiya checkpoint again on his way back home to Jerusalem. It was worse when his sons would call asking how long would it be before their father got home. This made me feel very guilty.

During another drive, I asked him why he didn't find a place outside the city in one of the suburbs on the Palestinian side of the checkpoint. He told me that he already had a house in Kufr Aqab. It has a garden. He bought it when the area was within the boundaries of Greater Jerusalem. "Then one day," he said, "I saw a man painting a big X on my fence. I asked him what he was doing and he said this is to indicate that the house has been moved outside the area of Jerusalem. Overnight I was chucked out of the city. I found a flat in At-Tur in an area that is so congested that one person complained that his neighbor's alarm clock woke him up."

Sami started again with another story aimed at distracting me.

"The other day," he began, "I was taking my two sons to Jerusalem from our home in Kufr Aqab. When we reached Qalandiya I got a call from a client for a job. I dropped off my two sons at the checkpoint and called my brother to pick them up on the other side. As I waited to see them going through on foot I saw a soldier beating one of them. I went over. I asked the soldier why he had done this.

"'Your son lied to me. He told me he has no identification card.'

"'But it's true. This is why he's carrying his birth certificate. Here it is. You can see he's not yet sixteen and not qualified to be issued an ID card.'" To me Sami commented: "They want to crush the spirit of the young. That's what they're after."

While I was trying to absorb the sinister behavior of the army, Sami, with hardly a pause, resumed his storytelling. "Imagine what I saw the other day when I went to fill up gas in Ramallah at the station near the Beit El settlement. Nearby, huge numbers of Palestinian police were standing in formation. I asked them why, and they said Abu Mazen, the Palestinian president, was planning to have lunch at Darna restaurant and they were waiting for him. Just as we were speaking, an Israeli tank rolled into the station, followed by a military jeep and an army personnel carrier. They parked at the station and several soldiers went to the upper floor above the station. They came down with a young man in handcuffs. They blindfolded him, threw him in the jeep, and drove away. The Palestinian police just looked the other way, waiting to take their president, their *rais,* to lunch.

"During the celebration for the forty-ninth anniversary of the unification of Jerusalem," Sami went on, "the police closed the roads leading to many parts of East Jerusalem where Palestinians live by placing a bus sideways blocking the road. I had to get the children from their school near the American Colony Hotel. I had to follow a long, roundabout route, park my car at the Ambassador Hotel, walk down to get them, and then go all around the new settlements to al-Zaim village and up from behind to El Tor. Some people had to abandon their cars and walk. The police take no account of what might happen in case of a medical emergency. They just shut the place up for the Arabs, and this on the day when they were celebrating the unification of Jerusalem. People call this Jerusalem Day our red day."

How so? I asked.

"In East Jerusalem the police use red ribbon to close off streets. There were so many streets closed off with red ribbon that we began calling this our red day. This is why my sons like to take every opportunity to escape to the Kufr Aqab house.

"Last night the constant hum of helicopters kept me from sleeping," Sami announced. "The army had come to arrest someone, and the young men began throwing stones at them. So they used tear gas. We had to close all the shutters to keep the gas from seeping into the house. The helicopters help the army a lot," he mused. "They see everything from above.

"During our last feast, the Israeli police prevented worshipers from reaching al-Aqsa mosque. Then they dumped sewage onto the streets so we would not be able to pray in them. They know that Muslims can only pray on clean ground. The police used to be different. We went to them to complain and expected to get relief. Not anymore. These days if you approach a policeman you run the risk of being shot at. Now they are racist."

I detected an uncharacteristically bitter tone in these words of Sami's. "Yesterday," he said, "a man flagged my taxi down. A policeman let me stop, then another officer came over to the Jewish American tourist and warned him in English (thinking I would not understand), 'He is not one of us.'"

In a somber tone Sami said, "I'm so tired of Jerusalem. All its people are bad and don't deserve this great city. The whole lot should all be evacuated and the city handed over to an international power. Then whoever wants to visit to pray there could use the houses of the former inhabitants, now turned into hotels."

Sami now fell silent. We drove on in uneasy silence, moving closer to the uncertain checkpoint, which would determine whether or not I was going to make it to the airport in time for my flight. The hills here looked decapitated, their tops flattened to accommodate settlements. They were lower than those we had passed earlier, with more open expanses of land between them.

As we began to approach the Rantis checkpoint, I saw that the land on both sides of the road was cultivated with old olive trees. The whole area was once owned by Palestinians. The slanting afternoon rays lit the limestone, and a glow bathed the olive branches, highlighting their silvery sheen. In the midst of the field beyond were spiny broom shrubs that shone with the sun like lanterns. How the settlers could argue that there was no one living in these lands before their arrival is truly bewildering.

Then Sami broke the silence.

"And yet some of these soldiers manning the checkpoints have a heart. One soldier noticed me coming to a checkpoint, getting checked, leaving and returning again and again in the same day. He finally asked me whether I ever get tired of all this. I could tell that he genuinely felt for me."

"And what did you say to him?"

"I didn't want him to pity me, so I turned it back on him, saying that if I didn't keep on going back and forth he would be out of work."

We were almost there. The time had passed with Sami moving from one story to another. We were now close to the Palestinian village of Rantis and the checkpoint—a beautiful area with low, undulating hills. My fear and nervousness were at their highest. Sami struck a lighter tone.

"Did I tell you what also happened on the last Jerusalem Day? It was an amazing sight. The municipality decided to construct a lift higher than a crane on the Mount of Olives. It had a sort of basket in which about ten people could fit. They were lifted so high up that they could see all of Jerusalem from on high. We watched this amazing spectacle as we were confined in our houses."

As I heard this, I smiled to myself. In one of my talks I had stated that Israel in this period was riding high. I was not aware how accurate this was. For a moment I considered telling this story in my upcoming talk in England. But then I realized I would not be telling any audience anything next week, because the soldiers manning this checkpoint were not going to let me through and I was going to miss my flight.

As we approached the Rantis checkpoint, I saw it all in my mind. With a few words or even just the movement of his hand, the young soldier would point his finger to me and order Sami: "Take him back. You should feel lucky that I'm not charging you. Just take him back." It would be so simple, and I would have to write to so many people to cancel all the planned events. So much effort and expense, gone for nothing. Sweat was trickling in rivulets down my back. I could feel that my undershirt was drenched. I looked at Sami, who remained calm and composed. There was no perceptible difference in his bearing as we approached the checkpoint. My admiration for him only rose.

Sami had saved the best and most engaging story for the end. He began, breaking through my line of thinking, saying: "Shall I tell you of the only time I lost my car keys and couldn't get back in my car?" I didn't answer. I was much too perturbed and preferred to remain silent. He continued: "I was driving near Jabaa. I had left my car to save people from a burning bus . . ."

He didn't have time to finish this one, though he kept on talking as if we were engaged in the most natural conversation and did not care at all about being stopped.

But I was not listening to Sami. Neither did I care anymore how the soldiers would perceive us and whether or not they would allow us to pass. My mind was now concentrated on the sign posted by the checkpoint. At first I thought I was hallucinating. I put on my glasses to make sure I was reading it right. It read: THIS CROSSING IS RESERVED ONLY FOR THOSE ENTITLED UNDER THE LAW OF RETURN OF 1950. Had it come to this, that passage through a checkpoint was reserved only for Jews, who were the only ones entitled under this discriminatory law? Many of those I saw passing unhindered indeed immigrated to Israel under this law reserved only for Jews, and made their home in the West Bank. Their government wants to deny me the right to pass because I do not qualify. Confronted with such injustice, what am I to do?

The spell was broken. I faced a much larger question than whether or not I would be allowed to pass through the checkpoint. What was the point of traveling all the way to London to tell others about injustice when I was so enmeshed in the logic of occupation that the possibility that I might be stopped at a checkpoint sent me into such panic? Was this what I had been reduced to after fifty years of occupation?

I looked at Sami. The sheen of perspiration was now visible on his brow. He too had been anxious, but he persevered. We drove through the checkpoint in companionable silence. He endured and will endure as he has for the past twenty years. I too cannot afford to abandon the struggle and must do what I can to end this occupation before it succeeds in utterly destroying us all.

OCCUPIED WORDS

LARS SAABYE CHRISTENSEN

PROLOGUE

Occupation is queue. Queuing is hell. Hell is reruns: every morning, more of the same. All kinds of delay, pain, and humiliation are gathered in these heavily guarded assemblies at the checkpoints around Jerusalem, where the lost faces lose face yet again.

OCCUPIED WORDS

At Ben Gurion Airport my suitcase is lost. It didn't arrive with the flight. It disappeared during transfer in Brussels, maybe already in Oslo. I know for certain that I carried it to the taxi in Anne Maries vei where I live, on the edge of the city, near the brook running down from the lakes of Nordmarka, the nature reserve surrounding the capital of Norway. It's not the end of the world. I can live without the suitcase. After all, everything I put in it can be bought again: socks, shoes, underwear, pencils, notebooks, clocks and watches, hat, phone charger, and a newspaper I didn't get to read before I left. And as I watch one last suitcase which doesn't belong to me glide past on the conveyor belt, which now looks like a dried-out riverbed, it strikes me: I'm a man without luggage. Everything in my possession can be replaced. My luggage is old news. This makes me agitated, even furious. I have to find someone to vent my anger on. It's obvious: the man behind the baggage service counter. I go over there to complain. I pour out my complaint. First I have to fill out a form: who I am. In addition, I'm repeatedly asked if I've really looked for it properly. So I haven't looked for it properly? Does the manager of the baggage service imagine that I don't recognise my own Norwegian suitcase, which I also packed myself? He has to check the ticket again. So he disappears for quite a while. There's another passenger missing his suitcase. He is even more agitated. It's the second time in a row it's happened. He's going to sue the airline, maybe even Israel, he is truly agitated. He gives me his business card. He travels around the world selling medical equipment. We can sue them together. Then we'll have a stronger case. But in airports aloneness reigns. Every passenger has his own case. Everyone is on his or her own. When the man I'm waiting for finally returns, I have to fill in yet another form: what my suitcase looks like. Suddenly I don't remember. It's embarrassing. It's like forgetting the colour of your loved one's eyes. I think it's blue. Yes, definitely blue, blue with a zipper and wheels. But these are vague memories, as if everything was long ago and not this morning, not today, not right now. Losing is laborious. The moment it slips away is short, but the time it takes is long. Losing increases the distances in you. You become a stranger no matter where you stand or position yourself. I sign at the bottom: Lars Saabye Christensen, author, blue eyed, 4 June 2016. June 2017 will be fifty years since the Six-Day War of 1967. The occupation of the Palestinian territories has lasted just as long. And that's the reason I'm here. To write about my impressions. Before departure, I got this bit of advice: you can tell airport security whatever you want, but don't lie. Anyway, I've no intention of lying. Telling the truth is good advice in most circumstances, except in obituaries. Hence I have to confess—and I use that exact word, *confession*, since I've noticed that my views, my attitude, are almost taken for granted, that a European writer isn't supposed to have a different opinion: Israel is the root of all evil. So I confess: I am a friend of Israel. I am willing to go far to be Israel's friend. It implies that I quite simply recognise

Israel's obvious right to exist, today, in the future. It implies Israel's duty to defend itself. It does not imply the right to torment people. There is no such right. No one has the right to do wrong.

I go through customs without being stopped. I have nothing superfluous. On the other side, my host, my employer, is waiting for me. He thinks I travel light. It's the other way around. An empty-handed man travels with a heavy load. We drive to Jerusalem. Since it's Saturday, one part of the city, the western, is silent and closed, while the shops in the east are open. We go to the main street and find a clothes shop. A young man is sitting on his knees in prayer. The shirts on the racks are garish, they remind me of the seventies or B movies. The young man continues his prayers, unperturbed between the till and the changing room. In the midst of the hustle and bustle of shopping, he's apparently found peace. Maybe his prayers are being heard. When I'm finally in the Ambassador Hotel, room 222, standing in front of the mirror before dinner, I see a strange man in a stiff, light yellow shirt with big lapels. He could be a restaurant musician, a bookmaker, a seller of Hoover bags. I try to make the words of the Swedish Nobel laureate Tomas Tranströmer my own: I am not empty, I am open.

A story, or rather an image, has haunted me all my life and therefore also left its mark on most of my writing. My mother, born in 1923, used to tell: she had a friend in the apartment building where she grew up, in Oslo. Her name was Rakel Feinstein. Rakel was Jewish. In October 1942 she knocks on the kitchen door, my mother opens, it's early. Rakel just wants to say that she's leaving now, but she'll be back soon. She doesn't come back. No one comes back. The Feinstein family is sent on the transport ship *Donau* to Stettin, Poland, and from there to Auschwitz. My mother always ended like this: I can still hear her footsteps down the stairs. When my mother died in 2009, I took over her story. Her memories became mine. Now it's my turn to hear these same footsteps that never turn back.

What's the use of a story like this, frozen in an acoustic image?

You shall not forget. You shall pass it on.

In the drawer of the bedside table there's a red circle with an arrow inside: DIRECTION MECCA. I am woken by the minarets, or maybe that's just something I'm dreaming. In any case it's strange. Being a stranger, in a strange land, does something to your thoughts. They seek an origin, a ground. That's what your thoughts long for. The thought longs for a direction to bend towards.

The next day is Jerusalem Day. And like most things in this region, this holiday is also ambiguous and full of contradictions. For some people it means liberation. For others, occupation. Settlers and their supporters will be marching from Damascus Gate straight through the Muslim Quarter of the Old City. I'm standing on the Via Dolorosa, waiting for trouble to ensue. It's five o'clock. Most of the shops are closed already. Last year they were damaged. A few peace activists, looking like peace activists all over the world, young, unassailable, and romantic, hand out roses. The message is old, the gesture likewise: the flower as a sign of good. There's a flaw in the symbolism, however, a permanent gash in this goodness: the flower withers. It lives for a moment. Then it withers in your hands. The first group arrives. I'm surprised. There are only young boys, dressed the same in white shirts, holding the Israeli flag high, singing and rejoicing. The next group is similar. I had imagined something different, middle-aged men maybe, older men, dour, religious, stern. Now it looks more like the celebration of a sports victory, or that these young people are done with their exams and have their lives, their entire wonderful lives, ahead of them, an unfurnished sky, freedom. It strikes me that these boys are happy. Their unity, their cause, are the sources of this happiness. I can't help but envy them. Then a peace activist gives a rose to one of the boys, virtually puts it in his hand, and all of a sudden this rose makes him vulnerable. And he reacts with a rage that in its force and precision almost resembles his joy. He smashes the flower against the stone step. He doesn't throw it away. That's too ordinary. Instead, he breaks the neck of the rose, and the dark red petals lie scattered along the cobblestones of the Via Dolorosa. Politics is dividing its own people. And this gesture is so violent that it certainly has a deeper cause than the evident, perhaps well-meaning, but at least well-mannered provocation the settler, the boy, is subjected to. And few things are worse than a well-mannered provocation. The rose threatens his very existence. There is nothing here which is neutral. Everything is loaded. Language is loaded. The language is armed and rearmed until the words are overloaded, until the words can't keep their word anymore and become action. The rose is a language that can immediately be translated to humiliation. Thanks are rendered into vandalism and destruction. And naturally I understand both expressions: the pious advances of the one idealist, the equally pious distance of the other. But who wins this discussion? The flower girl does. She is the clear winner. But it is the settler who carries the day. He has power on his side.

I remember another discussion, in the debating society of my high school in 1971. The radical youth movement was at the peak of its popularity. I'm referring to the Norwegian Marxist-Leninists, who during this short period shook hands with both Mao and Pol Pot, and if they could have woken Stalin from the dead, they would have taken both his hands too. The issue under debate was the Palestinians and the PLO. Could terror be justified in the struggle against oppression and imperialism? The answer was yes. If the cause was big and just enough and everything else had been tried, then aircraft hijackings were justifiable. In other words: war without limits, limitless war, not even civilians were to be spared. One of the participants actually said, I remember it verbatim: Terror isn't relevant in Norway yet, since it won't serve the cause. The cause? What cause? The word itself sounds unassuming, almost like an item on an overlong agenda. But the cause was greater than that. The cause was Utopia, the greatest thing of all, the classless society: the final exit, where Time encloses Justice like the shell encases the pearl. It was a cause that only had one side. Utopia is finite. Everything has already been achieved there. And these Norwegian utopians remind me of the boys marching on Jerusalem Day. They have zeal and unity in common. They have their sacred single-mindedness, their passion, in common. They have no doubts. Therefore, they are facing a disaster if it turns out that they're wrong. Therefore, they're able to murder a rose.

"When a Palestinian walking across the field feels threatened, maybe by a snake, a predator, or a thief, he immediately picks up a stone from the ground to protect himself. It's in our culture."

Those are the words of Bassem Tamimi, a well-known Palestinian activist. We're sitting with him and his wife, Nariman Tamimi, in their house in Nabi Saleh, which Amnesty International has called "a tiny village with a big voice." In the corner there's a rickety, half-empty aquarium containing three goldfish. Hanging on the wall is an embroidery that also used to hang in Norwegian homes, but that's a long time ago: GOD BLESS OUR HOME. Next to it there's another saying: PEACE AND JUSTICE. In the middle of the coffee table there's a platter of something that at first looks like dried brown fruit, but which turns out to be empty tear gas canisters, cartridges, shells. They are Israeli mementos: windfalls of metal. Glued to the flat screen is a photo I recognise: a small Palestinian boy crying in fear and pain, with an assault rifle pressed to his face. It's the couple's son. It happened last year. Now he appears in the background, together with his sister. They look like ordinary teenagers; with stylish hair, jeans, and a smartphone in the back pocket, they're busy, shy, and polite. I feel ashamed. Why shouldn't they look like ordinary teenagers? Are you supposed to stop brushing your hair because you're Palestinian? Are you supposed to stop dressing nicely because you are threatened?

Stones are defensive, not offensive.

Yet again one and the same object is split in two by words, in light and shadow. He who throws it feels threatened. She who is hit knows she is under attack.

Bassem Tamimi, who went on the barricades and is as convinced about the Palestinian cause as ever, although these days with a resigned intransigence, says: The two-state solution is an illusion. There is no solution. What will become of us? What will become of the Palestinian refugees around the world? There is no place for us. We feel alone.

Alone? I'm taken aback. Because the whole world thinks about the Palestinians all the time, more or less. The whole world talks about them, demonstrates for them, boycotts for them, and goes on strike for them. Ever since that meeting of the debating society in 1971, the world has cared about the Palestinians. People have been passionately devoted to their plight. People have been intransigent on their behalf. People have made the Palestinian cause into a lifestyle. People even dress like them. It is an absolute, superficial identification. And it hasn't really helped. On the contrary, things are getting worse. Idealism suffers defeat when the battle lines are drawn between all or nothing; that is, between good and evil. Maybe that's what Bassem Tamimi means with the loneliness of the Palestinians. With European idealism, everyone ends up lonely. Suddenly he starts talking about Gandhi and Martin Luther King Jr. When a middle-aged activist who spent years in Israeli prisons does that, then what you hear is a resigned human being. There is a kind of weary grief in his voice when he talks about peace. Peace isn't the same as peace either. This peace is a different condition in his language: corruption, limitations, delays, bureaucracy. This peace is a peace without justice. The Norwegian author and nation-builder Bjørnstjerne Bjørnson wrote: "Peace is not the best there is, but that you set your mind to something." I've always thought, what nonsense. And I still think so. But that doesn't rule out the possibility that Bassem Tamimi may be right. He emphasizes that all he wants is a normal life, just as most other Palestinians want normal lives.

And isn't that what Israelis want, too?

A thought, or rather a suspicion, strikes me: they don't know about one another anymore.

The house we're visiting is at risk of being demolished. For administrative reasons, according to the Israelis. And if not for administrative reasons, then for security reasons. Almost everything is for security reasons, apparently. If one person loves another it's probably for security reasons. I think Bassem Tamimi and his family could easily have put their signatures to the lines of Remi Kanazi, a Palestinian poet living in New York, and sent them to the prospective expeller:

> you don't want peace
> you want pieces*

But what kind of peace apostle is Bassem Tamimi? He speaks up for his, the Palestinians', cause, which obviously can't be faulted, but for an outside observer, like me, he nevertheless appears ambiguous.

---

* Remi Kanazi, *Before the Next Bomb Drops: Rising Up from Brooklyn to Palestine* (Chicago: Haymarket, 2015).

His language is carefully tailored, just as the photographs may be. What you see isn't necessarily true, but it's easily believable. All of it is easily believable. The table is set. It's the true propaganda.

Therefore, there's a darkness between the lines when Bassem Tamimi says that the third intifada must come and it must become global, and later, when I ask him how this global intifada will unfold, he answers: peacefully.

A few days before my departure from Norway, I saw an item in the papers: A small-town grocer had got himself into hot water. He had placed a crate of oranges outside his shop and put up a sign which just read ISRAEL. That was clearly wrong of him. The grocer shouldn't just remove these imperialist oranges, but also the sign; he should quite simply remove Israel. But shouldn't the people who insist on boycotting Israel be grateful instead? At the very least, here they could learn what tempting oranges they weren't supposed to eat. However, reason is not what counts in this matter. Apparently, the word *Israel* itself, the name of a democratic state, is enough to arouse anger, disgust, passion. You can talk matter-of-factly about ISIS. You can even show some understanding: ISIS is a monster created by the West. It is flagellation, European style. It is our bad conscience. ISIS warriors returning from Syria should get a second chance. They are good at heart. They should be pitied. It's a Norwegian article of faith: talk with someone for a long time, preferably in a hushed voice, and they'll become like us, eventually. But as soon as you talk about Israel, the tone is different, implacable, loud. Comparisons are made with South Africa. Comparisons are made with the Nazis. Anything can be said about Israel. And there's a lack of proportion, or a blind spot, in this increasingly hateful language, in which anti-Semitism appears as a shadow, a trace, a rumour being spread.

In the schoolyards in Oslo, *Jew* has become a term of abuse.

In the sixties, Israel was a role model. Radical youth went there to work on the kibbutzim. It was the new socialism. What has happened to language since then? Is it just a result of Israeli policies? It can't be that simple. We live in extreme times. Our language is being conquered by extremists. And when our language is occupied, attitudes change too, and sometimes the distance from attitude to action is short. The front lines move quicker than the thought. We can't keep up. Slowly but surely our views change, as when authors change the point of view in their novels without the reader noticing. It's a drama unfolding almost in secret. It's a drama which is met by a shrug of the shoulders, to the extent that it is recognised at all. It is the riddle of history: how brutalization and indifference go hand in hand.

The synagogue in Oslo, which is situated on the steep Bergstien near the beautiful and lush Saint Hanshaugen Park, was attacked by an Islamist in 2006. Thirteen rounds from an assault rifle. The court found that it wasn't terror. The Islamist was convicted of criminal damage. It is the new language, tailored, partisan, ideological: the true propaganda. Today the synagogue is under twenty-four-hour police protection.

By the way, I'm beginning to like my new clothes. The shirt is comfortable in the heat and the colour doesn't bother me anymore. After all, it's just a colour.

And then maybe I understand what Bassem Tamimi meant by the bureaucracy of peace: at Qalandiya checkpoint, which thousands of Palestinians must pass through to get to work in Jerusalem. It is five thirty. Hanna Barag, eighty-one years old, from the Israeli activist group Machsom Watch ("Checkpoint Watch") who is there to help, uses this expression: "the bureaucracy of the devil." This queue, mostly men, makes such a strong impression on me that I have to sort out my own vocabulary: occupation is queue. I know that this also has to do with Israeli security. I know that Israel has good reasons, better than most countries, to be on the alert. I know that there are two sides to every issue. But this apparently endless queue is one tragic side of two issues: Israel and Palestine. Here they are clear and distinct: power and powerlessness. Why does this queue affect me so strongly that I, too, must resort to the starkest of words? Queuing is something I can relate to. I hate queues. Queues are a waste of time. Queues are humiliation. Queues are the beginning of death. Queues are occupation. The column of men inches forwards, surprisingly disciplined, then the first gate closes, they wait, they don't know how long they have to wait, then they can proceed, but instead the men run, grown men run twenty metres to the next sluice, it is yet another humiliating race, as if they can recover everything they have lost during this stretch, time, money, land, honour. No one forces them to run, but they're nonetheless driven to it. Humiliation is the deepest wound you can inflict on people without taking their life. They have to live with something that's impossible to live with. Qalandiya checkpoint is like an everlasting airport: every morning Palestinians must stand in line to check in for work and board their life. Life here is delayed. You may carry only hand luggage. What I see is a society, the Palestinian society, put on hold. It is lost opportunities. It is waste. It is a tired tragedy in which Hanna Barag is a conciliatory figure. She relates that a soldier called her, this small, slight woman, "Arafat's whore." She couldn't get out of bed for a week. But Hanna Barag refused to be a victim of the war of words. She came back and has been standing here as a witness for the last sixteen years.

Another gate: the Humanitarian Gate. It's the checkpoint's fast track, for the sick, children, disabled people, and others in need of assistance. It doesn't open before six o'clock. By then the flight has already departed. I do know that it has to do with security. If someone in Israel says they want a divorce, it's probably for security reasons. Four hundred thousand Palestinians are blacklisted. But it is also a means of attrition. Attrition is a tactic: a slow, soundless war.

Israel is a triumph. In the course of a few decades, just a blink of history's eye, it has created a democracy, an army, science, a language, literature. Israel has managed this despite an almost impossible starting point, despite the hostility of the neighbouring countries, despite terror, which must have strengthened an Israeli habit of thought: to take nothing for granted, not even your own country. But is it nevertheless possible to say that Israel has become reckless? I think it is possible. Israel forgot about the resentment of the loser. Israel forgot the bitter memories of the Palestinians. Instead, Israel reminds them of their loss every single day. No one remembers better than the loser. To forget about it is playing with fire. I think: Can security become so extensive that it jeopardises security? Can security eventually become a security risk? One thing is certain: there aren't any certainties left.

When I return to my hotel room, I trip over something that wasn't there last time and take a tumble in the dark, hit my forehead against the bed and lie flat out on the wall-to-wall carpet. Is my nose broken? Something warm trickles into my mouth. Finally I manage to switch on the light. It's my suitcase. A greeting from the airline is attached to the handle. *Thank you for your patience.* I curse my luggage. I try and I try, but I can't get rid of it. My yellow shirt is flecked with blood. I throw it away with the other clothes. Then I shower, open the suitcase, and take out clean socks, underwear, light trousers, sandals, and a white shirt. I stand in front of the mirror. I don't recognise myself now either. Have I turned into a but person? Have I turned into the kind of person I despise, he who always says: I'm in favour of absolute freedom of speech, but. I'm categorically opposed to terror, but. I recognise Israel's right to exist, but. I don't want to be a but person, still attending the debating society in 1971, saying that the end justifies the means.

In *Haaretz* I read that the support among Palestinians for stabbing attacks on Israelis have sunk from 58 to 51 percent the last month. That's what you might call both good and bad news.

The day before I travel home to write this we drive to Hebron. Graffiti scrawled on a yellow barrier shutting the Palestinians out from Road 60 so that they can only use the old, neglected roads, grabs my attention: *A gift from Oslo.* So this is the local thanks for the Oslo accords: scorn. And later, inside Hebron itself, in what is known as Ghost Town, the most desolate streetscape I've ever seen, the settlers for their part have put up a sign in one of the closed-down shops, where the lock has rusted shut long ago and the dust drifting past recalls the violence and the sorrow: *These stores were closed by the IDF for security reasons after Arabs began the "Oslo War" [a.k.a. the second intifada] in September 2000, attacking, wounding, and murdering Jews on this road.*

The Oslo War?

Oslo, my hometown, is under attack from all sides. None of the parties is satisfied with Oslo. Oslo, the city of my birth, the setting of my stories, and the subject of my songs, is gradually being occupied. Language itself is being occupied. Oslo isn't a name anymore, but a rotten agreement, a conflict, a lost peace.

Is this the luggage I'm losing: My starting point, the only ground under my feet?

Then I take a closer look. It doesn't say *Oslo*, but *Olso*. Olso doesn't exist. It is an orthography of rage, an ideological misprint: the Olso War. I try to recapture my starting point, Oslo, here in these deserted streets of Hebron, where I'm suddenly reminded of a few lines by the great Israeli poet Yehuda Amichai. I don't know why, but maybe it is because poetry is a language that approaches the world from a different angle than all the assessments, statistics, speeches, and slogans, and with a different emotional reason than the passions of the moment, and which accordingly has its own purpose and agency, shining through the discreet beauty of these words:

> *Sandals are the skeleton of a whole shoe,*
> *the skeleton, and its only true spirit*
> . . . .
> *Sandals are the youth of the shoe*
> *and a memory of walking in the wilderness*

Between 2000 and 2007, five Israeli civilians, including an eleven-month-old baby, and seventeen members of the Israeli security forces were killed in Hebron. During this same period, Israeli security forces killed nearly ninety Palestinians. Walking on Shuhada Street, the main street of Hebron, has been illegal for Palestinians since 2000. And the few Palestinian families who still live here can't use their own entrance doors. They live in houses under lockdown. Now the settlers are here instead. They've built their own houses. They are, as they see it, back where they belong. It's their conviction. Israeli soldiers are protecting them. It looks like a war zone. A settler screams abuse. *May you get cancer in your hearts.* Another one approaches us to argue his cause, loud, rude and obstinate, his index finger dancing in front of our faces, closer and closer, but never too close. It is the same passion the young boy showed on Jerusalem Day, just in a different manner. An Israeli soldier intervenes. He is barely twenty and already tired and sad looking. Is this how he's supposed to spend his youth? I imagine he has his doubts at times: Who is he really protecting? We go to yet another checkpoint and are let through to the Palestinian area. The shopping street here is narrow and shadowy; only the colourful fruit in the stalls shed some light. I wonder: above us there's a stretch of wire netting, and in some places plastic. The carpet seller explains: the settlers living on the upper floors often throw garbage down at them; sometimes they even pour urine. I can understand the hotheaded settler. He is convinced he's right. It is his right to be wrong. But this? This isn't politics. This isn't ideology. This is evil. This is passion.

If you want to lose your faith, just go to Hebron.

Later that night I read in *Haaretz* about a terror attack in Tel Aviv. At least four people are killed at the Sarona Market by two Palestinians from the Hebron area. Soon Hamas praises the atrocity: this is only the first of many surprises we have in store. Time hasn't come to a halt. It has reversed, to 1967, just before the war, when Fatah said that every terror attack against Israel would remind the world about the word *Palestine*. The Palestinian leaders aren't just old. They are dead too. I can quote the same lines again: *you don't want peace / you want pieces*. The preliminary Israeli response: the entry permits of eighty-three thousand Palestinians to enter Israel during Ramadan are revoked. As a novelist, I'm obsessed with the sequence of things. The sequence gives the actions their meaning and shares out responsibility. Politics is a sequence as well. It's as simple as the logic of a child: you started it! Now they're losing count. It's as if the sequence is discarded and actions blend into one another. They lose their time and space. Israel points to the blood still flowing at the Sarona Market, June 9, 2016. Palestine turns to 1967, points to the occupation. The sequence, which is the arithmetic of possibilities, the geometry of hope, has become a vicious cycle instead.

I can't envisage anything but what I would call "a peace of the discontented." A two-state solution, if that's the way forward, would necessarily entail painful compromises. *Compromise*, a word blackened by European idealists, because it's too puny for them, is the most important tool of political craftsmanship. Big words rarely keep their word.

And heroes are a dime a dozen. They come and go. Compromise, on the other hand, demands visionary leaders. Compromise is boring. What's boring is what's true: meals, work, sleep, repetitions, in short— everyday life.

How easy it was to think this.

How easy it is to write it down.

Something else must be mentioned: What about the advance of Islamic fundamentalism, not just in Arab countries, but even in Europe? In this context Israel isn't Goliath anymore, but David. What about ISIS ravaging the neighbourhood, raising passionate zealotry to a new, historic level? What does that do to a conflict over an area the size of, let's say a Norwegian county? It makes compromise an alien concept in our occupied language.

Words bludgeon one another to death.

Two tracks cross in my story: Rakel, my mother's friend, who was sent to the concentration camp, and Ivan Osiier, who fled from Copenhagen to Sweden in 1943 and thus saved his life. He was born in 1888, married my paternal grandfather's sister, and was a beloved physician in Vesterbro. But above all, Ivan Osiier was a famous sportsman. As a fencer he holds the record for most appearances at the Olympic Games. He participated seven times: London 1908, Stockholm 1912, Antwerp 1920, Paris 1924, Amsterdam 1928, Los Angeles 1932, and, at the age of sixty, in London 1948, when he was part of the Danish épée team. His main fencing strengths were his precision and his effective parries. In addition, his powers of concentration allowed him to wait for his opponent to make a mistake. However, his most important Olympics were Berlin 1936. He didn't participate. On his own initiative he boycotted Hitler's games. Ivan Osiier said, "Fencing is a noble form of attack, but in defending myself I use all weapons." In 1986, twenty-one years after his death, he was inducted into the International Jewish Sports Hall of Fame.

Then I turn towards the synagogues and minarets one last time while the driver puts my old suitcase in the boot of the taxi. Yehuda Amichai writes in a poem:

The air over Jerusalem is saturated with prayers and
*   dreams*
like the air over industrial cities
It's hard to breathe

EPILOGUE

By the way, I had an appointment with an optimist in Ramallah, but he never showed up.

(TRANSLATED FROM THE NORWEGIAN BY
NILS TORVALD ØSTERBØ)

PRISON VISIT

DAVE EGGERS

WE HAVE ARRIVED AT EREZ BORDER CROSSING WITH ALL THE necessary permits and stamps and approvals to get me into Gaza. But the young Israeli man at the gate flatly refuses. He is sitting in a gatehouse, a structure no bigger than a backyard shed, and in every way he resembles a fast-food fry cook. He is thin and impossibly young, with just a few stray hairs on his upper lip and chin. He is wearing a black baseball cap with the letters DEA—the Drug Enforcement Agency, an American law enforcement arm—in large white letters. After he explains that I can't enter Gaza this day, he goes back to the work in front of him. Through his window we can see that he's drawing pictures of an idealized woman on a legal pad.

I'm with an Israeli guide, an ex-IDF soldier, and we have been traveling much of the day, looking at settlements and outposts in the West Bank. All day, using maps and talking very loudly, my guide has been making a good case for the theory that much of what we've seen is not the work of isolated settlers, zealots, and radicals, but rather a systematic plan, conceived and funded by the Israeli government, to encircle and cut off Palestinians from their land and their own people.

This is unsettling enough, but the enforcement of the myriad and byzantine rules and boundaries that make modern Israel and Palestine possible is equally or more troubling. All over the West Bank we have encountered checkpoints on roads, our car has been searched, and we have seen the refugee camps, and enforcing it all, and wearing the Israeli uniform are, invariably, soldiers who seem to be only months beyond adolescence. Scarcely filling out their fatigues, they appear alternatively blasé and terrified. And, like most nineteen- or twenty-year-olds, they are given to irrationality, caprice, and diffidence. In too many instances of IDF abuses, there is both the more rule-oriented systemic underpinning—the inherently inhumane essence of any occupation—and the capricious: very young soldiers making bad decisions.

This teenager in the gatehouse is one of these young people given too much unchecked power. When we ask him why I can't enter Gaza, even though I have every necessary permit and approval, he tells us that visitors aren't allowed to spend the weekend in Gaza.

"Never heard that one before," my guide says.

There is in fact no regulation that states that visitors can't visit Gaza on a weekend.

All week long in the West Bank, members of our group of writers have witnessed and heard testimony about the countless ways the occupation has made life less than human for millions of Palestinians—and, it's worth noting, for the Israelis who have to enforce the occupation. When laws are irrational, and paranoia is rampant, and ancient hatreds undergird both, life becomes a series of frustrations and humiliations, and humiliated people are either broken spiritless or, with nothing left to lose, are driven to acts of violent desperation. The young people tasked with enforcing these dehumanizing laws and regulations become, too, less human—they become callous, irrational, finding perverse pleasure in the wilful exercise of power.

Now, at the gate, we are experiencing just the smallest taste of this. Beyond the gate is the wall separating Gaza from Israel. It is twenty-eight feet tall and impenetrable. In front of us, visible about five hundred yards away, is a formidable guard tower, the same kind seen in the West Bank, threatening and impersonal, intended to intimidate. The wall is interrupted by a large modern building, looking like an airport terminal. Its facade is primarily glass, and it has an incongruously welcoming disposition. On its western side, the wall continues, and runs all the way to the Mediterranean.

I have been in a number of American prisons, and in most ways the entrance to Gaza resembles the entrance to a large maximum-security facility. There are the gatehouses, the walls, the guard towers, the changing and nonsensical rules for visitation, and now, as my guide and I look around for someone to appeal to besides the teenager in the gatehouse drawing pictures of women, I notice for the first time that there is a man pointing a semiautomatic rifle at us.

He is an Israeli soldier in a low guard tower, just beyond the gatehouse, no more than fifty feet away. He is pointing his Galil at us. He is wearing sunglasses, and has his cheek pressed against the gun in a way that means, or is meant to imply, that he is ready to use it. I point him out to my guide, and the ex-soldier shrugs.

"It probably isn't even loaded," he says. But this seems unlikely.

It is three thirty now, and the one actual regulation applicable here is that the Gaza border closes at four o'clock.

"If you don't get in today, we can try again Sunday," my guide says.

And though we argue with the young man in the gatehouse, he seems to be the only human at the border gate, and seems to have full and unchallengeable authority. My guide makes a flurry of phone calls to Israeli officials and journalists. No one he speaks to has ever heard of any regulation prohibiting weekend visits to Gaza. Finally he reaches higher-ups inside the glass building.

Ten minutes before four o'clock, a different Israeli soldier appears. He is some kind of military press officer, and he's as friendly as a small-town pharmacist. "Hello!" he says. He waves to my guide and ushers me through the gate. As we walk to the glass building that separates Gaza from Israel, he asks if I've been waiting long, if I've ever been to Gaza, if I've enjoyed my stay in Israel so far.

MINUTES LATER I'M SITTING AT AN OCEANSIDE PROMENADE IN GAZA City. The sun is bright and the sky is cloudless and blue. Hundreds of families are out, enjoying the day. Balloon vendors, followed by children and ignored by parents, carry great bursts of color pulling upward on tiny strings. Extravagantly painted fishing boats rock in the gentle current. Kites hover above.

I am with a man named Hazem, a fixer who guides visiting journalists through Gaza. Hazem is in his late thirties, with a wife and young children. Though the day is in the high seventies, he is wearing a sport coat over a sweater, and because he has worked frequently with British media, he speaks with a posh and lugubrious accent. We sit and watch the crowded waterfront, and I try to get Hazem to understand just how unexpected this is, this happy scene, these happy families, these children sitting on the sand eating ice cream, these groups of young men shyly eyeing groups of young women, this scene of idyllic normalcy in a region known globally only for its conflict, poverty, deprivation, and isolation. No one knows this side of Gaza, because no one can visit.

Since the election of Hamas in 2005, a political party considered far more radical than Fatah, its counterpart in the West Bank, Gaza has lived through three wars with Israel and the imposition, in 2007, of a blockade that prevents materials, from cement to fiberglass to fertilizer, from entering. Once, tens of thousands of Gazans were employed in Israel and the West Bank, but after the Second Intifada in 2000, the majority lost their work permits. When Hamas took control of Gaza, any remaining work permits were revoked. In the wake of the 2014 cease fire, a handful—five thousand—work permits have been issued, but still, unemployment has soared.

"The feeling is really bad," Hazem says. "It touches the soul in a bad way. The feeling that you can't leave. That no one can come here." Though Gaza has forty-two kilometers of white-sand coastline, and at one time was a destination for beachgoers—it even had a casino— Hazem can't remember the last time he saw a tourist in the Gaza Strip. "We are friendly people," he says, "but it's out of our hands."

In the days before entering Gaza, I'd met dozens of Palestinians in the West Bank, and not one of them had been to Gaza. Very few even knew anyone in Gaza. But invariably the perception of the place was one of privation and tragedy. And certainly, when I visited, in March 2016, Gaza was only two years past a brutal conflict with Israel. In that war, Israel fired tens of thousands of shells into Gaza, destroying 12,620 housing units and severely damaging another 6,455. Twenty-two hundred Gazans were killed, approximately 1,400 of them civilians. In the media, Gaza has long been depicted as a hellish place, a vast outdoor prison.

But then there is this waterfront. Jangly music grows louder from the promenade in front of us, and we see it's coming from tiny cars, built for children and bejeweled in gold and red and blue. For a few shekels children can get a ride on the cars, can be pushed around the pavement for a few minutes by surly teenaged men trying to make a living on a sunny afternoon.

An older man approaches, trying to sell us knives. They are kitchen knives with pastel-colored handles, and the salesman spreads them out like playing cards. Hazem waves the vendor off, but I make the mistake of showing the faintest curiosity, so the man remains in front of us. He takes out a piece of paper and in a fluid motion slices it in half. He offers this knife for the equivalent of one dollar. Hazem declines. The man offers two knives for the same price. After being rebuffed again, the man lowers the price to a dollar for all the knives he's carrying. For a moment, I consider buying them, just to appease him, and then think of the absurdity in trying to carry ten knives from Gaza through Israeli security. Hazem declines, and the vendor's hands drop to his sides. He looks away from us, scanning the promenade for the remote possibility of a sale.

HAZEM AND I HAVE HEARD ABOUT THIS CONCERT, A RARITY IN GAZA, featuring a new musical act. For months the group, called Sol Band, had been placing flyers around town, and had barraged social media with news of this concert, which was to be free to all. Since taking power in 2007, Hamas has not looked kindly on cultural gatherings like this, but there is some indication that its restrictions are loosening. In 2016, it has allowed a handful of films to be shown, though the movies are heavily censored and their showings closely monitored by what Gazans call the Hamsawis, the shadowy army of plainclothes spies and religious police affiliated with Hamas.

Concerts are rarer. To hold any concert in Gaza, permits from Hamas are required, and the Hamsawis are reluctant to issue permits, given the risk of inappropriate mixing between men and women. In any public gathering, especially a concert, women are to sit on one side, men on the other. No one is allowed to stand, in large part because standing might lead to swaying to the music, and this in turn might lead to dancing. And dancing is strictly prohibited. As is any kind of lewd comingling between the sexes, which of course would be facilitated by the dancing.

In the early evening, we enter the Red Crescent building, the second-floor ballroom of which has been converted this night to a concert hall. The muffled sound of amplified music fills the lobby. Hazem and I climb the polished steps to the mezzanine and see dozens of young Gazans socializing, their faces gray behind cigarette smoke. People taking a break from the show huddle in groups, male and female and mixed. The men wear skinny jeans, the women wear sparkly hijabs and new boots. Beyond them are double doors, and beyond the double doors are the thumping sounds of an amplified band in full swing.

At the doors, there is a jumble of young men serving as gatekeepers. Two are standing behind a card table, each of them holding what looks to be a guest list. Hazem says something about press credentials, and we're ushered in. The room is dark and packed with young Gazans. The mood is electric, even though the audience, four hundred or so men and women under thirty, are firmly planted in their seats. Ballroom chairs have been arranged in two sections, one male and one female. Hazem and I find the last few remaining empty seats, in the back row of the male section. Instantly a young woman carrying a baby slides into our section, a few rows ahead. She wears no hijab and sits between two men, their hips touching. Soon we see more women in the men's section, and men in the women's section.

Still in their seats, the audience sways to the music—recent popular tunes from Egypt and Lebanon. Onstage, the band is arranged like a tableau, well composed but unmoving. There is a keyboard player, a clarinetist, a drummer, and a conservatively dressed woman playing the oud. The lead singer takes a tentative few steps left to right, but the rest of the band plays with feet firmly planted. Certain songs elicit loud cheers, and the audience sings every word. They raise their phones to capture the concert, their blue screens high over their heads, and when a new song begins, they whoop and sing along. It all seems far removed, and far more liberalized, than one would expect to be permitted under the conservative rule of Hamas. For the single young men and women in the room, this is clearly the event of the month—maybe of the year. People continue to arrive and the hall grows more crowded. Friends look for friends. People get up, make room, sit down. Soon there are dozens of people standing behind us, and new people flow into the hall continuously.

Meanwhile, a blur of a man, wearing jeans and a sport coat, is at loose ends, darting through the room, looking like a concert promoter anywhere in the world. He's young and slick and nervous, walking up and down the center aisle, moving chairs, carrying new chairs, directing traffic, trying to find seating for everyone, checking his phone.

Because we've seen enough of the show, and because more and more people continue to stream into the hall, Hazem and I cede our seats to two women who have just arrived, and we leave. In the mezzanine, we run into two young women, both journalists. Because the circle of Gazan journalists and fixers is small, Hazem knows them both. One is Basilah*, with whom I have some American friends in common. In the haze of cigarette smoke and the buzz of the event of the season, we talk for a few minutes before the journalists want to go back inside to see the rest of the show.

Outside, the sky is pink and the air is cooling with the setting sun. The sound of drums overtakes the street, and when Hazem pulls his aging sedan onto the main drag, we find ourselves behind a wedding parade. A large open-backed cargo truck carries a dozen men—musicians playing drums and horns, issuing into the evening sky a rhythmic and delirious dirge. Following the truck is a caravan of six

---

* Names of this individual and many others whom I interviewed have been changed to protect their privacy.

cars decorated with balloons and streamers. They swerve through traffic, honking, pink balloons flying off caravan cars and drifting to the dusty roadside.

We follow the wedding parade up al-Rasheed Road as it hugs the coast and then turns east and inland. The road is abuzz with tuk-tuks and motorcycles and taxis. Barefoot children play on the rubble-laden sidewalks. Groups of teenage boys walk in the middle of the street, against traffic, defiantly causing cars to swerve around them. Old men on horse-drawn carts hug the curb. White lights from open shops line the streets. As we're following one wedding parade, another passes us going the other way. Like the one we're following, it features a truck filled with drums and horns, and is followed by a caravan of celebrants in sedans and trucks.

For a few hours this Thursday night, Gaza City is full of life and celebration, a coastal town electric with possibility. As confounding as was the idyllic waterfront earlier in the day, al-Rasheed Road on a Thursday night has an exuberant bustle to it that defies all the assumptions we make about Gaza.

It happens all weekend, Hazem says. The wedding parties drive up and down al-Rasheed, and end up at one of the many banquet halls on the waterfront. Marriage is expected of the young people of Gaza, and meeting this expectation, even though so few young people are employed, is difficult. Couples will spend upward of twenty thousand dollars on their wedding, and will live under the burden of this debt for many years. Children should come soon thereafter— children that again they have little means to support.

My hotel, the al-Deira, is located on the waterfront, and when Hazem drops me off, at nine o'clock, the celebrations continue. My room has a view of al-Rasheed's neon strip to the east and the black shimmer of the Mediterranean to the west. Just below me is an empty lot, where a steady string of men walking on al-Rasheed's sidewalk slip in and urinate against the wall. Next to the vacant lot is a restaurant calling itself the Love Boat, the words in English and set against a pair of red hearts. I'd seen the building earlier in the day, and at the time, I couldn't fathom what kind of business a sign like that would indicate, other than some kind of hourly hotel.

But now it makes sense.

It's one of the many banquet halls where the wedding parades end. From my hotel room, two stories up, I can see into the Love Boat's courtyard, and soon one of the wedding processions slows down and a flatbed truck full of musicians and drums, seven or eight cars following closely, enters. Thirty or more men in formal wear— the parties are segregated, male and female—unpack themselves from their cars and whoop into the hall. There are more songs, more drums, and soon the groom is led around the courtyard on a horse. Where did the horse come from? It is loud, even in the hotel room, even with the windows closed, and I assume I'm in for a long night.

I LIE IN BED, EXHAUSTED FROM THE DAY, TRYING TO SQUARE EVERYTHING that had happened in the last twelve hours. I listen to the whooping of the celebrants, the rumble of the road, the bleating horns, the insistent drums. I had been led to believe Gaza was a place of limitless sorrow, but now there is this. There is music, there are too many weddings to count. There are stylish young people smoking in the lobby of a concert hall. And there is the noise of a city that does not seem likely to sleep.

Only now do I remember something odd about my passing through the Erez gate. After the teenage fry cook denied my entry, and after the second officer led me to a green-glass building, I waited for a customs agent to process me. Like every other Israeli involved in every aspect of enforcement, she was very young, no more than twenty-five, wearing a crisp blue uniform. Sitting in a high glass box, she processed me efficiently, and I thanked her and moved on, into a vast second lobby. I was alone, and there was no clear indication of where to go next. I turned back to her glass box, and she pointed me to a nondescript door on the far wall. I expected this door to lead to some security check, but it led only to a strange hallway smelling strongly of the sheep that graze nearby. There were no guards or other travelers visible. This hallway led outside, where the smell of sheep and pigeon feces was overwhelming. I walked through an outdoor hallway, covered with a roof and fenced in on either side.

It twisted left and right for a kilometer, and all the while I assumed at some point I would arrive at a security area, where my bags and person would be X-rayed and examined. But this never happened. I was not stopped at either the Palestinian Authority or the Hamas checkpoint. When the hallway ended, there were only a handful of Gazan taxi drivers, smoking and waiting to take passengers across the buffer zone and into Gaza.

Trying to sleep, my mind conjures the masked faces of the soldiers I'd seen on the street that day, members of the al-Qassam Brigade. They were on the central turnabout of al-Rasheed Street, standing with legs wide, hands on their semiautomatics. Their uniforms were a swimming pool blue, their boots black, and on their faces they wore what looked like black ski masks. In the middle of the day, amid the rush of traffic, they had an appearance both nightmarish and routine.

The music outside continues. The thumping drums. The car horns. The whoops of young men. There is no reason to think it will end. But then it does. At the stroke of ten o'clock, it all ends and the street is quiet again. It is miraculous and strange, and the only logical explanation is Hamas.

Finally I drift into a jet lag–deep sleep, but soon I have a strange sense that someone is jiggling the doorknob of my hotel door. For a full minute the rattling of the knob is incorporated into a vague dream of mice scampering behind a shallow wall.

Now there is scratching at the keyhole. I'm still half-asleep, and still disbelieving that someone would actually be trying to get into the room. I listen, and picture the al-Qassam on the other side of the door. It makes no sense.

But now the person on the other side of the door is trying to work the lock. The sound before was an aimless scratching, a key trying to fit into a narrow hole. Now there is the determined sound of metal on metal.

Now I'm awake. There's actually someone trying to open my door. I remember that when I went to bed, I couldn't pull the dead-bolt over; it was stuck. So the door has no lock. All I could do was attach the chain.

The moment I remember this, the door swings open four inches and stops with a bang. The chain holds. "Huh?" I yell, because I can't think of anything else to say.

The door closes. Whoever it was who was trying to get in says nothing. I get up, go to the door, and finally get the bolt to work. I pull it right and it clicks into place. Now the door has a deadbolt and a chain, and I go back to bed. And, because everything here adheres to a logic all its own, I don't call the front desk. I don't call anyone. I immediately go back to bed and sleep the sleep of the dead.

"WE'RE VERY ANGRY. VERY DISAPPOINTED. VERY DESPERATE. WE JUST want to go and sing." These are the words of Basilah, one of the journalists I saw the night before at the Sol Band concert. We're sitting in the restaurant of the al-Deira Hotel, which overlooks the sea, and the day is sunny, the sky a brilliant blue, and the beach below looks peaceful and calm.

Basilah and I have mutual acquaintances in the United States, and they'd told me to bring her little luxuries that are hard to find, like lip gloss. I hand her a half-dozen containers of various looks and flavors, and her eyes grow bright.

Basilah is twenty-nine years old, and has been writing for various media outlets in the Arabic and Western worlds for the last five years. Because she's fluent in English, and is a skilled writer, her articles about Gaza have garnered an international audience. She is determined to make sure the world knows that there is a semblance of normalcy in Gaza. That there are malls, weddings, concerts.

"That doesn't mean that we're happy," she says. "We're not happy at all being in Gaza. Most of the people I saw at the concert, they are applying for student visas, they are losing their scholarships. They are thinking their chances are very, very limited. We are stuck in Gaza and we can do nothing about it."

With a median age of just over eighteen, Gaza has one of the youngest populations in the world. But though education is prized, there are few jobs for university graduates. And since the arrival of Hamas and its dismal relations with Israel, getting a visa to leave the country is exceedingly difficult. Because Gaza has no airport—its airspace has been controlled by Israel since 1967—Gazans wanting to study abroad must pass through Egypt or Israel, and because tensions are high between Hamas and both Egypt and Israel, neither country is currently inclined to allow Gazans student visas. And they can't see family members in the West Bank and Israel. In Gaza, they can scarcely find work. And every few years, it seems, Hamas engages in a disastrous fight with its infinitely more powerful Israeli neighbors, and this further limits Gazan civilians' ability to move in and out of Gaza, and curtails their access to goods, clean water, electricity, and opportunities.

Basilah and many other Gazans I met refer to Gaza as an "open-air prison," and it's difficult to argue with the description. On Gaza's northern border there is a twenty-five-foot wall separating Gaza from Israel. This barrier is forty miles long, and long stretches of it are thirteen feet higher than the Berlin Wall, and far more heavily fortified. On its eastern border there is a moat, then a low wall, and on top of it an electrified fence, dotted with guard towers manned by Israeli soldiers and patrolled by Israeli tanks. On Gaza's southern border there is another wall, separating Gaza from Egypt. This wall is ten miles long, and is much like the northern border with Israel. It is twenty-five-feet high and has fifteen guard towers.

On the last side of Gaza, the western side, there is the Mediterranean Sea. This is perhaps the most deadly and impenetrable border. Two navies, the Israeli and Egyptian, monitor the water with patrol boats, ready to sink any vessel attempting to go north to Israel, south to Egypt, or further than six nautical miles from shore.

So Gaza is a prison, and about 1.8 million people live inside this prison. They live in Gaza City, a bustling and cosmopolitan seaside city of more than half a million souls, and they live on farms and grow asparagus and almonds and cucumbers, and they go about life as best they can. There are nine universities and colleges. There are thirty-two hospitals. There are malls and galleries. There is Internet access, and wealthier people have cable television. The quality of water is substandard for some and terrible for others, and the electricity is not reliable; all but the elite can count on no more than eight hours a day. There are good restaurants. There are dinner parties, weddings, celebrations, births, parties by the seaside. But it is a prison.

We look down at the waterfront, and only then do I realize this is the beach where, in July 2014, an Israeli air force missile killed four boys in the middle of the day, in full view of dozens of observers, including a number of Western journalists. Four boys, aged nine to eleven, all of them unarmed and wearing shorts, were members of a fishing family called the Bakrs. They were playing in and around a small shipping container where their father kept his boat and nets. The IAF missile destroyed the container and killed them all. After an investigation, no Israeli soldiers were charged with wrongdoing; it was considered an honest enough mistake of war. Now as then, the waterfront looks as tranquil as would an Italian seaside village.

Basilah talks about the concert the night before. "I see the same people at all the concerts. The same four hundred people from Gaza City come to every show," she says. Often the concerts feature patriotic music, she says, bands singing about Palestine and the day when Gazans will return to their villages. "People shout 'Yeah, yeah!' and I'm like . . ." Basilah rolls her eyes. Basilah prefers the bands who are trying something new. I ask if a concert like the one last night, with its more secular focus, is evidence of an easing of restrictions placed on Gazans' social life.

"No, I don't think so," Basilah says. "Probably someone in the band has a relative in Hamas, and they got a permit. Hamas is not motivated to do *any* cultural event. They don't want these events, but they can't say no all the time."

If Gaza is a prison, it's a prison with three jailors: Israel, Egypt, and Hamas. For young people looking to place blame for their situation, "it's Israel first, Hamas second," Basilah says. The restrictions on their cultural life are oppressive and random. And widespread charges of corruption and graft have drained away any remaining goodwill the party had. They harass their own citizens on religious grounds, and, because the government is strapped for cash, they impose crippling fines for dubious violations. Last week, Basilah says, a taxi driver was stopped and made to pay fifty shekels—half a day's pay. When he refused, they impounded his taxi.

"Hamas, for god's sake," Basilah says. "You spend all these years in power and you do nothing. Your relations with other countries are like shit. People are committing suicide every single day."

She mentions a man who killed himself the week before. He had gone to the hospital and incurred a bill of two hundred dollars. But he couldn't pay it—he'd lost his job after the blockade—so Hamas took his identity card.

"They kept his card for two months," Basilah says, "and you can't live in Gaza without an identity card. Everywhere you go, they ask, where is your card?" The man was caught coming and going. The same party who took his card asked for it wherever he went. So he set himself on fire in front of the hospital.

"And no one cares anymore," Basilah says. "Even if you want attention, now there's no point to kill yourself. Too many people are doing it, so it has no effect anymore."

Basilah finishes her tea and looks out at the water.

"But we say, Okay, let's do something that breaks the routine of being always depressed, knowing that we're stuck in a prison. We're stuck in a prison, so let's sing and dance inside this prison."

THE COAST OF GAZA, ALL THE WAY NORTH TO EGYPT, IS RAVISHING—THE sea is bright blue, the white sand almost untouched. Hazem and I speed along the coast, a gentle breeze coming over the Mediterranean as we pass an endless succession of empty beachside restaurants. Before Hamas, the coast was used as a weekend getaway for Gazans, and before the first Intifada, the entire coastline was crowded with beachgoers.

But now it's empty. The conservative version of Islam favored by Hamas forbids women from wearing bathing suits, and frowns on men swimming shirtless, too. And because there are no tourists, we drive forty kilometers, from Gaza City to the Rafah Meena, and we see no more than a half-dozen humans on the uninterrupted white sand shore.

At the Rafah wharf, we find a long line of wooden fishing boats, pulled up onshore, painted in primary colors. Facing the boats is a row of storage lockers, used by fishermen to store nets and lights. In one of them, a group of men is sitting on overturned buckets, having lunch. They invite Hazem and me to join them, but we decline. We ask around for the leader of the wharf, and are directed to a large man named Bashir.

Barrel-chested, with a grizzled beard, sunburned skin, and a mouth full of broken teeth, Bashir is commanding but approachable. He wears a red-and-black plaid keffiyah over a faded peach button-down, its short sleeves revealing his deeply tanned arms. He has been fishing in the Mediterranean for decades. In the eighties he operated out of Haifa, and says "there were *too many* fish. We had to return them by the boatload." After the Oslo accords, he was relocated to Gaza, and began fishing from Rafah. Every few years since then, the restrictions on fishermen have grown tighter, and now, he says, is the most difficult time yet.

"The blockade is attacking all parts of life," he says. "People have no jobs, no work. They are desperate. Palestinian society used to be productive, farming and fishing. Now we are a consuming society, relying on others."

For centuries, Palestinians were fishermen, and until 1948 they were free to fish wherever they saw fit in the Mediterranean. In the decades after the creation of Israel, their freedom of movement has been increasingly curtailed. In 1994, the Oslo accords gave fishermen permission to fish twenty nautical miles west in pursuit of their livelihood. In 2006, Hamas captured and held an Israeli soldier named Gilad Shalit. In retaliation, Israel instituted a naval blockade, restricting the movement of any vessels to and from Gaza; the area in which fishermen were allowed was reduced to six nautical miles from shore. Now, depending on relations between Hamas and Israel, and depending on the mood of the IDF soldiers on the patrol boats, that six miles can be five, or three. Ostensibly, the IDF is guarding against the import or export of weapons, and against Gazan ships making their way to Israeli shores.

As we talk, there are about ten other fishermen around us, listening to Bashir. The day is breezy and clear. The sand on the wide beach is white and clean. Bashir points out to the sea, where we can see an Israeli patrol boat cutting across the horizon.

When IDF boats see a Gazan fisherman coming too close to the barrier, they are supposed to issue a warning via loudspeaker. If a verbal command to turn back is not heard or obeyed, the IDF is authorized to spray machine gun fire in the vicinity of the fishing boats—usually in the direction of the bow. When misunderstandings occur, things can escalate.

Gazan fishermen have been shot and killed. They have been detained and interrogated. Their boats have been impounded and stripped of vital equipment. Often their boats are sunk. According to the al-Mezan Center for Human Rights in Gaza, in the first half of 2016, Israeli ships targeted Palestinian fishermen seventy-one times, arrested eighty-three fishermen in twenty separate incidents, and wounded eleven fishermen. The Israelis have confiscated twenty-eight fishing boats in sixteen separate incidents, and destroyed fishing equipment in eleven separate incidents.

"It's not their right to put limits on us," Bashir says. "It's still our sea." Even so, given the lack of jobs elsewhere in Gaza, men come from all over looking for work. "There are more fishermen now," he says, "but fewer fish."

Bashir has had his vessels shot at and seized. His crew has been arrested, handcuffed, detained, and questioned at sea. Worse than the IDF, though, he says, are the Egyptians. Since the Muslim Brotherhood was thrown out, things have gotten far worse. The new government in place, led by Abdel Fattah el-Sisi, assumes that Hamas has been supporting uprisings and terrorism in Egypt, and treats every Gazan vessel as a possible terrorist conveyance. The Israelis will shoot in the direction of their boats, but "The Egyptians will shoot at us directly," Bashir says. Some interaction with one or the other navy happens every day, he says.

Gazan fishermen are not allowed to use sonar or radar, standard equipment for most fishermen around the world. And because their fishing grounds are so limited, Gazans catch far fewer fish, and now, though Gaza has forty-two kilometers of coastline, they import more fish than they harvest themselves. Over 90 percent of Gazan fishermen live in poverty and rely on international aid to subsist.

By now all of the other fishermen have left us. We are alone, and the wind is picking up. Bashir appears tired, and seems more interested in talking about the effect of the blockade on everyday family life than he is the dual navies that patrol the coast.

"When there is no work," he says, "it affects the social life, the family life. We can't go visit friends, we can't buy a gift for an occasion." Feeling this pressure, closed in on all sides and responsible for his family, he says, "A man might go a bad way."

AMIR WAS A FISHERMAN, AND HIS FATHER WAS A FISHERMAN, TOO. HIS people were fishermen as far as he can remember, but not anymore. We are sitting in his living room, sipping tea provided by his son Abed, a tanned, light-haired man in his late thirties.

Amir is wearing a gray *thobe* and moves with difficulty. He sits down against the wall and sets his cane on the floor in front of us. His face is oval, his chin narrow, his eyes tired. His skin is darkened by the sun, and the lines of his face are carved deep.

"Now I am an old person," he says, smiling grimly. At his next birthday, he will be eighty-one.

Periodically a girl of three or four peeks into the room. She is blond, as are a few of the other children in the village, which is strangely appropriate, given this place is called Swedish Village. In all of Gaza, there is perhaps no more fascinating and distressing place.

Amir was there when it was built. He was born in 1937, in a village of five thousand people called Hamama—the Arabic word for dove. Hamama was on the coast of the Mediterranean, about twenty-four kilometers north of what is now the Gaza-Israel border. He was eleven when Israeli troops overtook his village and drove its people into Gaza.

"It was maybe October or November," he says. "I was in the fourth grade of school, but school was off for that day. There were some Arab forces, troops from Egypt, Saudi Arabia, and from Sudan, and they were guarding the area. A month later they said, 'The Jews are coming. You have to escape.' We left and came here and we didn't go back."

When they arrived in Gaza, the United Nations gave the Ham-aman refugees tents, and they lived near the beach for the next four years, fishing and doing some light farming. Eventually they moved inland, creating a village of mud and brick huts. In 1965, a storm flooded the village, destroying most of the homes. UN troops, led by Swedes, helped them rebuild just off the beach, a few hundred yards from the Egyptian border.

The village is a desperately poor place, but Amir's home is clean and his sitting room comfortable and cool. We can hear the waves crash against the white sands of the beach outside. When the tea is gone, Abed brings orange soda and presents it with great ceremony.

"He has six kids," Amir says about Abed. "But he barely works. He makes twenty shekels a day from farming, but that's not enough. When the tunnels to Egypt were open, he could make two hundred shekels a day loading and unloading." But the tunnels were closed six months ago, and now things for this small village—no more than a thousand souls—are as desperate as they've ever been.

As is the case throughout Gaza, there is little work for the men. And then there is the troubling drop in fertility. Something has been preventing the young couples from having kids—it's been years since a new baby was born, though Amir says twelve young couples, all newly married, have been trying. And the kids there are, are getting sick. Amir thinks it has something to do with the sewage that pumps from Rafah into the ocean immediately next to the village. Or it could be the salinization of the well water.

"The closest clinic is Rafah," he says. But it costs money to get to Rafah, money they don't have in the village, so often the sick children stay sick.

Up to 2005, there was an Israeli settlement just east of Swedish Village, and I ask Amir what life was like with them so near. Because I'd spent time with my Israeli guide in the West Bank, and because the settlers of Hebron seemed so violent and unreasonable, I'm surprised by Amir's answer.

"When the settlements were here, it was good," he says. There was decent access to water and electricity, and Swedish Village was surviving. Abed was one of the young men employed by the settler-farmers. He became an irrigation expert. Then the settlers left. Then Hamas arrived. The water went bad. The blockade began, and jobs disappeared. Abed's job disappeared.

"I have six daughters," Abed says. He's giving us a tour of the village, and his eyes are worried. He shows us the site where there used to be a cemetery, but this was bulldozed some time ago by the Israelis. There is a boat on stilts that he says was being repaired but some of the materials they need to finish it are not available now, given the blockade.

In an alleyway, partially hidden by laundry drying on a line, there is a plaque that declares Swedish Village to be "a donation from the Swedes in the homeland and Swedish battalions of UNEF 25G and 27G. 1965."

A few yards from the plaque, across an expanse of garbage and a dirt road patrolled by the Gazan military, is the Egyptian border and the twenty-five-foot wall. Where the wall meets the shore, rising high above the beach, an Egyptian guard tower stands, cylindrical and sturdy. On the Gazan side is the Hamas version of a military installation, a makeshift wooden box on stilts that resembles a lifeguard shack.

The day is clear, and the sea is a bright cerulean. The beach is interrupted by a large pipe, set on rocks and directed like a cannon into the surf. We balance on the rocks until we can see the pipe's exit point. The smell is overpowering. This is raw sewage from Rafah being dumped into the sea.

"The smell," Abed says, "is far worse in the summer." Then, there is no place in the village to avoid the smell, and the flies and mosquitoes that come with it.

As part of the Oslo accords, a body known as the Joint Water Committee was created, to manage water resources in the occupied territories. But because of ongoing bickering, and not helped by the 2014 conflict, there are no effective long-term solutions to water treatment and the disposal of sewage in Gaza. Equipment that could help mitigate the problems has not been allowed into Gaza, for fear that it would be used by Hamas for military purposes. Ironically, the dumping of raw sewage into the sea affects the coastlines of Israel and Egypt, too. A desalination plant in Israel recently was closed apparently because the pollution from Gaza made the intake too dirty to desalinate. And of course the dumping of any freshwater into the sea is a breathtaking act of shortsightedness. This water, if treated, could replenish aquifers and be directed to agriculture and myriad other uses.

And even ambitious and well-intentioned plans are crippled by the wider context of dysfunction. The World Bank recently built a $73 million sewage treatment plant, but there is not enough electricity in Gaza to provide it with a reliable power source. It has yet to process any sewage at all.

We leave Abed on the beach and we drive back toward Gaza City. I look in the rearview mirror, where Abed is still standing at the waterfront. Earlier, Amir had said there was an era when you could tell the time in Swedish Village by the movement of the working men. You could tell the working day had begun when the men went off fishing or into the fields to farm. You could tell when it was five o'clock, with the men coming home for dinner.

"Now," Amir said, "because there is no work, the men go to the beach and just sit there."

AMONG ALL THE PEOPLE I'VE MET IN GAZA THUS FAR, THERE IS A CERTAIN grim resignation. People like Amir and Bashir have virtually no means of leaving the strip, and though they are outraged and heartbroken, and worry for their families and friends, they have come to terms with it. Basilah and Hazem, on the other hand, can more or less readily come and go into Gaza, and they are of the tiniest minority. Still, they are committed to staying in Gaza, perhaps out of a sense of loyalty to the people there, perhaps out of a sense of duty to make sure what happens in Gaza is duly reported, that the world knows what has happened and what will happen.

Talib and Amna are different. They are like Basilah in that they are young—Talib and Amna are both twenty-four—and well educated, but whereas Basilah is committed to staying, they badly want out. They have been trying for years to leave Gaza, and when we met were fighting fiercely to be allowed to pass through the Erez crossing to reach the American consulate in Jerusalem. And more so than anyone I've met in Gaza, they do not look like they belong here.

They walk into the al-Deira like a fashionable young couple in any contemporary metropolis—Paris, New York, Berlin. Talib, tall and bearded, is wearing jeans and an orange sweatshirt, nothing too noticeable, while Amna is comparatively the radical. Delicately beautiful, she strides into the restaurant wearing leggings, a loose sweater, and instead of a hijab, a wool cap. I ask if the restaurant is okay, if they'd like to go anywhere else, and they say no, they come here often. In fact, it's one of the few places in Gaza they can go, looking as they do. Because she rarely wears a hijab, and prefers pants to an abaya, Amna attracts attention everywhere she goes. Women glower and men hiss. "Are you proud of yourself?" is among the gentler things said in her direction.

She and Talib are harassed on the street by their countrymen and harassed by Hamas, too. Within seconds of sitting down and ordering lunch, Talib tells the story of when he and three friends were held for fifteen hours at the police station, interrogated and intimidated. It started when one of them was caught spray-painting lyrics on a wall. The lyrics were to a song by Mashrou Laila, a Lebanese rock band.

The four young men were kept overnight. Police took their phones and scanned them for contacts and evidence of forbidden acts. They were questioned until six a.m. and finally allowed to sleep. "Then my friend wakes up to someone holding a pistol to his head. Telling him, 'Wake up!' And making fun of him."

Another friend of Talib and Amna's, who works for a children's charity, was detained for six hours. Hamas, they say, has a particular suspicion of organizations that work with children.

"They took his Facebook account, asking him all these questions," Talib says. "'Why aren't you married?' If you have salary and are not married surely there is something wrong with you."

Talib and Amna were married a few years ago—not that they believe so much in the institution. "Marriage in Gaza, it's required," Talib says. "We were in a relationship, and we really suffered because of the culture and society. For three years we could not even be together, we could not sit in a restaurant in a public place. We can't have our own time. It's not love, it's acting for society. This is how it was. Unless we got married."

So they got married, and can now live together, but the expectations of family and society continue.

"Our families are pressuring us to have babies," Amna says. "A married couple is supposed to immediately have a baby in the first year."

"They're saying we have problems in our bodies," Talib says, laughing. "That there is something wrong."

Amna adds, "We say to them, 'We don't have a future here. To raise a baby in this prison? And what if there's another war? We would lose another soul.'"

During the 2014 siege of Gaza City, Talib and Amna live-streamed the Israeli air strikes from the eleventh-floor balcony of their downtown apartment. They were passionate about documenting the war, and speaking for Gazan civilians affected by a fight not their own. But the 2014 conflict solidified their commitment to leaving Gaza. Not just Gaza. They want to leave Palestine, Israel, all of it.

They have repeatedly applied for visas to leave, to no avail. In the last few years, Talib was invited to Poland, and tried to get there through Egypt, but was rejected by the Egyptians. He was invited to Ramallah, but his application for a permit was rejected by the Israelis. The last time Amna left Gaza was four years ago, when she was able to go to Jordan to visit family and celebrate a cousin's university graduation. For Talib, it's been eight years since he's left. That was January 2008, when Hamas activists destroyed a large part of the wall that divides Rafah between Gaza and Egypt. Thousands of Gazans poured into Egypt. They bought chocolate, sheep, anything they couldn't get in Gaza. After two weeks, the wall was repaired and the Gazans were sent back. That was the last time Talib set foot outside the limits of Gaza.

But now there is a new hope. Talib and Amna were recently granted a permit to come to the American consulate in Jerusalem to discuss a visa application to visit the United States. They have been invited to New York by the Institute for Middle East Understanding, a nonprofit that provides journalists with information about Palestine and the Palestinians. So in two weeks' time, if all goes according to plan, they will pass through the Erez gate and make their way to Jerusalem for an interview with an official at the US consulate. Then they have to turn around quickly; their permit states they have to be back in Gaza by six p.m.

The chances that they will be granted visas to come to the United States are exceedingly slim. From the American perspective, Talib and Amna, traveling together, would be a clear asylum risk. That is, the Americans would assume that once they arrived on US shores, they would apply for asylum. And Talib has another strike against him. He is a young Palestinian man, and his father is a well-known member of Hamas, who has for the last sixteen years been jailed inside Israel. His father's prominence helps Talib contend with Hamas harassment—it helped him the night he and his friends were held at the police station—but it has greatly limited his ability to leave Gaza. Will the Americans hear him when he says he has no allegiance to his father's politics, to Hamas, to Gaza, to even the larger Palestinian cause?

"I'm sorry," Talib says, "but this place is not Palestine." About residents of the West Bank, he says, "For sure if they tried to live here one year they would forget about any shit about Palestine."

He has never been to the West Bank and feels no connection to the people there. Hamas has been in power during most of his and Amna's formative years, and they have no allegiance to it and know they have no power to remove it from power. But they have occasionally joined in demonstrations meant to encourage cooperation between Hamas and Fatah. A few years ago there was a demonstration of young people hoping for better and more productive relations between the two parties. Hamsawis were everywhere, and the demonstrators were followed, photographed, videotaped, and intimidated.

Now Talib and Amna live in a state of surveillance and paranoia. This is why they are so content to be at the al-Deira, the rare haven in Gaza City where there is a semblance of sophistication and respite from being observed and judged. Here Amna can be something closer to the self she is at home, where she can dress as she wishes, and do as she wishes.

On her phone, Amna shows me some paintings she's made. In one, a self-portrait, she stands on the balcony of an apartment building while Gaza City burns all around her. In another, a bald woman looks out from the frame.

"My mother has breast cancer," Amna says. "Stage three. She's in chemotherapy. It's up and down."

It's at this moment that I make a mistake. Because Amna is a painter, and because I want to spend more time with Talib and Amna, I suggest we go to a gallery I'd been reading about. They politely agree, and we leave the hotel.

As we walk across al-Rasheed Road, though, something happens to Amna. She seems to shrink into herself. Already a wisp of a person, her shoulders now contract, as if hoping she could fold herself up and disappear. We walk up Ebn Seena Street, and already it's obvious the pressure she meets in public. Taxi drivers slow down to stare. Men standing in front of shops glare. As we walk, Amna positions herself between Talib and me, hiding, her head down. Finally, after a walk that seems interminable—it couldn't be more than ten minutes—we find the gallery, but it's closed. We decide to go back to the waterfront, to a seaside restaurant next to the al-Deira, and as we make our way to it, with every step, Amna relaxes a bit, until we are on the sand. When we're near, she smiles again. I tell her ten times how sorry I am.

This time we sit outside, in a crowded outdoor café on the sand. The tables are shaded by wide umbrellas in bright primary colors. When we sit, and people see Amna, the other patrons take notice and whisper among themselves, but soon look the other way. Though the patrons of this restaurant are among the liberal elite, Talib and Amna are still radically different from them. And sitting with me, the only Westerner here, seems like an invitation to trouble. But they are unfazed. They order fruit drinks, and Amna orders a hooka. She is the only woman there who does so.

"You ask about being isolated from the world," Amna says. "Here people are feeling pressure. There are no jobs. Young people study, they graduate, and they sit in their houses."

Amna and Talib recently visited a young woman who had doused herself with gasoline and lit herself on fire. The woman was in the hospital with third-degree burns all over her body.

"All her face was burned," Talib says. "Only her eyes were visible. She couldn't speak, so her mother was speaking for her. She wouldn't admit it was a suicide attempt."

"Suicide is shameful and forbidden in Islam," Amna adds.

"Also, Hamas doesn't want people to know that people are burning themselves," Talib says. "The stories we know in the media, these are people who suicide themselves in front of people." He cites the case of the man who climbed the highest building in Gaza, insisting he would jump unless the Palestinian Authority increased his salary.

"In the end, they convinced him that they would give him a salary, that it's okay to go down," Amna adds.

"He got fucked afterwards for sure," Talib says.

"There is another way of committing suicide," Amna says. "People are taking tramadol [an opioid]. They smuggle it into Gaza and there is addiction to it."

"Before Hamas," Talib says, "no one had heard about tramadol. When Hamas started to take over Gaza, now everyone can get tramadol."

The widespread assumption is that Hamas has a hand in smuggling tramadol in, and that the Hamsawis benefit from the drug trade. For many years people have assumed that Hamas knows about and benefits from the smuggling of hash, too. Though alcohol is hard to find in Gaza, hash is ubiquitous.

"Hamas likes to sell a lot of hash and get a lot of money for it," Talib says.

As they explain the connection between hash and Hamas, I look around, worried for them. We are surrounded by adults eating at tables no further than five feet from us.

"No one understands English here," Talib says.

"If they could understand what we are saying, we're fucked," Amna says, though without any apparent concern.

We talk about the two-state solution, the possibility that the West Bank and Gaza might somehow be connected.

"Of course for Gazans, if they open up this way, yeah this is good," Amna says. "They will have freedom of movement. But if you look at it, it's not freedom of movement. You just widened the prison more."

I ask if Hamas makes promises that things will get better.

"For ten years they have been saying that," Amna says. "Every war they say we will end this. And we will have an airport. And then the war ended and nothing happened."

Talib looks around to his fellow Gazans, their faces blue and red and yellow under their festive beach umbrellas, the bright Mediterranean beyond. "We're just animals in a cage. They're just feeding us to keep us alive."

THERE IS A MUSIC SCHOOL IN GAZA CITY, TUCKED AMID A NEIGHBOR-hood of apartments and storefronts. Hazem has arranged to meet members of Sol Band, the act we'd seen a few nights earlier. We're led into a comfortable practice studio on the second floor. The walls, painted teal, are covered in instruments—ouds and keyboards and tambourines. There is a drum set in one corner and an array of school desks and chairs all over the room. Against one wall is a roll of Styrofoam insulation, not yet installed.

Three members of Sol Band are here. Wasim Ali, the band's clarinetist, is twenty years old, a college student studying business administration. His hair is cut short and gelled, and he wears a sky-blue button-down and gray pants. On the night of the concert, he played the clarinet, but that's not his first instrument. At age twelve, he started on the bagpipes, and after that picked up anything vaguely similar—the accordion, any woodwinds that were handy. A month ago, he found a clarinet in the music school, and decided to teach himself how to play it. As far as he knows, his is the only clarinet in Gaza, and he is the only clarinetist.

Fares Anbar, the band's percussionist, is tall and thin, with a shrub of black hair growing high and rightward from his face. He is wearing a vest over a white shirt and jeans and, while sitting in a classroom chair, tends to sit with his legs akimbo, as if there were a drum there. He is nineteen and is also studying business. He and Wasim can think of only one man in all of Gaza who makes a living as a musician, so they're hedging their bets. Especially given that Hamas shut down their concert after one hour.

Majd Antar, the band's manager and promoter, sits next to them, slump shouldered and wary, like a teenager at the back of a classroom. A young man with a boy's face and a shock of black hair, he has just gotten back from the police station, where he'd been questioned about the concert.

"We made a mistake," Majd says. "At first we had paper invitations, and we distributed those. But then, twelve hours before the concert, we also announced it on Facebook, and too many people came."

The concert had been months in the planning. At first, Majd and the band had arranged to hold the concert in a venue called Roots, which had offered its space for free. But Roots had also recently hosted a fashion show that had, in the end, been seen as controversial in the eyes of Hamas. So Hamas officials suggested that the band have the concert at the Red Crescent building. The band members pooled their money to cover the cost to rent the new venue, $1,300, an amount equal to what any one of them could earn in a year. Majd and the band decided that the show would be free to attendees—it would be a showcase, a way to promote the band's name. It was a high-priced gamble.

"We hoped NGO people could come to the show, see what we do," Majd explains. "Maybe they want to organize something with us in the future."

After securing the venue that met Hamas's approval, the band had to submit an exact set list. The songs they proposed for the concert leaned, that night, slightly more toward romantic music popular elsewhere in the Arab world. After the election of Hamas, public musical performances have been greatly limited, and when they have occurred, the music has been limited to patriotic songs that celebrate Hamas and Palestine. Hoping for a temporary easing of these restrictions, Majd and the band expanded the scope of the set list a bit, and were surprised to see their application approved.

"I don't think the songs were the problem," Majd says.

The problem was the size of the crowd. The venue they rented could fit five hundred. Eight hundred people showed up. With so many people, even with Majd fretting and patrolling, they couldn't control the behavior of all the young people there. Sol Band's agreement with Hamas stated that men and women would be segregated from each other, that there would be no dancing or suggestive moving in their seats. But the audience began to mix, and to clap too enthusiastically, and move too much in their seats.

"At one point," Majd said, "a random woman got up on stage and took the microphone. We didn't know her, we didn't know what she wanted to say. She faced the crowd and told the people to calm down and be quiet. She'd seen some movements in the audience, and she didn't want the concert to be shut down."

But an hour into the show, Majd's phone rang. "It was a private number. He told me to stop the concert. I tried to explain to him, ask him why, what's wrong. 'It's immoral behavior, there is no segregation between men and women,' he said." Majd hung up. The band was still playing. The crowd was still electric. The event was an unqualified success so far, but he was about to have to shut it down.

He thought of how long they'd spent planning the show, how much money they'd invested. They would not get that money back. "Emotions were high," he says now. "Some relatives of the band members were sick or dead. The mother of one member had recently died. Another had a mother who went into the hospital that day for surgery. Another had a sister in the hospital." The fourteen members of the band had collectively worked so hard and sacrificed so much, and now, an hour into the show they'd planned for a year, it was over.

"I wanted to defy the call," he says, "but there were police there in civilian clothing, and they told me we had to stop. They were at the entrance, and they came, and we stopped.

"They called me today," Majd continues, "and they asked me to go to the office. I went there. They wanted to explain what happened. They were polite, actually. They respected me. They asked me to sign a pledge to not organize any party without a permit in advance."

Despite Hamas approving their permit in the first place, Majd sees no easing of cultural restrictions in Gaza. "It's not changing at all," he says. And there is no guarantee the band will be granted another permit to play in public. In the meantime, they can practice here, in this little room, and they can post preapproved songs online. Most of their fans are located outside Gaza, but the chances that any of these talented young people will perform outside the strip are very slim.

When I leave, Majd gives me a business card and a flyer, the one that advertised the show.

"The band works with own personal efforts to accomplish their goal," the flyer says, "and be what we are now, four years of work and still we have many of things in our bag, and that's a great proof of our determination to send our home, love, peace message covered with tunes of hope."

TALIB DOES NOT HAVE A VALID DRIVER'S LICENSE, AND HE AND AMNA think it too attention-grabbing for an uncovered woman to be driving a car, so they decide that I should drive the car they've borrowed from a friend. Driving in Gaza is not easy—the intersections have no lights, no stop signs, no signs at all, so at every intersection it's a matter of bluffing your way through four lanes of traffic. The most confident driver at any crossing wins the day.

We make our way through Gaza City and then speed along the interior highway—funded by the Qatari government—until we get to a small concrete village, where we turn east. For a few miles we drive directly toward Israel, past the last village and into farmland. We are a few hundred yards from the heavily fortified border, which should be unnerving, but because Talib and Amna are calm, and the day is bright and blue, it feels like a pleasure drive through the country. But soon we can see the low barrier up ahead, a few guard towers, the black stripe where the moat is, the barbed wire.

The dirt road we're traveling on ends, and we turn left, heading north along a dusty road, cutting through farmland on either side.

Ahead there is a Hamas guard tower. "Put your camera down," Talib tells me. It's the first time he or Amna has seemed at all concerned about Hamas since we met. We stop at the checkpoint and Talib gets out, explains ourselves to the soldiers, and we move on.

A half mile later, we stop at a ramshackle compound, overgrown with weeds and littered with broken machinery. A deeply tanned, diminutive, and wiry man emerges from the house. This is Jamal. He couldn't weigh more than a hundred and twenty pounds. A floppy hat with red and white horizontal stripes gives some shade to his tanned, heavily lined face, his sardonic eyes. He is wearing a secondhand T-shirt, created by and for settlers in the West Bank, bearing the cartoon image of a Hasidic Jew, with the words "A Hitchhiker's Guide to the Galaxy" in Hebrew. It's a souvenir shirt from a settlement called Otniel. Jamal acknowledges the irony of a Gazan farmer wearing a shirt from an Israeli settlement, and he does not care.

We sit on folding chairs in his courtyard, and he points out three tiny chicks, born the day before. They're being kept in a box at the foot of my chair, and over the next thirty minutes continually step over each other to get at the water dispenser he's placed at the ridge of the box. A few feet from the baby chicks is a large monument, looking like a tomb, covered with plastic bottles, buckets, and pieces of machinery.

"How do you like your tea?" Jamal asks us.

He disappears into the darkness of his low-slung home, and I ask Talib if he knows what the monument is.

"That's for his Italian friend," Talib says. "Vittorio Arrigoni. He was killed by radicals." Arrigoni, an Italian reporter and activist, had come to Gaza in 2008 to work with the Palestinian International Solidarity Movement. With the Arabic word for *resistance* tattooed on his right arm, he was on the first humanitarian boat to break the Israeli blockade, and later was injured by broken glass while serving as a human shield on a Gazan fishing boat. He spent many weeks living with Jamal, advocating for him and other farmers.

In April 2011, Arrigoni was kidnapped by a heretofore unknown group called the Brigade of the Gallant Companion of the Prophet

Mohammed bin Muslima. They demanded a prisoner swap with Walid al-Maqdasi, a Salafi radical being held by the Gazan government. During the negotiations, though, and before the captors' stated deadline, Arrigoni was killed. Two Gazan men were charged with the murder and are still in prison. The killing was denounced by Hamas and by Islamic groups around Palestine and all over the world.

Jamal returns with a tray, and we drink hot tea in the cool shade of his courtyard as he tells us a short version of his life. He is fifty-seven and was born on a farm. His father lived to be ninety, he says, so between them there is a hundred and fifty years of agricultural knowledge. When his father was a child, the family cultivated ten thousand dunams—a dunam being about one thousand square meters—a swath of land extending from where we are sitting far into what is now Israel. When his father was young, he was in the fields with one of the family's donkeys when there was suddenly yelling, confusion. This was the War of 1948. His family was driven into Gaza and they lost most of their land. Now Jamal owns ten dunams and rents another three hundred. He grows zucchini, grapes, watermelon, almonds, green peppers, tomatoes, and wheat.

We ask him about the IDF incursions. He shrugs. He has no problem with them. "The media are liars," he says. The bulldozers haven't violated anything, he says. He takes my notebook and draws a picture. "Here's the border," he says, and draws a straight line across the page. Next to it, he draws the one hundred–meter buffer zone. The bulldozers, he says, come into the buffer zone to clear debris and vegetation. He says their presence there is not new and not a problem—it has been agreed to between both governments. "It's fine. We see them, they go back. No problem."

He does take issue with the Israelis' new policy of spraying herbicides on his wheat to stunt its growth. We walk the fields, stepping between rows of zucchini and over a vast network of black irrigation tubes that Jamal can activate on his smartphone. When we get to the wheat, he shows us the stalks, which are about half the height as normal at harvest time. They should be one hundred centimeters, he explains, but the herbicides limit their height to forty.

"They don't want anything to grow high," he says about the Israelis. "No trees, no crops." They started spraying his land about eighteen months earlier. He's complained to everyone he can, including the International Red Cross, but has gotten no relief. We stand among his stunted wheat and look toward the border. Between us and the barrier is a field of yellow flowers. Jamal has been sifting wheat kernels in his hand, and now throws them on the ground.

The border's proximity makes his life fraught. He regularly hears gunshots—Israeli soldiers warning those who approach the barrier. Jamal can't go outside, by foot or by car, after dark. At night, the Israeli border guards are likely to perceive any movement as a threat, so he and the other farmers in the area stay inside. This is why he needs to be able to activate the irrigation by phone—manually turning on the water at night would be extremely dangerous.

Still, he has somehow made a life here, has in fact raised fourteen children here, some still in grammar school. Of his grown children, he says three of his sons are currently in college, and three of his daughters are married and have moved out. And, he says, "I have two stupid sons who are not educated."

This is Jamal's sense of humor, brusque and sardonic. Because he has equal disdain for just about everyone, Jamal is strangely likable and endearing. In the course of a few hours on his farm, he has equally dismissive words for the Israelis, for President Obama and President Carter, for the US Congress, for China, Russia, and anyone else purportedly working for peace in the region. He has the sarcasm of a man who has seen everything and has been let down by everyone. He is perhaps most dismissive of Hamas. "They do nothing. They're not our government." When I ask if they assist farmers in any way, through subsidies or tariffs or equipment, he scoffs. "No. Hamas, they are slaughtering us."

On our way back to his home, we pass a broken-down tractor with a smattering of bullet casings on its seat. Spent shells litter the ground of the compound, and bullet holes dot the border-facing side of his home. In the 2014 conflict, his farm was overrun by Israeli tanks and soldiers. His crops were flattened, his livestock killed. "It was like Hiroshima," he says. After the war ended, for three months there was no water or electricity. Gazan troops had to scour the land to be sure there was no unexploded matériel. Jamal lost the season.

We walk back toward the house, and pass a small field of corn. It's grown much higher than the stunted wheat. I ask Jamal what the Israelis think of this.

"Fuck them if they don't like it," he says. "If they had their way we wouldn't grow anything at all."

WALKING ALONE ON THE STREETS OF GAZA CITY IS A TEST OF THE SOUL'S capacity to trust. One morning I leave the al-Deira and head to the marina. I walk by the empty lot, where this morning a group of sanitation workers is cleaning it of debris, old tires, and garbage. On al-Rasheed Road, workers are cleaning up horse dung and candy wrappers. Somewhere there is the clop-clop of a donkey pulling a cart. The city is still asleep.

The night before had been another celebratory scene, full of joy and chaos. There had been wedding processions. There had been a group of seven men on horseback, perhaps going to one of the wedding halls. There had been crowds of young men, women in tight groups, older couples on romantic strolls. There had been the usual buzzing tuk-tuks and motorcycles. The adolescent boys on dirt bikes. The wild neon nightlife of weekend Gaza City.

And then there had been the bus. From my bed I heard a commotion and went to the window, and saw a tour bus stopped in front of the vacant lot. In front of it, there was a small car. Behind the bus, traffic was stopped because in the street, spilling over into the median, there was an argument. First it seemed to be between the bus driver and the driver of the vehicle—it was obvious there'd been an accident. But soon it was five men, pushing and arguing. Then ten men in a whirling circle, something like a human hurricane that kept growing. Now twenty men. Fifty. They spilled over from the northbound lanes into the southbound. Traffic on that side of the highway stopped, and the northbound resumed. Now the fifty men were on the far sidewalk, the scrum traveling far quicker than would seem possible. I watched for twenty minutes, until the mass of men finally cooled and dispersed. No one was hurt.

Then the fireworks began. At first it sounded like mortar fire. Then strafing bullets. But no, it was fireworks. Fireworks in the middle of Gaza City. They were loud and red. It seemed insane. They lit up the sky above the Love Boat and above the waterfront that had been shelled two years earlier.

But again, like the night before, and like every night, at the stroke of ten o'clock, all went quiet. Never could there have been a city that so quickly and dutifully observed a curfew—if there were an official curfew. More likely this was an unspoken thing, an understanding between the youthful population of Gaza, dancing and singing in their prison, and their disapproving, incompetent parents, Hamas.

The morning continues to awaken. Shopkeepers sweep their sidewalks. A pair of boys throw rocks at each other. I walk a few blocks down al-Rasheed and up ahead I see a group of police officers and al-Qassam soldiers. To get to the marina, I will have to pass them all. I count twelve officers in blue fatigues, black boots, and blue caps. They are gathered loosely, a few sitting on a bench. Nearby are two soldiers in masks, carrying AK-47s. I walk past them all, pretending to be a resident, one deeply preoccupied. I don't know if I should be more concerned or less.

I make it to the marina, where I find a spot near the dry docks. I watch the fishermen, most in sweatpants and sandals, as they work on their vessels. There is the sound of distant hammers working on repairs, the hoarse shushing of someone sanding a hull. In the harbor, there is the low buzz of outboard motors. Vessels leave the marina and head into the Mediterranean, to risk strafing and injury, detention and even death, for a few fish. The day is gray and indistinct. Beyond the marina, the horizon line is unclear.

ON THE WAY TO TALIB AND AMNA'S HOME THAT NIGHT, THE SUBJECT IS just what to bring. Wine is out, and there is nowhere near that we can buy a dessert. I am with two new acquaintances, the British journalist named Don McIntyre, and Silvia Ostberg Morales, the

Swedish-Guatemalan head of the Norwegian People's Aid office in the Gaza Strip. Don, a gentlemanly man in his sixties, has been coming to Gaza for more than ten years. We decide on flowers.

But first we have to stop at Silvia's apartment. She lives in a high-rise on al-Rasheed Road, with a magnificent view of the shoreline and the marina. Her apartment is spacious and well-designed, looking like the kind of place a successful executive might have in any prosperous city. This building and others like it were built in another, more optimistic time. Now electricity is uncertain and the running water is unfit for human consumption. Far below, we can see the vendors and walkers of the promenade I'd seen the first day with Hazem. From this vantage point, the possibility of Gaza City as an oceanfront vacation destination is strangely clear. The sea is beautiful, the day ending, the sunset a wash of oranges and reds.

The elevator worked on the way up to her apartment, but now, when we need to go down, it's out. The electricity has stopped. We walk down the five flights, unsure whether there will be power when we get to Talib and Amna's, whether they have been able to cook.

Near Silvia's apartment building, we stop in a small shop, something like a year-round Valentine's store, looking for a bouquet. The palette inside is all reds and whites and pinks, flowers and cards and teddy bears. We buy a small bouquet of white roses, and on the steps outside the shop, an elderly woman dressed in ancient, worn clothes, rags really, pushes a small bouquet of herbs in Don's face. She wants one shekel, about twenty-five cents, for the entire bunch. Don pays her and we get into Silvia's car.

Silvia is that rare NGO head who drives herself and travels with no security. Staff members from the UN, NGOs, and diplomatic missions usually operate within a strict cone of security—darting quickly between cars and compounds, seeing themselves as perpetual targets. But it remains unclear if there is any real danger here for people like us. There are the types of radicals, unbound and unpredictable, who killed Vittorio Arrigoni. Anyway, Silvia drives like she's back in Sweden—confident and unbowed.

Murad, Talib's brother, is a handsome young man of twenty-five.

Don and Silvia and I are all sitting on the floor of Talib and Amna's apartment while Murad looks on his computer for a video of the time, during the 2014 war between Israel and Hamas, when he saved the life of an old man, a Catholic, while Murad was out of his mind on hash.

"I was so high," Murad says.

The apartment is spacious and clean, located eight stories up, in a building dominated by the offices of media companies. After a dinner of sausage, stuffed zucchini, and rice, we look out the windows, where Talib and Amna watched the 2014 bombing, and Amna shows us her paintings, the ones I'd seen on her phone. In person, her painting of the siege is more vivid than any photos of the bombing.

Now Murad, wide eyed and quick to laughter, is trying to find footage of the time he ended up on the local news. The bombing of Gaza City had been going on for weeks, and Murad, like many other Gazans, lived with the perpetual expectation that he would die. The Israelis were targeting hard military installations, but they were also flattening buildings where Hamas operatives were known to live.

The Israelis have extensive intelligence networks in Gaza, so it's not difficult for them to know where a senior Hamas official might dwell. During the 2014 conflict, the Israelis would often choose to reduce such a building to rubble. In most cases, the Hamas official lived in an apartment building housing hundreds of other people, too, but the Israelis, to punish the Hamas official, would also leave hundreds of other people homeless.

When they flatten such a home, they're usually not intending to kill the Hamas official. In fact, the most recent IDF practice is to give residents of the building a courtesy call before the bombing, or drop a small signal bomb, a practice known as roof-knocking. This was a new Israeli policy, instituted during the 2014 conflict, meant to reduce collateral damage. They would call a resident of the building, informing that resident to leave their homes as soon as they could, and to tell everyone else who lived there. Then, fifteen minutes later, a missile would strike and the building would fall.

One night in 2014, Murad was sitting at a friend's house, high as a kite, when he got a phone call from a friend. A nearby apartment building was about to be leveled. Murad thought of an old man he knew who lived next door to the building about to be flattened. This man, Murad knew, would not be able to make it out in time. (Though the Israelis told the residents of the building, those who lived in other, nearby buildings were given no such courtesy call.)

So Murad got up, still high, almost numb, and ran to the building. He checked the time on his phone. He probably had six minutes before the air strike would hit. He ran into the building, flew up eight flights of stairs, and knocked furiously on the man's door. The man finally emerged, dazed, with no clue that his building would be rubble in minutes. Murad rushed him down the stairs and into the street.

We are sitting on the floor of Talib and Amna's apartment, looking at his laptop, and Murad finally finds the news footage. There is a video of fire, and ambulances and Gaza's Civil Defense firefighters. And then there's Murad, walking down the street, his face bright in the glare of the camera's light, and next to him is a tiny man, bald and no more than a hundred pounds, looking bewildered, terrified. In the footage, Murad does not look high. He looks very present, very much awake and aware, guiding the man down the street as flames bloom behind Gaza City's urban silhouette.

"But Gazans elected Hamas," Silvia reminds our hosts. She makes it clear that according to several international observers, the elections were fair and transparent, and that Gazans made their choice. She comes just short of saying "I told you so."

But, Talib says, he and Amna and Murad did not vote for Hamas. They did not ask to be raised here. They did not ask to grow up inside a prison, where the people grew so desperate they would elect a radical party like Hamas. They have no allegiance to any of it—not this party, not this city, not this country.

"Good night," the three of us, Silvia, Don, and I, say to Amna and Talib and Murad. "The meal was delicious. You were perfect hosts."

In the morning, Silvia and I will both be crossing the Erez border, heading back to Israel, where we will pass freely and continue on to Tel Aviv. From there, with our Swedish and American passports, we can go anywhere in the world.

In the morning Talib and Amna insist on driving me to the Erez gate. I had tried to take a taxi, but they wouldn't allow it. Today it is Talib driving, and we take the waterfront route, passing an endless array of buildings shelled during the 2014 conflict. Most are apartment buildings, and most are largely empty. But in many of these buildings, people still dwell, without windows, their laundry hung on the line, rubble to rubble, satellite dishes on the roof. A few have been painted in pastel colors, a recent project of an international NGO to beautify the waterfront.

We park near the Erez gate. We are early, so we talk about their upcoming visa interview. I don't know what to tell them. I explain what I know of asylum law, and tell them to call me if they need any help, any advice. But their situation is dire, and without parallel in the modern world. Though there are people around the world fervently wanting to move from oppressive governments, from poverty and terrorism and tyranny, it's only the Gazans who have absolutely no options to do so. As dangerous as it may be for North Africans to cross the sea to Sicily, or Syrians to cross the desert to Jordan, or Mexicans to cross to Texas, there are no walls that make those journeys impossible. There is always a chance. Even the Cubans of the Cold War—whose plight in some ways mirrored that of the Gazans, being victimized by a blockade and caught in geopolitics beyond their control or interest—had the option of the sea. If not Florida, there was the Dominican Republic, Haiti, elsewhere in the Caribbean.

The Gazans, though, are caught in a prison that has been perfected. It is impassable. They have no options but to ask permission and to wait.

Oddly, right in front of us is an outdoor mural, depicting a Gazan and an Israeli sitting at a desk. The Gazan is being interviewed by the Israeli, and the Israeli is attempting to get the Gazan to become an Israeli informant. The mural is strangely colorful, festive even.

The dialogue coming from the Israeli spy recruiter unspools from his mouth in a flowing wave of words, and the Gazan, sitting defiantly across the desk, is refusing to become a traitor.

Amna is with us, and I turn around to see that she's taken off her wool hat, revealing hair streaked with red. Her clothing and uncovered and dyed hair would attract too much attention among so many guards and Hamsawis, so she is sunk deep into her seat, almost invisible in the darkness of the backseat. Today she didn't drive, couldn't drive here, but yesterday she was a phenom. After we visited Jamal's farm, Amna had insisted on driving home. It was a long trip, over an hour, almost the length of Gaza, and she endured withering stares, children in the villages pointing at her, male drivers yelling at her and at Talib. All along, she stared straight ahead, never responding, never flinching.

I say good-bye to Amna, who stays in the car as Talib walks me through the first checkpoint. There is a line of Western aid workers waiting to go through customs. I see Silvia and two members of her staff, and I wave, and when I do, I drop the handle of my rollerbag, and its long handle makes a loud cracking sound on the linoleum floor. All the aid workers jump, startled, and then glare at me. To them the sound could have been gunfire, a bomb, anything.

Talib doesn't react. We say good-bye. I offer him money for gas, for photographic equipment. "No fucking way," he says, smiling. We lie about seeing each other again, and he turns to drive home with Amna.

After customs, Silvia asks me to accompany a German young woman, traveling alone. She has asthma and the heat is affecting her. We walk together through the kilometer-long fenced-in corridor through the buffer zone, and she tells me how she's working on a photographic series about circus groups. She's been to Afghanistan and Pakistan, too, and has just spent a week in Gaza, documenting a circus group whose members learned all they know by watching videos on the Internet.

Finally we arrive at the green-glass building, and go through security, through customs, and are in Israel. And I'm thinking about how exhausting it must be. To be Talib and Amna, living in a place that does not accept you, a place to which you have no loyalty or affection—everything you want in life is beyond the walls—and yet you cannot leave.

When we'd first met, at the al-Deira, we'd talked about meeting new friends, eventually saying good-bye. "We meet many internationals," Amna said then. "It's difficult every time to say good-bye to these people. We are always limited. We cannot see the real world outside. We cannot cross with you."

(Names have been changed to protect the speakers.)

EPILOGUE

I stayed in touch with Talib and Amna after I left. I introduced them to an asylum lawyer in San Francisco, who advised them as best she could from 7,000 miles away. They updated me many times about their status, but their prospects looked grim. Finally they received a visa from the United States, but still couldn't get a permit from the Israelis or Egyptians to leave Gaza. It was maddening. The barriers seemed insurmountable.

Then one day in October, I got an email. "We're in Brooklyn!!" Talib wrote. They'd bribed an Egyptian guard at the Rafah gate. It cost them $5000 but they were out. They traveled fourteen hours through the Sinai Peninsula and were finally free. With their Palestinian passports and their American visas, they flew to New York.

I was heading to Washington, DC, in November, and asked them if they wanted to meet in the capitol. They agreed, and we planned to meet on a Wednesday at the new National Museum of African-American History and Culture. It happened to be the Wednesday after the election of Donald Trump, who had proposed a ban on all Muslims entering the United States.

They had either come just in time, or at the very worst time.

SUMUD

EMILY RABOTEAU

1. TEL AVIV

I expected trouble getting through border inspection when I arrived at Ben Gurion Airport. In part this was because I'd had difficulty the first time I traveled to Israel, in the run-up to the second intifada. The problem then had to do with my middle name: Ishem. Evidently, it sounded vaguely Arabic. I was ignorant of my name's origin and strip-searched at the airport as a result. I'd since learned that it's likely a German Jewish surname. I was ready to share this information if I were questioned again about my identity. I'd also popped a half a Xanax. Like most airport agents, this poor woman looked like she suffered from hemorrhoids and would rather be anywhere else. I'm not sure what I looked like to her. An activist? A journalist? A threat? She examined my US passport. What was the purpose of my travel in Israel? she inquired.

My hosts had prepared me to be vague about this. I wasn't to volunteer I'd been invited here to write about the occupation on the occasion of its upcoming fiftieth anniversary, but rather to say I was writing about life in Israel and Palestine in general. The bulk of my trip would be spent in the occupied Palestinian territories, but I'd taken care to scrawl *ISRAEL* on the cover of my blank notebook above the date—June 2016—in the event my suitcase was searched.

"I'm here to visit an old friend," I told the agent, which was equally true. I wanted to know how Tamar was coping with her girls in this fucked-up realm, and, if I'm honest, to process with her how I was coping in mine, which was fucked in parallel ways.

"It's a long journey for just one week," the agent observed. "Why so short a time?" I wasn't fooled by the woman's conversational tone. I assumed the grilling was about to begin. I told her a week was as long as I could bear spending away from my two young children. Another truth, though I also felt giddy to be free, for a spell, of my son and daughter, and my country. Her face softened as she asked me their ages. "They're three and five," I answered. Just like that, she stamped my passport and let me through. "Have fun in Israel!" she called. I felt I'd been bestowed a magic cape with two contradictory but mutually advantageous traits: invisibility and power. I was a mother.

2. SUSIYA

It was unusually hot for June, and the heat was dry at the desert's edge. The semiarid South Hebron Hills were stubbled with scrub and thistles, and strewn with bone-colored rock. Though it was not quite summer and not yet noon, my guide, Ahmad S., estimated the temperature had climbed to 37 degrees, or as my mind translated it, almost 100. "Drink," the water lab technician reminded me. I lifted my bottle to my lips and without thinking, drained it. A first-world privilege, this—to be thoughtless about water. We were at the ankles of the West Bank, far off the grid, in the cab of Ahmad's dusty truck.

Ahmad, twenty-nine, Palestinian, comes from a town northwest of Hebron called Halhul. With his light-brown skin, gelled hair, gold chain, slim-fitting jeans, and Nikes, he could pass for one of the Dominican guys in my neighborhood back home in New York City. Apart from Ahmad's slick look, I found hardly anything familiar in the desolate landscape. We may as well have been driving on an asteroid. Judea, the right-wing Zionists call it. The apostle Mark called it "the wilderness." It was hard for me as an outsider to comprehend how such barren hills could sustain life. I'd been to Brazil's sertão, the steppes of New Mexico, and to Andalusia in Spain, where the spaghetti Westerns were filmed. None of those deserts was as dry as this. Yet to the north of us grew the vineyards of Mount Hebron, famed for its grapes since biblical times. The foothills to the west extended into Israel. To the east dropped the Jordan Valley, where the storied river (that the Israelites crossed) bottoms out into the Dead Sea. In Israeli settler parlance, and according to the Torah, God granted this land to the Jews.

We continued south, drawing closer to the area where the separation barrier peters out like the tail of an undulating snake. From the passenger's side window I saw an Israeli settlement spread out on a hilltop like a green mirage. According to the international community, the settlement is illegal.

"Throughout history, people always gravitate to the same places, wherever there is water," Ahmad said. "We have limited water here. This, as much as the rest of it, is the root of the conflict."

In close range, just off Road 317, lay our destination—the Palestinian shantytown of Khirbet Susiya, a ramshackle batch of tents, shacks, sheep pens, outhouses, a sad looking swing set donated by the EU, a lopsided dovecote, a solar panel array, and a stone monument to an eighteen-month-old allegedly burned alive in the West Bank town of Duma the previous summer when a group of masked Israeli extremists lobbed a firebomb into his parents' dwelling. According to Israel, the village of Susiya is illegal. All of its structures are under threat of demolition by the Israeli Civil Administration, the military arm meant to oversee daily life in Palestine.

Because I wasn't ready to look at the picture of the toddler's face inlaid in the monument as we rolled past it, I turned my attention to one of the most prominent of the village's "illegal" structures—a big white water tank on stilts. Along with the solar panels, the tank was supplied to the people of Susiya by the nonprofit Palestinian-Israeli organization Community Energy Technology in the Middle East (Comet-ME). Comet employs Ahmad, who holds a degree in laboratory science from al-Quds University. Its mission is to supply renewable energy and clean water services to some of the most impoverished and marginalized people in the occupied Palestinian territories.

Including Susiya, Comet currently serves about thirty villages in the South Hebron Hills. These small hamlets are mostly composed of clans of shepherds and farmers who dwell in caves and tents, living much as their ancestors have for centuries, separating the wheat from the chaff, except that in recent history they've had the bulk of their land grabbed. More recently, thanks to Comet, they've enjoyed a taste of electricity.

I knew about Comet because my best friend from childhood, Tamar, works there in development. She's the sole woman in a small team of quixotic physicist, electrician, and environmental-engineer cowboys who throw up wind turbines, water tanks, and solar panel minigrids in the face of a military occupation that has discriminated against Palestinians for the past fifty years. In addition to reconnecting with Tamar, I wanted to better understand the imbalance of power that would make such an organization vital. So here I was, shadowing my friend's colleague in the Holy Land. Ahmad parked on the unpaved road. We climbed out of the truck.

Today's task in Susiya was to test the purity of the water drawn by electric pump from a cistern of harvested rain into the tanks and then out through a network of pipes that snaked along the rocky ground, leading to taps and slow sand filters in the various tents. This system saves the village women the hours of labor it previously cost them to haul the water by hand. Before Ahmad got to work he took a long drag from his cigarette—one of the last allowed him during daylight hours before Ramadan, which was to begin the next day, or the day after that, depending on the fickleness of the moon. "In the spring, this is the most beautiful place in the world," Ahmad said. He must have read the look of misapprehension on my face. The most beautiful in the world, this place? "It's so *calm*," he said.

That seemed an odd word choice to apply to the territory of Susiya. The village gave off an air of impermanence, like a refugee camp or a site fabricated after a natural disaster, reminding me a little of the tent city I'd visited ten years before under an overpass in New Orleans, its population made homeless by Hurricane Katrina. In the past thirty years the village has been displaced multiple times, making it an international symbol for pro-Palestinian activists of how Israel maintains brutal control over much of the West Bank by confiscating land. Susiya falls under the designation of Area C, as does over 60 percent of the West Bank since the 1995 Oslo II accords—disputed land overseen not by the Palestinian Authority but by Israel's military. In a larger conversation comparing Israeli expansionism to Manifest Destiny in the United States, Tamar described Area C to me as "lawless like the Wild West."

Susiya has existed since at least 1830, but its Palestinian residents have been locked in a legal battle over land ownership since 1986. That's when archaeologists unearthed a sixth-century synagogue nearby with Hebrew lettering on its mosaic floor. The Palestinian villagers were evicted, their land expropriated, and the site turned into an Israeli national park run by settlers. Palestinians are prohibited from entering the park even though its grounds also include the remains of a mosque and the caves that people from Susiya once called home. When Susiyans relocated too close for the comfort of the expanding Israeli settlement (confusingly named Susya, as if to reclaim Susiya), they were again expelled. In the early 1990s Susiya's Palestinian villagers were herded into trucks by Israeli soldiers and deposited fifteen kilometers to the north under cover of darkness. Though some families scattered after being exiled, other stalwarts returned to their land, prompting escalating settler violence.

Susiya's residents were ousted yet again during the second intifada in 2001, in retaliation for the murder of a Jewish settler from a nearby outpost—this time under the pretext that the village posed a security threat. It didn't matter that the victim's killer didn't come from Susiya. Susiya's caves were packed with rock, its sheds demolished, its cisterns filled with rubble and debris, its olive orchards uprooted, its fields scorched, its livestock buried alive in bulldozed pens, to say nothing of the shepherds beaten and killed while tending their flocks. Many families fled to the nearby town of Yatta. What had once been a community of about eighty families dwindled to thirty, leaving Susiya even more vulnerable to attack. Under international pressure, Israel's High Court of Justice stopped the demolitions but never ordered the Civil Administration to concede Susiya's reconstruction.

These days, the State of Israel claims that the roughly 350 Palestinians who persist in the area of Susiya are trespassers because they've erected their tents without the required permits. And yet when villagers have submitted master plans to rebuild, their requests are systematically denied, as happens throughout Area C—meaning the people of Susiya live both hand to mouth and at the edge of ruin.

"This entire region is under stress," Ahmad put it, while grinding out his cigarette with his heel. "You don't sleep well if you spend each night dreaming of how to get through the next day when the soldiers may arrive to crush your house."

How could he call this nightmare calm?

We followed a line of laundry strung from one of the stilts below the water tank to one of the poles supporting a nearby tent. The tent walls were held down with tires; its floor was poured concrete. Inside, Ahmad greeted a middle-aged woman who served us tiny glasses of bitter coffee while three barefoot children looked on shyly from behind a stack of thin mattresses swarming with flies. I handed each of them a ballpoint pen.

"I hope those are magic pens that can write in English," their mother said dryly in Arabic. I loved her for offering that chestnut. It suggested this place wasn't a dead end. A clutch of chicks skittered about at our feet. Outside: the cry of a rooster, the bleating of a lamb, the blowing of saffron-hued wind.

Ahmad knelt by the water filter in the kitchen area and filled a test tube to check for contaminants while chattering good-naturedly about pH balance, microbes, chlorine tablets, and the generally high quality of this water. If all was consistently well maintained, he said, the product was as pure as what you would find in the municipalities. "As pure as what they drink in the Jewish settlements?" I asked.

"Just as pure," Ahmad said with pride.

I was struck by the mundane way he went about his job, as if it wasn't forbidden by Israeli authorities. I was also struck by the coziness of the tent and how readily it would buckle under the force of a bulldozer. It was made out of Styrofoam, plywood, nothing, and

brick. A sheet divided the home in half. Its few possessions were im-
peccably ordered. A handful of tin pots and a two-burner gas stove.
A broom. An *argileh* pipe. An electric fan. And most surprising of all,
given the basic conditions, a box TV set blaring an al-Jazeera tribute
to Mohammed Ali.

The boxer's young face filled the screen with dazzling braggado-
cio. He had died the day before. Ali seemed simultaneously out of
place and precisely at home in the West Bank. June 1967 is a water-
shed moment you hear referenced all the time in Israel-Palestine. It's
when Israel captured the West Bank, expanding its territory. It's also
when a US court found Mohammed Ali guilty of draft evasion for
refusing to serve in the Vietnam War, stripped him of his WBA title,
and barred him from boxing. He had concluded that the US govern-
ment was more his enemy than the Vietcong, who "never called me
nigger, they never lynched me, they didn't put no dogs on me, they
didn't rob me of my nationality, rape and kill my mother and father."
The TV special on al-Jazeera didn't go into all that history, but en-
countering Mohammed Ali in that tent made me think of his strug-
gle for the rights of full citizenship in direct relation to this woman's.

"Ask her what she will do when they come to destroy her home,"
I begged Ahmad before we left. The woman adjusted her head cov-
ering and gestured through the tent opening into the glare of day-
light at an unlikely rosebush I hadn't noticed growing in the rocky
soil, bedecked with bright pink blooms. Ahmad translated her an-
swer casually on our way out, as if it should have been obvious:

"She says she will stay right here and rebuild." In fact, the word
she'd used for her perseverance was *sumud*. It means steadfastness, but
it's also a political ideology that's developed in resistance to the occu-
pation since the 1967 Six-Day War. An icon of *sumud* often portrayed
in Palestinian artwork is the figure of the mother. With the image of
Ali flashing on the screen, I liked the idea of the mother as a similar
source of strength.

The temperature mounted as the morning wore on. We traveled
from tent to tent, hounded by a pink-eyed desert dog that Ahmad
suspected had rabies. In each tent we were graced by the specter of
Mohammed Ali on a Comet-powered television set. Nobody was

watching, per se. As at my mother-in-law's house in Jamaica, Queens, the TV was largely just background noise. *I'm the most recognized and loved man that ever lived cuz there weren't no satellites when Jesus and Moses were around, so people far away in the villages didn't know about them.* . . .

Ahmad went about checking the water meters to estimate daily use. The water crisis is rising for the entire Middle East due to increasing desertification, but here, in the poorest communities, the problem is most pronounced. Ahmad spoke in liters and cubic meters, throwing out statistics like the scientist he was. The daily allowance for domestic use by a family of five to ten people was no more than 200 liters, he explained, though the World Health Organization recommends 100 liters for just *one* person.

Even without a grasp of the metric system, I did understand that Ahmad's figures adhered to a stark and troubling scale that measured not just water consumption but relative human worth. In the remote communities of the South Hebron Hills, the average person has recourse to as little as 20 liters of water a day. That's far less than your average Palestinian, who (according to the Palestinian Water Authority) consumes 73, which is in turn less than half of the 183 daily liters consumed by your average Israeli. In fact, the Israeli settlements of the West Bank receive almost limitless supplies of water through Mekorot, Israel's government-owned water company. *Haaretz* reported in 2012 that Israel's 450,000 settlers used as much or more water than the total Palestinian population of about 2.3 million.

"It is not only that they have more water than us, but that they have *stolen* our water," Azzam Nawaja insisted when we visited his tent. Azzam was a shepherd in his fifties with a sophisticated understanding of the area's inequitable water use and a sense of outrage about its political leverage. He wore a red-and-white checked keffiyeh. His sun-creased eyes blazed when he spoke. The walls of his tent and the water tank outside it were decorated with Palestinian flags. One of Azzam's wives served me a glass of very sweet tea as Ahmad tested their water. Suddenly I was overwhelmed by the grandeur of her hospitality—how many precious milliliters did the glass contain?

"Have you seen how green it is up there by their nice villas?" the shepherd asked me, pointing out of the tent's mouth to the Jewish neighborhood about a kilometer away, one of five satellite neighborhoods comprising the settlement of Susya. Its greenery made it easy to spot, as did the red rooftops of its homes, its cell phone tower, and the utility poles connecting its overhead power lines. Azzam described its amenities. "They have lush gardens, watered lawns, and irrigated farms." He guessed they might even have a swimming pool. I agreed that it looked like an oasis.

"Have you seen our garden?" Azzam asked by way of contrast. He pointed first at a rosemary bush inside a car tire and then downhill at a stand of parched olive trees growing at strange angles from the rind of the earth. "They get water from an Israeli pipe that is prohibited for us to use. We don't have water to irrigate our crops. We're forbidden access to over twenty of our cisterns since they took our land, and we're forbidden to build new ones."

Azzam explained through Ahmad that in Susiya they reuse the water for cooking, then washing, then watering plants—not a single drop is wasted. Most years are so dry that there's not enough rainfall to fill the few accessible cisterns and the community must supplement its supply by buying water from Israel at a high price. A tanker truck that delivers this water requires a permit and is forced to take long detours to avoid Israeli military checkpoints and roads off-limits to Palestinians, resulting in further hikes to the cost of water. "Water eats up a third of our income," Azzam lamented.

Ironically, the water Azzam must buy from Israel comes from within the West Bank. Shared water sources in the slowly depleting Western Aquifer Basin have been under Israel's complete control since 1967. The mountain aquifer is the main source of underground water in both Israel and the Palestinian territories, but how Israel distributes that water is grossly imbalanced. This is what Azzam meant when he said they were stealing the water—not just on a small scale, but on a staggering one. A recent Amnesty International report revealed that Israel restricted Palestinian access to the aquifer's water while siphoning nearly all of it for itself. A recent inventory by the United Nations indicated that Israel's extraction from the Western Aquifer Basin was at 94 percent, leaving the Palestinians with a mere 6 percent.

The pink-eyed desert dog trailed Ahmad and me on our walk to the neighboring tent.

"We feel despair," Nasser Nawaja told me inside. He sat cross-legged on an unraveling floor mat and invited me to sit. "I hope we'll find some measure of justice through your pen."

Nasser is Susiya's unofficial spokesperson, an activist accustomed to talking about the local conflict to the international press. He was born over thirty years ago in one of the caves claimed by Israel as part of the archaeological park. Like Azzam Nawaja (the two men share a surname as part of the same extended tribe), he was consumed by the subject of water. Our meandering discussion of life under the occupation kept running back to it, like a river to the sea. Nasser still mourned the cisterns destroyed in 2001 with fresh hurt, detailing how they were packed with bulldozed dirt, poisoned with rusty scrap metal, "raped" by excavator drills operated by the IDF. He spoke about the shameful lopsidedness in the basic quality of life.

"For one thousand liters of water, we pay five times what they pay in Israel. Meanwhile, their water supply company funnels a pipe straight to the settlements through our land," Nasser said. "We asked Mekorot to give us an opening in the water pipe. We told them we'd pay for it, even though it's ours. They said, 'No. You're an illegal village.' They have all the water and electricity they want, even though it's *they* who are illegal. Let's put aside the international community that says so. Even according to Israel, some of these outposts are illegal." Nasser referred to the agreement reached twenty years earlier in the Oslo accords, after which there were to be no new settlements built. The number of settlers has tripled since that time. "It's illegal for Mekorot and the Israel Electric Corporation to supply outposts like this, and yet they do it all the time."

I asked Nasser how access to clean water and electricity through Comet had affected his family. He gushed about how it had made life easier, but still emphasized the differences in Susiya (the Palestinian village) versus Susya (the Israeli settlement). "The revolution of electricity is like a river that can't be stopped. This has given our dark life more light. Our children can study later, we have electric outlets to charge our cell phones, and it's made a small revolution in the lives of the women. For example, they no longer have to carry water or shake a goat's gut full of milk for four hours to make cheese. We have electric butter churns now, and the Internet.

"But there's no way to even compare what kind of power we have here versus what they have there. They're on an electric grid. We're still begging for permission to crawl out of our caves and work our land when it's clear they'll never give us permits to live here. I'm asking for the right to live in the twenty-first century, where people have already been to the moon and sent satellites to other planets."

"What do you do with your anger?" I asked Nasser.

The man looked thrown from his script. "It's hard to keep it swallowed up inside. For some people it spills out," was all he could say.

Outside Nasser's tent the desert dog had curled up inside a rusted-out car body, biting at the fleas on his bony back. Ahmad scooped up a rock to hurl if it pursued us. I must have appeared concerned for the animal. "It's part of our culture to throw stones to protect ourselves when we feel afraid," said Ahmad, apologetically. His work was done for the day. As we passed the toddler's monument on our walk back to the truck I forced myself to confront the child's face. His name was Ali Dawabshah. "My son started talking at eighteen months," I said. I remembered when signifier joined signified on my son's tongue, the charm when babble became "ba" became "bus." It slayed me that this child would never speak in sentences, that his mother would never learn what he had to say.

Ahmad hung back. He attended the movement of the dog as it slinked toward us with a growl in its throat. Ahmad threw the stone in self defense. I flinched when it struck the animal's hindquarter, prompting the dog to limp off behind a pile of tires. The man's shoulders sank. He admitted to feeling a little low, not because of the conflict in Susiya and throughout the West Bank, though that was cause enough for depression, but because tomorrow he'd start a month of fasting. The fatigue he knew to expect during Ramadan exhausted him already. Impertinently, I asked Ahmad how his body could take it. This was a question I would ask in many different ways of many different Arabs that week in Palestine—though by "it" I meant more than Ramadan.

Ahmad chose his words carefully. "We have resources deep within ourselves like a hidden spring. We draw from this to keep going even when we have no fuel."

Then, because he could see I was dehydrated, he pulled out a peach, seemingly from thin air, and told me to eat.

3. EAST JERUSALEM

Later that Sunday, I went to the Jerusalem Day parade. Tamar, a longtime resident of Jerusalem and a secular Jew, had zero interest in joining me for the festivities. "Try not to get trampled by the mob," she warned. She stayed at home to plan an upcoming *iftar* meal at Comet, where her Palestinian and Israeli coworkers could break the Ramadan fast together with some of the folks from the villages they empowered. Her activist boyfriend, Guy Butavia, escorted me instead, walking fast as a rabbit along King David Street toward the Old City with his video camera in hand.

We were going to witness the parade wherein thousands of ultra-nationalist Jewish celebrants proceed through Jerusalem, ending with a dramatic push through the Old City's Muslim Quarter. The city was divided after the 1948 Arab-Israeli War, with the west controlled by Israel and the east (including the Old City) by Jordan. Jerusalem Day commemorates the city's "reunification" in 1967, when Israel conquered East Jerusalem, but it's as much a provocation against Arabs as a celebration of unity. Over a third of Jerusalem's population is Palestinian, but they're not invited to the party. Most of them know to stay inside or risk getting beaten up or harassed. This year they marked the same date as the *naksa*, or "setback," commemorating their displacement after Israel's victory.

Guy referred to the annual tradition of "the March of Flags" as "the March of Hate." He's an activist with Ta'ayush (it means "living together" in Arabic), a group that uses nonviolent direct action to fight for Palestinian rights. Earlier this year he was arrested in connection with his activity, and spent some time in jail. As with the Black Lives Matter movement in the United States, filming unethical behavior is one of Ta'ayush's most effective tactics in battling state-sanctioned violence.

We trekked past Prime Minister Netanyahu's residence on Balfour Street, winding our way through the thickening crowd toward the nerve center of the Old City. We pushed through people beating drums and waving Israeli flags. They were mostly adolescents. Zionist youth groups, yeshiva boys, settlers, settler sympathizers, and messianic types bussed in from across the country. Riled-up children. They passed out stickers that said KAHANE WAS RIGHT, in reference to the late, infamous orthodox rabbi Meir Kahane, a member of the Knesset who endorsed annexing the West Bank and the Gaza Strip while expelling the Palestinians, along with a lot of other anti-Arab ideas that brought Israel to outlaw his political groups. In spirit, he reminded me of Donald Trump, who was scapegoating immigrants and agitating for a wall in an effort to "make America great again" back home. Although Kahane fell from grace thirty years ago, his writings have carried on as foundational texts for most of today's militant and extreme-right political groups in Israel. Some of Kahane's manifestos were on sale at the parade, including *They Must Go*, a screed whose title pretty much speaks for itself. Many parade-goers wore T-shirts silk-screened with images of a rebuilt Jewish temple, prophesied in the Book of Ezekiel as the eternal dwelling place of the God of Israel on Jerusalem's Temple Mount.

The site of the Temple Mount, or Haram a-Sharif ("the Noble Sanctuary") as it is known in Islam, was not far off. It was just through the Damascus Gate, inside the Old City, conquered by Israel on this day in 1967. There lies the holiest site in Judaism, the Foundation Stone, where some Jewish traditions hold that Abraham prepared to sacrifice Isaac and where Jacob laid his head and dreamed—the pillow of stone where heaven joins the earth. This rock is just as sacred to Muslims for being the place where the Prophet Mohammed is said to have ascended into heaven, enshrined by the eye-catching gold Dome of the Rock that sits on the ruins of the first two temples, like Susya on Susiya. The atmosphere grew more charged as we approached that mighty power source. The March of Flags would start at the gate and culminate at the last remnant of the Second Temple—

the Western Wall. The masses sang and chanted so loudly their voices grew hoarse. *The eternal people do not fear a long journey*, they belted. *Jerusalem of Gold*.

I remarked that it felt like a pep rally, one where everyone really believed in the team. "They're brainwashed," Guy said with great pity. Then he directed his lens at a unit of armed Israeli border police who'd blocked off a street entrance to an Arab neighborhood with a tank that would use its cannon to spray their bodies and homes with "skunk water" if they dared try exiting to protest the march. Skunk water is a putrid-smelling form of nonlethal crowd control developed in Israel to keep demonstrations in check. (Several police departments in US cities, including Saint Louis, are reported to have recently bought it in the wake of protests organized by the Black Lives Matter movement.)

"That's the smell of the occupation," said Guy. "It's worse than a skunk. It stinks like raw sewage and rotting corpses. It doesn't go away for days. It can make you sick. The term Israel uses for this is *sanitize*."

I thought of the fire hoses police targeted on nonviolent protestors, including children, in Birmingham in 1963. The pressure from their jets was strong enough to peel bark from a tree. "Why don't they just use water?" I asked Guy.

"Not cruel enough."

One of the police noticed Guy filming and put his hand on his assault rifle. We moved on, weaving into that amped crowd. "Get ready. It's about to turn ugly," said Guy. He braced himself to record the slogans, jeers, and acts of vandalism he'd witnessed at past parades: *Mohammed is dead*; *The third temple will be built and the [al-Aqsa] mosque will be burned*; *Death to Arabs*, and so on.

"Imagine they are storming through your neighborhood and you aren't allowed on the street, or to run your shop, or leave your house and they are chanting death to you and your prophet," Guy said. I acknowledged it would be hard for me, in that scenario, to turn the other cheek. Someone shouldered him, hard. A teenage girl.

"Why don't you point your camera at the Arabs throwing stones?" she spat at Guy, though the only Arabs in sight were shop owners being roughly steered out of the Muslim Quarter's market by Israeli police, to clear the way for the March of Flags. Guy thought it unsafe for me to be at his side, and directed me toward what looked like a secure perch from which to watch. Suddenly he was gone, swallowed up in the throng. Now I knew why Tamar warned me not to get trampled. There were 30,0000 people and two thousand police officers in attendance at this evening's parade. I climbed onto the post to the side of the steps leading down into the swarming plaza of Damascus Gate.

The revelers rode on each other's shoulders. Packs of boys dancing in horas. The next generation. They seemed like their voices had only just changed, and yet in no time at all they'd be required to serve in the army. The air was suffused with testosterone and great potential, enough voltage to power a city. "What are they singing?" I asked a sympathetic Hebrew speaker below my perch. *Worship God with happiness*, he translated. The air was electric. Their chorus reached a fever pitch. *God will defend us*, they sang, pumping their fists. I was touched by their expressions of faith and terrified of their zeal. *We will win*. It sounded to me like a battle cry.

As a mother I wanted to shake those boys by the shoulders for behaving like bullies. Such misguided ardor. They surged into the mouth of Damascus Gate. It felt like a desecration—not merely because they believed Jerusalem belonged to them alone but because their fanaticism was so close a surrogate for actual joy. I thought of Ali Dawabshah, and of my own children, whom I tell that the most important thing in life is kindness, to use their words and not their fists; who are black in the United States and therefore also endangered. An armed policeman stared me down with bloodshot eyes. I realized I was crying. I turned my face from his because I felt afraid.

4. IFTAR AT THE ELECTRIC COMPANY

On Wednesday, I went with Tamar to the Comet headquarters for the iftar meal she'd helped plan. It was just a dozen coworkers sitting down to supper at sundown in the desert at a table covered by a cheap plastic cloth. Arab and Israeli guys alike, who share the belief that power is a basic human right. Compared with the despair of Susiya and the furor of Jerusalem Day, I found this to be the truest expression of accord I'd seen my whole time here.

The festive mood swelled in the countdown to nightfall. The cool air was perfumed by the lavender shrubs growing beyond the veranda where the table was set. Our shadows grew elongated like figures in an El Greco painting, and then our shadows were gone. Twilight, the magic hour. "Is it time yet? Can we eat now?" asked twelve-year-old Yusef. He sat at the table next to his father, Ali A., a shepherd from one of the off-grid communities Comet services, a place called Tuba. Ahmad S. consulted his watch, and then the slip of the moon in the indigo sky. He clapped his hands. He looked so much more energized than he had on our depressing day in Susiya. His eyes twinkled like the stars that were starting to show. It was time.

Ahmad uncovered the dishes of mouthwatering Arabic salad with tahini, grape leaves, soup, kibbe, and roasted chicken. Like a maître d', he brought out a platter of lamb and served it with flair. The other project managers and technicians were in equally high spirits as they broke their fast to dig into the feast, to make toasts and joke with each other in Arabic and Hebrew. *Habibi*, they called one another. Is there another word on earth as tender as this? *My darling.* Even as an outsider, I felt inside their circle, just as I'd often felt as a girl when invited to Shabbat dinner at Tamar's house. Yusef felt at ease enough to joke that by my age I should have five sons at home, not just the one. Through Tamar, I ribbed the boy back. "Why? So I could have four more like you to smack in the head for telling me how to live?" I tugged that rascal's earlobe and he grinned.

Comet's Israeli cofounders, the physicists Elad O. and Noam D., were smiling, too. There was cause for their organization to celebrate, though it wasn't the express reason for tonight's iftar. In the eight years since Comet first electrified Susiya, it had largely succeeded in its mission to electrify the South Hebron Hills. That is, most of the so-called cave dwellers in this part of the West Bank were now connected to an alternative energy source—the wind or the sun. Since 2008 Comet has erected 10 small wind turbines, 569 solar panels, and over 100 household water systems like the ones I'd gone to check with Ahmad, serving approximately 2,500 Palestinians in its effort to help them remain on their land. While continuing to keep up these existing systems, Comet's next stage will be to expand its reach beyond the South Hebron Hills and establish new ones. This expansion offers an alternative to the State of Israel's. It strives not to take but to give, not to extinguish but to illuminate.

Earlier that day I'd sat in on a planning session to serve a previously unserved community. Tamar asked me to keep its name a secret, off the Civil Administration's radar. Elad showed the team a slideshow graphing peak electric consumption loads, and they discussed how many kilowatt hours per family per day they could realistically provide. The community in question is semiurban, different from the rural cave and tent dwellers traditionally served by Comet. Working there brings with it a set of new challenges—most notably, higher expectations from their minigrid. The people will likely want more power than Comet can supply. Comet provides modest energy services on average of 2 to 2.5 kilowatt hours per family per day. (The average American household uses 30.)

For all the prosaic nuts and bolts about generators, hard stops, and photovoltaic arrays, it was hard not to consider this conversation's biblical overtones. We were in the Holy Land, after all, and these guys were deciding how much power to bestow. That level of responsibility seemed to me almost supernatural. The underlying question was, how should power be put to use? Maybe because I felt a little lost in all the kilowatt talk, or because of the dreaminess of the landscape, my mind wandered to Genesis. *And God said, Let there be light, and there was light.*

The engineers seated at the table weren't gods, of course, but men. Men having a philosophical and practical argument. For the moment they disagreed about how the money for the electric service in the new community should be collected. Comet is a unique NGO in that it is also, sort of, a utility company. The people Comet serves pay electric bills, and the money is deposited into a savings account, to be used ten years or so down the line to replace the batteries. "It's to prevent a swamp of donor dependency," Tamar explained. "And it gives people a stake in their energy grid."

Whereas Noam felt a local committee should be established for collecting the funds, Elad believed the people would consider Comet more of an authority if each family paid Comet directly, the way they'd always done it, with Wasseem A., Comet's maintenance manager, going door to door or tent to tent every other month to give each household a prepaid meter card in exchange for fifty to one hundred shekels. I wondered, was the organization becoming more faceless as a function of its growth?

"I don't see Comet as an electric company but as a social project," Noam insisted. He was a contemplative man in his sixties with a short gray beard, wire-rimmed glasses, and a hand-rolled cigarette. Elad said they were the closest thing to an electric company these people were going to get. He was twenty years younger than Noam, and wore a Groucho Marx T-shirt that read "Those are my principles, and if you don't like them . . . well, I have others" in Spanish. (One of his principles is that we who take electricity for granted have done absolutely nothing to deserve it.) The men seemed to reach a compromise. There would be a community committee, but Wasseem would be on it, and Comet would have a stake.

Noam felt satisfied by this arrangement but stressed, "If you want to empower somebody, you give *them* the power." After dinner his tone grew more wistful out on the veranda as he reminisced about Comet's early days. Having cheerfully inhaled the meal, the Muslims in the group had left the table to bow toward Mecca in prayer. They used trash bags as makeshift prayer mats. Among them: Ahmad, Wasseem, and Moatasem H., a young technician clutching the Quran, who sometimes awakens to the sound of bulldozers rolling up to demolish parts of his village before coming to work in the morning. It was quiet now. Not the sound of a muezzin, or TV, or traffic, or gunfire, or anything but the wind turning the blades of the tall white Comet turbine standing nearby.

Noam rolled a cigarette. Above us gleamed the waxing crescent moon. Before us on the horizon a string of faraway Ramadan lights blinked in the growing dark. They sparked a warm feeling in me. I felt grateful to be reunited with my old friend in this faraway place, liberated from the responsibilities and anxieties of parenthood in uncertain times. The Ramadan lights sparked a fuzzy feeling in Noam, too. He spoke to me and Tamar about the first time he saw Susiya lit up in the night almost ten years before, the fatherly joy he'd felt at having helped supply its first light.

"Susiya is completely different today than it was ten years ago. At that time they were very vulnerable. Activists would stay the night to protect them from getting beat up or evicted. They were at the bottom of the barrel, looked upon as uneducated. Now they're building their position in life. They've learned how to sell their story. Usually, after you install energy, the first thing they'll do is buy a TV. It doesn't matter that I'm not in favor of that choice, or that I dislike when they squabble over who'll get hooked up first, who gets the first fridge, or the eventual air conditioner. It's their choice how to develop themselves. This is our belief. On this point, Elad and I agree."

Tamar added that Comet didn't get into issues of gender inequality. As a woman, this was sometimes hard for her—she smiled awkwardly at me, for example, when Moatasem wouldn't shake my hand on meeting me, but she also knew it wasn't her job to make him accept it. "Empowerment means letting people live their lives as they choose to live them," Noam repeated, "even when giving people tools to argue means they may argue with you." I understood we were no longer just talking about electricity, infrastructure, or social justice. We were talking about free will and its brightest corollary—hope.

Elad had somehow ripped his trousers. "The occupation did it," he cracked, and everybody burst out laughing. The Muslims returned loose-limbed to the table. It was time for dessert. We stuffed ourselves silly with *qatayef*, coffee, and dates until at last we were full. I gazed up at the sky, now punched through with a thousand stars, and streaked with meteors. Its perfect clarity made me gasp. That night felt free in part because no veil of light pollution obscured it. We were at the edge of the world, in the Milky Way. We were that far off the grid.

JOURNEY TO THE WEST BANK

MARIO VARGAS LLOSA

1.

In the 1970s I was quite active in the defense of Israel, getting myself involved in many polemical exchanges. At that time in Latin America it was fashionable, not only amongst the far left but also the moderate left and a great number of centrist and right-wing organizations, to attack Israel. Israel was accused of being a "pawn of US imperialism," an instrument used by the United States to destabilize "progressive governments" in the Middle East and counteract the influence of the USSR in the region (which was very strong, especially in Egypt).

I don't know how many articles I wrote, lectures I gave, and manifestos I signed in those years opposing this caricatured vision of Israel, and affirming that it was a pluralistic and democratic society, the only state in the Middle East where there was freedom of expression, freedom for political parties, and truly free elections. I pointed out that what had made Israel's existence possible, apart from Zionism, was not "US imperialism" but rather European anti-Semitism, with its long and bloody history leading up to the Holocaust and the murder of six million Jews perpetrated by the Nazis.

From that time I have often been to Israel—on one occasion to receive the Jerusalem Prize, which I am very proud to have been awarded—and my ideas about the need to defend its existence, with secure borders, have not changed one iota. I have many friends there, and generally we share the same views about Israeli policy towards the Palestinians. I am very critical of this policy not only because it seems to me right to be so, but also because I feel that the ever more colonialist bias of recent governments—I am referring to the governments of Sharon and Netanyahu—may be terribly prejudicial to Israeli democracy and the future of the country. Nothing degrades the political life of a nation more than sliding down a nationalist or colonialist path.

My opinions on Israeli policy towards the Palestinians have subjected me to many attacks, of course, especially from Jews living outside Israel; Israelis, in general, seem less intolerant and have a less narrow outlook than their supporters abroad. But I want to point out that my criticisms of the Israeli government's Palestine policy are the same as those voiced, in Israel, by tens of thousands of Israelis themselves. It is true that these internal critics are not sufficiently numerous to win a general election. But they exist, they are there, sometimes demoralized, but always active, and they—I call them the righteous ones—are for me the best guarantee of a different future for Israel, of peace and friendship with their neighbors and of coexistence and cooperation with the Palestinians.

I am and will always be against the "academic boycott" that threatens Israel. I will always be against "collective punishment" in which the righteous ones often pay for the misdeeds of the sinners. More so in this case, because it is absurd to penalize universities in Israel for the excesses of their government. Universities are often the best foci of resistance to the policies of Netanyahu, the places where the most constructive ideas and initiatives are developed in favor of a just and sensible agreement between Palestinians and Israelis.

2.

"Israel's biggest problem is the settlements in the West Bank, that is to say, the occupied Palestinian territories," Yehuda Shaul tells me.

"I think that there is a solution and that I will see it in place before I die."

I tell my Israeli friend that one has to be very optimistic to believe that anytime soon the 377,900 settlers on these invaded lands—who have created Bantustans, fencing in the 2.9 million inhabitants of the Palestinian cities and keeping them isolated from each other— will withdraw in the name of peace and peaceful coexistence. But Yehuda, who works tirelessly to highlight what the majority of his compatriots refuse to see—the tragic situation in which Palestinians live in the West Bank—tells me that I might be less skeptical after the journey that we will make together, tomorrow, to the Palestinian villages in the mountains south of Hebron.

He and I were in those mountains, almost the furthermost border of the West Bank, six years ago. Back then, the village of Susiya had about 300 inhabitants and seemed destined to disappear, like others in the region. Now there are about 450 inhabitants because, despite all the misfortunes they have suffered, a number of families that had fled have now returned. It seems that they, like Yehuda, are optimistic, inured to the atrocities.

The harassment that Susiya and the neighboring villages have suffered for many years has not ended. Quite the reverse. I am shown the recently demolished houses, the water wells blocked by rocks and rubbish, the trees cut down by the settlers, and even videos of settlers attacking the inhabitants with metal bars and clubs, as well as of the arrests and mistreatment meted out by the Israeli Defense Forces. In the community center, one of the few buildings left standing, Nasser Nawaja, a leading community organizer, shows me the demolition orders that, like swords of Damocles, hang over the buildings not yet destroyed by the bulldozers of the occupiers. The pretext for demolition is that the fragile dwellings are illegal because they do not have building permits. "It's madness," Nasser says. "When we ask permission to build or to reopen the water wells, they refuse us and then they demolish the houses for having been built without authorization." For this reason, in this village, like others in the region, the farmers and shepherds do not live in houses but in tents and lean-tos made of canvas and tin, or in the caves that the soldiers have not yet blocked by filling them with stones and rubbish.

Despite everything, the residents of Susiya and Jinba, the two villages I visit, are still there, resisting the siege, supported by some NGOs and Israeli solidarity groups such as Breaking the Silence, to which Yehuda, who has invited me here, belongs. In Susiya I meet a very pleasant young man, Max Schindler. He has come here for a few months as a volunteer, and he teaches English to the children in Susiya. Why does he do it? "So that they can see that not all Jews are the same." In fact there are many like him—these righteous ones—who help the Palestinians present their claims in court, who provide medical aid and build alternative energy systems, who protest against the abuses. Amongst them are writers like David Grossman and Amos Oz, who sign manifestos and demand that human and civil rights violations stop, and that these villages be left in peace.

Though at least fifteen homes in the ancient village of Jinba were destroyed, solidarity efforts helped stave off complete destruction. Now Jinba's existence depends on a final ruling by the Israeli Supreme Court. In Jinba is an enormous cave, as yet untouched, which, I am told, dates back to Roman times. It is today under threat of demolition because, along with twelve other villages, it is in an area that the Israeli government has declared a firing zone. As in Susiya, in Jinba I am surrounded by barefoot, skinny children who have not, however, lost their joy. One girl in particular, with large, mischievous eyes, falls about laughing when she sees that I cannot pronounce her Arabic name.

You need only to study a map of the occupied territories to understand the rationale behind the Israeli settlements: they surround the large Palestinian cities and obstruct their contact with each other, impeding free movement. At the same time, they expand the Israeli presence and split up and fracture the territory that, supposedly, would constitute a future Palestinian state, making this proposition impracticable. This proliferation of settlements seems designed intentionally to make the two-state solution unworkable, despite the fact that every Israeli government says it accepts the idea. Why else would all Israeli governments, of center, left, and right, the only exception being the last Sharon government, which removed the Israeli settlements in Gaza, have permitted and still permit the existence and systematic growth of illegal settlements—some secular but many more ultrareligious—which are a constant source of friction and make the Palestinians feel that the already reduced space they inhabit on the West Bank is being continuously stripped away?

I don't pretend to read the secret mind of the Israeli political elite. But it is enough to follow on the map the way in which the illegal settlements have encroached on Palestinian territories over the past few decades to see a tacit or explicit policy to encourage and protect them. This is not just a cause of constant friction with the Palestinians. It is a reality that every day makes the establishment of two sovereign states more difficult, perhaps already impossible, a reality that makes the proclamations of the Israeli authorities in support of a two-state solution sound like empty utterances, devoid of truth, pure noise.

There is probably no more dramatic case of such disruption than the five settlements established in the heart of Hebron. Approximately eight hundred Israeli settlers in the heart of a Palestinian city of two hundred thousand! To protect them, approximately six hundred and fifty Israeli soldiers mount guard over the old city that they have sealed off, "sterilizing" its streets—closing all the shops, the main entrances to houses and businesses—to such an extent that walking there is like traveling through a ghost city, without people and without a soul. I wandered through these dead streets eleven years ago; the only thing that has changed is that the racist insults against Arabs, which used to adorn its walls, have nearly disappeared. But everywhere there are the same checkpoints manned by soldiers, and there is still the ban on Arabs walking on the main market street, or driving through the other streets of the center, which means that they have to make an enormous detour across town to get from one neighborhood to another. The Israelis traveling with me—there are four of them—tell me that the worst thing of all is that now nobody even speaks of the horror that is Hebron and the tremendous injustices committed there against two hundred thousand inhabitants in order, apparently, to protect eight hundred invaders.

Unlike other neighborhoods in Jerusalem that are as immaculately clean as those to be found in a Swiss or Scandinavian city, the Palestinian neighborhood of Silwan, in the east, close to the Old City and the al-Aqsa mosque, seethes with rubbish, foul-smelling puddles, and all kinds of waste materials. I wonder if such filth is not a matter of coincidence but rather part of a long-term plan to remove the fifty thousand Palestinians who still live here and replace them with Israelis.

The settlers began infiltrating the Silwan neighborhood of Batan al-Hawa in 2004, when they managed to build one of the tallest buildings in the neighborhood. The settlers who have moved into various Silwan neighborhoods come from two settler organizations: Elad and Ateret Cohanin. There are not many settlers: some seven hundred spread across seventy-five houses. But they have established a beachhead which can keep expanding.

If you want to know where the settlements are, you just have to look upwards. The Israeli flags fluttering in the gentle morning breeze indicate that they have been encircling the area, as in the mountains south of Hebron, isolating and entrapping the entire neighborhood. According to Israeli NGO reports, there are different ways in which these settler groups have managed to take over houses: claiming to possess old documents showing that the previous owners were Jewish; buying properties through Arab front men; going through the courts to have properties seized through the absentee property law or, in extreme cases, waiting for the owners or tenants of disputed houses to go on a trip or simply leave the house, then forcing their way in. Once the settlers are inside, the Israeli government sends the police to protect them, because of course this trickle of settlers in the ocean of Palestinians would be in danger. The trickle will become pools, lakes, seas. The religious settlers who have put down roots here are not in any hurry: eternity is on their side. This is how Israeli enclaves have spread across the

West Bank, turning it into a gruyère cheese; this is how they are growing in Arab Jerusalem also.

Appearances are maintained, as in the rest of the nation: Israel is a very civilized country. In Batan al-Hawa there are fifty-one Palestinian families threatened with expulsion because they live in houses that the settlers claim were owned by Jews in the 1800s.

When I ask Zuheir Rajabi, a resident who defends Palestinian rights in the neighborhood and who is my guide on this visit, if he has faith in the honor and neutrality of the judges who must make these rulings, he looks at me as if I were more idiotic than my question. "Do we have any other option?" he replies. And he continues his explanation. He is a sober man who has been in prison several times. He has three sons, aged seven, nine, and thirteen, each of whom has been arrested at some point, and a little daughter, Darín, who is six, who clings to one of his legs. His house is surrounded by two settlements and he has received various offers to sell it for much more than it is worth. But he says that he will never sell and that he will die in the neighborhood; he is not afraid of the threats he receives from his neighbors.

I ask him if the settlers in Silwan have children. Yes, many, but they rarely go out, and if they do, they are escorted by police or the private security forces that protect the settlements. I think about the terrible cloistered lives of these children, locked up in these houses, and I think about the lives of their parents and grandparents who are convinced that by perpetrating this injustice, they are carrying out a divine plan and will earn their place in Paradise. Of course, religious fanaticism is not exclusive to a minority of Jews. There are also Palestinian fanatics who blow themselves up, setting off bombs in buses or restaurants, who aim missiles at kibbutzim in the south of the country, or who try to knife soldiers or innocent passersby, crimes that serve only to widen the gulf, which is already vast, that separates both communities and puts them at odds with each other.

On our walk around Silwan, Zuheir Rajabi points out a building several stories high. The entire place has been taken over by settlers save for one apartment which is occupied, against all odds, by a Palestinian family of seven. Up to now they have stayed on, despite having their water and electricity cut off, and, Rajabi tells me, needing to knock on the front door to have the settlers let them in.

While we are talking, without my noticing, we have been surrounded by small children. I ask whether any of them has been arrested at any time. A boy with a cheeky, naughty look puts his hand up: "Me, four times." Each time he was held for just a day and a night. He was accused of throwing stones at the police, but he kept on denying and denying, and they did not take him to court. His last name is Sirhan, and his father, Samir Sirhan, had an incident with a settlement security guard, who shot him and left him to die in the street.

I am telling these sad stories because, I think, they give a fair idea of the burning problem facing Israel: the problem of the settlements, the increasing occupation of Palestinian territories which has turned Israel into a colonial, overbearing country and which has done so much damage to the positive, almost exemplary, image that it had for a long time throughout the world.

From the first time I came to Israel, I felt an enormous affection for this country. I still believe that it is the only place in the world where I feel a man of the left, because among the Israeli left there is still an idealism and a love of freedom that has disappeared from the left in many parts of the world. I have been saddened to see how, in recent years, local public opinion has become more reactionary, which explains why Israel now has the most ultrareligious and nationalist government in its history and why its policies are becoming daily less democratic. To denounce and criticize these policies is therefore not just a moral duty; it is also, in my case, at the same time, an act of love.

4.

Yehuda Shaul is thirty-three but he looks fifty. He has lived and still lives with such intensity that he eats up the years the way marathon runners eat up the miles. He was born in Jerusalem, into a very religious family, and he is one of ten children. When I first knew him, eleven years ago, he still wore the *kippa*. After completing his military service and returning to civilian life, he took stock and thought that since his compatriots were unaware of the ugly things that the army was doing in the occupied territories, it was his moral duty to make them known.

To this end on June 1, 2004, Yehuda and other soldiers founded Breaking the Silence, an organization dedicated to collecting testimonies from ex-soldiers and current soldiers. In exhibitions and publications aimed at informing the public in Israel and abroad, they display the truth about what is happening in the Palestinian territories that were occupied after the 1967 war. (This year is the fiftieth anniversary of the occupation.) Before they are distributed or exhibited, texts and videos go through military censors, because Yehuda and his coworkers do not want to break the law. They now have over a thousand testimonies.

Until relatively recently, thanks to the democratic safeguards in the country for Israeli citizens, Breaking the Silence could operate without problems, although it was strongly criticized by nationalist and religious sectors. But since the most recent government, the most reactionary in the history of Israel, came to power, a very strong campaign has been waged against the directors of the organization and its activists both in Parliament, with statements from ministers and political leaders, and in the press, accusing them of being traitors and seeking to outlaw the organization. There have also been many insults and threats on social media aimed at the activists. Yehuda Shaul does not feel intimidated. He says that he is a patriot and a Zionist and that he is committed to what he does.

There is in Jewish history an uninterrupted millennia-old tradition: the tradition of the righteous ones, men and women who emerge at moments of transition or crisis and make their voices heard, against the tide, indifferent to unpopularity or to the risks they run by acting in this way, to expose a truth or to defend a cause that the majority, blinded by propaganda, passion, or ignorance, refuses to accept. Yehuda Shaul is one of these people, in our times. And, fortunately, he is not the only one.

The imperturbable journalist Amira Hass is still there. She went to live in Gaza to document firsthand the experiences of Palestinians, day by day, in her chronicles in *Haaretz*. Thanks to her, some years back, I spent an unforgettable night in the cramped and asphyxiating warren that is the Gaza Strip, in the house of a Palestinian couple involved in social action. And her colleague Gideon Levy, a tireless writer, whom I meet again after a long time, still fighting for justice, pen in hand, but less optimistic than before because all around him, every day, the numbers who defend rationality, coexistence, and peace are shrinking, and there is a relentless rise of fanatics embracing single truths and a Greater Israel which would have nothing less than God on its side.

But on this journey I have got to know other people, equally pure and brave. Like Hanna Barag, who, at five in the morning, at the Qalandiya checkpoint, choked with fencing, cameras, and soldiers, showed me the suffering of the Palestinian workers who, despite having permits to work in Jerusalem, have to wait hour after hour before they can get through to earn their living. Hanna and a group of Israeli women position themselves every morning in front of these wire fences to denounce the unjustified delays and protest against the abuses being committed. "We try to get to the ones in charge," she tells me, pointing to the soldiers, "because these people don't even listen to us." She is a diminutive old woman, full of wrinkles, but her clear eyes shine with a blinding light and decency.

Salwa Duaibis and Gerard Horton, two lawyers—she is a Palestinian, he is half-British, half-Australian—are members of a humanitarian organization that monitors the trials in military tribunals of young Palestinians between the ages of twelve and seventeen who are accused of threatening the country's security. Salwa and Gerard devote their days to documenting injustices perpetrated against these children.

Yes, there are many righteous ones, though not enough to win elections. The fact is that for a number of years now, they have been losing elections, one after another. But they are not bowed by these defeats. They are doctors and lawyers who go to work in half-abandoned villages and defend victims of abuse in the courts, or journalists and human rights campaigners who record violations and crimes and bring them to public attention. There is ActiveStills, an association of photographers made up of very young men and women, who capture for eternity, in images, all the horrors of the occupation. Although the official press does not publish their photos, they exhibit them in small galleries, on street billboards, in semiunderground publications.

How many are the righteous? Thousands, but not enough to rectify the shift in public opinion that is pushing Israel more and more towards intransigence, as if being the leading military power in the Middle East—and, seemingly the sixth-largest in the world—were the best guarantee of its security. The righteous know that this is not the case, that, quite the reverse, by becoming a colonial power that does not listen, that does not want to negotiate or make concessions, that believes only in force, Israel has lost the prestige and honor it once had, and that the number of its opponents and critics is not diminishing but rather growing by the day.

Two days before leaving, I have dinner with two other righteous men: Amos Oz and David Grossman. They are magnificent writers, old friends and both tireless defenders of dialogue and peace with the Palestinians. The times they face are difficult but they are not disheartened. They joke, argue, tell stories. They say that, all things considered, neither of them could live outside Israel. Gideon Levy and Yehuda Shaul, who are there as well, both agree. In all the days I have been here, this is the first time that a group of Israelis has been in total agreement about something.

(TRANSLATED FROM THE SPANISH BY JOHN KING)

PLAYING FOR PALESTINE

ASSAF GAVRON

IN A 2009 TV COMMERCIAL FOR THE ISRAELI CELL PHONE CARRIER Cellcom, a jeep drives alongside a gray concrete wall, which looks exactly like the separation barrier between Israel and the West Bank. Suddenly something lands on the hood of the car. The soldiers jump out of the jeep in alarm, but then one of them reassures the others, "It's just a soccer ball." The commanding officer orders a soldier to return it, and the soldier kicks it over the thirty-foot-high cement wall. A few seconds later it arcs right back over, and this time the soldiers shout, "Come on guys, game on!" The feel-good melody swelling beneath their voices has soothed their tension.

"And everything is sweet and cool!" the singer tells us, to make sure we get it. Again and again the soldiers kick the ball to the other side of the wall, and it comes back. In the end, a narrator announces, "What does everyone want, after all? Just a little fun!"

A few days after Cellcom's commercial first aired, Palestinians from Bil'in decided to examine the scenario it depicts and what it might look like in the real world. In their video, the same beachy, acoustic soundtrack plays, Palestinians juggle a soccer ball and then kick it over the fence. In return, the Israeli soldiers shoot tear gas. The clip ends with a close-up of the ball, stuck in the barbed wire.

It is easy to analyze how Cellcom's commercial reflects the desires, conscious or not, of Cellcom's customers: all we want is to have a little fun, to play a little game, but we don't want to see the faces of what might actually be happening on the other side of the proverbial pitch. We want it behind a wall of protection.

You might wonder how a large company could be so tone deaf. I've certainly wondered, and I think the answer lies in soccer. Cellcom would not normally have dared to step into the political minefield of the West Bank crisis, but soccer defuses the mine, because everyone loves to play. The game is the pure representation of freedom, fun, and community, the most popular sport on earth, one which everyone loves, no matter one's race or religion. However, the Palestinians in their video force us to confront a different side of the story: everyone loves to play, but not everyone can.

If the conflict in Israel and Palestine is the summertime pickup game that Cellcom suggests it is, then who is winning, and who writes the rules? The stories of the soccer players themselves shed light on these questions. Sameh Maraabah, a rising star in Palestinian soccer who led his team to second place in the West Bank league last year, is one player who has learned how fickle success can be in the profession he might have once thought of as a "sport."

On April 28, 2014, when Maraabah tried to cross the border from Jordan to the West Bank on the way back from training camp with his Palestinian teammates, he was arrested by Israeli authorities. According to Shabak, the Israeli security services, when Maraabah was in Doha, Qatar, the location of the training camp, he met a man called Talal Sharim, a former Hamas member turned Israeli prisoner, who had been released in the Gilad Shalit prisoner swap. Shabak alleges that Sharim gave Maraabah "money, a cell phone, and written messages" to deliver to a man whom Israeli newspapers called "a senior Hamas activist." Limor Livnat, then Israel's minister of culture and sport, sent a letter to international soccer's governing body, FIFA, decrying the exploitation of soccer for terrorism, and Maraabah was sent to jail in the Nablus region for eight months.

Immediately after his release, in January 2015, Maraabah was invited to join the Palestinian national team on its trip to the Asian

Football Confederation Cup in Australia. At the Allenby Bridge border with Jordan, he was arrested again. After being held for five hours, he was sent back to Qalqilya while his team went on to lose all three of the games it played.

Maraabah's next trip was to Malaysia, that June, for a World Cup qualifier. As if for the sake of routine, he was stopped at the Allenby Bridge. This time the rest of the players protested, organizing a spur-of-the-moment sit-in at the border crossing, announcing they would not move until Maraabah was allowed to pass. Meanwhile, officials from the Palestinian Football Association contacted FIFA and asked for help. Eventually Israel issued a permit for Maraabah to cross, and he scored two goals in his team's 6–0 victory over Malaysia in Kuala Lumpur.

To be sure, Maraabah is far from the first athlete to have his life upended by Israeli authorities, nor is his example the most egregious; rather, it's alarming because of how typical it is, an occupation story in a nutshell. The West Bank is filled with such nutshells—wherever you turn you will crack one beneath your shoe.

Arrests of youth and adult soccer players in Palestine are so common that they don't even make the news. The players are usually accused of stone throwing, and are often held for up to eight months before they are released. Husam Karakre, a sixteen-year-old player from al-Bireh, is still in detention at the time of this writing. Soldiers broke into his family's home one night and arrested him for allegedly throwing stones at IDF vehicles. Six players from one team, Beit Umar, were arrested last year, and the team was relegated to a lower division at the end of the season. Then there's the story of three players, Muhammad Qweis from the Mount of Olives in East Jerusalem, Sami al-Daur, who lives in the town of Samu'a near Hebron, and Fadi a-Sahrif from Gaza, and their border troubles. A-Sharif, who played for Hilal Gaza, was injured in a game and was granted a permit for knee ligament surgery in a hospital in East Jerusalem. His friend al-Daur, originally from Gaza, asked a-Sharif to bring him his laptop computer, and coordinated with Qweis, who had dislocated a shoulder and was being treated in the same hospital, to get the laptop to him. The three were arrested and imprisoned for a week, the laptop was scanned thoroughly (nothing suspicious was found), and al-Daur was expelled from Samu'a back to Gaza, losing his place on the team and thus his livelihood.

Mahmoud Sarsak, a player from the south of the Gaza Strip who had signed a two-year contract with a team from the West Bank, was taken by Israeli authorities out of the cab that was driving him from Gaza. He ended up serving three years in jail but was never tried. Only a 101-day-long hunger strike and the intervention of soccer fans and players from around the world (including Celtic FC fans in Scotland and the veteran French soccer players Eric Cantona and Lilian Thuram), the heads of FIFA, and Amnesty International could bring about his release. Interested in asking Sarsak about what happened? You can find him selling falafel in London.

You cannot ask the Palestinian soccer legend Ahid Zakut anything. He was killed in his home by an IDF jet fighter missile during Israel's "Operation Protective Edge" in 2014. He was a star in the 1980s and 1990s and played on the first-ever Palestinian national team. He coached Riadi Gaza to a championship title, and went on to become a popular sports show presenter on Palestinian TV. He had no relationship with Hamas or connection to politics. But Israel has blurred the lines among politics, soccer, and war, if indeed they ever existed.

Israeli authorities exert power over Palestinians, be they professional soccer players or not. Israel controls not only its own border crossings but also those between Jordan and the West Bank. It also controls the narratives that its domestic media propagates.

Israel's strategies for marginalizing Palestinian soccer illustrate the fight over the narrative. A Palestinian meets a Palestinian in Qatar. A Palestinian receives money from a Palestinian in Qatar. These facts are undisputed. But what is their meaning—was it a terrorist rendezvous? Is a Hamas member always and only a terrorist? Is a released prisoner (who was released in a deal before finishing his term) necessarily a terrorist? Is a sum of money always meant for terrorist activity, or could it be a donation to a soccer team? Would a terrorist group deliver money, a cell phone, and "written messages" through a soccer player? The Israeli answers to all of the above are yes. The Palestinian answers are no.

Israel's suspicions are understandable, and at least partly justified. But to throw up our hands and say that there's no way to approximate the truth would not just be defeatist but also wrong. I don't know whether the money was meant for running the Qalqilya soccer club, as the Palestinians claimed, or for Hamas terrorist activity, as the Israelis did, but I tend to believe one story over the other. Why do I believe the Palestinian side? Because over the years I have stepped on many nutshells, many stories, in which Israel exerted too much power and showed too little fairness. A whole life living this conflict has taught me that on the Israeli side the finger is light on the trigger, its power is blinding, and in the name of security, the nation often loses its way.

THE PALESTINIAN SOCCER LEAGUES ARE NOT WITHOUT THEIR RIVALRIES. As in every country, "derby" games between neighboring teams are especially explosive: al-Amari refugee camp versus al-Bireh in the Ramallah region, Tulkarm refugee camp versus Tulkarm city, Silwan versus Hilal al-Quds in Jerusalem, Balata refugee camp versus the Askar refugee camp in Nablus. Yet Palestinian anger over the occupation trumps even these rivalries. Take the case of what, in recent years, has been the most bitter rivalry, the one between Shabab al-Khalil and Shabab al-Thahriyeh. Both are among the strongest teams in the Palestinian league—al-Thahriyeh won the 2015 championship and al-Khalil the 2016. Both teams come from the Hebron area, which, as the home of half of the twelve teams in the first division, is considered Palestine's soccer city. The derby between al-Khalil and al-Thahriyeh is called the Palestinian El Classico, after the match between the perennial Spanish titans FC Barcelona and Real Madrid. In recent seasons some of the Palestinian El Classicos have ended in blows between the fans in the stands, virtual blows on social media, and damaged cars outside the stadium.

The Palestinian El Classico that took place on October 30, 2015, was different. It was during the wave of violence that swept the region that fall and winter. During the "Knives Intifada," attacks by young Palestinians, mostly improvised, some lethal, were met with a fierce, mostly lethal response by Israeli security forces and nationalistic vigilantes. Hebron was a hot spot for attacks, and between October 1 and the day of the al-Khalil–al-Thahriyeh derby, more than sixteen locals were killed—almost half of all Palestinians killed in that period. One of the victims, killed exactly two weeks before the game, was the twenty-year-old Basil Sidir, who was known for being Shabab al-Khalil's number one fan—he appeared at all of the team's practices and games, leading cheers with a huge drum.

Before the game, both teams released a joint statement, asking all the fans to wear black in solidarity and in mourning and respect for the dead. In addition, the fans were asked to sing pro-Palestinian chants together, instead of their respective teams' songs. The fans responded with an altercation-free game. When the al-Khalil fans chanted "We will give our soul and blood for al-Aqsa," al-Thahriyeh's fans replied "We will give our soul and blood for Palestine." Shabab al-Khalil won the game 2–1, an important win on the way to the title, but there were very few celebrations. Posters of Basil Sidir were raised by fans in the stands, and his drum was hung high in the air.

THE POWER OF SOCCER TO UNIFY, ITS POWER TO PROJECT NATIONAL PRIDE and national identity—even when those nations are no longer on the map—is an old phenomenon. In the Soviet Union, the most important teams were the team of the people (Spartak), the team of the army (CSKA), and the team of the security services (Dynamo), and to this day fans keep their identities according to this division, many years after those security forces have been dismantled. The Barcelona soccer club in Spain is undoubtedly the leading symbol of Catalan identity and ambition for independence. Perhaps even more prominently, Bilbao Athletic has opted to represent the Basques, allowing only Basque players to play for the team. In Glasgow, Celtic FC is the Catholic team and Rangers FC the Protestant (and in their charged Old Firm derbies you can spot Israeli flags on the Rangers' side, and Palestinian, as well as Basque, flags waved by Celtic fans, whose religion's second-class status in England and role in the long battle over Northern Ireland aligns them with independence struggles). In 1990, fan violence in games between Red Star Belgrade and Dynamo Zagreb in the Yugoslavian league was one of the triggers for the civil war that broke out the following year, a war in which mobs of Red Star soccer fans led by a Serbian criminal known as Arkan turned into vicious militias which went on to carry out ethnic cleansing.

In another example of professional soccer pitting the occupied against the occupiers, Algeria in 1958, midway through the war of independence against the French occupation, formed a national team. The National Liberation Front (FLN) recruited supporters among the Algerian community in France, and in a secret operation in April of that year, nine players of Algerian descent who played in the French league (two of whom were also on the French national team) left to join the newly created Algerian team. The defection of those Algerians—residents and citizens of France—to their homeland showed the commitment of the Algerians to independence. Despite FIFA's refusal to recognize it, the new team played close to eighty international games. At the end of the Algerian War, it became the official national team. Its players were heroes not only to Algerians, but also to a world freeing itself from colonialism—Ho Chi Minh met with them in Vietnam, and Zhou Enlai met with them in China. They were invited to play around the world and became an enduring symbol of the power of sports to resist and highlight political injustice. To this day, young French players with dual citizenship debate which national team to join, even though one of them, France, is among the strongest teams in the world. Still, the other team might be closer to their hearts.

The power of soccer to create a space that could allow the foundation of a new state has not escaped the attention of politicians, including those in Palestine. The Palestinian perhaps most inspired by the FLN's successes is Jibril Rajoub, who has harnessed the power of soccer to unite a population, even if not to the full satisfaction of his people.

A seasoned politician, Rajoub is more revered for his savvy—and the success it has brought—than for his candor. It's enough to read a selection of his quotes from recent years to understand why: he speaks in belligerent anti-Israeli rhetoric when inside Palestine, positioning himself as a man of the people; while in speeches and interviews in English—those that primarily reach Israeli and American audiences—he waxes conciliatory about his peaceful aspirations for the end to violence, positioning himself to outsiders as the kind of Palestinian leader who will help stabilize the region. His resume, a virtual history of modern Palestinian resistance, also speaks to his political savvy. Rajoub fought in his youth in the PLO against Israel, took part in armed attacks in the seventies, was sentenced to life in an Israeli jail and released fifteen years later in a prisoner swap, but not before he developed an impressive command of Hebrew and English. When the PLO became the political movement that created the Palestinian Authority in the 1990s, he was there alongside Arafat and filled a number of roles in the newly formed security services. But given soccer's role in legitimizing marginalized groups and fueling revolutionary impulses, it seems that Rajoub, the chairman of the Palestinian Football Association since 2006, is now in his most influential political position yet. In the decade in which he has worked in sports, possibly the toughest period to date for Palestinians under occupation, Palestinian soccer has achieved its greatest successes. And as always seems to be the case, the breakthroughs are more national than athletic in scope. Though there has been a Palestinian Olympic team since 1996, now the entity of Palestine has become a recognized member of FIFA with its own national team.

When Israel prevented players and coaches from several Arab states from entering the West Bank to take part in the West Asian youth championship, Jibril Rajoub did something brilliant and controversial: he demanded that FIFA suspend Israel's membership in the organization. Later, after his plea went unanswered, he compiled a list of five demands confronting Israel's breaches of FIFA's founding principles: (1.) that Palestinian players and staff and their equipment be granted freedom of movement between Gaza and the West Bank (FIFA rules forbid the restriction of movement of soccer players because of their nationality); (2.) that football clubs based in settlements be banned from the Israeli league (FIFA rules state that a football association cannot include teams that are based outside the state's official territory); (3.) that the Israel Football Association fight racism in stadiums; (4.) that Israel issue construction permits for soccer stadiums and grounds in the Palestinian territories; (5.) that taxes and other restrictions on importing soccer equipment to the Palestinian Authority be lifted.

Rajoub did not stop with these statements. He gathered a team of Palestinian and Latin American lawyers to support his demands, and galvanized public opinion in the occupied territories and around the world. After Israel rejected the demands, Rajoub put forward a proposal to expel Israel from FIFA, and a vote was set for May 29, 2015.

In the weeks and days preceding the vote, the story became the center of attention in Israel and beyond: newspaper headlines, op-ed pieces, and current-affairs shows talked soccer and FIFA more than ever before. Israel and Palestine fought to sway FIFA delegates as if they were UN delegates in disguise. The international human rights organization Avaaz published an online petition in favor of Israel's expulsion that collected sixty thousand signatures, half of them from the Palestinian territories and the other half from all over the world. On the day of the vote, thousands of Palestinians went out on the streets with soccer balls, balloons, and red cards that protestors "issued" to IDF soldiers. The scenes of nonviolent resistance were live-streamed around the world, and they inspired outpourings of support. Palestinian leaders had, it seemed, found a new tack, one that Israel could not resist by crying "security" and calling attention to Palestinian attacks on innocent civilians.

According to the Palestinians I have spoken to, the majority of FIFA delegates supported their case, but then a problem came from an unexpected direction. On the same day of the vote on the Palestinian proposition to suspend Israel, another vote was to take place at the FIFA convention: the election of the organization's president. Prince Ali Bin Hussein, brother of Jordanian King Abdullah, was running for the position against Switzerland's Sepp Blatter. Delegates from the European countries did not favor the Jordanian candidate, but he offered them a kind of compromise. In return for their support, bin Hussein would put pressure on the Palestinians to back off. It was a seductive offer. These delegates were eager to end what had become a major diplomatic scandal, but didn't want to be seen as suppressing Palestine's initiative. They wanted bin Hussein to do their dirty work.

At first, Rajoub fought fiercely against the Jordanians, but thirty minutes before the vote, Rajoub withdrew his proposition. Many Palestinians who are familiar with Rajoub's career in the Preventative security forces, and his role as PFA head, believe his decision was tainted by corruption and international pressure. They believe, and have written, that he sold out the cause for his political career.

Disappointed Palestinian organizations started a new campaign: a red card for Jibril Rajoub. The people felt betrayed and angry. Rajoub, anxious about losing the people's support, summoned anger of his own. After several days of posturing, both sides decided to take advantage of the momentum they had achieved and negotiated a reconciliation: in return for backing off, Rajoub was promised that a special FIFA committee would examine Israel's compliance with FIFA rules and human rights. The Palestinian organizations promised to work together to help the committee.

Israel's political might carried the day, but the values of soccer—opportunity for the underdog, consistent rules applied to all—also had their moment. The message that came across was that Palestinians want to play soccer, but are not allowed to do so.

THE FIFA COMMITTEE FINALLY MADE IT TO THE PALESTINIAN TERRITORIES in May 2016. It was headed by Mosima Gabriel "Tokyo" Sexwale, himself a fascinating character. A black South African from Soweto, he was a member of the ANC who had fought against apartheid and sat in jail alongside Nelson Mandela, and after apartheid had risen in the ranks of the South African government. His ambitions to replace Mandela as president were ultimately thwarted, and he started a successful career as a businessman in the diamond mining industry. He acquired his nickname in childhood after becoming a karate champion.

Sexwale visited, among other places, the village of Beit Liqya in the Ramallah region, and was present with Rajoub at a special tournament organized for the FIFA delegation. The location was carefully picked by the Palestinians: Beit Liqya was home to a new soccer pitch built two years earlier and officially inaugurated by FIFA president Blatter but, owing to an Israeli prohibition, had never been used.

About two weeks after Sexwale's visit, I traveled to Beit Liqya with Hilmy, a village resident who told me he used to work in construction in Tel Aviv, to see what had happened to the stadium. We left Jerusalem, traveling north to Ramallah, wound our way through an hour and a half of bypasses and rough roads, passed village after village, and maneuvered around restricted highway 443. When we arrived at Beit Liqya, Hilmy pointed to a hill and said that beyond it was Abu Gosh and Ma'ale Hachamisha. I know those hills well; that's where I went to high school. Had we been able to travel directly, we would have arrived fifteen minutes after leaving Jerusalem.

Hilmy showed me the old soccer field on the southern side of the village, a dry earth pitch with two rusty goals. Here young people used to play daily, but since Israel started constructing the security barrier in 2004, it had become the site of clashes between the IDF and villagers protesting against the barrier cutting through their fields and orchards. The skirmishes reached their tragic peak on May 4, 2005. According to Hilmy, an IDF helicopter landed on an overlooking hilltop and unloaded soldiers. Children who were playing on the pitch that morning started throwing stones at the soldiers, who chased the kids and opened fire. Two boys under the age of fourteen, Uday Assi and Jamal Assi, were shot and killed. They are buried next to the field.

Following this incident, the village decided to build a new soccer field, far from the violent fighting zone of the barrier, on the western side of the village. Money was raised. The mayor brought in an engineer and a lawyer, and they started working on the paperwork. After surveying and measuring, they submitted a detailed construction plan to the Israeli Civil Administration in Beit El. Israel refused to approve the plans, offering no explanation. Outer Beit Liqya is in Area C, the part of the West Bank that remained under Israeli military and administrative control after the Oslo accords. Israel virtually never approves Palestinian construction in Area C. So even though the pitch has been laid out at the site for two years, there are no changing rooms and no stands and no games played there, because Israel won't allow it. As hard as I try, I can't find any explanation for how this structure could possibly harm Israel. On the contrary, it could help deescalate the violence that has attached itself to—and eclipsed—the game of soccer.

Tokyo Sexwale heard the story of the field and met children from Beit Liqya who asked him to help them find a way to play soccer. According to Palestinian journalists, Sexwale said that preventing children from playing the game is a crime that international sport organizations must not ignore.

IN 1996, I TRAVELED TO RAMALLAH FOR THE JERUSALEM MAGAZINE KOL *Ha'ir*, to write about the Palestinian national soccer team, which had been formed a few weeks earlier. My article begins with a quote from the local newspaper of Macclesfield, England, where the Palestinian national team played its first proper game, losing to an amateur English team from a regional league: "Without an organized league, training structure, and travel permits for eight key players from the Israeli authorities, this national team was not a real threat even to our second team. But the Palestinians made some friends and put a few smiles on faces, especially the performance of goalkeeper Galam Salem, who looked as if he had lost his invitation to the tea party, jumping to and fro, not necessarily in the right direction." Later in my article, an official of the Palestinian Authority's Sport Ministry explains, "The grass ruined our players in England. It was slippery and wet and cold, they slipped on it every time." The official also detailed the difficulties suffered at the hands of the Israelis: refusal to let the Gazan players travel to a West Bank training camp, refusal to let some players leave the country, a twelve-hour delay at Tel Aviv airport (and the missed flight that resulted). "It would be no exaggeration to say," I conclude, "that from Palestine, the neighbor's grass looks much greener."

Twenty years on, it is easy to tell what has changed (there are organized Palestinian leagues and the national team is winning international matches and doesn't slip around on the grass) and what hasn't (the Israelis still delay Palestinians at the border and refuse to grant travel permits for players), but what stands out for me rereading my article is the light tone I imbued it with. Yes, I relayed miserable airport and permit stories, but I also did my best to capture the sense of hope I felt. Something new was beginning. Just three years had passed since the Oslo agreement; there was a Palestinian Authority; and it had established its own "civilian" ministries, including one for sports. The national team was brand new. The players and politicians I interviewed spoke about a future in which the team would play all over the world, would beat the national teams of the neighboring Arab nations, would beat Israel. And I, the Israeli reporter, was perhaps somewhat patronizing, but also interested and encouraged. The hope surged through me, too. After thirty years, the occupation looked like it might be in its final days.

Now, fifty years into that occupation, the tone with which I once wrote about Palestinian soccer feels bizarre. This time in Ramallah, Beit Liqya, East Jerusalem, Bethlehem, and Hebron, no one joked with me, no one mentioned a future match against Israel. When you travel for a grueling hour and a half and arrive at a village which is located beyond the hill and see a soccer field that the people are forbidden to use, a field built to allow children to play in safety, far from the pitch where their friends were killed, the disappointment feels absolute, the complications insoluble.

THE NATIONAL TEAM OF PALESTINE FOUGHT FOR A TICKET TO THE 2018 World Cup in the Asian qualifying group A. It finished in third place, trailing Saudi Arabia and the United Arab Emirates, and ahead of Malaysia and East Timor. The thrashing of the teams below it and draws with those above were not enough to qualify for the World Cup, though they did raise Palestine's FIFA ranking thirty places, from 140th in the world to 110th. But, as always seems the case with Palestinian soccer, the competition was merely a sideshow. The most interesting story took place away from the pitch.

The Saudi Arabian national team was expected to arrive at their game in Palestine in the middle of 2015's violent fall, in November of that year. The Saudis tried to switch the game to neutral ground in Jordan, their reasoning being that Saudi Arabia had no relations with Israel and therefore its team was not willing to pass border checkpoints manned by Israelis. The Saudi act was supposedly pro-Palestinian and anti-Israeli. However the Palestinians were eager to host a home game against a major team like Saudi Arabia in order to send a message to the soccer world that they were no longer the charming footnote they once had been, but were now a strong national team, one with a home in which it hosts its games. Jibril Rajoub opposed the Saudi decision vehemently and told FIFA that it could not force Palestine to play away from home. A couple of weeks before the game, FIFA made an announcement recognizing the Palestinians' right to host games on their land, a right that could not be revoked. The Saudis increased their pressure, aiming it in all directions: at FIFA, at President Abbas, at the Jordanians, even at Hamas, who announced at one stage that they *supported* the Saudis.

Why would an organization fighting for the freedom and independence of Palestine oppose the Palestinian national team's hosting a soccer game in its home country? There were rumors that the Saudis had bribed Hamas. But as is the case with so much of this brand of soccer politics, definitive answers elude us. Rajoub continued to resist, and twenty-four hours before the game was supposed to take place in al-Ram, it looked as if the Saudis would suffer an automatic 3–0 loss for failing to appear. Rajoub said, "If, for the Saudis, supporting the Palestinian struggle is so important, and normalization with Israel is so dangerous, I'm sure they would be happy to sacrifice three points and have their Palestinian brethren get them." But the Saudis kept pressing for a change of venue, and at the last minute, possibly following instructions from President Abbas's office, the Palestinian security forces announced that they could not guarantee the safety of the Saudi players. It was now too much for Rajoub to fight against. The game moved to Jordan and ended in a 0–0 tie.

It was another diplomatic defeat for Rajoub after yet another heroic stand for the rights of Palestine. Another story in which the Palestinians showed that they would not allow themselves to be eternally portrayed as victims, but rather as a people trying to build success, pride, national identity, and a civil society. Soccer inspires all these possibilities. Yes, Palestinian soccer has suffered due to many crimes of the occupation, but it also has the power to create whatever is waiting beyond occupation. Here is a national team representing a state that does not exist, that has no airport or control over the movement of its players, that is never certain where it will play, which players will be allowed to attend and which won't. But at the same time, it is a team participating in tournaments, achieving better and better results in them, positioning itself and its people as a national entity that exists on the world's stage.

THE PALESTINIAN NATIONAL TEAM CREATES PALESTINIAN IDENTITY AND pride in another way: as an institution that unites Palestinians from all over the world. West Bank Palestinians with Gazan Palestinians, Palestinians living within Israel's borders and carrying Israeli passports with second- and third-generation Palestinians who emigrated to different parts of the world. The unity is reflected in the backgrounds of the Palestinian soccer players: Ahmad Awad, who was born and grew up in Sweden, recently joined Palestine's national team; Yashir Pinto is the latest recruit from Chile, a country that has created a pipeline of players of Palestinian descent to the league and the national team. (Famously, there is a team founded by Palestinian immigrants in the Chilean first league that features on its jerseys a map of Palestine in place of the number 1.) In the current team there are also six players who carry Israeli passports, among them Muhammed Darwish from Fureidis (who previously played ten years in the Israeli league), Ahmad Abu Nayeh from Sakhnin, and Shadi Shaaban from Acre (who played for the Israel national youth team). There was also the late Azmi Nasser, a native of Nazareth who coached the town's team in the Israeli league before becoming the coach of the Palestinian national team.

Palestinians take great pride in their league. Salman Amar, a coach born in Beit Safafa, an Arab neighborhood of Jerusalem, is just one example. Amar, who holds Israeli citizenship, played most of his career as an iconic right back for the Israeli team Hapoel Jerusalem and later coached it. Then, earlier this year, he transferred leagues without even moving out of Jerusalem—when he accepted an offer to coach the Palestinian team Hilal al-Quds, he simply drove down to the Palestinian part of Jerusalem.

Hilal al-Quds, a club with a decorated history that includes winning the championship in 2012, was in the middle of a terrible season. Placed at the bottom of the table, far behind its rivals, it seemed destined for demotion. But under Amar's guidance, the team turned the season around, emerging victorious in most of its remaining games, and avoiding relegation to the second division. Amar also led Hilal al-Quds to the Palestinian cup final. In a conversation in Beit Safafa, Amar spoke mainly about the incredible experience of working in the Palestinian league, characterizing it as going "back to my roots." Even though he was delayed for hours every day in the Qalandiya checkpoint on his way to practices and games in the Faisal al-Husseini International Stadium in al-Ram (despite being a Jerusalem team, Hilal must play in the West Bank because some of its players are barred from entering Israeli-controlled East Jerusalem), his feeling was of a homecoming. Coaching in Arabic and traveling to players' weddings in Jenin and Nablus reconnected him to life in the West Bank, and conversations with players charged the experience with emotion. "In the Israeli league the players speak about their girlfriends. Here you have players and staff from refugee camps. They speak of arrests of their brothers, of sleepless nights."

Israel is trying to divide the Palestinians, geographically and historically. Gaza is divided from the West Bank. The Israeli Palestinians are divided from those in the occupied territories. Part of the Palestinian struggle is to blur those divisions. "Either we're all Palestinians, or we aren't," says Amar. Like him, most Palestinians I talk to are puzzled when I ask if Israeli Palestinians are welcome in Palestine and not seen as collaborators with the enemy. They are, after all, still Palestinians, they tell me. This is why players with Israeli passports are welcomed into the Palestinian league and onto the national team. And this is why it is so meaningful that Salman Amar, an Israeli citizen and former Hapoel Jerusalem player, led his team in a Palestinian cup final. It demonstrates how futile Israel's policy of division is; how it only strengthens Palestinians' bonds and inspires them to cross borders, like the French citizens opting to play for Algeria over half a century ago.

The road to the end of the occupation is long and winding. We've been on it for fifty years now, and I'm not convinced it won't require another fifty. But the occupation *will* end. And until that day, I suggest that anyone who wants to know where things are going follow Palestinian soccer. Using the power of the game, it is pulling the wagon, slowly, out of the mud.

(TRANSLATED FROM THE HEBREW BY THE AUTHOR)

LOVE IN THE TIME OF QALANDIYA

TAIYE SELASI

A T THE EDGE OF RAMALLAH, JUST UP THE ROAD FROM THE OFFICE of the UN High Commissioner for Human Rights, the Darwish Museum sits perched on a hill, overlooking the city of Jerusalem. The building itself is beautiful: small, modern, minimal, impeccably landscaped, its terraced garden a nod to the typical terrain of a Palestinian village. It is a lovely visual metaphor—the work of the Palestinian architect Jaafar Touqan, himself the son of a poet—and a fitting tribute to Mahmoud Darwish.

Palestine's beloved national poet was born in the Galilee in 1941, seven years before the Israeli army invaded and razed his village. After fleeing the violence, his family returned in 1949 to what is now northern Israel. The poet spent his twenties in Haifa, then traveled abroad to study. When he joined the PLO at thirty-two, he was banned from reentering Israel. His celebrated literary career unfolded primarily in exile. When Darwish passed away at sixty-seven, the mayor of Ramallah decreed that the nation's poet would be buried next to the Palace of Culture, a park and memorial erected in his name.

It is here, on the southwestern outskirts of Ramallah, with the sun setting over Jerusalem, that I begin an inquiry, quite unintended, into Palestinian-Israeli love.

I'VE COME TO RAMALLAH WITH A DIFFERENT AIM: TO EXPLORE THE city's nightlife—that is, to understand how young Palestinians, my peers, pursue pleasure in the midst of occupation. Zaher, one of my guides for the evening, meets me in the center, proposing that we swing by the museum en route to Orjuwan, a lounge nearby. Darwish's grave sits atop a regal set of limestone steps, but Zaher's favorite spot is the infinity pool tucked into one of the lower terraces. It is a narrow pool with a narrower platform—what appears to be a stone diving board—protruding to its center and surrounded by small lights. When Zaher and his friends were at university, he says, they would come to this pool in the dead of the night. In turn, each would walk to the end of the platform and speak (or shout) his mind. Shrouded in darkness and silvered by moonlight, they'd yell into the water, the black, the night—unburdening themselves with their faces unseen.

"What did you shout about?"

"Usually about a girl I liked."

RITA IS THE NAME MAHMOUD DARWISH GAVE THE GIRL HE LIKED. Zaher shares this casually. "Everyone knows that Darwish's lover was Israeli." "The national poet of Palestine had an *Israeli* lover?" I am incredulous. "Who was this Rita?"

Zaher doesn't know.

But, as of two years ago, many do.

In August 2014 the Arab-Israeli filmmaker Ibtisam Mara'ana released the documentary *Write Down, I Am an Arab*, named for the refrain of Darwish's famous poem "Identity Card." At one point in the film a recording of the enigmatic poet's voice plays: "Rita is a name that I chose. Rita in all my poems is a Jewish woman. Am I revealing a secret?"

In part. As Zaher suggests, long before the release of the documentary, Darwish fans knew that the Rita in poems like "Rita's Long Winter" and "Rita and the Rifle" was his lover. Though the poet claimed that he'd created the alias for artistic reasons, he never hid the fact that Rita was Israeli, destined to join the same army that had destroyed and occupied his homeland. In his 1973 memoir *Journal of an Ordinary Grief,* Darwish writes:

> Between sand and water, she said, "I love you." And
> between desire and torture, I said, "I love you." And
> when the officer asked what she was doing here, she
> answered, "Who are you?" And he said, "And who
> are you?" She said, "I'm his sweetheart, you bastard,
> and I've come with him all the way to the gate of this
> prison to say goodbye. What do you want with him?"
> He said, "You should know that I'm an officer." "I too
> will be an officer next year," she said. She brought out
> her military induction papers. The officer then smiled,
> and pulled me away to prison.

Rita's true identity would remain a secret for some forty years; in 2014, six years after Darwish's death, she "outed" herself in Mara'ana's film. An Israeli of Polish origin, Tamar Ben Ami was working as a dancer in Haifa when she and Darwish met.

A dyed-in-the-wool romantic, I am instantly intrigued. It can be difficult not to compare Israel with its historical precedents—for example, the apartheid states of pre-1964 America and pre-1994 South Africa—and I find myself searching for a parallel: a renowned brown intellectual with a white partner. There is, of course, Frederick Douglass's second wife (Helen Pitts) and Amiri Baraka's first (Hettie Cohen), Richard Wright's two white wives (Dhimah Meidman, Ellen Poplar) and Alice Walker's husband (Mel Leventhal). Perhaps because my own family is composed of so many so-called interracial couples, I have always been moved by these figures: activists whose revolutionary politics do not dictate or delimit their emotional attachments. Leaving aside the personalities involved, one might view such relationships as a hopeful act, proof that one can denounce the grotesque political systems that seek to divide human beings while, in the most personal way, affirming the shared humanity of the same.

That Mahmoud Darwish, who so tirelessly condemned the Israeli state's dehumanization and deterritorialization of the Palestinian people, could nevertheless see the humanity of his Israeli lover: this says something. At least it says something to me.

By the time I discover Rita I've spent a week in Israel and occupied Palestine, observing the effects of systematic disenfranchisement and recognizing them as the classic aims of the apartheid state. In the more isolated pockets of Palestine (*isolated* meaning not rural, or not only, but stranded, ringed with settlements) the prospect of an interfaith relationship is unthinkable precisely because human contact has been so violently curtailed. There, in places like Hebron and Nabi Saleh, where Israeli soldiers and settlers relentlessly harass Palestinian villagers, one can scarcely imagine circumstances under which a civil, let alone sentimental, encounter might arise. The strategic dehumanization of the Palestinian population has replaced the possibility of love with the pervasiveness of hate—not only for fully cognizant adults but, more devastatingly, for their children.

When, for example, on our first day in East Jerusalem, an armored bus of Jewish children pulled up to the barred front gates of their settler family's building, what struck me most were not the guns strapped to the chests of the policemen who escorted the children to their door, but rather the looks on those children's faces. These were Israeli children taught to fear—and, as a logical extension, to hate—Palestinians, much as white children were once taught to fear African American bodies, white South African children, black ones. It is the go-to strategy of any apartheid state: the indoctrination of children and the absence of empathy it ensures. A white child taught to fear a brown one will not speak to that child, play with that child, learn anything of or see the humanity in that child—and will most certainly never love him. In this sense a bedtime story is as potent a weapon as state-sanctioned violence or court-upheld law: history's most brutal segregationists have all begun their work at home.

Learning of Darwish's Jewish lover, I am suddenly heartened by a thought: that the unraveling of Israel's segregationist fabric might begin at home as well. To imagine an interfaith romance in Hebron, where mere encounter carries the promise of violence, is impossible.

But on the sandy beaches of Tel Aviv? In the leftist, activist, secular (vegan) circles of bohemian Jerusalem? In this glittering city of Ramallah, where high heels seem more common than hijabs? Darwish's story is cinematically romantic—handwritten love letters from a Palestinian poet to an Israeli dancer!—but I can't believe the West Bank version of *West Side Story* so rare. In a week I've met so many open-minded activists: Muslim and Jewish, highly educated, antioccupation, precisely the kind of people who wouldn't see faith as a barrier to love. Just as interracial marriage is unremarkable among the educated elites of the coastal US, I wonder now if relationships between liberal Palestinians and Israelis are common.

And so I ask.

"Do Jewish and Palestinian citizens of Israel ever date?" I ask Zaher as we head to Orjuwan, stop number one on my one-night tour of West Bank bars. Leaving the museum, I am suddenly less interested in Ramallah nightlife than in Haifa romance—although, by the end of the evening, the proximity of the topics will come clear. Nightlife around the world is the domain both of the wealthy, that is, the leisure class, and of the liberal. To explore the swanky clubs of Ramallah is, on the one hand, to explore occupied Palestine's moneyed class, a demographic as commonly ridiculed as it is globally ubiquitous. Women teetering on their designer heels, men leaving their luxury cars with valets, purple-tinted lights and pink-tinted cocktails: elite nightlife looks and smells the same worldwide. The problem with elite nightlife in *beleaguered* places is precisely this: that it flaunts the standard excesses of the few in the face of the standard sufferings of the many. All that I've heard and read of Ramallah points to this familiar problematic: the massive chasm between its upper-class residents and occupied Palestine's poor. Certainly, leaving the museum at sunset, I am struck by the palpable affluence of the place; with its luxury condos and manicured palms, Masyoun Heights feels less like the West Bank than West Hollywood. In part, my interest in Ramallah nightlife stems from an abiding curiosity about the global politics of privilege. To what extent does a society's elite seek to remedy or to maintain that society's inequities? Is there not something intrinsically off about sipping poolside cocktails at Snowbar while knowing that, beyond the pine trees, children are being evicted from their homes in East Jerusalem?

Any investigation into what we might call a club scene in the developing world must attend to these questions of social inequality. Equally interesting, though, are questions of social transgression. At the other end of the nightlife spectrum, far from the neon lights and saccharine drinks, lies the social space known as the underground. If nightclubs offer society's elite a stage on which to display their privileges, they also offer society's rebels a playground for exercising their freedoms. *This* version of nightlife favors rule-breaking behavior over consumerist performance; however famous, underground clubs exist to house, and to hide, transgression. Whatever practices a society considers taboo—the consumption of drugs and alcohol, homosexuality, *female* sexuality—take root in these darkened spaces. I want to visit Ramallah's clubs because I want to meet Ramallah's rule breakers: youth with a measure of privilege, yes, but also with a spirit of nonconformity.

I am specifically interested in meeting women, ones whom the Western media rarely portrays: educated twenty- and thirtysomethings living "modern" lives in Palestine. My father spent over thirty years in Saudi Arabia; in my experience, one of the biggest misconceptions about the region is that no educated, empowered woman would willingly choose to live there. Knowing this to be false, I am keen to speak with women who have the means to travel but who have nevertheless chosen to live in Palestine or Israel and who do so on their own terms. Hence, Ramallah. In the conservative Muslim culture that distinguishes most of Palestine, a woman swilling Taybeh and smoking *shisha* is making a statement. On my night out I meet, as I've hoped, thrillingly brazen women charting a course between honoring family traditions and defining individual boundaries.

"My mother knows that I go clubbing," says one, Layla, lighting a cigarette. In her early thirties, single, employed by a Ramallah-based NGO, Layla typifies the six women who have joined me for the night. "She doesn't *like* it, but she accepts it. I studied well. I work hard. I'm a good daughter. One day I'll get married. But that day is not tomorrow." These are women after my own heart. They like to flirt, to drink, to smoke, they tell me, laughing. They like sex. In this they are no different from their single male friends. Some lie to their parents and brothers about frequenting Ramallah's clubs, uninterested in being shamed for their unapologetic pursuit of pleasure. Others demand that their families accept their lifestyle as an expression of a twenty-first-century femininity as Muslim as it is modern. For both groups—those who confide in their families and those who cannot—Ramallah's club scene offers a safe space for all behaviors.

All except for one.

"Have you ever dated a Jewish man?" I ask this gathering of free-spirited women. Silence. The energy at the table shifts. A ripple of nervous chuckles. No, never, five of them say, raising their eyebrows and stirring their drinks. "*Would* you date a Jewish man?" The answer is the same. No, never. I ask if they've heard of Darwish's Israeli lover Rita.

"Of course. But he was a man," one says.

"And very young at the time," adds another.

No one seems keen to discuss the topic further. "It isn't done" would appear to be the general sentiment. At this table full of rule-breaking women, one rule stands: Arabs don't date Jews. Only later does Fatima, who has kept quietest, explain why. A British-born Palestinian, Fatima has recently moved to Ramallah from London. When the others go to the bar for drinks, she shyly comes to sit next to me. Lowering her voice, she confides that she had a Jewish Israeli boyfriend in graduate school. She doesn't want the others to know, she says, because she's found that Palestinians judge her harshly, condemning her for having "slept with the enemy"—an accusation she has levied at herself. In the course of her yearlong relationship she never stopped wondering whether her boyfriend saw her as his equal, whether his attraction to her was a form of exoticization, a sexualized curiosity about the Other. Fatima's anxieties recall those I've heard from brown women in other contexts: African American women dating white American men, West African and Indian women dating

British. In my observation, where the man in a couple belongs to a socioeconomically dominant culture and the woman to a historically disenfranchised one, questions of power arise very quickly. Is the white man acting out a fetish of the brown female body, a perverse conflation of social privilege and sexual dominance? Does the brown woman betray her antioppression politics by "submitting" her body to a member of the oppressing class? Added to the power imbalance inherent in any man–woman relationship in a patriarchal setting, ethnic inequality will most always destabilize a romance in a racist one.

Of course, the distorting effect of power disparity works on the minds of men, too. Days after meeting Fatima I sit down with Esther, a Jewish graduate student, in Jerusalem. For two years she has been with Diaa, a Palestinian citizen of Israel educated in the United States. Much like Fatima, Esther speaks of her relationship in nervous whispers, reluctant at first to talk to me, wary of being overheard. While Esther's parents adore Diaa ("my father is always texting him in Arabic"), her grandmother refuses to meet him, devastated that Esther has chosen such a fraught path. Diaa's parents, meanwhile, have no idea that Esther exists. They live in a small Palestinian village, she says, where everyone knows everyone else. Though Diaa suspects that his parents are open-minded enough to accept his relationship, he fears that the rest of their village is not. Not wanting his parents to be ostracized by their community, he has spared them the burden of knowledge. When Esther and I meet, she and Diaa have recently returned from their first trip to the States. With palpable sadness she recounts their return to Tel Aviv.

"We were going through the first security check in Turkey and he said to me, 'If they bother me, just keep going. Don't wait for me.' And when we landed in Israel, there they were. Right at the door as you walk off the plane. I don't know if they somehow knew he was on the flight. They stopped him instantly. Before anything, before he'd even taken a *breath* of the air of this land. I was freaked out. I know they have their little prisons at the airport; I didn't want to leave him. So I walked a few steps, then I kind of waited, and they noticed. They called me over and asked for my information, too.

"Nothing big happened. But when we walked away, he was really upset with me. He didn't want me to put myself in the position of protecting him. Something about the incident made him feel so weak, so uncomfortable. It's such a crazy thing. I *do* get this protective feeling. I *do* feel my social power in comparison to his, in these moments. And I *do* feel: 'Maybe it's good for them to know that he's associated with a good Jewish girl. Maybe then they'll leave him alone.'"

Both Fatima's and Esther's accounts would seem to underline a primary complication in Palestinian-Israeli relationships: a racialized imbalance of power. Without wishing to generalize, I would imagine that the issue is exacerbated when the man is Arab. The versions of Jewish and Muslim culture that appear to have achieved social dominance in Israel and Palestine are markedly conservative ones, especially where gender roles are concerned. For an Arab man, whose culture privileges a patriarchal model of manhood, the idea of needing protection from any woman—much less a Jewish woman—must be anathema, I propose to Esther. She agrees. And yet the countless forms of intimidation and violence inherent to the occupation make any other dynamic impossible. How does one *not* try to protect a loved one from persecution? How to move through the world as a unit when one's freedom of movement is so grotesquely different from one's partner's? The same questions arise in relationships between Arabs with differing citizenships, Esther explains. Diaa's previous relationship, with a Palestinian woman in Ramallah, ended because he holds an Israeli passport and she does not. "He couldn't give up his citizenship, the right to see his family." I ask if any of her friends—all of whom know of and support her relationship with Diaa—are in interfaith relationships themselves.

"Not anymore. For most people it's just too hard."

The silence with which my question was greeted in Ramallah begins to make more sense. It is not, as I've feared, that my Palestinian and Jewish peers have drunk the Kool-Aid, accepting the purported Otherness of their neighbors. Rather it seems that, whatever natural instinct toward intermixing may exist, the legal and logistical barriers are astoundingly, discouragingly high. Indeed, despite the parallels that can be drawn between interfaith dating in Israel and interracial relationships elsewhere, something in my whispered conversations points to a unique dynamic. That something is the threat of physical danger.

"I would never date another Israeli," Fatima says. "It was hard enough in London. But here I'd be endangering myself and, worse, my boyfriend." Fatima's current partner is a US-educated Palestinian activist (the only man, she notes, who did not stop dating her on learning of her Jewish ex). I have been told that both Israeli and Palestinian authorities use blackmail as a form of political control over Palestinians—taking photographs of citizens in compromising positions, then threatening to publicize those images if the citizen doesn't collaborate—but I am shocked to learn that interfaith dating constitutes a compromising behavior in 2016. My Ramallah hosts are much more willing to speak openly about *this*: the very real danger faced by Arabs and Jews who have fallen in love. Their stories are horrifying: of Palestinians photographed with Jewish partners, then threatened: "If you don't inform, we will send these photographs to your family."

I have been naive, I see, to conceive of Palestinian-Israeli relationships in terms of liberal politics alone. Even for the twenty- and thirtysomethings whom I envisioned as champions of a defiantly humanist position, the risk of harming one's family seems an impossibly high price to pay. It is one thing not to have met your girlfriend's woefully bigoted grandmother. It is another thing entirely to face physical and political intimidation on account of whom you love. By way of analogy, interracial dating in the United States simply cannot compare, at least not in a twenty-first-century context. The barbaric antimiscegenation practices of the twentieth century, or the present-day criminalization of homosexuality in the developing world, comes much closer. If the story of Darwish and Ben Ami speaks to a beautiful possibility—the transcendence of apartheid politics at the level of human interaction—the fear in Esther's and Fatima's voices betrays an uglier reality: the trauma experienced by those Palestinians and Israelis who dare to love.

On August 17, 2014, shortly after *Write Down, I am an Arab* was released, twenty-six-year-old Mahmoud Mansour, a Palestinian citizen of Israel, married twenty-three-year-old Morel Malka, a Jewish convert to Islam. Religious intermarriage is not recognized by the state of Israel; were Malka a Jewish Israeli and not a Muslim convert, her marriage to Mansour would have been invalid. Still, the union offended the right-wing Israeli organization LEHAVA, its name a Hebrew acronym for "Preventing Assimilation in the Holy Land." In early August, LEHAVA published Mansour and Malka's wedding invitation on its Facebook page, urging antiassimilation demonstrators to storm the banquet hall with banners and megaphones. Fearing for their safety, the couple sought a court order banning protestors from their wedding. They succeeded only in obtaining an order that barred demonstrators from coming within two hundred meters of the celebration. Hundreds of police were deployed to prevent violent confrontations between antiassimilation protestors and counterdemonstrators: hundreds of the former, dozens of the latter. Malka's father refused to attend his daughter's wedding, while LEHAVA's chairman accused her of "marrying the enemy."

It is on these grounds—that Jewish women who date Arab men are betraying the state—that LEHAVA created its infamous hotline in 2013. The telephone service, intended to "save the daughters of Israel," allowed anonymous citizens to expose Jewish women suspected of dating Arab men. A recorded message offered callers three options: "If you are in contact with a goy and need assistance, press one. If you know a girl who is involved with a goy and you want to help her, press two. If you know of a goy who masquerades as a Jew or is harassing Jewish women, or of locations where there is an assimilation problem, press three." While *goy* is a derogatory term for any non-Jewish man, LEHAVA makes clear that *Arab* men are the danger—a view commonly aired in conservative circles. A week after our night out, one of my companions in Ramallah sends me a link to a skit from a right-wing satirical program on Israel's Channel 1. The two-minute video begins with an Israeli American woman introducing herself as Chloe and cheerfully describing Amir, the Arab man she's just begun dating. The five ensuing sequences depict the stages of Chloe's relationship, as the bubbly Israeli goes from wearing a minidress and holding a beer to: (1) wearing a long dress and drinking water; (2) wearing a headscarf and holding cooking pots; (3) wearing a full abaya and holding a baby; (4) wearing a niqab and holding several babies; (5) being absent. She has been killed. The iconography recalls the visual language of the antebellum South, where African American men were considered (and murdered for being) a threat to "pure" white women. In the Israeli antiassimilation narrative, it is not the Arab man's body that threatens to annihilate, but his culture: oppressively patriarchal and inherently violent. Though the aforementioned hotline no longer exists, LEHAVA's website still offers visitors the opportunity to "report cases of assimilation." According to my hosts in Ramallah and Jerusalem, groups like LEHAVA intimidate mixed couples, defending, as they see it, the purity of the Jewish state.

The same sentiment exists in Palestine. Just as Morel Malka, the Jewish-Israeli bride, is said to have married the enemy, Ibtisam Mara'ana, the Palestinian-Israeli filmmaker, has been condemned by Palestinians for marrying a Jew. Notably, Mara'ana has said that she made the Darwish documentary not to expose the poet's romance but to legitimize her own, a two-year relationship with a Jewish Israeli of Canadian origin. Four years before revealing Rita's identity in *Write Down, I am an Arab*, Mara'ana released *77 Steps*, a film about the challenges she and her boyfriend faced as a Palestinian-Jewish couple.

"One of my biggest fears was whether Arab society would accept the film," she said. "To convince myself . . . I created a 'safe answer' to throw at anyone attacking me for exposing my relationship with a Jewish man. This 'safe answer' was that if Mahmoud Darwish could write love poems about his Jewish loved one, then it is perfectly fine to make a movie about my relationship with my Jewish boyfriend, a controversial act in both the Arab Israeli and Jewish Israeli societies."

A controversial act indeed.

Surely the greatest feat of any apartheid government is convincing its population that to love, that most human of acts, is in fact to betray. In every oppressive society there is a demographic—the young, the students, the artists—that will reject the ideology of dehumanization on which protracted oppression and occupation rely.

None of the Jewish activists and students whom I meet in Jerusalem, Jaffa, or Tel Aviv can be made to believe in the fundamental inferiority of the Palestinian people. No amount of Palestinian Authority propaganda will convince the intellectual clubbers in Ramallah that *all* Jewish Israelis wish them ill. And yet with precisely the same logistical maneuvering that has chipped away at Palestine's borders, the occupying state has eroded the likelihood of interfaith relationships even among the most open-minded Muslims and Jews. There is nothing accidental about this outcome. It can be easy to dismiss organizations like LEHAVA as representing an extremist fringe, as reprehensible but as exceptional as, say, Germany's anti-immigrant group PEGIDA. In reality, the antiassimilation project flourishes at all levels of Israeli society: from courtroom to bedroom to classroom and beyond.

In 2015, for example, a novel called *Borderlife* was added to Israel's literature curriculum. Written by Dorit Rabinyan, "one of the country's most respected authors," *Borderlife* tells the love story of a Palestinian painter and an Israeli translator. Including this kind of narrative in a high school curriculum does much to naturalize interfaith dating in the minds of youth. For precisely this reason the Israeli Ministry of Education banned the novel from schools, arguing that Israeli young people could be encouraged to pursue relationships with Arabs by the book. Though two members of the curriculum panel quit in objection, and though the ban was widely criticized, it has held. Witness: the enforcement of personal prejudice at the level of the state.

Religious intermarriage is not recognized in Israel, much as interracial marriage was once criminalized in the United States. One cannot make a direct comparison between the two; the marriage of a mixed faith couple wed outside Israeli borders is, for example, recognized within them. But though such a union is legalized in theory, it is not legitimized in practice—and it is in the context of the manufacture of social illegitimacy that comparison proves instructive. The US legalized interracial marriage in 1967, when the Lovings (that fabulously named couple) appealed to the Supreme Court to declare antimiscegenation laws unconstitutional. Richard Loving was white,

Mildred Loving black; theirs was the country's first legal interracial marriage. What I've always found most interesting about the Loving case is the history of the laws that it overturned. Before there were *anti*miscegenation laws, miscegenation itself had to be invented. According to etymologists, the word was coined in 1863 in response to the abolition debate. The fabricated word combined the Latin *miscere* ("to mix") and *genus* ("kind"), where the reference to *genus* was intended to underscore the allegedly biological differences between nonwhites and whites. The irony, of course, is that all human beings belong to the same genus (*Homo*) and the same species (*Homo sapiens*). By definition, there can be no such thing as miscegenation among *people*. Religion is a less slippery concept than race if only in that the former can be said, per force, to exist. But in the Palestinian-Israeli context the two often blur together. To invalidate inter-religious marriage (and, more important, to illegitimate interfaith romance) is to problematize interethnic love—that is, to invite one to forget that the Other, enemy or lover, is a human being.

Through a combination of formal policy, cultural production, and violent intimidation, the state has succeeded in racializing love—the most egregious act of dehumanization possible. Invariably, a single image comes to mind when I think of the dehumanization of the Palestinian people: men packed together like caged animals at the border crossing in Qalandiya, grimly preparing for the checkpoint rush. It is impossible to see photos like this without confronting the extent to which the architects of the occupation have ceased to view Palestinians as human beings. Though there are many Israelis who do uphold the humanity of their Arab neighbors, the danger associated with *loving* them succeeds in obscuring the singularity of humanity itself.

What Palestine's national poet knew is that, as soon as one sees the other as human, not only love but *nuance* becomes possible. Concluding his 1973 musings on Rita, Darwish writes: "The following year the [1967] war erupted and I was put in prison again. I thought of her: 'What is she doing now?' She may be in Nablus, or another city, carrying a light rifle as one of the conquerors, and perhaps at this moment giving orders to some men to raise their arms or kneel on the ground. Or perhaps she is in charge of the interrogation and torture of an Arab girl her age, and as beautiful as she used to be." What Esther knows, what Mahmoud Mansour and Morel Malka know, what Tamar Ben Ami knows, is that fear is as instrumental to hate as nuance is detrimental. In discovering Darwish's Israeli lover, I rather childishly wish to have found some ray of hope, some proof that love might somehow triumph over all the hate I've witnessed. I do not wish to imagine Darwish's lover as a conqueror, a torturer. And yet Darwish did because he had to. Still he saw her beauty. In speaking with Jews and Arabs about the thorny subject of interfaith love, I learn that my thinking lacks nuance. With Darwish I am obliged to see the matter for all its ugliness *and* its beauty, resisting the urge to simplify while retaining the right to grieve. I have asked a question and received an answer, not the one for which I hoped, but a harsher truth born of a haunted, hardened landscape. Love between Jews and Arabs *does* exist, but must fight violence and bigotry for its survival. Or, said more hopefully, violence and bigotry do exist, but love between Jews and Arabs does, too.

IMAGINING JERICHO

COLM TÓIBÍN

I N JUNE 1992, ON THE NIGHT YITZHAK RABIN WAS REELECTED IN IS-
rael, I was in Jerusalem. When darkness fell, I went alone to the
Western Wall. I walked through the security barriers and down
the steps. The Wall was floodlit and people in black clothes were
praying up close to it. The sound of the prayers was intense and mes-
merizing. Some of the men with black hats and hair curled down the
sides of their faces were almost in a trance. Some were reading, some
reciting. The atmosphere was laden with reverence and emotion.

After a while, I went and sat on my own close by. The strength
and force of what was going on at the wall was intense, filled with
fervor.

Over the previous two years, as Eastern Europe opened up, I had
spent time in the countries that had been on the other side of the
Iron Curtain. In cities such as Bucharest, Budapest, Prague, Kraków,
and Warsaw in 1990 and 1991, the fate of the Jewish population was
not memorialized. The Jewish population, which had once been an
essential thread of the fabric of these cities, was simply a palpable
absence, surrounded by a desolate silence. My efforts to find where
the Warsaw ghetto began and ended, for example, were met with
bafflement. No one I asked seemed to know.

It was hard, then, and indeed in Jerusalem and Tel Aviv in 1992,
not to keep in mind how little Ireland, my country, had done in

response to the plight of the Jews of Europe. In December 1942 Eamon de Valera, who was both the Irish prime minister and foreign minister, received a telegram from Chief Rabbi Herzog of Palestine, whom he had known when Herzog was chief rabbi in Ireland between 1921 and 1936. It read: REVERED FRIEND PRAY LEAVE NO STONE UNTURNED TO SAVE TORMENTED REMNANT OF ISRAEL DOOMED ALAS TO UTTER ANNIHILATION IN NAZI EUROPE GREETINGS ZIONS BLESSINGS. Herzog followed this in January 1943 with a long telegram that referred to "five million threatened with extermination."

The Irish authorities dithered and made enquiries, but in general they did nothing, as even more alarming telegrams came to de Valera from Herzog.

During the war years the number of Jews allowed into Ireland "may have been as few as sixty," according to Dermot Keogh in his book *Jews in Twentieth-Century Ireland*.

It was hard not to think of this as I watched the figures praying at the Western Wall. It was hard also, in reading about the early years of Israel, not to be reminded of the revolutionary generation in Ireland in the years leading up to the 1916 rebellion—their idealism, their belief in culture, their sense that they were making a better life for Irish people in the future.

And it was difficult too in thinking about the fate of the Palestinians who suffered in the creation of Israel not to remember the history of dispossession in Ireland, of Irish Catholics in the sixteenth and seventeenth centuries being removed from their land. This was a history whose legacy was still poisoning life in Ireland even as late as 1992.

But in Ireland things in 1992 were changing. John Hume, the leader of constitutional nationalism in Northern Ireland, had developed a mantra. Everywhere he went, he said: "There is no such thing as territory. There are only people." And: "You do not make peace with your friends. You make peace with your enemies."

Slowly, tentatively, the parties in Northern Ireland had begun to move towards ending the conflict. What was striking about John Major and Tony Blair, who oversaw this process from London with considerable energy and care, and indeed their Irish counterparts, was that no matter what atrocity was committed by any of the terrorist armies, it did not stop them in their efforts to negotiate and talk, even with those close to the perpetrators. Each spate of killings almost seemed to spur them on to find a solution so that there would be no more killing.

In the week before the 1992 elections in Israel, as a guest of the Israeli government, I had spoken to politicians of every hue and had spent days and nights listening to arguments about the internal complexities of Israeli politics, some of which had close connections to Ireland. It seemed to me, however, that the fierce arguments and the many differing opinions on factions and personalities in Israel served almost as a means of distraction from the threat from the Arab world, and, more important, as a way of keeping the burning question of how to make peace with the Palestinians at bay.

Many people I met in Jerusalem and Tel Aviv wanted to talk about anything except how they were going to make a settlement with their immediate neighbors in East Jerusalem, the West Bank, and Gaza. Many secular Israelis seemed more concerned with the demands coming from religious Jews than they did with the plight of the Palestinians.

Nonetheless, during the week I had met candidates from the left wing parties who did want to discuss the Palestinians; some of them, had run a campaign based on their readiness to form a pact with the Palestinians. Among those I saw also was Yossi Beilin, whom I remember as the most open and intelligent politician, passionately engaged in attempting to find a reasonable solution, to take the desires and needs of the other side into account. On the other hand, I had also met people who wanted Israel to be a religious society, and wanted no dialogue at all with anyone, least of all the Palestinians.

As I walked away from the Western Wall on election night, I bumped into a man with whom I had had dinner a few evenings earlier. He had been born in England, but had come to Israel with his family; he had not, he said, voted for Rabin or any of the left-wing parties and now he was on his way to his local police station to get his equipment to do vigilante duty in the city center for the evening. I walked around with him for a while. Some of his children had become very religious, he said, and he seemed happy about this. I noticed a hardness in this man's views, a determination, a sense that he would do anything to hold on to what Israel had achieved.

I wondered what someone like him would do or feel if negotiations with the Palestinians began, negotiations which would have to conclude with the Israelis ceding rights and land, and losing a sense that they fully controlled what happened within the borders of Israel, Gaza, and the West Bank, the borders which had been created in 1967.

That same night in Jerusalem, as the results came in, my friends who supported the left-wing parties were jubilant. Rabin had won, and would hold power, they hoped, with the help of Meretz, the most dovelike of all the Jewish parties. They raised their glasses to the possibility of peace that night in Jerusalem, and it felt good until I began to move among these people and ask them specific questions. Did this mean that they would demolish the settlements in the West Bank? Did this mean that they would allow Gaza to be part of an autonomous Palestinian state with the West Bank? A real state? With an army? A police force? What about Jerusalem?

These were liberal Israelis on the night of an election victory, and each time a specific concession to the Palestinians came up, they were doubtful, and when Jerusalem itself came up, they were sure, they would not give up Jerusalem.

The next day I went to the West Bank with an Israeli military expert. I had imagined the settlements to be in the wilderness, in the middle of nowhere. But Israel is a tiny country, and if you drive for just fifteen minutes out of Jerusalem, you are quickly in the disputed territory, and another half an hour and you are in the place that the Palestinians want as their state. As we passed through Arab villages, the military expert scoffed at the notion that at some point in the future Palestinians would have the right to stop him and his driver.

As we stood on a hill overlooking the Jordan Valley, we saw herds of goats being tended by a solitary Palestinian sitting on an opposite hill, the man working in the same way as people have for thousands of years. I pointed out the herdsman to the Israeli expert, but he was too busy explaining potential strategies in the event of an invasion.

He explained how quickly an Arab force could overrun the West Bank, how vulnerable Jerusalem and its Jewish citizens were, and how vigilant they would have to be at all times in the future.

In the distance to the right, there was shimmering light over an area that seemed fertile, with many shades of green. This area stood out against the muted brown desert color all around it. As the man spoke about security and strategy, I kept looking over, wondering if it was an oasis, or what city or town it could possibly be. When I asked the military man what it was, he told me it was Jericho. Can we go there? I asked. No, he responded, it is not of much interest.

In the years that passed, whenever I met anyone from Israel or the West Bank or anyone who had visited the country, I asked them about Jericho. From that vantage point that day, it had seemed alluring, magical. I imagined flat-roofed houses with shaded patios inside. I imagined ancient mosques and Coptic churches and even older signs of habitation, a rich archaeology, places where Cleopatra and Antony had lingered, places haunted by the snarling echoes of Herod's voice, the place where Jesus had cured the blind beggars. I imagined calm, shaded squares with palm trees and coffee shops, people moving slowly in the heat, markets filled with produce, a sense of traditional life that had continued uninterrupted for many centuries.

No one who had been there confirmed this view of Jericho, however; no one saw it as a haven of peace and ease and tradition. Most were of the view, in fact, that it was really not worth visiting.

SOME MONTHS AFTER I WAS IN ISRAEL FOR THE ELECTIONS, I TRAVELLED to Tunis, where I did two interviews with Yasser Arafat, who was the leading representative of the Palestinian side, or at least the one whom most people recognized.

I was told when I arrived in Tunis to go to a certain hotel and wait there. Eventually, I was informed, I would be collected from the hotel and taken to meet Arafat. I remember that I was asleep when the phone call came. I had been waiting all day and it was dark now. I picked up the phone without switching on the light. "Now," a woman's voice said. "Now. We're in the lobby now. Come down now, immediately!"

I didn't have time for a shower. I splashed water on my face and then dressed as quickly as I could. I grabbed my notebook and my key and ran to the lift. As I waited I realized that I wasn't wearing a tie. If he'd been a head of state, I would have worn a tie: I decided to go back and put on a tie.

When I came out of the lift into the lobby a woman in her twenties stood watching me. There was a sort of controlled, intense fury in her bearing. I was late. I had not come down immediately. I must hurry.

I followed her out of the hotel into the dark street, where a car was waiting. The glass was smoked, so I could not see who else was in the car. A guy in a leather jacket stood at the driver's door, waiting. His look was bored, expressionless, but alert at the same time. At her signal, he got into the driver's seat and I got into the backseat. The photographer I was working with was already there. We set out at speed through the streets of Tunis. There was silence in the car.

Later, I discovered that the villa in which Yasser Arafat was staying lay close to our hotel, much closer than this first tense journey suggested. Eventually, having wound our way around the city, we came to a small hill with villas in their own grounds on either side. The car pulled into the right. There was a sentry box with a few army officials, and there were several burly civilians studying the car as it stopped, as though they had been waiting for it.

They watched us intensely when we got out of the car and stood in the small garden in front of the house. The man detailed to search through the cameras and photographic equipment tried to hold a machine gun as well. When he found he couldn't do this, he put his machine gun between his knees and attempted to keep it in place there, but it was too much for him and he had to hand his gun over to one of his waiting colleagues.

As the search went on, more men in their twenties and thirties came and stood around, looking at the cameras, looking at us. Some of them were armed, but others seemed to have no special function.

After the search we went into the house. In here, there was an air

of silence and sanctity. There were more men in a long room, part of
the hallway to the left of the entrance, watching us. On this first visit
to Arafat's house, I noticed this group of men, between a dozen or
two of them, all of them in their early twenties, I guessed, all of them
tall and good looking, some of them sitting slouched, some standing,
observing things silently.

We were led into a room to the right that had two long, thin
tables running down the center parallel to each other, and a number
of chairs. At each end of the room was an alcove. Yasser Arafat was
out of sight in one of them, speaking on the telephone, and I was led
to the other, where there was a sofa and some easy chairs, and told
to sit down. There was still an air of uneasiness and control. When
they discovered that I had a letter for Arafat from London, it had to
be taken out and opened in case it contained some special poison.

You could tell he was coming. It was as though the air in the
room changed, became tense. I stood up. Everyone watched Arafat
as he walked towards his desk, and he was aware of this. He looked at
no one, but seemed deeply conscious of his status in the room, enjoy-
ing his own performance, and the sense of awe and admiration that
his presence that night among his minders and advisers conjured up.

When he saw the photographer's lights, he gestured and smiled
as if to say: *All this for me?* He was wearing his customary headdress
and olive-green uniform with a pistol in a holster. He sat down at
his desk. I was motioned to move to a chair at the side of the desk.
Several older men sat on the sofa close by, as Arafat began to read a
pile of faxes which had been placed in front of him, carefully going
through each line, dead serious, like a businessman looking at a deal,
or a prime minister at a brief. He had a red felt-tipped pen in his hand
and he wrote notes and instructions on the top right-hand corner of
each page. There was silence in the room until he had finished; a
young man came and took the faxes away.

And then Arafat looked up at me and his face broke open into a
smile; the smile was friendly and unsuspicious, but it had a combative
edge to it, as if to say: *Who are you and what do you want to know?*

I told him that I was an Irish journalist working for an English
magazine. He laughed and looked around at his minders and advisers.

He nodded his head and smiled, as though the idea of this genuinely amused him. He repeated it. And then he stopped and examined me quizzically again. He was ready for questions. I wanted to start with something vague and general. I asked him if he saw more hope now for a solution to the problems in his country than he had a year ago. He hesitated and thought about it for a moment. All the charm was gone from his face: he was thinking.

His English was slow and careful, but he seldom made mistakes. A few times his advisers sitting on the sofa filled in phrases for him, and his press assistant helped him with words he did not know.

"I am a pragmatic man," he said. "It is not a matter of being hopeful or not. Our people are suffering from the daily oppression, the occupation, the daily crimes, the daily breaching of the Geneva Convention. I'm going to say that we were expecting something of Rabin. I expected that the Israeli masses voted for peace."

He spoke quietly with gravity and authority. It was a speech he had obviously made many times before, but this did not stop him exuding a controlled anger and a sadness in a tone that sounded heartfelt and sincere. It was like watching an actor in one of the great tragic roles use every inflection of his voice and every turn of his face to hold the audience.

He went on to talk about what the Israelis were doing, not only establishing more settlements in disputed territory, but committing crimes "against our sacred and holy Christian and Muslim places."

"To be a good Muslim," he said, "you have to be a good Christian and a good Jew." His country, he said, was the cradle of so many religions, traces of which existed in so many cities, towns, and villages. He looked straight at me as he preached religious tolerance, as he emphasized that he studied the Old and New Testaments as well as the Quran. He was not a fanatic; that was the message.

In that interview, he was no longer the internationally known terrorist, fluent in the bitter language of aggression and revolution, but he was someone ready to make a deal, using the soft language of concession and reconciliation. He and his organization had come to realize that they could not retake Israel, so the only option was to see how they could share power with the Israelis, make a compromise.

His tone, as we spoke, was melancholy but gentle, filled with layers of understanding. He was sure, he said, that the Israelis wanted peace, and he and his followers were prepared to negotiate to live side by side with the Israelis. Towards the end of that first meeting he nodded to an aide who brought in two small boxes to the room and left them on the long table. They were presents for me and for the photographer: carved versions of the Last Supper, made in Jerusalem. Icons from our religion. It was important for Arafat to establish beyond any doubt that he was tolerant, ready to accept a faith other than his own. In that first interview, that was his aim, to establish himself as someone whom the international community could trust.

At the end of that interview, I asked him about the city of Jerusalem. How did he visualize it in the future? He looked at me, puzzled as to how I would ask such a foolish question. "Jerusalem is our capital," he said. Who will police Jerusalem? I asked. "The Palestinian government," he said. The tone was matter-of-fact and clear, as if what he had just said was perfectly obvious.

When Arafat told me that he wanted a Palestinian government of the future to control the policing of Jerusalem, I thought of the Jewish people I had met the year before in Jerusalem and Tel Aviv. I had a sense as he spoke that he had no idea how hard it was going to be for him to negotiate from his current position of powerlessness and dispossession. I wondered how his melancholy charm might work in detailed negotiations.

I asked Arafat if he were given the West Bank as a Palestinian homeland, would he also want an army? He grew indignant at the question. "Why have the Israelis the right to have an army and we not? An army and control of foreign affairs is one of the most important characteristics of an independent country." During an interim period of self-government, he saw the possibility of having no army, but after that, there would have to be an army, even if it was a small army.

There in that house in Tunis, in his long and restless exile, in the room with all his cohorts around, I wondered if there was a way to explain to Arafat how afraid even the most liberal Israelis were of him and his followers. But he was talking again about justice and self-determination and then he stood for a photograph. The photographer asked him if, despite everything that had happened, he saw hope for the world. He had been laughing, and I thought that like most politicians he would say yes, of course. But he didn't. He shook his head and said no. He seemed downcast as he talked again about the tragedy of his people, "two-thirds of them homeless, stateless, one-third under occupation."

Yitzhak Rabin, with whom Arafat won the Nobel Peace Prize in 1994, was assassinated in 1995. The new emerging Israeli leadership, figures such as Ariel Sharon and Benjamin Netanyahu, were less interested in a two-state solution, or the rights of the Palestinians, and more concerned about the security and destiny of Israel. The decade after I visited Israel for the elections and went to Tunis to interview Arafat was a time when attitudes hardened, a time when things began to seem intractable, when polarization and sometimes savage violence, including a spate of suicide bombings perpetrated by the Palestinians, and the use of live ammunition by Israeli soldiers, took the place of imaginative solutions and a will to settle differences. In 2008, Yossi Beilin, whose influence had been waning considerably, retired from politics.

Within a decade of the interviews I did with him, Arafat was to become a strange, powerless figure. As the Oslo agreement unraveled, he would be confined within his Ramallah compound by the Israeli army. He died in a hospital near Paris, France, in November 2004 at the age of seventy-five.

By 2016, as I prepared to travel to Israel again—this time my trip would be organized by Breaking the Silence—no one I spoke to, no book or article I read, saw any possibility of a solution. Now, as I dreamed of seeing Jericho and walking in its shaded streets, I also knew that to see Jericho, as I still wanted to do, I would have to see other things too. I would have to witness what was happening in the West Bank, in the occupied territories, as well as see my dream city.

In that first visit, I realized, I had paid attention to Israel as a haven for a people who had been persecuted over many centuries, and to the idea of Israel's security. While I had shared Israelis' sense of relief at having founded a state, I had not paid enough attention to their sense of destiny, which at times had an edge that was relentless and complete enough to suggest that no one else's destiny mattered. I realized that I should have listened more carefully when left-wing Israelis spoke about the problems their country faced from the religious right. Had I done so, I would have learned something about the reason why, even though they spoke about peace, the Israelis continued to build settlements in the West Bank—more than a hundred between the election of Rabin in 1992 and 2016.

Many of these settlements were called outposts, since they did not have official approval. Despite their being unofficial, however, they were provided with electricity and water by the state. The Israeli army also provided the settlers with a protection that took the form of aggression both mild and intense against the Palestinians who lived close by.

The reason why the settlements continued in the areas of the West Bank still held by the Israelis after the Oslo accords has a shadow element that is economic. Most settlers do not come from wealth and few enjoy the relaxed, privileged lifestyle found in parts of Jerusalem and Tel Aviv. The impulse to settle in the West Bank comes, however, not merely from an urge to find cheap housing, or even to colonize the West Bank as a way of ensuring Israel's security. Rather, it comes from a sense of religious destiny, a belief that this territory belongs to the Jewish people as a gift from history; it was where they believe they came from, and now it is a place to which they return as though of right. In September 2013, Benjamin Netanyahu, for example, justified the occupation of the city of Hebron by Israelis by claiming that Hebron was "the city of our forefathers."

Indeed, many of the 400,000 Israeli settlers in the West Bank believe that God gave them the land they have decided to settle on, and God, with the help of the Israeli state, is ready indeed to give them more.

The gradual creation of Israeli settlements in the West Bank after the Six-Day War in 1967, when the Jordanians withdrew from this territory, was done piecemeal; it was unofficial and then official; it was provisional and then part of an elaborate design; it arose from a dream, but it soon became fixed and hard and menacing. It was utopian, invoking a legacy that was thousands of years old, but it was also practical, militaristic, detailed, determined, and merciless.

Hebron, the largest Palestinian city in the West Bank, has five small Israeli settlements, the last of which was set up in April 2014. In Hebron, there are 200,000 Palestinians, 850 Israeli settlers, and 650 combat soldiers to protect the settlers.

One of the settlers appeared when, in July 2016, with a small group, I tried to visit the grave of Baruch Goldstein. Goldstein had entered the Cave of the Patriarchs in Hebron in February 1994, wearing his army uniform, and opened fire in the mosque, killing twenty-nine Palestinians and injuring one hundred and twenty. He, in turn, was subdued and killed by Palestinians inside the mosque.

The settler who appeared was large and threatening. Soon, two other figures arrived, one a woman who began screaming at us, and another a man who blocked our path. Each time we tried to move forward, all three stood in the way, moving to the right if we did and to the left if we did. Soon a policeman came and there was heated discussion, which left me free to go to look at the gravestone of Baruch Goldstein, which had small stones placed on it by those who had recently come to visit. The inscription on the gravestone called on God to avenge Goldstein's blood, and went on: "He gave his life for the sake of the people of Israel, the Torah, and the Land." It concluded: "His hands are clean and his heart pure."

Every account of Hebron over the past hundred years is peppered with stories of the killings of Jews by Palestinians and of Palestinians by Jews. Each side can list the atrocities and single murders that have taken place.

In the late nineteenth century there was a small Jewish population in Hebron, but, when sixty-seven Jewish people were murdered by Palestinians in 1929, the rest of the Jewish population left the city. There were no Jews in Hebron again until a small settlement began in 1968, when Israelis, having got permission to stay briefly in the Park Hotel in the city, refused to leave.

Hebron is organized by the Israelis according to an elaborate system of control, with a complex maze of checkpoints and rules. On certain roads, for example, no Palestinians are allowed to drive. In other areas, no Palestinian shops are allowed to remain open.

More than a thousand Palestinian housing units have been aban-
doned, and two thousand Palestinian businesses closed. Of these,
more than a thousand were closed during the second intifada, from
2000 to 2005, and almost five hundred closed by military order. In
the city center there is 70 percent unemployment. The old gold mar-
ket is a rubbish dump now, the rubbish having been thrown down
from one of the Israeli settlements above it.

There are roads marked "sterile," meaning that no Palestinians at
all can walk on them.

ON MY FIRST VISIT TO HEBRON, I WAS SURPRISED WHEN THE POLICEMAN
at the park where the tomb of Baruch Goldstein is sited suggested
that we leave the area. He did nothing at all to deal with the settlers
who were, for no legal reason, blocking our path. Five days later, I
was even more surprised when a group of settlers emerged from a
civil building close to the Tomb of the Patriarchs in Hebron. In full
view of the army and the police, one of them, a young man, began
to kick the photographer I was working with. The kicks were high
and hard and focused so that one of the cameras was smashed to
pieces.

When we asked the security forces what they were going to do
about this, the police who had been watching it said that they had not
seen it. A number of army officers then appeared and made desultory
enquiries, but they did not ask us for statements or for a description
of the assailant.

In a place called Qawawwis in the South Hebron Hills on a Sat-
urday morning in July 2016, a Palestinian sheep farmer—whom I'll
call Ibrahim—has been detained by the army, whose soldiers keep
the engines of four jeeps running while they work out what to do
with him. On the other side of the jeeps is an Israeli outpost, which
was founded in 1998.

The problem is this: while the farmer can graze his sheep on these
uplands, which are his, there is one piece of land not fenced off, close
to the outpost, which is disputed, on which his sheep are not entitled
to go. Unfortunately, the grass there is more plentiful than the grass
on the other side of a small path. So the sheep have gone there to

graze. In order to remove his sheep from this small piece of land, the farmer has had to walk on the disputed land.

It is clear that the sheep will always want to go to this piece of grass, and the farmer knows this will bring trouble.

There is no suggestion that Ibrahim is a security threat. His problem, effectively, is that he is Palestinian. His family has been using this land for generations.

There is no doubt this morning that the farmer has set foot on this disputed land, but it is hard to think of how he could have removed his sheep from the land without stepping on it. The army waits for the police to come.

The sun is hot. Hours go by. The farmer talks about his fear of the people in the outposts and of the army. He has been in hospital, he says, five times arising from injuries received at the hands of the settlers and the army. He alleges that while detained by the army on a previous occasion he was not only beaten up but also stabbed lightly with a knife. The settlers, he says, also attack his sheep.

Obviously, in another country, he could call the police, but he lives under military law, and the police and army support the settlers in the outpost who live under civil law, but in fact the settlers live as though there is no law at all.

Ibrahim, who lives nearby in a small makeshift hut, has seventeen people in his family. The aim of both the settlers and the authorities is for this man and his family to leave here, to move to one of the cities, such as Yatta, in Area A, which is, as a result of the Oslo accords, under the rule of the Palestinian Authority. (Area A, indeed, is set aside for Palestinians, and a system of transport had been designed so that Israelis never have to travel through or even see most Palestinian towns and cities.)

This morning is another small moment in the slow harassment of Ibrahim. The land around is rocky, the area is remote and desolate looking and also very beautiful. There is something almost comic about the scene, how serious the young army men look as they gravely walk back and forth as the sheep gently graze away from disputed land, as the piece of disputed land which is causing all this trouble appears not much larger than a suburban garden.

It becomes less comic in the farmer's hut when one of his family members shows me his plastic stomach, the result, he says, of being shot by one of the settlers when he was grazing sheep in 2001, three years after the settlers arrived. He spent, he says, fifty-four days in an Israeli hospital and was finally taken to Iraq for a new stomach. There was, he says, no action taken against the settler who shot him.

Nearby, there is another Palestinian family whose house and farm buildings have recently been demolished, the demolition once more having been invoked by antiquated law. The scene is like a disaster area. Since it is midday, the sun is fierce in the sky, and the family must take shelter in one small makeshift tent. Some of the young women are also sheltering under an old truck. To rebuild will take time and ingenuity, as no machinery will be allowed to approach the site. Everything will have to be done by hand, with the risk that any new building will also be demolished.

Once more, there is no question of the family here, who are farmers, being a security risk. The problem is that they are too close to the Israeli settlement of Susya and too close to an outpost. The aim, once more, is to get them to leave.

When I ask one of the older men where the family originally came from, he tells me that he used to live inside Israel until 1948. After 1948, the family moved to Susiya al-Qadim, where they lived in caves. But in 1985 archaeologists came. For about a year, the man says, they remained in the caves while the archaeologists worked, but the archaeologists then fenced off the area and evicted any Palestinians who were living there.

A few days earlier in another site close to an Israeli settlement in the South Hebron Hills, I had visited a Palestinian family whose cave, which they had built themselves, had been demolished by the Israeli army. They were now living in a makeshift tent. Once more, when I asked them where they had originally come from, they said that they had lived in the caves in Susiya al-Qadim but had been moved in 1986 by the archaeologists who blocked the entrance to their cave with stones.

Susiya al-Qadim is now an archaeological park, a National Heritage Site. A brochure describes it as an "Ancient Jewish Town" and offers the site for "Weddings and Bar/Bat Mitzvah ceremonies in the ancient synagogue courtyard." It also advertises a "covered event hall [which] holds up to 150 people."

A cave in which audiovisual material is now displayed was the cave where the family whose cave was later demolished by the Israeli army had lived. The son of that family, Nasser Nawaja, now the father of three children, was born in the cave where there are now benches where visitors can sit to watch a video.

The site itself is a fascinating example of an early Jewish settlement. The synagogue was built between the fourth and the seventh centuries and was in use until the ninth century. The floor of the synagogue includes a mosaic in Hebrew. The contours of the site provides valuable clues about Jewish social patterns and religious rites centuries after the destruction of the Second Temple.

Although on the site itself there is a single reference to a mosque and there is a clearly marked outline of where the mosque was situated, there is no mention of the mosque in the promotional brochure. Although it has been suggested that Arabic inscriptions were also found at the site, there is nothing about this at the site itself or in the brochure. Nor is there any mention of who was living on the site at the time of the excavations.

Instead, the brochure suggests that Susiya was a sort of prototype for a modern Jewish settlement. For example: "In attaching the houses one to the other and creating a joint external wall a sense of security and defense against the desert dwellers was obtained." This suggests that the Jewish inhabitants of Susiya were under attack in some way, and yet there is no evidence anywhere in the site of violence or violent attack. The site seems to have been abandoned by its Jewish population rather than attacked.

When the brochure reads, "It is probable that all of the town's inhabitants took part in the construction of the defense belt," it is hard to imagine what evidence the writer could have for this, but it is easy to read this as a sign that the Jewish people who lived here in the distant past organized building communally, as though Susiya were an early kibbutz, or indeed an early outpost or settlement.

There are several references in the brochure to "security," and one to "the high security needs of the inhabitants." But the brochure gives no evidence of what these needs might have been and nothing at all about what the excavation of the mosque shows, or what the very existence of such a Jewish village in a time of Islamic rule might imply.

It is clear that the heritage of Susiya, while mainly Jewish, is also complex and multilayered. The ghosts that walk on these old stones are not merely Jewish ones. But the archaeologists are working in a time when re-creating the past and invoking its power and its echoing presence are crucial weapons in the efforts to make the settlers feel that they have returned to a place that was once theirs. They do not wish to know that Susiya, like most other places in the world, also once belonged to other people too.

Indeed, the creation of the park itself involved the expulsion of Palestinian families who are, thirty years after their eviction, still living in appalling conditions nearby. Moving the Palestinians out in order to open such an impressive and important site to visitors might seem reasonable, but it appears less so since an outpost of Israeli settlers has arrived to live inside the boundaries of the park. The settlers are there under the full protection of the Israeli army.

The idea that the Israelis care about every single inch of this territory and have plans for it is striking. The soldiers and the settlers who watched the lone shepherd that morning in July 2016 viewed his brief presence in a small piece of grassland with immense seriousness.

Sometimes, the Israelis' sheer attention to detail and the thoroughness of the security forces and planners are impressive. It is easy to feel this, for example, in Hebron itself, easy to feel how careful and detailed the security system is until someone takes you into the city by a series of narrow paths, across waste ground, thus avoiding checkpoints. And then you realize that the system merely looks impressive, and is designed to impress, but it doesn't really work and is, in fact, not designed to work. It is there for other reasons.

It is easy, for example, for Palestinians to enter parts of Hebron banned to them by using the Muslim graveyard. Nobody actually cares whether the Palestinians enter or not. But the stores and markets are closed; the doors of the Palestinian shops are sealed up. The place has been brutalized. The army is moving up and down the empty streets. That part of the plan has been carried out with care and efficiency. A society that once prided itself on making the desert bloom is now involved in making a ghost town of a great old city.

In the weeks before I went to Hebron, a young girl had been murdered by a Palestinian in the Kiryat Arba settlement just outside the city, and another Israeli had been murdered on the main road leading to town. The government response was to seal off parts of Hebron lived in by Palestinians and seal off other towns and villages as well. One Saturday, I noticed an Israeli bulldozer creating ditches, all the more efficiently to close off a field that led to a village. Three days later, as I passed again, I saw a truck bringing supplies to the village driving blithely across the same field that had been sealed off. It had not really been sealed off. The bulldozing had all been done for show.

THE CITY OF JERICHO, LIKE RAMALLAH, IS IN AREA A, WHICH MEANS that it is under the control of the Palestinian Authority. With a population of twenty-three thousand, it is the oldest inhabited city in the world. A tourist brochure outlines the rich and complex heritage of the city, which includes Hellenistic and Roman remains, signs of Byzantine and Islamic habitation, and a synagogue from the sixth through seventh centuries AD.

Because of its mild climate in the winter, Jericho has become a place of refuge for rich Palestinians who live in Ramallah and East Jerusalem. On the outskirts of the city, some very grand modern houses have been built by Palestinians who have money. Also, because Palestinians are not allowed to use the airport near Tel Aviv and must travel to Jordan and use the airport at Amman, Jericho is an important stop along the way.

The place was not the haven I imagined, however, but an ordinary, slightly sleepy town with a main square, the old mud houses replaced by modern buildings. Nonetheless, I did find a small, relaxed café, plus an efficient barber shop.

On the outskirts of Jericho, however, are the ruins of Hisham's

Palace, a massive desert outpost created by the Arab Umayyad caliph Hisham Bin Abd al-Malik, from the eighth century, with signs of a sophisticated heating system, some sculpture, and some exquisite mosaic work, including the very beautiful *Tree of Life*, with two gazelles on the left-hand side of the tree standing alone and free but the gazelle on the right-hand side being attacked savagely by a lion.

When the guide told me that the flower motif at the edge of the *Tree of Life* was replicated in the mosaic floor of a synagogue nearer the city, I was interested in this, but the synagogue is now closed and cannot be visited.

As in Ramallah, there are conflicting versions of what the Oslo accords have meant. On the one hand, the accords have resulted in the withdrawal of the Israeli army and the building of hospitals and schools in Jericho. (And in Ramallah, they have meant the arrival of banks, with quick mortgages and easy credit, and thus a sort of boom.)

But on the other hand, in Jericho, once I began to talk to people, I discovered that many problems persist, not least the complex problem of getting across the border into Jordan, but also the problem of who owns the water here and who is allowed to make use of it.

Palestinians have to travel to Amman to use the airport, a journey that the Israelis make difficult. There are two checkpoints between Jericho and the border, and luggage must be transported separately. A journey of ten kilometres thus takes hours rather than minutes.

In the streets of Ramallah and Jericho, there is the illusion of freedom, and in Ramallah now there are some fine restaurants. It is when Palestinian citizens attempt to exercise their freedom— including the freedom to leave the country and then come back— that the problems begin. And the problems also begin with water.

There are five water springs close to Jericho. The city can use one of those, while the Israeli settlers, of whom there are six thousand in the Jordan Valley, use the other four. Even in Area A, which is, in theory, controlled by the Palestinian Authority, the Israelis do not allow Palestinians to dig wells. Since the Jordan Valley is fertile and valuable, more than 80 percent of it remains in Area C, under Israeli control. In 2011, according to the Israeli NGO B'Tselem, "the average household water allocation was 450 litres per person per day for the Israeli settlers and 60 litres per person per day for Palestinians. (The World Health Organization recommends a hundred litres per person per day.)"

Since only the city of Jericho itself is in Area A, then Area C surrounds certain parts of it. Many of the houses of the older Palestinian inhabitants in Area C that are close to Jericho are under demolition orders, and some indeed have been demolished recently and left without electricity and water.

Jericho will be an enclave, surrounded by Israeli power and Israeli settlements. Slowly, then, as Israeli outposts and the slow harassment of the Palestinian population by the army and the authorities increase, as the West Bank becomes two countries, with some roads essentially for Israelis only and others only for Palestinians, with settlements and outposts surrounded by the army for protection, with 62 percent of the West Bank under full Israeli control, with just a few towns and cities under Palestinian Authority control, the West Bank will have been successfully occupied, the Palestinians will have been surrounded and corralled.

What is essential then is that lines of communication between Israeli leaders, even leaders in civil society, and those who lead their communities in the Palestinian-controlled areas be kept open. There will, at some time in the future, have to be dialogue, an appreciation of what the history of suffering has been and has meant for both sides.

Instead, there is silence, suspicion, and distance.

On my last day in Israel, as I waited in the airport, I picked up a copy of the *Jerusalem Post*. At the bottom of page 3, there was a headline: "FM blocks Beilin from meeting Abbas."

The article said that Yossi Beilin, who had been involved in the negotiations which led to the Geneva Initiative of 2003, as well as the Oslo accords (Geneva was a failed initiative which would have involved an almost total Israeli withdrawal from the West Bank, a non-militarized Palestinian state, and Jerusalem divided between Israel and Palestine) goes with others from the Israeli side of those negotiations "every month or so to meet with their Palestinian counterparts."

"We always get proper authorization [since Israelis need this to legally enter Ramallah], and we have never been turned down except during war like in July 2014," Beilin said.

Beilin's application to visit Ramallah was turned down by the Israeli Defense Minister for "security reasons." Neither Beilin nor anyone else could think what these "security reasons" could be. Stopping Yossi Beilin, a figure whose record in seeking agreement between Israel and Palestine has been brave and distinguished, from meeting with members of the Palestinian Authority seems counter-productive and petty.

Like much else that is happening in the West Bank, including things I witnessed while I was there, this may satisfy some set of short-term goals, but it is hard to see any long-term strategy involved which will bring justice or create anything other than hardship and bitterness. The strategy seems merely tactical, and it is hard to see the tactics as anything other than cruel and self-serving and shortsighted.

THE END OF REASONS

EIMEAR MCBRIDE

HAD NOT THOUGHT ABOUT THE WORLD FOR A VERY LONG TIME AND, of all places, here had seemed easier to ignore. But I am driving down to Jericho now, and, for the first time in a week, I breathe. Not because I have become accustomed to the hassle of checkpoints or seeing young men and women, still teenagers some, looking out at me from behind guns that they know how to use. Not because I have stopped noticing how grown men and women close themselves up behind a mask of quietude in order to cope with their every movement being at the whim of those same youngsters. The red signs at every turnoff into the West Bank, warning that the government forbids entry and that entry is dangerous, have not ceased, in a whole variety of selfish and unselfish ways, to alarm me. Quite to the contrary, I am only beginning to see, learning how to look, and my sense of alarm is off the charts.

I have not forgotten the modernist concrete barrier bulletproofing the road winding over into Hebron. And I will not forget, cannot forget, the madness of what I saw there. Family homes turned into lookout posts. Front steps opening onto streets where their owners may not go. The guts of once busy shops and markets left flapping in the sun. The bullet holes and furrowed walls where tanks have squeezed improbably through. Patrolled by soldiers and the ever voluble settlers eager to impress their point of view. The places where life was, children played, people called to each other and thought of as home and, once perhaps contentedly, as the boundary of their whole world, stand empty. Desolate. Turned into rattraps now, and cages. Sealed behind soldered doors. Closed off for hours, then days, then years at a time. Street names mauled and replaced so the very memory of their ever having existed becomes debatable, then fabled, then gone. The sheer effort, in this place, to make history die. I stood on a hill, looking out across the city, listening carefully for its particular sound, but there was such quiet. I have never heard so many people live in silence before. Later, down again and at a checkpoint to the other side, the man who'd volunteered to guide us through lost his rag with the young soldiers who had decided to make us, for no discernible reason, wait. In the heat. And I got so polite inside myself. Willed him to stop being antagonistic with them. Forgot how fast I like to walk. Hate security in airports or the time lost in call centre queues while he, along with everyone he knows, spends his life waiting for that arbitrary Stop to be Go. Not ten minutes. Hours of the day. Years of life. Wasting in the delay.

Inside, finally, and there was the sound. The press of people herded into too little room, and open eared I went through the streets. Only after a while thinking to look up and consider the mesh that was the sky. Covered in filth. Bags of shit. Bottles and nappies and every kind of rubbish in every place, leaking in, dripping through. Thrown down on people from the bright white settlements built above, on top of them, in buildings that were once their own; surely a far cry and gleaming domestic heaven when viewed from the squalor inflicted below. The indecency of it. The disgrace. Can even the fervent belief that such mass dispossession is a gift from God really justify this? Then the screaming of the settlers waiting for us when we emerged from the checkpoint on the other side, best summarised as "You've been talking to terrorists and liars. Your eyes do not understand what they have seen," is overwhelming, and in one way, of course, they are right. I can make no human sense of what I witnessed on those streets. But I know my eyes saw what they did and can never unsee it again.

Now, though, I am driving down to Jericho, and, for the first time, the country opens wide. All week, until now, the rain has poured down and today is blue skies with no cloud as far as the mountains in front of us, then away into Jordan on our right. And if my boots are still wet with the mud of Susiya and Umm al-Khair, I can live with that. The harping cold of those remnants of villages is slipping off me now. I wonder how it is today for the toddlers I saw there. Life doesn't just look worse in the rain. Yesterday their parents noticed a car stopping nearby for its driver to make notes and knew this meant someone would soon be back to demolish their homes again. As I took a photo of a man's goats grazing in the rubble of what had been his house, he said "Hey, take a picture of my son." But when I did, he said "No, where his kitchen should be, where his toilet was." When he put the child down, his baby shoes soaked up the wet from the tile fragments surrounding the skeletal remains of a squat loo and the thin line of debris dividing it from where a kitchen must have been. And I took the photo. And looked at the little sodden feet. I couldn't imagine how they would ever get dry in that tiny tin shack where this little boy, along with his whole family, now lived, and they hoped would not be torn down again soon. From where I stood I could easily see into the warm, well-built homes of the settlers beside, who were obliging their close neighbours to live in this foulness, who must've looked out every day through the well-fitted glass of their comfortable kitchens onto this shameful site. And although I was familiar now with the many justifications for why the settlers have decided their fellow human beings deserve to live this way, why Palestinians have brought this situation on themselves by insisting on their right to remain on their own land, I did not understand. The ideology, the tacit encouragement—to support its own territorial ends—of the state, the problems solved by attempting to force outward migration, even the opportunist's chance for land, my brain knows how to get around. What I do not understand is the human choice settlers make and the certainty with which they seem able to choose for others what they would never choose for themselves. Presumably it helps that a state machine, which has lost the run of itself, works only in their favour.

But we are nearing Jericho, talking about all kinds of things in the car. Two women in the front, mother and daughter. Mother just a few years older than me and her daughter in her late teens. Me and the translator in the back. Their English though is excellent, a product of the elder's childhood exile in the United States. I can hardly imagine her history, growing up in the South and being "the brownest people on the street." But when the Klan planted a burning cross on their lawn, her father—a former member of the Popular Front for the Liberation of Palestine—went out and blew it up. And we laugh about programmes on TV, especially the *Curb Your Enthusiasm* episode called "Palestinian Chicken." She likes that one a lot. I ask about marriage. "I met my husband during the first intifada," she says. "I was in my teens, he was throwing stones, and I thought that was kind of sexy." I'm pretty sure in my teens I would have too. She'd like her daughter to marry but expects her to choose. Education is vital. Her daughter also thinks so. They are liberal, articulate, wearing jeans. Her daughter wore a headscarf for a while, for solidarity. She doesn't anymore. She doesn't think it means that now. And then they talk about their cousin. A boy of only sixteen. Kidnapped, beaten, murdered, burned alive. The injustice of what happened in the investigation of the crime. Undercover agents beating up other family members, then detaining them without charge. The boy's own parents accused of perpetrating the murder themselves, as a homophobic "honour killing." The stress of the state-serving media slander and, on top of all this, the awfulness of the grief itself. There is nothing I can say. I have never known anyone killed in this way. I have never known a family who has had to endure this. I wonder how much comfort they take from the justice that was finally wrung from the state. Maximum sentences are what the perpetrators must live through now but change nothing of what the victim's family must live with, and without. As I listen I am so conscious that for me this is just one more terrible thread in a pattern I am still learning how to read. But for them, it is a nightmare that will never go away, an inescapable agony at the very centre of their lives. How must it be to wake every day to the knowledge that they, along with their whole society, have no place of refuge, nor expectation of respite, from these deep injustices and horrific crimes? All that is human in me recoils from this. Does not want to believe there are those who seek to justify it, who feel it can be justified, that the modern state—which has forced itself into the position to preside over such abuses—willingly continues to do so and then blames its victims too.

But "I don't need your tears" a woman in Nabi Saleh said, after I'd watched a home video of one of her relatives dying horribly, bloodily, from a tear gas canister being fired into his face. And it's true, the emotion of well-meaning outsiders like me is of no worth. It's certainly a hindrance, once descended into hysteria and insults on the Web, to reaching those who must, most urgently, be affected. Those people on the other side whose rejection of occupation would count, whose voices would have to be heard, who need all our encouragement to risk becoming more than the sum of their—not always unreasonable—fears.

So we go through Jericho and see its giant key painted in white with the words *We will return* . . . Then on out into the Jordan Valley to Ras al-'Oja and the Bedouin women living there.

In plastic chairs we sit in a ring arranged under trees. Women in colourful hijabs, old men smoking, and glasses of tea. The huts they live in scarcely more than that. Carpets on mud floors. Breeze blocks covered in tarpaulin and plastic. Their lowness keeping out the wind and the sun. Chickens and goats running around. The heat almost kills me but balmy for them and I'm unsure where to start. I've inkling enough though that what I thought I'd ask won't be answered in a mixed crowd. Under occupation, I've learned, there is no space for the personal, not when speaking to foreigners anyway. There is barely air. So instead I ask the women to tell me about their day to day. What's a normal one? Milk the goats. Bake bread. Get the children out to school. What kind of education do you have? University level. What, all of you? Of course. Women as well? Yes. And they are surprised that I am. When we were chased off our ancestral lands in forty-eight, they explain, some of us fled to Jordan but those who remained decided that, as a people, we must educate ourselves. Our level of education is a beacon to the Arab world. Today I hear this time and again. But the conversation turns and they tease about finding me a husband among them. When I say I have one, and a child, a woman my age says she has eight and is the first wife of three. She says she doesn't mind because the others do things her way. The other wives agree, and I'm pretty sure I would too if she were in charge of me. With her husband sitting there, playing henpecked though, I know I won't learn much more. What happens if a marriage is unhappy? The family sorts it out, of course. So I look out across the fields. The season is still green but, not far off, there stands a white concrete building with its tell-tale antennae. Is that a settler outpost? I ask. And it is. They will be coming soon. What do you think about that? What can we think? We are afraid. This village is under demolition orders already, while they have every comfort the state can provide. Mains water and electricity, while we are beaten for trying to collect water at all. The violence always and the threat of it. "Would it ever be possible, in the future, to integrate?" "We'd live with them," they say. "But they won't live with us." It's a line I've heard many times this week, along with the—surprising to me—preference for a single state. It's explained simply, and of course makes sense, this is their homeland, all of it. How can they give up on their dream of the freedom to travel it? See the cities they've not seen in years. Catch up with friends and family members. Go paddle with their children on the beach in Jaffa. This is a country they love, so I ask about love. In this terrible situation, what can it mean, love of country, family, sister-wives even? "It's everything," the first wife says. "For me, love is everything."

Later we go to another village. It's been arranged that I'll speak to a group of local women and the leader of the women's council there. After I've been welcomed, but before I am left alone, the man who arranged the introduction advises me not to "ask about the occupation. The women will be too intimidated to speak openly about that." But the very minute he closes the door, that's exactly where they start. There is no work in this village and their lands are being eaten out from under their feet by the ever-widening jaws of the settlement. And although the settlement grows daily, the villagers themselves have no right to build. They must cram what breeze-block floors they can onto their already crumbling houses beneath. So families are crowded on top of each other in dangerous buildings. Freezing in winter and boiling in the sun. No adequate sewage, clean water, or medical attention. An elegant and eloquent young woman says, "I'm a trained social worker but I spend my life picking onions." With their own lands appropriated and the fathers of their children unable to find jobs, or forced into outward migration, these women's only available option is to work as manual labourers in the settlements nearby. It's a thirty-minute ride just to get there every day, in a trailer, open to the elements rain or shine. Every woman in this room, young and old, regardless of education, family situation, or physical ability, must pick and pack and clean onions to make ends barely meet. Six a.m. to two p.m. for ninety shekels, from which the overseer extracts his own commission. Fifteen-minute break a day, is all. No health care provision or compensation for those injured on the job. And the work is riddling them with health problems. Carpal tunnel syndrome and what the constant bending does to the discs in their backs. Breathing problems from the constant intake of unfiltered, noxious air in an enclosed space. And these are greenhouses they work in, so they're hot. No job security or benefits, of course, and what causes them all great distress is being forced to leave their young children home alone, constantly. One woman says, "I cannot go on. My health is broken. I can no longer work. I am in constant physical pain and I have only come out to ask if you can do something. I beg you, please do something for me." She becomes so agitated and I am so obviously useless that she has to leave.

For a while there was an NGO out of Bethlehem helping them start a microenterprise of their own, in the hope of providing an alternative source of income to the hated settlement work. They set up a wedding business. Providing chairs. Photography. Catering. Music. For a time it worked and hope happened, then the NGO moved on. Without the experience of keeping a business going, it folded soon after that. For a while they talk about the dearth of leadership, about the wilful passivity of the West, about Arafat and what he made them dream, then how he allowed those dreams to be betrayed. And what lifts, like mist, is the rage in them. The visible rage at this maze which they find themselves trapped in. Rage at the waste of their good minds, and their talents forcibly left to rot. The waste of the painstakingly acquired educations and skills which can bring them no benefit. The sheer frustration of ambitions that have nowhere to go and, because of that, living constantly in the shadow of what most people would consider to be unlivable: the unending decay of hope.

In a coffeehouse in Ramallah, I sit with three women, all of whom are smoking like trains. They have agreed to meet me to help fill in the gaps. They are long-term advocates for Palestinian women's rights. Passionate but also dispassionate. Apologetic that some of their number have backed out because they feared "breaking the BDS by meeting you." When I protest that I'm not Israeli and this project receives no government funding from there, they say they know, and think it is a shame, but the social repercussions of falling foul of the BDS movement are so great that some people have become afraid of speaking out to foreigners who are involved in projects that include Israelis. I think this is an unfortunate consequence and am all the more grateful to those who have come. They are all highly educated, liberal, without headscarves on and scornful of their fellow female activists who have started to don them. They are, in fact, pretty enraged that those in headscarves lay claim to a superior commitment to the cause. They see it as a sign of how women have been conned into forgoing their battle for equal rights until the greater war has been won. So here is where I hear about domestic abuse and its victims' near-total lack of recourse. Even where there are shelters, the occupation regime's movement restrictions make the victims' ability to access them virtually nil. Contraception is available for married women, but hard to choose unless their husbands are in agreement. As for the rest, "sex before marriage does not exist." So for any woman unlucky enough to find herself pregnant and unmarried, the future is very bleak indeed. "Honour killings" are a real threat. Abortion is expensive here and the quality of treatment often poor. They say these are problems within the purview of the Palestinian Authority to address but it chooses not to, and even when it has—as in a recent law forbidding honour killings—implementation rarely moves beyond lip service. Fighting for an end to the occupation is the only struggle the PA will admit. But these women think Hamas has destroyed the struggle anyway, by pairing the legitimate fight for rights, justice, and self-determination with fundamentalist ideology. That was never what they were fighting for, and they object to the perception that this is what they are fighting for now. Before I leave them I ask that most awkward and impossible of questions: What can I do? Nothing, they say, except go home and tell everyone what you have seen and heard.

On my last day I walk around West Jerusalem. It's a world I nearly know. People just being, getting on with their lives, and I've half-stopped noticing the guns on display everywhere. It's only when I arrive at the protest known as the Women in Black that I'm slammed back to reality again. Every Friday, for twenty-seven years, this group of Jewish Israeli women have come to silently protest against the occupation. They are mostly elderly now and all they do is stand holding placards made in the shape of black hands with the words STOP THE OCCUPATION printed on them. I stand with them for, maybe, an hour, the last one of that day. And the fury this simple act of defiance provokes is incredible to behold. Drivers slow down to give the finger, honk their horns, and shout "Traitor!" at them. A man—young enough to be most of the women's middle-aged son—stands on the opposite curb and for the whole hour shouts how he hopes that they get raped. That rape is what they deserve. This is normal, they say, we're used to it, over the years we've had much worse. I admire their tenacity and their self-control. Occasionally he is flanked by young soldiers who smirk but do not speak. He garners slaps on the back and sometimes raises likewise vocal companions from the passing crowds. And he is completely comfortable where he stands, screaming these obscenities in public to a crowd of women who are silently asking their government to stop their illegal occupation, nothing more. The hate they provoke though, has much to say, I think, about their fellow citizens' consciences. Because everyone is implicated here; at one time or another, most have served. It reminds me of what another activist said, earlier in the day; that this visceral anger is a good sign because it means, somewhere inside, these angry people are ashamed, and that, at least, is a start.

As I settle down on the plane back, to the now almost unbearable freedom of my life, and start drinking the strongest drink I can find,

I realise I don't know how to begin understanding, never mind writing about, what I've seen and heard. I can liken it only to witnessing a people trapped in the mouth of a machine and knowing that, very soon, it's going to clamp its jaws shut. I think of the terrible courage of the people I have left behind. The Israeli peace activists who choose it, in spite of the social, political, and legal toll it takes, and the Palestinians, who are forced to live their every moment bravely because they have no choice. I fear what life holds for all of them and I know enough now to fear for their lives. And I fear the impossibility, even if one day the occupation ends, of their shared, or separate, future capacity to overcome this past.

Then I think of the car journey back from the Jordan Valley, when we had already passed through Jericho again. In the front seat the young girl opened her laptop up, and tried to find some signal, to prove to me that Arabic really does contain twenty-six synonyms for the word *love*. As we drove she found them listed on a website somewhere and, all the way back to Jerusalem then, one after another, she slowly read them out loud.

HIGH PLACES

HARI KUNZRU

Jerusalem was first established on the hill on which you are now standing, almost 4000 years ago, during the Canaanite period (Middle Bronze Age II). . . . A journey to the City of David is a journey to the source. The City of David was the first capital of the tribes of Israel and the spiritual and political center of the Jewish nation. Many of the books of the Bible were written here and from the small mound of the City of David came forth the belief in one God and the basic human values taught by the prophets that have inspired the entire world.

The City of David is the place where Jerusalem was born—the place where it all began.[*]

WHAT MORE MEANINGFUL PLACE ON EARTH COULD THERE BE than this? It seems extraordinary that archaeologists have pinpointed the site and a modern tourist facility has been built on it, so visitors can stand on the very spot where much of the Bible was composed, where David danced in ecstasy before the Lord, and the powerful idea of monotheism first made its way into world history. Yet here I am in East Jerusalem, reading a wall text, standing

---

[*] Text on the wall of the City of David archaeological site.

on a windy platform built out over a maze of ancient stone founda-
tions clinging to the side of a hill. I have returned to the source.

The City of David is an archaeological brand. In the gift store you
can buy City of David mugs, bags, jigsaw puzzles, coloring books,
a T-shirt with CITY OF DAVID: DIG IT! written in a fun, funky font.
The City of David lyre logo (1 Samuel 16:23, *"And it came to pass,
when the evil spirit from God was upon Saul, that David took an harp, and
played with his hand"*) is everywhere, on the uniform polo shirts of
the guides, on signs that hang from houses on the route of a history
walk that takes visitors through the streets near the site. The location
of a new dig is enclosed by boards with imagery of happy, smiling
people, boys on lyre-adorned Segways, friendly archaeologists in lyre
caps helping elated white children sieve and wash soil to recover
fragments of their Middle Eastern cultural heritage.

Monotheism's ground zero is just outside the so-called Dung Gate
of the old city of Jerusalem, near the Western Wall. Charities pay for
young diaspora Jews to come here, so they can learn about their past.
The government pays for soldiers to come here, so they can learn
about why they fight. From the lookout you can see the necropolis on
the side of Jabal al-Zaytun (otherwise known as the Mount of Olives)
and, on the hill opposite, a slightly down-at-the-heels-looking neigh-
borhood, with washing lines strung over flat roofs and trash tumbling
down a steep slope behind the houses. After a while you may notice
the minaret of a mosque. If you are there at prayer time something
startling flows over these stones, so saturated with Jewish history and
culture. Muezzins call from all around, their keening voices instruct-
ing the Muslim faithful: *Hasten to prayer, hasten to success, prayer is better
than sleep. . . .* It becomes apparent that there are mosques in several
nearby locations, not just on the opposite side of the hill.

Competing with the muezzins' amplified call, the tour guide
raises his voice. "David says, you know what? I feel so bad. I live in
a great palace here, made out of cedar. But the Ark of the Covenant,
the holiest thing imaginable, is just sitting in a tent. . . ." He's wear-
ing a *kippa* and carrying a red clothbound book of scripture, a prop
that seems unnecessary, for he narrates his story fluently, giving his
ancient kings and courtiers a folksy American-accented patter. As we
listen, I can feel Yoni Mizrachi fidgeting beside me.

"What are they actually looking at?" he whispers. "This place he's calling the palace of King David? Some stones, and a man telling a story. How do they know if he's telling the truth?" Mizrachi is an archaeologist who has spent his career working on excavations around Israel. While there is nothing to absolutely disprove their claims, in Mizrachi's opinion, "There is nothing here to tell them where they really are. Nothing to say what the purpose of all this is."

NADAV WEIMAN IS A BROODING, DARK-HAIRED THIRTY-YEAR-OLD WHO served as a sniper's spotter in an elite reconnaissance unit of the IDF. He came, he says, from a military family. It was expected that he would serve "at the tip of the spear." One of his jobs was to conduct so-called straw widow operations, taking over Palestinian homes all over the West Bank for use as temporary military posts. His team had the authority to choose any house that seemed suitable to them. Under cover of darkness, they would enter as quickly as possible, waking the family and concentrating them in one of the smaller rooms, usually a bathroom or one of the children's bedrooms. While one soldier stood guard, the others would open a tripod near the largest window, hang camouflage nets, and set up a sniper rifle and observation equipment. Their role was to provide cover for other units operating in the city. A straw widow could last overnight, or for two or three days. During that time, the family could not leave.

Nadav did this three or four times a week. He estimates that on any given night in the West Bank, there are probably ten units doing the same thing. Forty or fifty families a week. More than two thousand families a year, having the same experience, the soldiers breaking in, adrenalized and violent because they have no idea about what could be waiting for them in your house, perhaps smashing the lock on your front door, taking the window out of its frame, breaking things as they move your furniture. Your children terrified, having to ask permission to go to the toilet. Hours, even days, unable to go to work or to school. The rage that comes from helplessness, of being unable to protect those dearest to you, of seeing your parents deferring to the young conscripts, eighteen or nineteen years old, who are lounging about in your home.

The logic of the occupation doesn't see this metastasis of resentment as a negative. It is part of a tactic, the creation of "a sense of persecution" among the Palestinian population. I hear the phrase used several times by former soldiers. It is, it appears, an IDF term of art.

So what am I looking at?

A deep hole, beneath what was once a parking lot. I can see some walls, a few fragmentary columns, a mosaic floor. It's by far the most visually impressive part of the City of David site. I assume that I'm looking at the remains of ancient Judean houses.

—It's a Roman villa, says Yoni. From about the third-century CE. It was probably destroyed in an earthquake.

—So this isn't anything to do with David?

—No.

We walk back to the place where the tour guide was telling his breathless story about the ancient king.

—Well, says Yoni. We can say that's a wall. He pauses. In my admittedly limited dealings with archaeologists, I have come to know what that pause means. It is the scrupulous hesitation that signifies *As for the rest, we don't know.*

—A wall. A palace wall? The wall of the palace of King David?

—I would be inclined to say it dated to the twelfth or eleventh centuries BCE, and was constructed by the inhabitants we call Canaanites. It's possible that it dates to the tenth century BCE, which biblical tradition marks as the beginning of the House of David.

—But a palace wall.

—You can see it's a thick wall. Perhaps it had a defensive function.

Little by little, Yoni dismantles the origin story being retailed to the tourists by their guide. There is, in Yoni's opinion, no archaeological evidence to link this place to the biblical King David. No artifacts, no inscriptions. The site is a jumble of ruins from every period from the early bronze age to the Ottoman period. They don't exist in neat strata, but are jumbled together in ways that make assigning dates to individual features very difficult. There were, for example, significant remains from the period of the Umayyad Caliphate, but those have been removed, so that the focus of the site falls solely on the people whom modern Israelis are taught to claim as their ancestors. As for monotheism, there's the small matter of the female votive figurines, thousands of them, made of clay and found in strata from the times of the Kings of Judea. They have heavy breasts. They are assumed to have a religious function.

—Mother goddesses? From the time of David?

Yoni's pause seems to stretch out forever.

Five a.m. There's a fierce February chill in the air. Men are climbing out of minivans and running to get in line at the checkpoint, jostling as they enter a large, metal-roofed shed. They have their hoods pulled up, their hands jammed into their pockets. They smoke cigarettes and carry plastic bags containing their lunch. Thousands of Palestinians must pass through this place every morning, workers entering Jerusalem from the West Bank.

If the checkpoints and the so-called separation wall did not exist, the journey from Ramallah to Jerusalem would take around twenty minutes. As it is, for Palestinians it lasts several hours. For those requiring emergency medical care, the delay can be much more than an inconvenience. Down the road is another checkpoint, used by Jewish settlers, who can drive through freely, rarely having to stop for inspection. When erecting the wall, the Israeli planners made special environmental provisions, carefully moving a population of rare irises and creating tiny passages for animals. Many Palestinians were, on the other hand, cut off from their farmland or their water supply, or simply had their homes and businesses demolished. What traces of all this will archaeologists find a thousand years from now? What will they understand to have been the function of this structure?

> *So David dwelt in the fort, and called it the city of David. And*
> *David built round about from Millo and inward.*

2 Samuel 5:9

Once you've seen the ruins and perused the trinkets in the gift shop, you can walk out of the main site of the City of David, taking what appears to be an official trail down a street of picturesque stone houses. Sign boards bearing the ubiquitous lyre logo give their names: the Tirah House, the Tamar House. They have the feeling of land-marks, pieces of heritage. They also have prominent security features. Intercoms, heavy doors, high fences, multiple security cameras.

Once you've got used to the pleasing honeyed stone, the security cameras are the most prominent features of the streetscape, at least until you turn a corner and see that on the roof of one house is a guard post, manned by a sour-looking young security man with a semiautomatic weapon.

Why are all these precautions necessary, in a place where tour-ists are being encouraged to wander? The answer lies in the lyre. Before it was the logo of the City of David, the lyre was the logo of the organization that runs it, the Ir David Foundation, commonly known as Elad. Its founder, David Be'eri, is a former special forces commander who got to know the area during the first intifada, when his men conducted operations across the West Bank. Archaeology is not Elad's primary concern; or rather, archaeology is only a means to a political end. As the group puts it on its website:

> The Ir David Foundation is committed to continuing
> King David's legacy as well as revealing and connect-
> ing people to Ancient Jerusalem's glorious past through
> four key initiatives: archaeological excavation, tourism
> development, educational programming and residen-
> tial revitalization.

What is King David's legacy? Music? Smiting Philistines? It's a phrase with a feel-good ring but little content, except that it clearly has something to do with Jewish tradition. Behind the anodyne phrase *residential revitalization* hides Elad's primary agenda. The ruins that it has branded as the *Ursprung* of the Israelite people were found beneath Silwan, a Palestinian village that was annexed into Jerusalem in 1967. An Elad board member, Adi Mintz, told *Haaretz* in 2006 that the organization's goal was "to get a foothold in East Jerusalem and to create an irreversible situation in the holy basin around the

Old City." That is to say, Elad's purpose (as another spokesman put it, in conversation with a reporter for the *New York Times*) is to "Judaize" Silwan, acquiring homes and property by a variety of means and placing ideologically committed settlers in them to create a "Jewish presence." Coupled with the archaeological invocation of a primal Jewish past, the hope is that this will bind Silwan to Israel, so that in any future territorial negotiation it will appear to be a "natural" part of the Jewish state. The tendentious "educational programming" offered by the City of David, "geared towards Israeli students, adults and soldiers" to "reconnect them to their history and heritage" reinforces this message. Our history. Our land. Elad is a political project conceived by a trained military strategist, an apparatus for capturing territory.

Duvdevan is one of Israel's most mythologized military units. The nickname means "cherry," the fruit that goes on top of "the cream," as the IDF special forces like to term themselves. Established in 1986, shortly before the outbreak of the first intifada, Duvdevan was formed to infiltrate Palestinian urban areas undercover with the objective of identifying, locating, and then capturing or killing terrorists. Be'eri, who is a former student at yeshivas associated with the far right of the Israeli settler movement, became the unit's deputy commander. This is how he got to know Silwan, a neighborhood where his teams operated.

According to *Shady Dealings in Silwan*, a report commissioned by the Israeli NGO Ir Amim* about settlement activities in Silwan, after he left the military, Be'eri continued to move through the urban terrain of Silwan, sometimes posing as a tour guide. He looked for houses and land that had been passed back and forth in relatively recent history, land that had some documentary history of Jewish ownership. It was a feat of historical research that relied on two primary sources—records of a purchase made by Baron Edmond de Rothschild in the early twentieth century on behalf of the Palestine

---

* Following the publication of the report authored by journalist Meron Rapoport, Elad filed a lawsuit in Israel against Ir Amim. The suit was settled, without retraction.

Jewish Colonization Association, and records of land that had belonged to a community of Yemeni Jews that had formed in the late nineteenth century and been violently dispersed in the wake of Arab rioting in 1929.

According to Ir Amim's research, Be'eri got to know the terrain inch by inch, meticulously recording any property he felt he could plausibly claim as Jewish. He secured a quasi-official role as a locator of Jewish property for the Jewish National Fund, the group that flyers American neighborhoods with pictures of happy folk planting trees, and which has a deep involvement in evictions and forced displacement. Be'eri also cultivated contacts in the Ministry of Housing, the Office of the Custodian of Absentee Property, and the contractors overseeing the redevelopment of East Jerusalem. While he was identifying his target houses, Be'eri secured financial support to "Judaize" additional parts of the historic basin of East Jerusalem. When he was ready, he acted systematically, petitioning various authorities to have Palestinian residents removed from their homes.

Many houses, many lawsuits. Litigation lasting years. The Ir Amim report describes the practices used by the settler groups: Palestinians cajoled into selling, shabby houses in Silwan bought by Palestinian front men or anonymous front companies, companies with neutral names and pockets deep enough to pay extravagant sums, many times what those houses would otherwise be worth.

Gradually Elad has become almost inseparable from the Israeli state in Silwan. The Jewish National Fund signed over its absentee interests to the settlers for a nominal sum, and the legal and planning systems worked in concert to grow the City of David inside the community. One house, five houses, a dozen houses, family homes suddenly declared vacant, or their owners absentees. The letter of the law, always backed up by force. They would arrive and take possession of the expropriated houses under the protection of guards, who stood watch as they mounted the cameras and welded heavy security doors onto their new forward operating bases.

For Elad, the cherry on top is control of the past. Of the urgency of the historian's task, Walter Benjamin famously wrote that one must be convinced that "not even the dead will be safe from the enemy" if that enemy is victorious. In 1997, over the initial cautions of the Israel Antiquities Authority, Elad took over responsibility for the archaeological ruins in Silwan from the Israel Land Authority. Eventually, however, the Israel Antiquities Authority came on board with the transfer of a supposedly important site to a private nonprofit organization, which, in the eyes of some, had little or no credibility in the world of academic archaeology, and in 2008 the director stated that he couldn't see a problem with Jews discovering more about their heritage and "didn't like bringing politics into archaeology." Elad was now the law in Silwan, a law always tending in one direction, towards the erosion of the Palestinian presence on its hillsides.

There are facts and there are facts on the ground. Ancient history grows out of the barrel of a gun, and reportedly out of offshore accounts in Panama. Between 2006 and 2013, Elad took in $115 million in donations. At the opening of the City of David visitor's center, the guests included Roman Abramovich, the owner of Chelsea football club, Lev Leviev, who made his fortune processing and mining diamonds in Angola and apartheid-era South Africa, and the former Soviet refusenik Natan Sharansky. The Nobel Peace Prize recipient Elie Wiesel served as chair of Elad's International Advisory Council.

PALESTINIANS FIND IT ALMOST IMPOSSIBLE TO GET BUILDING PERMITS IN East Jerusalem, but in Silwan Ateret Cohanim, another settler group operating in Silwan, has thrown up a six-storey tower, far taller than anything around it. It is a fortress, with metal bars on the windows and a huge Israeli flag draped down the facade. The reality of life for its inhabitants is grim, surrounded by people who hate them and whom they seem to yearn to displace. They have named the place Beit Yonatan, after the imprisoned Israeli spy Jonathan Pollard. One afternoon I watch the children returning from preschool, in a van with wire mesh over the windows, spattered with paint and dented by stones. A border police patrol waits outside the house, alongside a team of private security guards. A father emerges from the house and welcomes his little son with a tender kiss. I have a boy that age. I kiss him just like that. I cannot help but ask what sort of man would choose to put his family in such a situation. A dozen armed guards to get you in and out of your home? Only a fanatic would make his child endure such a life. In justification, the settlers point to the historical presence of Yemeni Jews in Silwan, Zionists who arrived in the 1880s and were expelled in the upheavals of the early twentieth century. The Palestinians of Silwan tell stories of settlers attacking their children, of police personnel who have orders only to discipline them, never their Jewish antagonists. Their own violence is clearly visible on the bodywork of a settlers' school bus, the strain on the wan little faces peering out from behind the mesh.

In 2010 David Be'eri was filmed running over two children from Silwan with his car. Elad claimed its director had been surrounded by a stone-throwing lynch mob. The video showed four boys with stones, two of whom were hit and injured. An investigation cleared Be'eri of wrongdoing.

A PALESTINIAN IS NEVER INNOCENT. THE TECHNICAL TERM USED IN THE Israeli military is *uninvolved*. A Palestinian is either involved or uninvolved. But in this place, who can really say they are uninvolved? I meet Palestinians. I listen to them discuss politics. All I can do is record, scribble down fragments of a conversation that has been going on for half a century.

—We need a Palestinian Gandhi.

—Are you joking? The Gandhi times have gone. How can you have Gandhi with these settlers?

—Gandhi took thirty years.

—Thirty years! We don't have the luxury of time.

Conversations in cafés, in a Ramallah conference room, a chopped-down olive grove, a Red Cross tent on farmland in the South Hebron Hills.

—If it's an occupation, it needs to end so we can build our state. If we're too weak to make a state then it's a civil rights movement and we need to gain our civil rights. Our right to freedom of movement, our water rights. . . .

Conversations. Burning cigarettes. Sipping tea.

—Once we were part of the General Union of Palestinian Women. We were one of the founding organizations of the PLO. Women participated in all forms of struggle. After Oslo we were very optimistic. We thought we were heading towards the end of the occupation. The implementation of the two-state solution. We were aiming very high. We were looking for secular laws in which the rights of women are respected. But the role of women has been deteriorating since Oslo. I maintain we had much more democracy under armed struggle than we do now. We were activists. Now we are NGO employees. Before Oslo, these organizations were the government of the Palestinian people, giving services, mobilizing people. With the arrival of the donor community they became more professional, they became the agents of the donors. Now I spend my time writing reports and arguing about where I put the donor's logo.

Smoking, looking out the window at a communications antenna, a line of red-roofed settlement houses on a hill. Her eyes moving back and forth, as if looking for a place to put her bitterness.

—I have only one child. I had to wait a long time. Fifteen years. I had to have a lot of operations. And I am not ready for him to die because of some stupid Israeli soldier. So sometimes I keep him inside. But I cannot keep him inside. He is a teenage boy. He wants to go. What can I do? The settlers are running Israel now. They want to kick us out of the country. I see it coming very soon. Now the world is concerned with Syria and the Israelis are showing their true face. They are savages. They will kick us out. I bet none of these human rights defenders in Europe will say a word. The least we can do, we are doing. Which is to stay here.

Conversations, cigarettes, sipping bitter tea.

[Speakers: Ala Hlehel and Lama Hourani, Sam Bahour, Lama Hourani]

I am in Hebron, standing in the "sterilized zone" of Shuhada Street. It is a ghost town, the bustling market emptied of people, the shops sealed. This is my house, shouts the settler at my colleague, the sardonic Palestinian journalist. I have better papers than you do. I have title to my house. I bet you don't have papers.

I ask the settler if he was born in Hebron. No, he says. Brookline, Massachusetts.

AH, PAPERS. LOOK OUT OVER THIS UNHOLY LAND AND THINK OF PAPERS. Deeds, assignments, documents with signatures and seals. It is early spring. The valleys are green, but the hilltops are barren and rocky. Look out over this land and think of law. How do you take the land, if you believe it is yours by right? You need to do it by law. You need papers. Throughout the West Bank, almost every relevant agency of government collaborates to create or perpetuate insecurity for Palestinian landowners. Elad is far from the only organization that solicits money from sentimental diaspora Jews and uses it to research and fight court cases, dunam of land by dunam of land, house by house. This is not your house. Before it was your house it was my house. Now it will be my house again. My house, our house, my people's house, my father's house, with its tiled red roof and its guard post and its security camera.

But there is more land. Land that is cultivated by Palestinian fellaheen, grazed by Bedouin herders. To take it you need papers, so you look back further in time, until you find older laws that will justify what you want to do. Look back to Ottoman times, to the Land Code of 1858. For the Ottomans, to own land meant to exploit it, to cultivate it. All uncultivated land reverted to the state. Look again at the land. At the green below, the rocky hilltops. Those hilltops are not cultivated land. Invoke the old Ottoman laws and, at a stroke, all those high places now belong to the state. The state can now give it to those who will make use of it, who will build red-roofed houses to look down on the old fellaheen villages.

The land belongs to the cultivator. Who cultivates the land? Come down from your new red-roofed house, with your automatic rifle slung on your back. Come down and ask to see the farmer's papers. Does he have title? Does the shepherd have a paper to prove his right to the pasture? He says he has always been here. Before his always comes your always. Before it was his house it was your house. Come down from your red-roofed house and bring a court case. While the case is in progress, the farmer can't carry on cultivating the land. That wouldn't be just. It wouldn't be right to let him farm land that might not even be his. If he tries, you chase him off with your gun. Perhaps the state decides this unfarmed land is vacant and reassigns it to you. Perhaps you begin to cultivate it yourself. You can cultivate it by planting a seedling in a rusty barrel and placing it on the ground you wish to claim. You don't have to water it, or do anything much at all. In the eyes of the law you are a cultivator, making the land bloom.

Ali is a shepherd. I meet him in the South Hebron Hills, a middle-aged man with a flock of twenty or thirty goats. He grazes them by the roadside, a narrow strip of green. He can't go up the hill, because he will be trespassing. He can't graze them in the field with the stunted seedlings in the rusty barrels. Once that was his village's pasture, but not anymore. It belongs to the settlers, who are making it bloom. There is good pasture near the settlement, but he consti- tutes a security risk, and he fears they would shoot him if he went there. So he uses the strip by the roadside, where the trucks thunder past, bringing produce from the settlements to sell in Tel Aviv and Jerusalem.

This is not Ali's land. Maybe it never was. The land always be- longed to the men from Brooklyn and Melbourne and Johannesburg and Kiev. All those years that his father and grandfather roamed these hills grazing their goats, and they never realized that the real owners had yet to arrive.

TWO ORTHODOX BOYS, WEARING *KIPPA*S AND BLACK TROUSERS AND DRIP- dry shirts and scuffed thick-soled shoes. They stand on the wall at the viewpoint at the top of Mount Scopus, surveying the Jordan Valley far below. In the distance lies the Dead Sea, just a sliver of hazy gray blue. Nearer you can see a black ribbon of road, and the settlement of Ma'aleh Adumim. One of the boys laughs and begins to stride down the hill. The other, shivering slightly in the cold, slips on a green New York Jets sweatshirt.

—Hey, he says, turning to us. Is one of you a tour guide?

He speaks English with an American accent. Hagit asks him what he wants to know.

—My buddy is walking down to the highway. How long will that take? He says he can do it in five minutes.

—It will surely take him longer than that. Maybe twenty minutes, half an hour? I've never done it.

—Okay. Thanks.

He stands and watches. After a while he takes out his phone and begins to shoot video, talking to his friend, the hands-free wire dangling down by his waist.

—I'm looking right at you! Yes, I am. Pose! That's right.

This is what mastery looks like. Two carefree boys, surveying the terrain. Who gets to survey the land from high places? Who gets to walk down to the highway, ignoring paths or boundaries? Who gets to walk just as far as he wishes to go?

> This is why that [sic] we opted for the methodology of walking through walls . . . like a worm that eats its way forward, emerging at points and then disappearing. We were thus moving from the interior of homes to their exterior in a surprising manner and in places we were not expected, arriving from behind and hitting the enemy that awaited us behind a corner.

The speaker is an Israeli paratroop commander called Aviv Kochavi, interviewed by the architectural theorist Eyal Weizman in 2004. During the 2002 attack on Nablus, Brigadier General Kochavi's troops advanced into the city through aboveground "tunnels" which they blasted through the dense urban fabric of houses, shops, and workshops. The soldiers avoided the streets and alleys of the city, moving horizontally through party walls and vertically through holes blasted in floors and ceilings. Thermal imaging technologies allowed them to "see" adversaries on the other side of solid barriers, and 7.62 mm rounds could penetrate to kill on the other side. Much fighting took place in private homes, and the civilian population was profoundly traumatized.

A retired brigadier general called Shimon Naveh, who taught at the IDF's Operational Theory Research Institute, told Weizman of the IDF's interest in the philosophical work of Gilles Deleuze and Felix Guattari, particularly the concepts of "smooth" and "striated" space:

In the IDF we now often use the term "to smooth out space" when we want to refer to operation in a space as if it had no borders. We try to produce the operational space in such a manner that borders do not affect us.

Elad's multidimensional project to smooth out the Palestinian space of Silwan seems entirely continuous with these French-theoretical military tactics. They are an organization that has grown out of war, a very modern full-spectrum war in which the distinction between combatants and the civilian population is blurred, and the battlefield could potentially be everywhere, including inside civilian homes. Elad's attack is slow, but it is happening. It is unfolding at the pace of spades and excavators, the pace of planning hearings and court dates and fundraising galas, an assault on an urban area slowed down to the speed of archaeology.

Elad's latest tactic in Silwan is burrowing. It has already built a tunnel (billed as "the pilgrims' route") to connect the City of David to the Temple Mount, and the highlight of their tourist offerings is the chance to walk underground along part of an ancient aqueduct system, through which water still flows. Other tunnels are confidently identified as the work of King Herod, or as hiding places for Jewish rebels against the Romans. The new tunnels (no doubt supplied with their own attractive biblical backstories) are worming in all directions under Palestinian Silwan. Part of their routes are secret. Residents complain that they are seeing cracks in their walls, in the foundations of their houses. They wonder whether it is because of the tunnels that in several places the streets have collapsed.

IN THE TOURIST SHOPS IN JERUSALEM'S OLD CITY YOU CAN BUY PICTURES of Temple Mount with al-Aqsa and the Dome of the Rock airbrushed out. You can buy pictures of the Temple itself, coming down over the Western Wall like a returning UFO, a structure made of Hebrew text, of scripture.

In Silwan there is—or was—a wall, the front wall of a house on which a muralist had carefully painted, in English, a famous line of the great Palestinian poet Mahmoud Darwish. *My homeland is not a suitcase and I am no traveler.* The worm soon arrived in the guise of municipal workers, sent to erase the "graffiti." Local people prevented them. So the mural stayed, at least for a while.

—June 2016

STORYLAND

LORRAINE ADAMS

O little town of Bethlehem,
How still we see thee lie;
Above thy deep and dreamless sleep
The silent stars go by:
Yet in thy dark streets shineth
The everlasting Light;
The hopes and fears of all the years
Are met in thee tonight.

'M A CHILD, AND THIS CAROL IS MY FAVORITE. I WANT TO SINK INTO ITS
dreamless sleep beneath its silent stars. Also, it's about me in a way
"Joy to the World" isn't, because Bethlehem is about a bambino
born in an inch of a town, just like I was in a miner's hospital in a
Pennsylvania coal patch. The story implies that insignificant begin-
nings aren't determinative. It's outlandish but possibly true: yes, even
a child swaddled in a feeding trough for animals can embody the
hopes and fears of all the years.

I visit the actual Bethlehem in 2011. I arrive during the day, so
there aren't any stars. The only everlasting light I can locate is the sun
bleaching out the mundane sprawl of asphalt roads. I squint under its
broiling heat, walking across Manger Square to the Church of the

Nativity. Inside, tourists are queued to kiss the spot where the holy manger is believed to have been—a dubiously authentic location at best, seeing that it was chosen out of several caves rumored to be the birthplace of Christ three hundred years later by the frail and confused eighty-year-old mother of Emperor Constantine.

I never make it to the manger. The church itself, divided into quarters by quarreling Christian denominations, lacks the beneficent mystery I'd hoped to find. Their centuries-old antipathy reaches a risible donnybrook a few months after my visit when a Greek Orthodox monk inadvertently pokes his broom into the Armenian Apostolic part of the church floor, prompting a mop brawl between sixty clergymen that Palestinian police have to break up with batons.

After the church, I take a five-minute walk down passageways lined with souvenir shops selling Baby Jesus T-shirts and crèches made in China. Skeevy men try to hustle me to buy rosaries. To avoid them, I hurry out of the kitsch toward open air.

There I find the sublime. I'm in awe. I'd heard about it. Now I see it. It's a wall. It's so high, made of sequoia-big panels of concrete, that I feel like I'm a toddler all over again. At thirty feet, it's roughly the same height as the walls I saw as a kid around Pennsylvania's Eastern State Penitentiary, the prison that my mom told me housed Al Capone. Only now I'm on the inside, smack up against it—my hand touches it from time to time—this rough, matte gray, articulated python of irrepressible power. I can't stop walking along it. It's fourteen miles long around two-thirds of Bethlehem, but I want to do the whole thing. Plus, it's covered with the most opulent graffiti I've ever seen, far better stuff than the subway cars of my teenage days in 1970s Manhattan. I come upon a clever reversal: the artist Banksy has painted a girl in a pink dress and pigtails frisking an Israeli soldier. I look above them and see four feet of electrified wire on the crest of this whale of a wall. Every so often I pass a guard tower where young soldiers from Israel look out through small, dirty windows.

BETHLEHEM IS DANGEROUS. THAT'S WHAT THE WALL SAYS. IT SAYS TERrorists live in Bethlehem. Before the Wall, they got in their cars and blew themselves up on buses in Jerusalem or Tel Aviv. Everything about that is awful. But even worse, they incinerate children with these suicide vests. One of them is a girl named Hodaya Asraf. You can find her life story on YouTube. Here's Hodaya as an infant, a pumpkin of adorability. Here are her little brothers holding her hands while she toddles in a pink-trimmed onesie on an outdoor deck. Here's her grandma from Greece in a scarf bobby-pinned to her head, nuzzling precious Hodaya. Here's her mother and father bussing her at her birthday parties, here's balloons, here's bad cake, here's dancing. Here's her bedroom with the purple beanbag chair. Little Hodaya, dead at thirteen, her killer, twenty-two, a Jew-hating madman, who came from Bethlehem.

All you can say is build the Wall. All you can think is that Hodaya's story about Bethlehem is the new Bethlehem. The Bethlehem of "O Little Town of Bethlehem" is gone. The guy who wrote it came to Bethlehem on a horse in 1865. It took him two hours to ride the six miles from Jerusalem that now takes twenty minutes. Never mind that it takes Palestinians four times that long to cross checkpoints and take circuitous routes along the Wall.

You should listen to another story about Bethlehem. It's from the Torah. It's about Rachel. She went into labor on the way from Jerusalem. "Rachel died and was buried on the way to Efrat, which is Bethlehem." (Genesis 35:19) But the midwife told her she'd given birth to a son right before her soul left her, so that was a consolation. Not much of a story? There's more. There's an ancient commentary called a midrash that embroiders on the story, adding that her other son Yosef prayed by her grave when he was on his way to slavery in Egypt. "Mother, my mother who gave birth to me, wake up, arise and see my suffering." Rachel replied, "Do not fear. Go with them, and God will be with you."

IT'S JUNE 9, 2016, AND I'M ON MY WAY TO RACHEL'S TOMB. I'M COMING from Jerusalem, just as she did. I'm in a Kia and I've got a guide who says he's an anarchist and a former Israeli Defense Force soldier. He looks a lot like Jesus Christ, or at least like the one painted in the sixth century in Saint Catherine's Monastery on Mount Sinai, not the blue-eyed one hanging on the wall in my grandmother's coal patch kitchen that was the handiwork in 1941 of an advertising illustrator from Chicago named Warner Sallman. That Jesus has sold five hundred million copies.

When we get close to Bethlehem I see the Wall looming ahead. I can't help it, I feel the same reverential dread and awe I did five years ago. This side of the Wall around Bethlehem is pristine, no graffiti. We take a banked turn and all of a sudden the Wall is on both sides of us. I'm in a cement canyon. It curves for some time, and then we come to a three-way intersection. We're here.

There are so many children. There are the soldiers, who have to be at least eighteen but look more like sixteen to me. They wear olive uniforms with heavy military gear sagging around their skinny waists. They suffer from acne, carry machine guns, and have expressions that convey that they know they should be serious but why should they because there are maybe ten new clean buses parked in the cement canyon intersection and pouring out of them are boys in yarmulkes doing what boys do, which is shoving each other, flinging themselves against each other, pointing, snarking, shouting, or moping. The point of being there is to do these things and not to go to Rachel's Tomb on a class field trip. The point is to be noticeably cool or safely ignored. The girls are doing what girls the world over do. They stand in clusters watching the boys.

I can't see the tomb. It's behind a fortress that grows out of the Wall. My guide points to a red squiggle on the map, a Muslim cemetery, and a refugee camp called Aida. I look back at the scene on the ground. All of this—the special road, the walled canyon, the walled intersection, the fortress, and the soldiers—so Israeli schoolchildren can go to a tomb of a woman they believe symbolizes the holiest mother of Judaism and do so unmolested by Palestinian children throwing stones. It's not that simple, according to politicians, diplomats, military analysts, historians, theologians and cultural critics, but it's also that simple.

So let's see what this tomb looks like. I go through the door for women. At first all I see is a small room with women seated on benches, mumbling Hebrew from palm-sized prayer books. One or two have their necks thrown back and the little books' pages rest open on their faces, covering eyes, nose, and mouth. Some are up against a perforated screen and they're davening so strenuously it looks as if the bitty books will start flying. Through the screen I see a sarcophagus covered in white satin. Some of the women remind me of Mennonites, the plain people of the Pennsylvania Dutch on my father's side of the family. They wear turbans that look like bonnets, long gathered skirts, and prairie aprons. Some are praying to have sons because Rachel did after she was childless for a long time. Even so, just like Jesus's manger, this may not be the spot Rachel's buried. Some archeologists think she was buried north of Jerusalem near what is today called al-Ram.

I see the boys outside at the buses again and remember Moayyad al-Jawarish. His story is in a book about Bethlehem written by a former *Newsweek* journalist named Joshua Hammer. I recall how Moayyad lived just outside Aida camp, a few yards from where I am right now. It's 2000 and he's thirteen. He's the son of an unemployed pipe fitter and the goalie on his junior high soccer team. His parents told him not to join a schoolboy march to Rachel's Tomb to protest Israel closing it to anyone under forty-five. He promises them he won't. But then, a cool kid from a tougher camp called Duheisha casually asks Moayyad if he's going. It would be embarrassing to look weak in front of this boy. So he joins about four hundred boys with backpacks singing Palestinian songs as they walk-run towards the tomb. A boy from Duheisha camp smashes the windows of a Ford Transit van, sprinkles gasoline inside, and throws in lit matches. Quickly, Israeli soldiers surround the area. Their snipers get on top of a Kando gas station. Moayyad and his best friend are freaked out so they scramble to a field to lie on their bellies in the high weeds. But then Moayyad's best friend gets a call on his cell phone: twenty soldiers are coming through the Muslim cemetery behind them. "Time to go home," he tells Moayyad. They stand up and start running. Straightaway, his best friend doesn't feel Moayyad beside him. He looks around, confused. Then he sees Moayyad, facedown in the weeds. What is he doing? Is he stupid? They need to get out of there. He yells at him to get up. He drops down to the ground, out of breath, spitting, "Moayyad!" Then he sees the blood, shiny and spreading in the yellowed under-grass. He bursts into tears. He doesn't understand completely yet that a sharpshooter drilled a round into Moayyad's head, a shot so precisely delivered that Moayyad was dead when he hit the ground.

I'M JUST OUTSIDE AIDA CAMP IN BETHLEHEM, WHERE MOAYYAD LIVED, on the other side of the wall. There's a metal panel in the wall; when Israeli soldiers lift it by remote control, you find yourself at Rachel's Tomb. Aida camp boys still come here from time to time to demonstrate. I look up and see cameras. Soldiers sit in Jerusalem and watch the boys. When needed, they use a slender cannon attached to the top of the wall near the electrified wire to spray the boys with a liquid called the Skunk. I experienced its aroma on a dirt road where boys demonstrate north of here. It smells like sewage and sulfur, and not surprisingly, skunk. The Israeli research and development company Odortec developed it in cooperation with the Israeli police department, to replace "conventional tactics—from physical force all the way to teargas and water cannons." Its website says it's nontoxic, organic, and drinkable.

I have a Palestinian guide now. This one is tall, gray, and distinguished. He reminds me of a professor, with his white polo shirt tucked into his pressed khakis. He says he was on this street walking during the weekly Friday demonstration when he got sprayed with the Skunk. He wasn't throwing rocks. He was going to a store. It took multiple showers and three days' time for the putrid stink to leave his body. He's matter-of-fact about this. He's not a complainer. As we walk he says he's not so sure the Israeli soldiers prefer the Skunk over tear gas. "I went on YouTube and saw a video of them saying, 'We will throw tear gas at you until all of you die—children, women, old people.' And so on. I hear this myself coming from them. So that's the kind of war we have over here."

Now we're inside the camp. It feels like a miniature town created especially for children—the United Nations first set up tents here, then concrete sheds thirty-four-feet square to shelter a family. Lots of them are painted sherbet colors to relieve the monotony. The bumpy road's so narrow it doesn't look like it was made for grown-up cars.

The hush comes from the fact that it's a Friday during Ramadan. Everyone is fasting, not even letting themselves have a glass of water. They'll drink and eat after sunset. I can sense everyone around me conserving energy.

Parents often excuse their children from fasting, so here are two boys huffing on bikes. One has training wheels. Four boys are playing marbles on the street near a manhole cover. A fourteen-year-old girl looks chic in black leggings and black T-shirt. She's fasting. Are you hungry? She shrugs. "No." Are you thirsty? She shrugs. "No." What's it like living here? She shrugs. "I like it." What do you want to be when you grow up? She looks off into the near distance as if I'm an idiot. "A teacher."

Farther along we happen on a friend of my guide. He's what my miner grandfather would have called a working stiff. He hasn't shaved and his beard is growing in with flecks of gray. He's carrying two rubber hoses in his hand to fix his mother-in-law's gas oven. And he has a story to tell. "The situation is very bad. My family were shepherds over there," he says motioning to a place over the Wall, which has now reared up again to our right. An artist, not Banksy this time, has painted twenty-foot-high boys throwing rocks at the actual guard tower.

"Our land was taken by the settlement of Efrat," this working stiff tells me. "They confiscated it."

How long did his family own this land?

"Since the time of the Turkish people."

The Ottoman Turks ruled over the land where we're standing from roughly 1486 until 1917, when they were trounced by the British in a brief campaign. When Israel was created in 1948, jurisdiction over the fields of this working stiff's family fell to Jordan. In 1967, Israel defeated Egypt, Syria, Iraq, and Jordan in the Six-Day War, wresting the Gaza Strip and Sinai from Egypt and the Golan Heights from Syria. Jordan lost East Jerusalem and the West Bank, which contains Bethlehem and this man's fields. That's when the occupation, now in its fiftieth year, began.

I turn to my working stiff and ask, What's been your experience with the settlers from Efrat?

He gestures west toward the water reservoirs associated with King Solomon of Ecclesiastes. "I was working near Solomon's Pools. On building a new pumping station." His tone is nonchalant. "The settlers from Efrat came," he says. "They threw stones at me."

Were you hurt?

"The settlers were there, so the Israeli soldiers came."

That must have been a relief.

He shrugs. "Not really."

Well, they protected you from the settlers.

"They came to protect the settlers. They hit me with tear gas and shot at me. I was lucky. I got away."

PALM TREES ARE SWAYING IN THE SOFT WIND, LOUNGE MUSIC IS PLAYING, and customers fill the round glass tables. Young Israeli Defense Force veterans are sharing stories about their tours of duty on the veranda of the Ambassador Hotel in East Jerusalem.

Yehuda Shaul, now thirty-three and a giant of a man with a bushy beard and steel-rimmed spectacles, served in Bethlehem in 2002 when settlers and soldiers attacked the working stiff. "We have settlers and Palestinians who operate under different legal systems. Even though under international law our mission is to protect the Palestinians. As soldiers in the field, our mission was not that. It's to protect settlers."

And yes, 2002 was also the year thirteen-year-old Hodaya died in the bombed bus. "It's March, we call it Black March," Yehuda begins his story. "Almost every single day a bus explodes in Israel and you can't escape it. It's a Wednesday night, Passover, there's a suicide bomb in the Park Hotel, thirty Israelis are murdered. My phone rings. I'm called to duty. All of a sudden the doubts vanish. This is why we're serving. To protect our country and get terrorists. Not protect crazy settlers." His unit operated in Ramallah during Operation Defensive Shield and was later ordered to join different operations, among them the Deterrence Path operation in Bethlehem for three weeks in June 2002. One night stands out.

"We're enforcing curfew. Driving the streets of Bethlehem in our armored troop vehicles. Nobody's on the street, nothing's going on. We come up on a Palestinian kid, four or five years old, eating watermelon up on a balcony. My deputy commanding officer says something like, 'He's collecting intelligence on us.' I think, 'He can't be serious.' Then he throws a tear-gas grenade at the kid."

"Why?" I ask, startled.

"Why not?" Yehuda shrugs.

So it was sheer depravity? Maybe there's something I'm not understanding.

"Sheer depravity."

He goes on. "So we storm a house. In a few minutes the whole house was destroyed and broken to pieces. After fortysomething minutes we found a pistol and a cartridge from an AK-47. There was lots of excitement, 'We found a weapon!' The company officer shows up, he was a decent guy, he came in, I still remember I was standing at the entrance to the house, he saw all the destruction, he said to no one really, to himself, 'Why does it always need to look like this?' I heard him, I said to myself, 'Wow. He's completely right.' I froze there for a minute and when we came back to the base he put the entire company in a room and he screamed at us and showed us a documentary about American officers who murdered a Vietnamese village in My Lai. And I was crying."

Another person at the table wants to know about the everyday tension, not the dramatic incidents.

This time Ori Erez answers. He's twenty-nine now and works as a plant biologist. "In my experience there was no tension, because imagine yourself, encountering, oh, I don't know—a cockroach. Is there tension? You're big and strong, and he's . . . not. He can run away maybe, but in the end when it comes to one-on-one he doesn't have a chance. That's how I felt. I was always on the right side of the gun. And they were on the wrong side of the gun."

Another vet who recently served, Dean Issacharoff, adds, "Look, you are being fed 24/7 that this is the single greatest thing that ever happened, that the Jewish nation can now—never again, like the Holocaust, never again—and you're being shown how strong, how big and strong Israeli troops are and they are so good and righteous and do the right thing and so you never question it . . . I told it to my soldiers and I told it to myself and I actually believed it."

MY MOTHER WAS THE DAUGHTER OF A LITHUANIAN COAL MINER, AND she had no illusions about what our family would have done during the Holocaust if they'd remained in the rural town of Alytus instead of immigrating to Pennsylvania in 1905. Maybe she was realistic because she saw concentration camp newsreels when she was only thirteen. Throughout her life she read any book on the Holocaust she could find. I remember her sharing *The Book of Sorrow* by Yosif Levinson. He described how armed Lithuanians murdered 1,279 Jewish children, women, and men and disposed of their bodies in big trenches in the Vidzgiris Forest.

No matter where my mother was, she wanted to know how and why the unthinkable could happen. So when we finally went to Lithuania, she made a point to see the Vilnius prison where the Soviets tortured members of the Lithuanian resistance. We were there around the time the photographs of Abu Ghraib were released. As we stood in a cell with hooks on the walls where they hung prisoners, she said: *All of us anywhere are capable of the worst.*

A few years later, when my husband was wooing me, one of the first things he showed me was the letter on onionskin paper his father had sent to his mother when his unit was among those liberating Dachau. Milton gave Harriet every detail he could of what he witnessed, and he closed by saying, "If you see any of this in the newsreels, it's true, it's not propaganda."

My husband's family had immigrated to the Lower East Side of Manhattan at the turn of the last century. Relatives who hadn't left Romania perished in the Holocaust. We decided one summer to see Auschwitz-Birkenau. We'd spent the day and at the end of it walked along the train tracks that led to the gas chambers. We paused as the sun set over the ruins of the crematoria.

We heard singing. We followed the sound, and it led us to nine or ten teenagers, who'd formed a circle with their arms on one another's shoulders draped with Israeli flags. They stood on the charred ground and were singing the *Hatikvah*, Israel's national anthem. *Hatikvah* means *hope* in Hebrew. The poem it was based on was written in Romania in 1877, not long after *O Little Town of Bethlehem* was composed.

> *Our hope is not yet lost*
> *The ancient hope*
> *To return to the land of our fathers*
> *The city where David encamped.*

TO GET TO THE SETTLEMENT OF EFRAT FROM THE CITY OF DAVID, A HIGH-way drive of fifteen minutes is involved. The Wall soars on the right. In the jumble of development, I learn to identify settlements two ways. They are built on hills and always have terra-cotta roofs. Maybe they're trying to evoke Tuscany or Andalusian Spain. As the car zooms south, the vibe becomes sterile; thousands of identical domiciles accordion into the mountaintops, forming a ring around Bethlehem. If the block called E1 gets built as planned, they'll reach to the Dead Sea, bisecting the Palestinian homeland.

The entrance to Efrat is west and south of Bethlehem. I realize as we drive up to the security booth that somewhere along the way the Wall disappeared. I see a pole barring our way attached to the booth, but whoever's in it doesn't stop us, just flips the pole upward. I've seen better security in gated communities in Florida. We coast past landscaped terraces with majestic pine trees, delicate flowering bushes, weeping figs.

City Hall feels like Portland, Oregon; it's thoroughly secular, satisfyingly rustic. To be honest, everything looks perfect. The hallway's aglow with indirect lighting. Through a sequence of glass doors I see unremarkable people peaceably conducting city hall business in well-designed rooms. Here's the mayor's office. His secretary is wearing that long-sleeve T-shirt under a short-sleeve top I've seen around; it's in fashion for Orthodox ladies. Her bangs poke out of a white knit beret that doesn't do much for her. But she couldn't be nicer.

She ushers me into Mayor Oded Revivi's office, a corner one, with glass windows overlooking the planned splendor that is Efrat. A cobbled sidewalk disappears into a sea of green trees like the yellow brick road, while beyond it agricultural fields fall in graduated slopes along a valley to the horizon. A few clouds in the blue sky, but not many.

In comes the mayor. No signs of fanaticism, just a preppy button-down, navy trousers, and black loafers. It's clear right off that Oded's sort of handsome and definitely funny. He gets a satellite map of Efrat, and starts in.

"Established in 1983, with a city plan of being a city of thirty thousand people. Today in Efrat we have ten thousand people. It hasn't reached its full potential yet." But wait, after years of settlement building freezes under George W. Bush and Barack Obama, Israel declared some Palestinian land as "state land," thereby performing the legal sleight of hand to make Efrat bigger and let it eat into the Bethlehem governorate. The Israeli government granted 1,100 permits for new dwellings, which, Oded shares, "is extremely unique and extremely outstanding. There's no city in the whole of Judea and Samaria that got so many building permits. Some say because of my political connections. I tend to put that in doubt."

Oded, born in Jerusalem and a lawyer by profession, came to Efrat in 1994 after he married. His Messianic reason? They couldn't afford to buy a house in Jerusalem. Their four-bedroom Efrat apartment with a garden would have been double the price in Jerusalem. So if it's not his political connections that won Efrat the right to expand, if it's not to fulfill a biblical yearning for Judea Samaria, what is it? "Because we didn't build for a long time, there were a lot of building plans that had passed the preliminary stages that were already to be implemented to be built immediately.

"So when you came from Jerusalem," he's saying, "you saw on the left-hand side the most remarkable, outstanding candidate for many architectural awards, the security fence. It's there. You can't not notice." The Wall. He calls it a security fence. But still, he's going right to the heart of the matter.

"It was supposed to be built over here," he says, pointing to the map. "They never completed it. This was the first place where Arabs and Jews united together against building the fence under the belief that you don't need high fences to create good neighbors."

It's hard not to like Oded and his pragmatic belief in his own essential goodness. I want to jostle along buoyantly with him, partaking of the brotherhood between him and his Palestinian neighbors. See, Efrat has olive groves inside city limits that their Palestinian owners are free to tend. Of course, Efrat's doctors treat Palestinian villagers in their state-of-the-art ER. Please understand, Efrat's expansion is legit because Jews owned land here prior to 1948. Look, Efrat has a forested park where village kids can play.

He drives me over to the park. I can reach out and touch the Palestinian village of Wadi an Nis. "When I bring tourists over here and I show them the proximity, they usually faint," he relates. "Because when President Obama talks about a two-state solution and I invite him over to come and see the reality, you have to see the proximity in order to understand the complexity."

Complexity.

About those olive groves—what about my working stiff, stoned by Efrat settlers at Solomon's Pools?

About Wadi an Nis—of Efrat's total 538 acres, 423 were confiscated from the village. What's left of it is water-deprived (thirty-two liters of water a day, when the World Health Organization says the minimum should be one hundred) and has an unemployment rate of 55 percent.

About that park—there's barbed wire around it.

So I ask Oded, Why does he think he has a claim to this land where Efrat's outstandingly poised to expand? "Because I'm in the shoes of the Jordanians who have been here in the past, of the British who have been here in the past, of the Ottomans who were here in the past, they were all sovereign countries to rule this land." He sees my face, maybe it's not as jollied along anymore. "So now Israel is here," he says. "You are right. It's been fifty years of vagueness of not making decisions. But that's at least a legal argument that was decided to determine—"

I have to interrupt. "I get the legal argument . . . now I ask you, just Lorraine to Oded, just you and me, what do you think about that? Do you have any doubts or troubles about it?"

"I might have doubts. I might have trouble. I don't think that's the level of the question. The level of the question is how can we live, one beside another, and build a relationship that we can determine the use of this land. Plus, settlements only constitute four percent of the West Bank. That's it. There's plenty of land for everyone."

ONE OF THE MAYOR'S NEIGHBORS IS MAZEN FARAJ. HE SEES EFRAT illu-minated with its swan neck streetlights from his cinder block home in Bethlehem's Duheisha refugee camp, the tough one that was home to the rough kid who shamed thirteen-year-old Moayyad into join-ing the march to Rachel's Tomb.

It's pitch black at four a.m. when Mazen rises for the day. He needs that much time to get through the Israeli checkpoints in time for work. He slips on his Docksider shoes, lights up a cigarette. He's striking enough to pass for a Marlboro man, the brand he chain-smokes.

His job is to tell his story. His destination most days is Israeli high schools. None of them are in Efrat. Settlements are excluded from the work he does—by mutual agreement with the Israelis who part-ner with him, who want their children to consider the complexity.

So he waits in the long lines moving Palestinians through rows of narrow cattle yard pens at checkpoints. He sees the way Israelis live well. He understands how Duheisha's schools can't compare with the ones in Israel where he talks to distracted teenagers.

He tells them how he was born in Duheisha in 1975, how his mother died of cancer when he was six months old, how his father, "a man with a beautiful heart," took over his mothering. How when he was eight, he started asking his father why his family of thirteen lived in a steel-roofed shack thirty-four square feet. Why they didn't have water all the time in the summer or electricity most of the time in the winter. His father explained it all started when he was only six and ran from his village because of the war and found himself in Duheisha. He was supposed to be there a couple of years at most.

But two years stretched into ten, twenty, thirty, and forty. By then, Mazen was thirteen, and he started throwing stones at Israeli soldiers with other Duheisha kids, "to say that we exist, that we are still alive. And we want our life back. We want our freedom. And we want to live a normal life like anyone around the world."

The day Mazen turned fifteen, Israeli soldiers captured him. "That first day they just put me in a small place: less than three feet. . . . They shouted at me and beat me. They sometimes let me stand for days without eating or drinking, without a bathroom, without many things.

"I believe in myself. I can do it. It's okay. It's amazing to be there especially when you are fifteen years old. They put handcuffs on you. You stand. Sometimes I did not know what the time was, whether it was day or night. I did not know if it was morning or afternoon. You are far away from the world. I was in this situation the first time for more than one month.

"They just wanted me to say 'I am a dangerous one and I want to do something against them.' I am not. I can't believe that. What is the maximum they can do? They can kill me. That is it. To suffer? I am already suffering in the refugee camp. To be hungry? I am already hungry. It is the same."

He spends his high school years in Israeli prisons, getting captured and released five times between the age of fifteen and eighteen. "So when they finished the first intifada in 1993, they have a peace agreement, Oslo agreement, and it was signed on the balcony of the White House by Arafat and Rabin, and when they announce it they just say that after a few years you will have your new Palestinian state. But again a few years has become more than twenty years."

Peace talks sputter out in 2000 and again boys and young men take to the streets. Mazen isn't interested anymore. His father, his brothers, none of them take part. "Too many people get killed. You can smell the blood in the streets. Just killing, killing and the revenge, the revenge and the settler violence without mercy."

One night in 2002, in the middle of curfew during Israel's thirty-nine-day siege of the Church of the Nativity in Bethlehem, Mazen, who's twenty-seven at the time, gets a call. "The body of our father is in the hospital. We want to go to the hospital and they just say, 'It's not allowed. You have to wait until the morning.'" The body of his sixty-two-year-old father arrives by truck the next morning. The soldier who killed him used a tank-mounted Browning .50 caliber machine gun. The bullets are a half-inch thick. The soldier fired so many into his father's torso it was little more than mush.

In Efrat, Oded pulls his car into one of his elementary schools and guides me to a wide hall with floor-to-ceiling windows. Against them are nine enormous glass tanks filled with—I'm guessing confetti. School's in session and kids are bouncing and jostling around us.

The glass tanks are the brainchild of a history teacher. She wanted to teach kids about the Shoah without the sickening newsreel images. "She came up with an idea to have the kids collect one and a half million buttons. Why a million and a half?" Oded asks, raising his voice above girls whooping in navy pleated skirts down a flight of stairs. "Because a million and a half kids were murdered in the Holocaust."

Buttons are better than the movie *Paper Clips*, he says, because these buttons are all different, like a million and a half snowflakes, or fingerprints. The kids found a lot of them, but eventually, buttons started pouring in from all over once the project made it to YouTube. It took over the hearts of millions of people. The consummate power of the Wall, the way it paralyzed me, gives way. What was I thinking? I wasn't. I was just reacting. No, these vitrines of buttons constitute the most sacred site in my Bethlehem.

A memory flashes inside me. I'm in Bethlehem five years ago, sitting in a café. A literary reading is over and it's time for questions and discussion. At first everyone is polite, then less so and soon it's a free-for-all, everyone arguing and commiserating the way oppressed people do when they're together, just them. They're thinking out loud about why the world doesn't feel obligated to help them when it sees the Wall and the checkpoints and the lopsided kill ratios showing ten times as many Palestinians are killed as Israelis. Where is the unshakeable international consensus? Where is the Palestinian state? It's been more than fifty years, what are we doing wrong? I'll never forget someone standing up, she looked like she was just out of college, and saying, "We just don't have as good a story as they do. What's better than the Holocaust?"

MAZEN IS THE COEXECUTIVE DIRECTOR OF A GROUP OF STORYTELLERS called the Parents Circle Families Forum of the Bereaved Palestinian and Israeli Families for Peace and Reconciliation. It's a gallimaufry of a name, and won't ever fit on a bumper sticker. Yet like Efrat's button project, people from all over have contributed to keep it going, even if so far the group has been able to recruit only seven hundred Israeli and Palestinian families who've paid the ultimate price—losing their Hodaya, their Moayyad, or their father, as Mazen did back when he was twenty-seven. Their latest promotional spot asks: If we've paid the ultimate price and can believe peace is the only answer, why can't you?

Now forty-one, and a father himself, Mazen invites me to his house in Duheisha camp. There's no water the day we meet. I go to the kitchen sink with his wife, turn the faucet, and three or four drops leak out, then nothing. She reminds me of my aunt Marge, whom we all used to call "crazy clean." Marge scrubbed every scintilla of her coal patch house because she knew the Welsh hated on Lithuanians for being dirty. Mazen's wife knows Israelis feel the same about her. So water or not, the cinder block house I'm standing in is immaculate. They've been waiting for water since Monday. Today is Friday. If you look out the window, you can see Efrat's carrot-top roofs in the sun. At the touch of a hand, water flows through their sprinklers, dishwashers, washing machines, Jacuzzis, and swimming pools.

She doesn't mention any of that. She's preoccupied with her daughters back in the living room, which she's decorated with striped pillows, sectional sofas, and family photographs. She's resisted the bling most Arab homes I've visited tend to pile on.

Here's Alma, eighteen months, stumbling around barefoot in a floral jumpsuit. Here's Salma, eight, named after Mazen's mother. Her shirt has a nerdy girl with big glasses on it. Each knee has a

Band-Aid, each foot pink socks. Zuhra, who will be ten in August, has the same nerdy-girl shirt and a cascade of Rapunzel hair. Mazen wants me to know they're going to a Christian school far better than the one he went to. This house, it's double the size of his father's UN shed. Zuhra is learning English, and French. She's seated quietly. I can tell she's old enough to be shy.

We continue to talk about the night his father was killed and the Israelis forbade him from seeing his father's body. "'Forbidden,' this word. 'Not allowed.' In Arabic it's *muharram*. As a Palestinian and as an Arab and as a Muslim I have two *muharram*s in my life. The first one comes from the religion, traditional culture—'not allowed' to have a girlfriend, 'not allowed' to drink alcohol, 'not allowed' to be free and do whatever you dream about or think about. And the other 'not allowed' and 'forbidden' was from the Israeli occupation. Not allowed to live, not allowed to exist, not allowed to have your state, your rights, your freedom. And the most important thing—'not allowed' to have your respect as a human being."

He thought about revenge after that night. Instead he went to a bereavement group meeting and heard Rami Elhanan talk about losing his fourteen-year-old daughter to a suicide bomber in 1997. He learned that Yitzhak Frankenthal, whose nineteen-year-old son was kidnapped and murdered by Hamas in 1994, had started the group. After some time Mazen started to see Israelis who lost their children were more like him than unlike him. He has made it his life's work to join them and argue publicly that their common grief can be the basis for peace.

It's important. But Zuhra, the oldest, has other things on her mind. I can see her across the room, eyeing my iPad. Zuhra, I call. She shrugs. Zuhra, I call again, determined not to be an idiot this time. She comes over. But she's only a little interested in the iPad. After a few selfie videos, she's hankering for something else. What is it?

"Will you come to my room?" she whispers in my ear.

We go.

The first thing I see is a twin bed. The spread boasts cherries, hearts, strawberries, and butterflies. Now I see two other twin beds.

The spreads all match. Three to a room. Better than thirteen, as Mazen had. He's followed us in, but he's letting Zuhra have center stage. Then I see what she wanted to show me. What she can't believe exists.

The far wall of the bedroom is papered over in its entirety with a scene from Walt Disney's *Cinderella*. The motherless young lady isn't dusty and worn, as the Brothers Grimm would have it. She's life-size and radiant in a cerulean chiffon ball gown with opera-length gloves. Other young princesses with hair flowing a lot like Zuhra's are wearing medieval dresses the color of emeralds and rubies. One of them is black. One is Arab. One is either Ashkenazi or a daughter of Pennsylvania; it's hard to tell exactly which. They waltz across Zuhra's wall, powerfully saccharine, utterly commercialized, the un-hip rejoinder to Banksy's graffiti on the Wall inside the little town of sweet baby Jesus.

Zuhra is holding her hands together below her chin, she's looking down at her feet, but her smile isn't shy. She knows this is the holiest site in all Bethlehem.

THE SEPARATION WALL

HELON HABILA

1. THE WALL

In history and in literature, walls have always appealed to the popular imagination. In his short story "The Great Wall of China," Kafka shows this abiding popularity of walls using the example of the building of the wall in China. The wall was ostensibly built as protection against "raiders from the north." It took many generations over many dynasties to build, and it involved the entire Chinese nation, making the people who actually engaged in the building into popular heroes. They were protecting the fatherland, devoting their time and skill and resources to saving children and the women from depredating "others." Kafka's narrator describes how the people celebrate the builders as they travel to their stations: "Every countryman was a brother for whom they were building a protective wall and who would thank him with everything he had and was for all his life. Unity! Unity!"

This passage, with its careful register referencing "unity," and "countryman," and "brother," captures the nationalist and populist ideology behind the building of security walls. There is nothing new or original about walls; they have always been there, from the Wall of Jericho to Hadrian's Wall to the Berlin Wall to Donald Trump's imaginary wall on the Mexican border. There is something visceral and primeval in us that yearns for the protective presence of a wall. But walls aren't always solely for the protection of citizens; they serve a variety of other functions. They have been used as militaristic symbols of impregnability, and permanence.

In the movie *Avenge but One of My Two Eyes*, director Avi Mograbi tells the story of the siege of Masada by the Romans in 73 CE, and how the Romans, unable to penetrate the fortified settlement, decided to build dykes and a circumvolution wall around the settlement. Their message: We are not going anywhere. Today, Mograbi is trying to show, Israel is behaving like the Romans did, and the Palestinians can be compared to the besieged Jews of Masada. With the separation barrier, which was initially presented to the public as a temporary measure against Palestinian attacks, Israel is telling its Palestinian and Arab neighbors (in concrete terms, if you will), "We are going nowhere."

I sensed that overwhelming message of permanence the first time I stood under the wall. I felt overwhelmed and diminished, like an ant. Where I stood, near the Shuafat refugee camp in East Jerusalem, the wall towered over twenty-six-feet high. The dimensions and the materials of the separation barrier vary from place to place, but they are usually tallest and sturdiest in the urban areas, like here in East Jerusalem. Thick slabs of concrete shot out of the ground and into the sky, running in a meandering curve around the camp. I was on the Israeli side of the wall, meaning inside the wall—though at times it was hard to say what side was inside and which outside. The Shuafat refugee camp, like other Palestinian refugee camps, is among the oldest such camps in the world, with a population of about eighty thousand uprooted Palestinians. I imagined what it'd feel like to live under the shadow of this giant concrete slab, waking up to its concrete view every morning, and going to sleep at night to the same view. "It is all right," a resident I asked this question said. He looked at the wall as if seeing it for the first time. "We get used to it."

MOST ISRAELIS DO NOT REFER TO IT AS A WALL, THEY CALL IT THE SEPA-ration barrier, or the security fence, because a major portion of it is only fencing and barbed wires with a stretch of space around it; in some places it is only a strip of road patrolled by the border police. But Palestinians are less euphemistic: they call it the Wall; some call it the Wall of Apartheid. Originally planned to run a total length of 490 miles when completed, the line traced by the separation barrier is more than twice the length of the Green Line, with about 85 percent of it cutting at times as far as eleven miles into the West Bank.

Critics of the wall claim that it is a tool for Israel to unilaterally expand its territory, much as the architects of the East Jerusalem plan envisioned when they called in 1967 for "maximum territory, minimum Arabs"—hemming in the Palestinians into ever-shrinking urban centers. The wall will isolate about twenty-five thousand Palestinians from the larger community. For if Palestine is a nation in the making, then its borders are still fluid and negotiable, and the more Israel encroaches into this nonexistent border, the more it would seem reasonable and neighborly when it eventually gives back a portion of what it has taken.

Construction on the wall began after the second intifada broke out in 2000, when suicide bombings and attacks on Israeli civilians increased dramatically. Proponents of the wall call it a necessary security buffer between Israel and the West Bank. The figures generally confirm this—according to most sources, between 2000 and July 2003, before the completion of the "first continuous segment" of the wall in the north, seventy-three suicide bombings were carried out from the West Bank; however, from August 2003 to the end of 2006, only eighteen attacks were carried out.

2. THE CHECKPOINT AT QALANDIYA

To get out of their neighborhoods and into Israel for work, most Palestinians wake up early, some as early as two a.m., to be among the first at the checkpoint when it opens at four a.m. I got to the Qalandiya checkpoint as it was opening. There were men and women already in line; a few were seated on the red iron benches, the only furniture in the warehouse-like building that, together with the military kiosks and the turnstiles before the kiosks, form this, the biggest checkpoint in the West Bank.

Palestinians who hold West Bank IDs must have a permit to pass through the checkpoint into East Jerusalem and Israel for work, medical care, education, or for religious reasons. The checkpoints, acting together with the walls, control population movement, they control labor, they control commerce, they control privilege. There are about thirty-two major checkpoints between Israel and the West Bank; then there are uncountable smaller, or "flying," checkpoints, which can be erected by dragging large concrete blocks into the middle of the road at any time, or by closing the ubiquitous yellow gates that stand at the head of any road leading to a Palestinian village or town. The flying checkpoints are arbitrary, they are unpredictable, and they serve their purpose: to keep the Palestinians off balance, to make the Israeli presence felt. And to control terror attacks. Yet despite the walls and fences and checkpoints, about fifty thousand Palestinians go illegally into the Israeli territory daily to work—proving that the wall is not as insurmountable as it is made to appear, and that its primary purpose cannot be for security, but for something else.

At Qalandiya, not all must pass on foot through the turnstiles. East Jerusalem residents can cross in their cars, which have yellow license plates. But West Bank residents, with some exceptions relating to old age, must have a permit to cross. The easiest way of getting a permit is to get a job in Israel, and for that you must be over twenty-two, and married, and your name must not be on any blacklist—the conditions accrete, almost as afterthoughts, one upon the other.

This was an example of control through bureaucracy, Hanna, my guide, told me. There were currently between two hundred and three hundred thousand Palestinians on the secret blacklist.

"How do you get on a blacklist?" I asked her. First of all, you don't have to have done anything wrong. Anyone in your extended family can be punished for the wrong of another member living in another town; that family member can be someone you've never even met before, but as long as he or she is related to you, you can get punished for his or her wrongdoing. This is the concept of collective punishment.

It is also an excellent way to turn innocent people into informers. If you have a family of five, or ten, an extended family, all depending on you, and suddenly your means of livelihood is threatened, you'll do anything to safeguard your job, including turning informer. Also, getting a pass might make you feel grateful—perhaps after going through all the hoops and obtaining a permit, you'll feel as if you are special, a chosen one.

Hanna belonged to a group of elderly Jewish women, Machsom Watch, trying to help somehow, even if it meant speaking against their own government. She was over eighty and had worked as a secretary to David Ben Gurion in the late 1950s and early 1960s. She and the other women took turns volunteering at the checkpoints, trying to protect the Palestinians, some of whom didn't speak Hebrew, from arbitrary harassment by the soldiers manning the checkpoints.

"People shouldn't be treated like animals," she said.

To show me what she meant, she took me round to the very front of the line. Here the men and women were trapped, single file, in the cage-like passage leading to the turnstile, admitting one person at a time. "Look over their heads, see the barbed wires. They say this is because the men would sometimes try to climb over each other to go first, behaving like animals. Tell me, who wouldn't behave like an animal if he had to go through this same thing every morning?"

But to these Palestinians, the barbed wire was the least of their worries. The worst was to get to the kiosk, to hand over your ID card and work permit and magnetic card, only to be told you couldn't pass, that your permit had been revoked for some reason. And the soldiers were not obliged to tell you the reason.

A big-jawed Palestinian man had been hovering on the edge of our little group as we talked to Hanna. He was dressed like the others in jeans and a jacket. He looked worried, and he kept following us, then pulling back. Finally he approached Hanna and started to speak to her in Hebrew. He said he had been turned back at the checkpoint.

"Why?"

He didn't know why. Had it happened to him before? No. He was over fifty, he had been going through the checkpoint for years. He lived in Beit Hanina. Yes, of course he had a family, wife and children and parents. This had never happened to him before. Hanna took his pass and saw that everything was in order. She said sometimes they could just tell you there was a glitch with the machine, that you were blocked, just to play with your mind. The aim was to keep needling you, until you snapped. Then they threw you in jail, one less Palestinian out there.

3. A VIEW OF THE WALL FROM AIDA REFUGEE CAMP

Standing on the roof of a house at the Aida refugee camp in Bethlehem, I could see the arched entrance to the camp with a huge key logo on top of it. The key of return, they called it. Palestinians have been described as a people without a land, a nation of exiles and refugees. The Aida camp seemed to underscore that view. It also underscored Edward Said's opening line in his essay "Reflections on Exile": "Exile is strangely compelling to think about, but terrible to experience."

Aida is home to over five thousand Palestinians, uprooted from their homes after 1948. In that time, multiple generations have lived here; the camp has grown from a village of tents to a city of concrete, with buildings piled on top of buildings because here growth can only be vertical. Young families build their homes on top of their parents' homes; the house on whose roof I was now standing housed seven families.

"But it is all a temporary arrangement," my host and guide, Munther Amirah, said, laughing. "Temporarily permanent" seemed to be a running joke among the Palestinians. Their exile was supposed to be temporary, the separation barrier was temporary, the occupation was temporary, the settlements were temporary, and they had all been temporary since 1948, since the creation of the state of Israel. The only thing permanent was the hope that the Palestinians would return to their homes in Jerusalem. That was the meaning of the key of return—it was a symbol of hope. It was the key to each and every home left long ago, still waiting, pristine, the pots and pans

and toys still intact as they were left, waiting to be touched and uti-
lized by their real owners; the olive trees waiting to be watered and
plucked by the hands that planted them. That is the myth of return.
It is a narrative encouraged in order to keep hope alive. But of course
harsh concrete reality keeps intruding at every turn. And life in the
camp has become something of a balancing act—balancing myth
with reality. On one of the walls, there is a painting of an olive tree,
and under it a line from a poem: *If the Olive trees knew who planted them
/ their oil would turn to tears. . . .*

FROM THE ROOFTOP WHERE WE STOOD, NOTHING SEEMED MORE REAL
than the concrete wall of separation a few meters away, with its huge
tower, a staple feature of the separation wall. There were soldiers
inside the tower, watching, monitoring, waiting. There was graffiti
on the wall, showing the faces and names of young men and women
killed or incarcerated in the course of the struggle; there were scenes
of resistance and dates and numbers—one was the number 194, refer-
ring to the UN resolution that is commonly interpreted as granting
the refugees a right of return. A right that kept hitting the concrete
wall of Israeli determination not only to keep them here forever, but
to make their stay here as uncomfortable as possible.

"Why?" I asked.

"Why? Simple. They want us to go away. To disappear," Amirah
said.

The wall meandered and curved, for as long as the eye could see;
facing us was a part of the wall that had been chipped and hacked at,
cutting through the concrete to show the iron armature embedded
inside. Protesters had attempted to break down the wall in 2009.
A purely symbolic gesture—there is no breaking this wall, not by
ordinary human hands. The act had sparked a reprisal by the Israeli
military, which had invaded the camp, barricading the entrance and
throwing tear gas. My guide, before we came up to the roof, showed
me a patched section in the wall of this home where soldiers had
cut a hole to access the building, and then progressed from house
to house, making a hole in each wall, thus avoiding exposure in

the streets, where they'd have faced heavy resistance. In one of the houses a woman, Noha Quattmesh, a mother of five, had resisted the intrusion, and was reported to have asked the soldiers, "Why do you cut through my wall to come in? Why not use the door?" She threw open the door, and inhaled tear gas from a projectile shot by soldiers outside. She died.

Exile is difficult to experience. Earlier we had gone to the cemetery, located at the entrance of the camp, to view her grave and that of a boy recently shot dead by Israeli soldiers. His name was Abdurrahman; he had just returned from school, wearing his backpack, and, as many Palestinian kids do when they see Israeli army vehicles, he had thrown stones at a passing Israeli army jeep. They shot him dead. He was thirteen years old. On the grave there were pebbles painted in the colors of the Palestinian flag, red and green and white, and a flag itself, and then a picture of the boy. For people like him, whose names are etched into the headstones here, there would be no return.

To our right the wall intrudes in a fingerlike projection into the Palestinian side.

"Why does the wall dip that far?" I asked.

"That is an Israeli holy site. Rachel's Tomb. It is popular for tourists, so they had to move the wall to surround it."

Rachel, famous in the Old Testament for weeping for her children and refusing to be comforted, would have wept over the bitterness and bloodshed caused by the seemingly innocuous progress of a wall over a seemingly undistinguished piece of land. From here we could see the Palestinian community of al-Wallajeh, in which a few of the houses were trapped inside the wall, on the Israeli side. This phenomenon of a community caught on the "wrong" side of the wall is one aspect of a multifaceted apparatus known as a "seam zone."

Although they lived on the Israeli side, the families inside the wall could access schools and health care only on the Palestinian side of the wall. And even though the distance between al-Wallajeh and Bethlehem was only a few kilometers, the residents of those houses in the seam had to circle many miles away to their designated checkpoint, and then from there to here, doubling and tripling the real distance between the two points. The separation barrier had overnight shifted borders and elongated distances. In some areas, Palestinian towns, cut off by the wall, were connected to each other only by tunnels controlled by Israeli security forces. These islands of Palestinian population have been likened to South Africa's apartheid-era "Bantustans" or townships—densely populated areas created by the colonizing power for the uprooted "natives," easy to monitor and control through a pass or permit system, and close enough to exploit for cheap labor.

4. THE SEAM ZONES

Alon Cohen-Lifshitz is an architect who works with Bimkom, a human rights organization founded in 1999 by Israeli professionals, mainly architects and planners, with the aim of advancing the development of Israeli planning policies, making them more just and respectful of human rights, including in East Jerusalem and the West Bank. Alon had been trying to explain to me what a seam zone was; now he was taking me to see one. He took me to the village of Beit Ijza. Here he showed me an extreme example of how the seam zone manifests—a single Arab home is cut off from the rest of the village, and the Israeli settlement of Givon HaHadasha is wrapped around the single home. The entire house is caged in with a high fence and barbed wires. A thin passage connects its residents to the rest of the village. Only the family living in the house can come in through the gate; visitors have to get a special permit to enter. The intimidation and harassment the family endures from the encircling settler community can only be imagined—we could see pieces of garbage that they said had been thrown into the compound from over the fence by the settlers.

The seam zones were created, according to official narrative, to protect Israeli settler communities and holy sites that lie east of the Green Line and west of the separation barrier. Many settler communities are placed deep inside the West Bank, in and around Palestinian communities; in some cases, fences and special security zones have been erected on private Palestinian land in order to protect the settlers. In other cases, including the seam zones, the separation barrier has cut off Palestinian farms and lands close to the Israeli border from their owners, and has de facto annexed these lands into Israel. Both cases seem to be evidence of Israel's persistent attempt to take over more land inside the West Bank.

FOR PALESTINIAN FAMILIES IN THE SEAM ZONES, LIFE CAN BE ISOLATED, lonely, and cruel.

Arab al-Ramadin al-Janubi is a Bedouin village trapped in the seam zone. It is only a few miles away from Qalqilya and used to be part of five loosely linked villages, two of which have been cut off by the wall. Al-Janubi and the other village, Arab Abu Farda, now find themselves marooned on the Israeli side. A few squalid houses made out of scrap metal and wood form the entire village. The population is over three hundred, our host, Hassan, tells us. He is thirty-five and was born and raised here. The Bedouins are traditionally nomadic; their lives are structured around the grazing needs of their livestock. How does it feel to be trapped in a seam zone, with no livestock? Hassan shrugs. He has never really known the nomadic life. He knew that the family moved from two previous locations before settling here. He turns to his father, a seventy-year-old man listening and nodding, for help. Three kids, two girls and a boy, all Hassan's children, ages ranging from ten to three, sit on a mat next to the old man, looking at us shyly. The old man remembers that they came from Bir Saba (known to the Israelis as Be'er Sheva), with a stop in Hebron, before coming here. They bought this land in the 1990s, though they had been here since 1967.

Life here isn't easy; it is a closed military area, so they need permits to continue to live in their homes. Even though they are on the Israeli side, they are not allowed to cross the Green Line, and they can't have weddings or celebrate festivals because they can't have visitors, even family members—visitors from the Palestinian territories need permits to visit, and special permits to stay overnight. They used to get water from the nearby Israeli settlement of Alfei Menashe, although today their water comes from the nearby Palestinian village of Hableh, and they get their electricity from the Palestinian side under the fence. The men work in Qalqilya and in the nearby Israeli settlement. They run their own primary school in a rectangular building with wooden windows, but for secondary school the children have to go to the Palestinian side through the checkpoint. Every day. They walk to the checkpoint and then take a bus to school in Qalqilya. Each child must have his or her permit.

"What if a child loses his permit?" I asked. Then all the children would be detained at the checkpoint until a parent came to identify the child. And if a seam zone dweller falls ill and has to go to the hospital on the Palestinian side, the ambulance must wait on the other side of the checkpoint, the Palestinian side, and the patient is taken in a cart to the ambulance.

"Life must be hard living here," I said. They shrugged. "We get used to it."

At the moment they had a demolition order on their homes. The other day a military officer came and offered to move them to the Palestinian side, but they refused.

"Why?"

"This is our land. We don't want to move."

The officer was angry at the refusal and promised to make life uncomfortable for them. Most seam zone communities are separated from their farms and water wells, which they can then only access through special gates called "agricultural gates." For that, they need to apply for special permits, which are always temporary, and which can be denied with no explanation. In her book, *Time in the Shadows*, the Palestinian academic and author Laleh Khalili describes the byzantine nature of the permit system in the seam zones:

> A quarter of all applications are denied, and the appeal process is profoundly complex and differs across different permit regimes. Access is granted only through the sole gate recorded on the permit, and nighttime access requires additional permissions. Permits expire after varying periods. Donkeys, automobiles, and work

vehicles may or may not be allowed in the seam zone, depending on specificities, although this is also arbitrary. Some gates allow entry by villagers for farming their lands, whereas other gates allow only merchandise to pass to and from Israel. Some gates open two or three times a day; others are closed randomly and without any previous notice. The hours of operation of the gates are erratic. More recently, privatization of some of these crossing points has meant that "civilian security guards" are in charge of some crossing points alongside or instead of soldiers or border police. The dizzying complexity and arbitrariness of the measures create disorientation, confusion, and uncertainty, excellent techniques for maintaining control over civilians.

FROM AL-JANUBI, ALON TOOK ME TO A FARM IN JAYYUS TO DEMONSTRATE the problem of the "agricultural gates." We wandered about a bit before a young man pointed us in the direction of the farm, and we found the owner and two young men plucking loquat fruits off the trees and arranging them in cartons.

"Where do the fruits go?" I asked the owner, Sharif Khaled.

"Ramallah," he said. All around were orchards belonging to Palestinian families who lived across the wall in Jayyus and Qalqilya. There were olive trees and orange trees. Alon told me the farms here were among the most fertile in all of Israel-Palestine. Khaled plucked a bunch of fruits and handed them to us. "Eat, please."

He was happy to see Alon, who told me he used to bring his children here to help Khaled with the harvest. Alon was one of a handful of Israelis I had met who continue to build bridges between Jews and Palestinians despite the Israeli government's efforts to dissuade such actions. For instance, Israelis are forbidden by law to visit most Palestinian urbanized areas, and many Palestinian peace activists are denied permits to enter Israel, all under the guise of "security."

"How old do you think I am?" Khaled asked. Seventy-three, it turned out. This farm had been in his family before he was born; he had two farms on this side of the wall, totaling forty dunams (One dunam is 0.24 acres). He was one of a lucky few whose farms were mostly on the Palestinian side of the wall, in Jayyus—four farms, in Khaled's case. To visit this farm on the Israeli side, he needed to have a permit. Which was why he was in a good mood today, his agricultural permit had just been renewed, following the Israeli military's recognition of his ownership of the land. He took it out and showed us. A long piece of paper, with his biographical data on it. Valid from February 2016 to February 2018.

"This is very good. A whole two years," he said.

Before the Israeli military recognized Abu Azzam's ownership of the farms, he had been granted a permit for only three months. The permit stated the gate he must use, which was open only during three slots—6:30 to 7:00 a.m., 1:30 to 2:00 p.m., and 5:00 to 5:30 p.m.—seven days a week. Was it hard to get the permit? Oh yes. He had to prove this was his family land with an Israeli "land ownership document" which costs thirty-eight shekels, then he had to prove that he was one of the heirs of the land with a valid inheritance order, and that the land was on the other side of the wall—this was done by showing a current map of the farm. Finally, he attached to his application for permit a certificate from the Jayyus municipality to prove that he still uses the land and that he did not sell it.

Two of his sons had applied and were denied permits to visit the farm. Khaled was one of five brothers, and he was the only one still living in Jayyus. The others had left—one currently lived in San Diego.

"Why is the whole permit system so hard?" I asked Alon later. That was the whole point, he told me. To discourage these farmers from using their lands, because any land unused for a period of three years could be taken over by the government. Legally.

"Why are you against the wall?" I asked him.

"Walls are not the answer," he said. "Walls can never solve the Israeli-Palestinian problem." Bimkom, he said, was against all barriers, including gated communities, because they violated people's freedom of movement and caused untold suffering. The route between Qalqilya and Jayyus used to be only five kilometers long, using agricultural paths, before the barrier was erected, making the use of these paths impossible. Now a Palestinian must travel an average of fifteen kilometers to get between the two places.

But still, Jayyus was one of the few Palestinian villages that had been able to challenge the expropriation of its land by the separation barrier. They took the Israeli government to court and were able to have the course of the wall altered. Jayyus, along with other villages and the Association for Civil Rights in Israel, won two decisions: in 2009 Jayyus recovered 2,488 dunams of land, including land belonging to Abu Azzam, and one water well, after the course of the wall was altered.

Organizations like Bimkom and individuals, both Palestinian and Israeli, have been challenging Israeli government policies in the West Bank. Some of these challenges have borne fruit. In some areas, the building of the barrier has been suspended since 2014 due to court cases brought by Palestinian communities. In Qalqilya and Jayyus, about three thousand dunams of land was returned to the community. But the poster child for successful struggle against the incursion of the wall into community lands remains the town of Budrus.

The story of this tiny town's resistance to the wall is captured in the documentary film *Budrus*, by the director Julia Bacha and the organization Just Vision. The movie tells the story of the peaceful resistance to the encroachment of the wall into the village's land. If the wall had continued as planned, it would have taken 1,200 dunams of land, including three thousand olive trees. The wall would have cut in half the village cemetery, and would have passed right in front of the village school, hemming in the already tiny, claustrophobic village. In 2003, residents of Budrus, led by Ayed Morrar, decided to protest, peacefully. Women lay in front of bulldozers, children sang, men marched, and soon foreign and Israeli civil rights activists joined their ranks. International media took notice as Budrus carried out fifty-five demonstrations against the wall, lasting over eleven months, and won. Their peaceful marches and shrewd use of the media to publicize their struggle became a model for other towns like Bil'in and Nabi Saleh.

The Israeli government stopped building the parts of the wall,

Alon said, "because they know they'll lose in court, and they don't want that. Many cases show them they cannot do what they like."

"So, is that the end of the barrier?" I asked.

"No. They are waiting, thinking what can we do? It happened in 2004, in the South Hebron Hills, the route was changed entirely after such challenge. They changed tactics and said, okay, we'll build only along the Green Line; then in 2004 they said, oh, but we need to protect the roads, so they set up barriers along the roads, cutting off Palestinian access to farmlands and grazing ground."

But the important thing was that a precedent had been set. The wall can be challenged. Activists like Ayed Morrar, like Alon Cohen-Lifshitz, like the residents of Bil'in and Ni'leen and international organizations and volunteers, continue to pressure Israel to live up to its democratic ideals. Israel faces an existential threat, by its very location in the midst of enemy countries, but building walls is never going to solve the Israel-Palestine question. When you build a wall between yourself and others, you are basically saying that you have stopped listening and seeing. You have cut off contact. And how can there be understanding without contact?

A HUNDRED CHILDREN

EVA MENASSE

IMAGINE THE CHILD AYA*, EIGHT YEARS OLD, LYING IN BED BETWEEN her siblings, dreaming of a rumbling, grinding monster. The monster crosses over from the dream to rage outside the window, and she wakes up. Women's screams stab her ears, harsh light pierces her squeezed-together eyelids. A strong arm grabs Aya and carries her away; from the smell of soap and coffee she knows it's her mother. In a frantic gallop she flies through the air, out from the brightness into the night, where a few harsh lights glare like cruel white suns. Her father, her uncle, her big brother, and her cousins are lying facedown on the ground, a thicket of gun barrels aimed at them. They don't move, but somehow Aya knows they're alive.

The motherly arm sets her down, and then it's Aya who hurries after her mother, tugging at her clothes and trying to drag her away from the soldier she's clinging to, pleading. The soldier laughs, another soldier extricates him. He shakes off Aya's mother like some kind of insect. Now the bellowing monster looms like a gigantic scorpion, stinger raised. From up above it hacks away at the house where a few minutes before Aya was sleeping between the warm bodies of her siblings. There's a crashing, a crunching and smashing,

* All of the characters in this essay are fictional, and any resemblance to actual persons, living or dead, is coincidental.

and merciful white dust rises, veiling the scene. The mother screams, the father and brothers are lying on the ground, the aunt with the kohl-rimmed eyes stands off to the side, holding up her iPhone as tears run down her cheeks. But she's filmed everything bravely; for the rest of their lives they'll be able to watch their house being razed. Their first house being razed. Others have lost still more, first and second and third houses, then the corrugated iron shacks that they built themselves, God knows how, and finally even the tents of the international aid organizations. But that's not here, that's in the Jordan Valley, far removed from the Green Line, where no one is watching at all and they can do as they please. But whether here or there, they always come at three in the morning.

We'll build a new house, Aya's father will say the next morning to the strangers with the cameras, raising his fist. By then he will have changed his shirt; the other one was all dirty and wet in front. The strangers will nod, looking concerned, and meanwhile Aya's cheeky brothers will tug at their trousers and say "whatsyourname" "whatsyourname?" giggling whenever one of the strangers bends down, shakes their hands, and says "Tom" or "Steven" or "Karen." Aya's little sister has climbed into the black cistern that once stood on the roof and now lies demolished in the rubble. She stands inside it, drumming her fists on the plastic and shrieking with delight. Three of the strangers hold up their cell phones between themselves and Aya's sister, their faces stony.

AYA LIVES IN A VILLAGE CALLED WALAJEH. THE FIRST VILLAGE, OLD WA-lajeh, once stood on the opposite hill. But in 1948, the year of the catastrophe, Walajeh was forced to move, the whole village, with bag and baggage. The Green Line was drawn down the valley between Old Walajeh and Walajeh, a line that has been fought over heatedly for decades in faraway countries where different laws apply. But that hasn't changed anything over here, hasn't made even a blade of grass grow in a different direction. Here the Green Line doesn't mean a thing, it's just an obligatory stroke on all the maps.

The relocation of the village of Walajeh back in 1948 ought not to be pictured as an orderly affair. War was raging; the survivors fled far into Jordan. Later, the ones who dared to return built the new village on the opposite hill. There they watched as bulldozers came and collapsed the abandoned village to a heap of stones, as their olive and pomegranate orchards, their almond, apricot, and lemon trees were seized. But there was enough land left for them on their side of the hill.

Nineteen years later, in the next war, the Blue-Whites overran the invisible Green Line and occupied the entire country. The people of Walajeh, who are "Red-Greens," cursed their own leaders, calling them incompetent and corrupt, but in the end farmers are just happy if they can work their fields again without getting shot.

SINCE TIME IMMEMORIAL, THE RED-GREENS HAVE BUILT THEIR VILLAGES to embrace the hills, not to ride them. The Blue-Whites, by contrast, "took the hilltops, their houses are a honeycomb, with the buildings marshaled next to each other in a rigid plan," writes the great Palestinian author Raja Shehadeh. That changes everything; the biblical landscape is now crowned with beige cement like dabs of icing, and the highways cut imperious swathes in between.

One of these honeycombs looms right above Walajeh. It's called "Har Gilo." The inhabitants aren't bad people, just people whose many privileges include not having to think about them. They aren't the kind of fanatics who lodge themselves right in the middle of the Old Town of Hebron, spinning barbed wire around their homes and schools like militant caterpillars. In this clean-cut settlement with the clean-shaven, heavily-armed security man at the entrance, they have IT jobs and children and comfy station wagons. They're young, modern, and thrifty; compared with Tel Aviv or Jerusalem, Har Gilo is reasonably priced. The air is even better than the view. These well-educated young people aren't even exactly aware that they're living in a settlement.

This country, you see, is made up of two different countries. They are superimposed on the same place like two noncongruous maps, and for fifty years, it must be said, the Red-Greens have been on the bottom, with much less air to breathe. There are two systems for everything: different roads, different license plates, different-color identity cards. Different jurisdictions. Different checkpoints for people with very different privileges: at one checkpoint the ones with the "right" license plates are waved through almost as casually as though this were Europe's Schengen zone; at the other one the men with the wrong-colored ID cards stand in a pen several yards long, made of iron bars and ringed by barbed wire, so they can't climb out. In this humiliating position, caged like wild animals, they wait patient and helpless like Kafka's surveyor to learn whether they'll make it to the Castle this time. But even if they succeed, all their Castle means is that after an endless wait they can go to their badly paid job in a bakery or a restaurant kitchen, or the construction workers can erect the Wall with their own hands, or build new honeycomb houses on the land that once belonged to them.

And there are even two kinds of roofs in this country: on shoddy flat roofs black cisterns clump together like aphids, while the others have tidy red tiles evoking Europe. These roofs don't need water tanks; here, as in other civilized parts of the world, the water pressure is adequate.

And not just the languages are different, the terminology differs as well: when the Blue-Whites build houses in the occupied territories, they're called settlements, and when not even their own government has authorized them, they're called outposts. Still, the same government sends soldiers quickly if they need protection. Meanwhile, the Red-Greens live in old-fashioned villages, cities, and towns.

There is just one common feature: almost everything built since the beginning of the occupation is illegal, either by international law or by Blue-White law, because an occupation is normally a temporary state. In a provisional arrangement, by its very definition, no construction permits are given to the Red-Greens. People need houses all the same. So they build them, with their bare hands and the help of their neighbors, using everything they can find. But all of them, with a few anomalous exceptions, are illegal, and have been illegal for the past fifty years. But only the houses of the Red-Greens get torn down. By the month, by the week, sometimes several each night. Whereas the settlers' houses are torn down so rarely that whenever they are, it makes headlines. And it may goad Blue-White fanatics into carrying on their "Price Tag" campaign. The "Price Tag" campaign is a threat ostensibly aimed at their own government, the message being: Go ahead and tear down our houses, the houses of the true patriots. You'll see the price you have to pay. Many wondered if the July 2015 arson attack in Duma was one of those retaliatory actions: at dawn, when it's usually the scorpion-like bulldozers that come, a Molotov cocktail was tossed into a Red-Green house, and a couple and their eighteen-month-old baby died in the fire. The four-year-old survived, an orphan with no siblings, and will need a lifetime to recover from the injuries.

BACK TO THE FRIENDLY YOUNG FAMILIES OF HAR GILO. THEY DON'T even think this is a settlement, they think it's a suburb of Jerusalem. As for Walajeh, the little village growing wild half below and half behind them—they probably think it's a slum, if they notice it at all. All those heaps of rubble everywhere! Next to one of the fresh heaps, where the dust still gleams white, Aya and her siblings play in the sun.

Soon there's going to be a big nature park down in the valley. All that needs to happen first is for a bit more of Walajeh's inhabitants' land to be expropriated. For decades the fields of Walajeh have systematically been taken away from the owners, using such a colorful bunch of rationales that one has to admire the Blue-White lawyers' creativity: pre-1917 Ottoman laws, military firing zones, fields left unused for too long. Also: deed registrations that are unclear, or have vanished, or been declared invalid; security concerns far too classified to be explained, or, again, almost a sardonic touch: a nature park. What objections could anyone have to that? Plenty, if all you have left is that one olive grove.

But the young families from Har Gilo are looking forward to the park! Soon they'll be picnicking amid natural splendor with their friends from the capital. Meanwhile, the people of Walajeh, halfway down the hill, will be cooped up behind a fence several yards high, staring from a safe distance at what used to be their fields.

I imagine fourteen-year-old Elad, living in Har Gilo, Row Two, in a three-bedroom honeycomb. But right now his favorite place is Hebron, the historic city where he has relatives. I imagine that Elad's mother isn't happy about that, though the relatives are her own brother and his sons. She's constantly worried. And so Elad doesn't tell her about his heroic exploits with his cousins. There are certain things mothers don't understand; for instance, that the demands of patriotism are directly dependent on where you live. In boring old Har Gilo you have time to play Game Boy, but in Hebron you have to struggle, even if you're just a boy.

After school the kids in Hebron hang around near the holy places, where the tour busses arrive, Jews from all over the world, chirpy Taiwanese Christians wearing pink baseball caps so they don't lose sight of each other (as though that were even possible), and timid Germans with roughly carved wooden crosses dangling over their checkered bellies. The enemy busses, the left-wing snakes with their followers from Central Blue-White, are smaller and less conspicuous. But the main actors in this play have known each other for years, so it takes just a few minutes before the teenage boys identify a bus full of critics, and the game begins.

Like all games, it has clearly defined rules: get in their way however you can, spoil their tour of the city. Only touching is off limits. So these teenagers silently stretch out their arms and spread their fingers, almost a welcoming gesture, but in fact meaning just the opposite. As human barriers they stand in front of the guides of the small groups that come not to pray at Abraham's grave, but to show this brutally divided city, this witches' cauldron whose lid is held down with tremendous effort by the Blue-White military. They come because many of this doubled country's problems come to a head in the Old Town of Hebron: religious fanaticism, military intransigency, and the resulting radicalization of the oppressed Red-Green majority. But the few hundred settlers who see themselves as a bastion of religion don't appreciate this sort of human rights tourism. And their children don't appreciate it either.

And so the settlement kids plant themselves in front of the hulking guide who used to be their protector in a previous life, when he was stationed here as a soldier.

THE GREAT ISRAELI WRITER AMOS OZ, WHO THREW STONES AT BRITISH soldiers himself as a child and yelled "British go home," describes himself as a "cured fanatic," writing: "Traitor, in the eyes of the fanatic, is anyone who changes."

The guide, the ex-soldier, is one of those changed people. He hasn't become a pacifist. But he was unable to bear what his army, his country, was doing day after day as an occupying power. And every week he takes other interested citizens to Hebron to show it to them.

That is why these kids are blocking the path of the traitor, their own soldier. He has to zigzag around grinning children. Whenever he holds up a photo or a map, they crowd up and hold their hands in front of it, hiding the illustrative material by becoming an illustration themselves.

Now this gets the attention of the active soldiers, who are lurking everywhere in small groups. They approach unobtrusively, as though gliding on tracks. The guide raises his voice ("Here you can see that the front doors are welded shut, the occupants can leave their houses only out the back way, or from the roof"), realizing that the group's attention is slipping away from him. The boys grin at each other. They raise their arms with the outspread fingers, like windmills, a ballet of arms. The members of the tour group shake their heads. I imagine that the boys consider it a good day if at some point one of these out-of-town voyeurs loses his cool. Some jerk from Haifa, Netanya, or Brooklyn will yell at the kids, tell them to behave themselves, in the end he might even grab one of them by the arm and push him aside, but they can always count on the group's cameraman, the littlest one, a ten-year-old, he always films everything with his cell phone. And then they call the police.

I imagine that at first Elad was afraid to play along. But the worst thing that can happen is that the soldiers might drag you away. Once Elad's cousin yelled, "Are you grabbing me like an Arab?" Elad remembered that. Now he always yells, "I'm not a filthy Arab, arrest these left-wing traitors here instead."

The best thing is when Oded, Elad's uncle, comes—and he almost always comes when people in Western clothing start taking pictures of the concrete blocks, as tall as a man, that chop up the alleys of the Old Town, with *Death to Arabs* spray-painted on them.

"Talk to us," Uncle Oded demands, "listen to the other side! They're lying to you, they're hiding the truth from you," he shouts. "That guy over there, your Arab friend, he's from a family that shot one of our babies. Do people like that get to have human rights?"

And the coolest one of all is Moshe, ancient and pious, a great-uncle or great-granduncle. He's so old, no one's going to do him any harm, and he's so angry that his sidelocks nearly stand on end. He dashes outside as soon as he sees one of those left-wing snakes with their groups, and every time he has to pull himself together not to snatch at their T-shirts. But he yells and rages, he knows all about them; for instance, that the mother of one of the activists committed suicide. "If you end up with a kid like that, all you can do is kill yourself!" Sometimes Elad almost worries that one of these days it might make them stop coming.

When there's nothing happening, no activist busses, the Hebron kids bombard the marketplace. The buildings in the Old Town are divided horizontally, one group upstairs, the other downstairs, with entrances on different sides. The stairwells are cemented shut. With their surveillance cameras, the Blue-Whites keep an eye on everything from above. The Red-Greens still have a few scattered shops down in their narrow alleyways, and they put up gratings, nets, chicken wire over them to protect them from stones and rubbish from above. That doesn't matter. The right projectile can sometimes get through the nets, and big stones can at least shake them so that the people below duck and hold their hands over their heads. In some places it's starting to get dark down there, dark forever. Elad, who likes to tinker, thinks a lot about what kind of objects block the most light. Water canisters, flattened boxes, tarps, old cloth. Square yard by square yard. At some point you people down there will be living in endless night. And then you won't even be able to see those colorful sweets of yours.

OF COURSE THE BOYS DON'T JOIN IN THE GIRLS' GAMES, THAT'S AN INTER-national norm. But they go and watch on Saturdays, when they don't have school but the others do. These big boys' little sisters stand outside the Red-Green girls' school and wait for the other girls to come out. And then they push and throw stones, and human rights freaks from Europe, big pale or salmon-pink grownups from the north, awkwardly throw themselves between the two groups and try to protect the little girls with the headscarves. And the soldiers stand by and watch, because they have an unambiguous mission in this sick, ambiguous city: to prevent violence against the eight hundred Blue-Whites. The violence committed by the few Blue-Whites against the two hundred thousand Red-Greens is none of their business, none whatsoever. Certainly not when little girls are beating up little girls. Then the soldiers daydream about their next cigarette break and shrug their shoulders, every single damned Saturday afternoon, when the little Red-Green girls' school lets out and the chase begins.

IN WALAJEH, THE VILLAGE THAT WILL SOON BE ENCLOSED BY A WALL AND a fence the way a stone is held by a fist, one Red-Green has pulled off a spectacular, absurdist victory against the occupiers. Let's call him Abu Mustafa. He has three children and a couple of goats. And his house is the only one outside the line along which the fence will be built. Walajeh is a peaceful village, not a hotbed of terrorism, and the people don't demonstrate every week, like people do in other places. But one reason all these walls and fences are being built is so that if there is a new uprising, the Red-Greens can be shut out quickly and effectively. Picture an enormous crane truck piled high with cement blocks. In the event of an alarm, it will trundle through the occupied territories and dump several of the blocks outside the entrance to each village. And everything is shut tight.

At any rate, Allah lent his aid, Abu Mustafa successfully fought off all orders to tear down his family's house and resettle them, and now, believe it or not, the soldiers have built him a tunnel under the fence. Soon he'll get a gate and a key to go along with it. So that, walled out twice over, he can go into the village, for example if he wants to do some shopping or pay a visit. Or if he wants to leave Walajeh. You see, that he must do via the official exit. Anyway, from his house he could do nothing but clamber up the steep slopes.

And so Walajeh, this village of 2,500 people, will be shut in a coffin just as West Berlin once was. With the distinction that the Berlin Wall was meant to keep the shut-out East Berliners from fleeing into the fenced-off freedom of the West. Whereas here the farmers are being kept from their fields, which even now they can reach only with great effort, by taking detours, and soon, if the whole green valley is turned into a nature park, will no longer be allowed to tend them. But Walajeh has yet another problem, compared with which Abu Mustafa's private tunnel is just a grotesque escapade.

If we picture the fence around Walajeh as a circle with just one opening, and Abu Mustafa's house as a little bulge, there's also a line cutting straight through the circle. It is the Jerusalem municipal boundary. Part of the village belongs to the capital, part to the occupied territories. In other words, this village, which has already hopped over one border, the Green Line, has been saddled with an additional border. A lot depends on whether or not a house is located on the territory of the capital. Red-Green inhabitants of Jerusalem are able to work anywhere in Blue-White, which means far higher wages. It means that their license plates (yellow) and their ID cards (blue) are the "right" colors. It means that they don't have to stand in iron pens at five a.m., worrying day after day that for "security reasons" the computer will refuse to let them go to work. It means access to the Blue-White social security and health care system. Let us say a fictitious Mahmoud is injured when his house is declared illegal and torn down. Because from 1967 onwards the demolished house stood in the right location, Mahmoud, with his blue ID card, can be treated in a Blue-White hospital. Only he's unlikely to win his case against the soldier who injured him.

It is easy to see what that means for a small community, when one person is able to reach for the lifesaver that the vagaries of the border have put within his reach, while his next-door neighbor cannot. Some take advantage of it, some refuse on principle. And others don't even have that choice.

And we haven't even spoken of the true tests of solidarity faced by the families in all the little Walajehs in this carved-up country. The ten-year-old boys who are arrested for throwing stones and beaten up in prison, who then "confess" to something, incriminate someone else, and forever after are the school cowards, the traitors. Or the other children like the pretty little girl who angrily shook her fist at a soldier, became famous when the picture went viral, and got a medal from President Erdogan of Turkey. One is a traitor, one is a star. In all the little Walajehs there may be a dramatic lack of water, proper garbage disposal, legal security, justice, freedom of movement. But there's Internet everywhere.

When I first came here, I thought I knew about borders. In Vienna, where I grew up, very near the Iron Curtain, it was a harsh but clear-cut affair: watch towers, barbed wire, us over here, them over there. As children, we were afraid that "they" might attack us, might cease to respect the border. The moment a siren howled, six-year-olds said to each other with serious faces: "The Russians are coming." But the Communists cared about that border even more than we did—they had cooped up their own people behind it. Just as the Iron Curtain fell, seemingly without warning, I was growing up. My coming of age coincided with an infinitely blissful sense of liberation, of setting out into the world that once again had other directions beside west. Borders have fascinated me ever since. How they suddenly vanish, and sometimes linger all the same. In the Thuringian Forest, along the former border between East and West Germany, the mouflon still keep to their old sides, a quarter of a century after the fall of the Wall. No one told them that the land mines and spring guns have been removed, and so they avoid the former death strip.

In the West Bank, which some call Palestine and others call Judea and Samaria, the concept of the border as I knew it has lost all validity. It has less to do with Here and There than with Above and Below, with In Front and Behind—a tangle of two different-colored threads that the reckless construction of settlements tangles more and more inextricably. These borders are much more dangerous than borders elsewhere, for they are constantly in motion. And that means that they are everywhere—above all, to cite an old saying, "in people's heads."

I wonder whether one of those kids from Hebron with their sense of infinite strength might wake up one morning, at the age of forty-five, say, as a businessman in a hotel room in Atlanta or Tokyo, in Moscow or Tel Aviv. Whether he might glance at something or smell something that reminds him of those days. Might look at it differently for the first time in decades, that summer of dares, when the world was so splendidly black and white, when it was hilarious to see old women flinch as he and his friends tossed trash and stones onto the grating over their heads, and when his pretty little cousins made girls of the same age fear for their lives.

I wonder whether children like Aya, dragged out of their beds in the middle of the night because the army has come to bulldoze their houses, will ever forget that moment. Or whether these children will relate differently than I to a tattered sofa lying in the rubble, simply because they've seen them so often. Whether only I, coming from a peaceful world, think that a wrecked sofa looks so human, so distressingly intimate.

But even as I try to think of the future, the military-green present just goes marching on. For six years no more houses were torn down in Walajeh, just south of Jerusalem. Then, suddenly, three were torn down in one night. And now the order has come for twenty more to be torn down. Twenty Ayas. Most families have four or five children. Twenty times five.

(TRANSLATED FROM THE GERMAN BY ISABEL FARGO COLE)

VISIBLE, INVISIBLE: TWO WORLDS

ANITA DESAI

THE INVISIBLE VILLAGE

We have arrived, we are told, at the village Susiya. The dust stirred by our vehicle settles. We look around—and see nothing. Where is the village Susiya? Here is only dust, stone, rubble, and the white heat of the sun.

Blink, and you will see the caves where people once lived but have been bulldozed, smashed, their entrances blocked with rocks. So now there is only a blue tarpaulin or two, held up by sticks. Once there had been a cistern to collect sparse rainwater, but someone has driven the rusty chassis of a defunct car into it. So now they must buy a tanker of water to fill a container for them; they are waiting. Once they grew a little wheat by hand, having no implements, harvested and stacked it. Then the settlers came and set fire to it, so now there are only ashes. (If they fail to cultivate the land for a few years, whether based on fear or for other reasons, "Ottoman law" can be invoked and the land taken over.) They had once owned the land but then the authorities arrived with sheets of corrugated tin and built a shed in front of which they erected a sign: ARCHAEOLOGICAL SITE. So now their land is taken and archaeologists will come to dig for their remains. The people who live here still have been given their sign: they are considered dead, gone.

But a spot on the lunar landscape reveals itself as a tree: the lone tree of the village. Under it is seated a group of dark shapes: women sheltering from the noonday sun. From their folds a little girl emerges, a pretty child with a face like a flower. She extends her hand, offering the small hard green fruit in it to us, the visitors. Then, from under a tarpaulin, a boy, her brother, comes out with a tray—tea for the visitors.

Where have they come from—this small hard green fruit, this tray of glasses with hot sweet mint tea? These are ghosts of a past in which hospitality was gracious, a tradition. Is it what the archaeologists will find on the site of their excavation?

THE VISIBLE SETTLEMENT

These are the settlements lately built, of great blocks of pale limestone, one piled on top of another on a raised outcropping of rock, ringed by walls of concrete topped with barbed wire. Each house with an air-conditioner attached to its facade like a watchful eye. These are fortresses and the settlers inside it are safe. Sometimes the children of the fortress come to the wall and lean over it to spit on the ghost children of the invisible village below, then depart with shouts of laughter.

THE INVISIBLE CITY

Shuhada Street in Hebron once had a short wall built along part of its length—the broader half was where Israelis might drive, the narrower half where Palestinians might walk. Now the wall is gone but the entrance to the market is sealed, the shops shuttered. The residents of the apartments above the shops had cages installed over their balconies to protect them from the rocks hurled by settlers. Then the entrances were sealed. To exit, they had to climb down ladders at the back. Curfew could be declared for days, and had been for months in the earlier parts of the Second Intifada. A long, circuitous route would have to be traversed on foot to bring back a carton of milk, bread, or perhaps medicines. Slowly the number of residents dwindled.

Among the abandoned houses on Shuhada Street you may find just three or four that are still inhabited—by residents who refuse to leave, instead living the lives of ghosts who will not go away.

Witnesses then, these ghosts.

Two brothers, seated on an upholstered sofa that might once have furnished a grander house, now stranded. Once they had gone out to attend to businesses, to work. Now they go nowhere. One brother had his back broken in a beating by soldiers. He traveled to Jordan to have four vertebrae in his spine replaced, so now he is back, with a record on film of the surgery. His brother had had rocks flung at his head by settlers; he had lost his teeth; the dentures pinched but he was not complaining. He removed the dentures to reveal his tooth-less gums: evidence.

Also, they had computers on which to show films of the violence around them: one of a woman who had gone to stop soldiers from beating her son and was flung to the ground. Another, recently taken, of young settlers climbing into an apartment from the roof and seizing and flinging the furniture they found—tables, chairs, beds—into the street below, to cheers from the watching settlers. Calls to the police had gone unanswered. The broken wood would come in use: the festival of Lag Ba'Omer was coming up, huge bonfires would be lit. Many gathered to watch.

A boy, eleven years old, stick thin with a face as white as a sheet and eyes deep sunk and dark, brings the two men, his father and his uncle, cigarettes. It had taken a long time to persuade him to go out for them, after the time he had the bicycle he was riding in the street knocked down by soldiers who demanded, "Why do you have a knife? Why are you throwing stones?" He had neither a knife nor a stone on him, but they took him to their post, blindfolded him, and tied him to a chair and held him for two hours. When they tired of his crying and sniveling, they let him go, shouting, "You are not allowed on the street again today. If we see you, we will lock you up." He had come home weeping, then had hidden in his room and refused to come out.

His father had pulled him to his feet and told him, "Come with me. We will go out on the street and we will walk. Never be afraid to be free. Come," and he had led him down onto the street to teach him to be free.

In the apartment next door is a young man who goes to college, studies literature. From his open face, lively eyes, and ready laughter, it is clear he remains free. In a way. He loves the literature he reads, would like to go abroad for graduate studies. But he will not, because his mother and sisters cannot be left to fend for themselves. So physically he is not free, no, but his face and his eyes are lit with another kind of freedom. The kind the settlers must fear.

At regular intervals these residents have a visitor. They know him well. Each time he asks them, "When will you leave? Here, I promise you a million dollars. An American visa. American citizenship guaranteed. Take it, and leave. Why won't you leave?"

The remaining residents stare at him, silently. Some others have accepted his offers and gone, but they continue to refuse. All he can find in their faces, their silence, is their refusal.

AT THE JERUSALEM WRITERS FESTIVAL, A CONVERSATION BETWEEN Colum McCann and David Grossman.

McCann: "So why don't you leave?"

Grossman: "Because here I am relevant."

THE VISIBLE CITY

Not far from Shuhada Street, the Visible City, a settlement. Not so much a fortress, this one, as a sleek city suburb. The apartments have balconies with flowers, the yards have trees. There are cypress trees, there is bougainvillea. Cars come out of the gates, they are driven to shops and schools, they take people to work. The sun shines. How normal it all is.

But the apartments must have windows and out of those windows the residents can look across the street to the old city, the ghost city. When they do, what do they think? Or do they not think, just hope that it will disappear in a cloud of dust, like a ghost?

FROM THE INVISIBLE TO THE VISIBLE WORLD

One must go through a checkpoint. One must have a pass, an entry permit, a work permit, ID. One must be there at four a.m. if one needs to be at work, or at school, by seven a.m. One must pass through turnstiles guarded by soldiers who might do their best to bar entry or at least delay it. Men must remove belts, shoes, women must prove they have a doctor's appointment or there is a family crisis or it is a day or an hour when it is permitted to visit the mosque. It cannot be on any day or at any time. Nowhere is time and the calendar observed with greater ferocity.

Out on the land it is fences that separate farmers from their fields. There are gates that will be opened at certain times, for a certain period, so the farmers may tend to their crops, their vines, and their flocks. If a farmer misses the time allotted to him, he will find the gate closed. If it is open, he will find it is not a direct crossing to his land; the route devised for him is the longest one possible to make. So gradually his vines and crops will wither, his flocks disappear, and the land become fallow. Then, by "Ottoman law" it can be appropriated—and "settled."

Don't these people understand that they are not meant to be? That they are ghosts, without lives, without a future? So why do they insist on continuing to exist? And suffer?

HIP-HOP IS NOT DEAD

POROCHISTA KHAKPOUR

MY TRIP TO ISRAEL-PALESTINE WAS MY FIRST JOURNEY BACK TO the Middle East after thirty-four years. My family, Iranian refugees, left Iran just before I turned four, shortly after the revolution. The Iran-Iraq War was well under way. I had not properly been in the region since, other than a dizzying stopover at the Dubai airport en route to Australia, which really could have been any travel hub in the First World.

The night before my flight to Tel Aviv I was restless in my bed in New York City's Harlem. For months I'd felt equally agonized and excited about this trip. Just six months before, I'd gone to the first Muslim country I've been in since Iran: Indonesia, and I'd found myself mesmerized by the sound of Islamic prayers over loudspeakers, streets full of women in colorful veils, and people who not only were interested in but delighted by my background. The last time I'd been surrounded by women in veils and heard the sound of the call to prayer was when I was a toddler in Iran. My memories of that time are tense and turbulent and, in the context of my new home in America, even shameful. Indonesia somehow made me feel more Iranian, in the best way. But just weeks after I left, the Sarinah shopping mall in Jakarta, right across from my arty boutique hotel, was attacked by terrorists. In the months that followed, I read about one terrorist attack after another, all over the globe. Every week it felt like I had a new country to hashtag with "#PrayFor."

Israel-Palestine, of course, seemed menacing well before all this. I had long argued the issue with people I barely knew on Facebook; I fought about Gaza without understanding much about the region. And as the only Middle Easterner from a Muslim culture flying in from abroad for this trip—and one who was outspoken on all issues involving the Middle East online—it frightened me that my hosts took my fears about safety seriously.

At several points I considered not going.

Still, in another way, this trip felt like a homecoming. My assignment was to cover Palestinian hip-hop. It had been fourteen years since I had covered the hip-hop beat, my first area of interest as a journalist. As a young writer in Manhattan, I lived for shows and did CD reviews and feature interviews for all sorts of music publications, concentrating on hip-hop. Now I longed to learn more about the hip-hop scene in a region where people looked like me and my family.

Meanwhile, my hosts were fixated on the fact that my US passport listed Iran as my birthplace. *This will likely be a problem*, my liaison said to me over e-mail several weeks before. My hosts arranged a VIP escort for me at Ben Gurion Airport, in hope that this would get me through without harassment. This felt strange to me: It had been fifteen years since I'd become an American citizen, just two months after 9/11. Certainly the American portion of my hyphenated identity could protect me from the Iranian?

AT THE AIRPORT, A WISECRACKING OLDER WOMAN IN A SUIT AND BADGE approaches—she is my escort, and she helps me with my bags, and seems delighted that I am from New York. "Good city!" she says, but when she looks at my passport, she frowns.

"Iran?!" she says.

I nod.

"Oh dear. This could be a"—and here comes the word everyone uses—"problem."

I nod. I am prepared.

But I am not quite prepared for the three and a half hours that I am detained in a holding area in the airport, with half a dozen other Arab-looking people. Inexplicably, a group of Midwestern women who are part of a school trip are detained too.

"No idea why we would be here!" one of them declares to no one in particular, laughing nervously. Within half an hour, they are on their way.

The rest of us wait silently, staring at the ground. There is a television monitor blasting the news, but I am lost in other thoughts. When I finally look up at the screen, I see footage of Syrian refugees waiting at some border.

My escort, the only Israeli in the holding area, paces back and forth.

"Iran is a problem here," she repeats, with a shrug.

I am questioned not once, not twice, but three times by three different agents in cramped offices. They look things up on their computer as they ask me questions, and I wonder if they are googling my name.

"What are your parents' names?"

I tell them.

"What about your father's father?"

I pause. I never met the man. He died in the 1950s, when my father was seven. His is the most Muslim-sounding name in my family history: Assadolah. I almost feel like they know this. I realize it's a name I've never said out loud, and when I do it's almost a whisper.

They ask me to repeat it.

I say it again.

Their nods feel knowing.

Two out of the three interrogators ask me why I am here. As instructed by my hosts, I tell them I'm working on a book. I do not discuss my itinerary, which includes stops at checkpoints, settlements, and refugee camps. I realize too late that the printed-out e-mail I am holding in my hand contains these very instructions.

"Why does it say not to tell us of your itinerary?" he asks, eyes fixed on the papers in my hands.

I panic but try to seem calm: "Because it's not set. They keep changing it. We wouldn't want to tell you the wrong thing."

He looks at me skeptically and I will myself not to look away. He returns to his computer. I am amazed he could make out the print.

Back in the holding area, I ask my escort what would be the worst-case scenario. She says she is not sure, but she has seen many people put back on a plane and returned.

Eventually without much explanation I am released. My hosts meet me, and give me a nice tour of Jerusalem. I fall in love with the Old City. There is a beautiful white dustiness to the city, a gentle, aged quality: the ruins come to life. I try to forget about my hours at the airport, though when I see the Israeli soldiers and police officers, many of them young women with full makeup, giving off an aura of both boredom and toughness, I feel anxious again.

Back in my room, I try to go to sleep early, but outside there is noise. For a moment I wonder if I am hearing the call to prayer, but I soon realize it's another sound: celebration. On the terrace below my balcony, there is a wedding party going on. Women in jeweled and embroidered veils, wedding cakes, children running around, and that sound: the elated wails of a full-throated singer belting love ballads. In the secondhand joy of these moments, I soon forget my airport experience entirely.

AFTER MANY DAYS OF EMOTIONALLY TAXING VISITS TO AREAS UNDER OC-cupation, I return to Tel Aviv—this time for hip-hop. Tamer Nafar, arguably the first Palestinian rapper, invites me to a screening of his and Udi Aloni's film *Junction 48*, playing at a Tel Aviv movie theatre. He tells us to pick him up for breakfast before the showing. I am thrilled at the prospect of a fancy Tel Aviv breakfast with a Palestinian hip-hop celebrity.

But Tamer, who barely says hello to us when we pick him up, does not want to go to some fancy Tel Aviv restaurant. Instead, he takes us to the heart of Lod, twenty minutes from downtown Tel Aviv, where he grew up. Lod is a mixed Palestinian and Jewish city inside Israel, rough around the edges, the way Brooklyn used to be.

The café he suggests is a bare-bones greasy spoon, empty but for us. The waiters know him well. They bring us a no-nonsense breakfast of bread and hummus and coffee and we chat.

Tamer Nafar, thirty-seven, turns heads everywhere he goes—he is well-known to everyone, it seems, in Israel-Palestine. He is also hard to miss: very tall, somewhat chic, and a bit goofy, but still with that hip-hop swagger, in the Jay-Z urban-nerd sort of way. He scans the room, as if on the lookout for something. He is nervous about his film, almost a biopic, in which he stars.

He is more at ease reminiscing about the 1980s and his introduction to hip-hop. "We all watched Fresh Prince. And everyone was a Michael Jackson fan. For me he was the first gangster rapper before NWA." He recalls asking his Ethiopian Jewish friends what lyrics meant, stopping any black person on the street for guidance with American rap. He became hooked on Tupac, which, in turn, helped him improve his English. Ultimately it was Slim Shady–era Eminem that became his favorite.

In the late 1990s, after seeing Jewish rappers perform in Tel Aviv, Tamer started writing lyrics in Hebrew. Shortly after that, he started rapping in Arabic too. He formed the group DAM with his brother Suhell and their friend Mahmoud Jreri. The name means, in Arabic, "lasting forever" or "eternity" and in Hebrew it's the word for "blood." It's also an acronym for "Da Arabian MCs." DAM's music caught on. For two weeks, one of their songs was number one on Haifa radio, the first time local rappers were on the charts. The music, at that point, was essentially mixtapes, since Tamer and DAM had no access to producers. By 2000, he was performing in front of both Jewish and Palestinian crowds.

His biggest hit came in 2001, when he wrote a song called "Who's the Terrorist." In it, he argued that the Israeli military and the state were the primary perpetrators of terrorism, not Palestinians. The song was downloaded one million times in a single month, and it led to offers from record companies. DAM signed with Red Circle and EMI Arabia, and started touring and earning real money for the first time.

DAM was a family affair. Tamer and Suhell's father came to their shows, even though he was a devout Muslim and was confined to a wheelchair. In 2013, while Tamer and Suhell were away on tour, their father died. Tamer's first child was born the month before. These two events happening at almost the same time changed Tamer. "I wanted to quit music—I wasn't inspired anymore," Tamer says. He wanted to be with his family in Lod.

Lod, Tamer tells me, as we drive through the nicer part of town where he now lives, not far from the other, rougher side of town where he grew up, was and is a center for the Israel–Palestine drug trade. Tamer himself was never involved in drugs—never even smoked weed, though he hung out with drug dealers and drank a lot. He never smoked, because, he tells me, "a lot of my friends who smoked a cigarette ended up with a needle in their arm, so I didn't want that."

His music is full of clever observations, tongue twisters, and unpredictable slant rhymes, like early Jay-Z meets early Kanye. There is always humor and there is always politics, sometimes deep ironies tucked in the dark comedy. For instance, in "Mama I Fell in Love with a Jew" the hook goes "Her skin is white, my skin is brown / She was going up, I was going down." In "Who's the Terrorist" the rhythm feels very Eminem, and Tamer's rhymes feel like a manifesto: "Who is a terrorist? I am a terrorist? / How can I be a terrorist if I live in my homeland? / Who is a terrorist? You are a terrorist / You have taken everything I own in my land."

I realize that not long ago, I'd seen a very funny music video of his single "Scarlett Johansson Has Gas." In 2014, Johansson had attracted worldwide criticism for appearing in an ad campaign for SodaStream, which was then produced in an Israeli settlement. Tamer's response came in his hit song: "Saving the world from all them boring details / Whatever she sells, count me in on presales / Even if it's in a settlement, do we care? / About reality, my reality / First they moved me here and now they wanna move me there."

Even with all the international and mainstream success, a project as personal as *Junction 48* was a big step for Tamer. It's described as "a love story of two young Palestinian hip-hop artists who use their music to fight against both the external oppression of Israeli society and the internal repression of their own crime-ridden, conservative community." In it, Tamer plays Kareem, who lives in the ghetto of Lod and dreams of becoming a rapper. This is, in many ways, Tamer's *8 Mile*—he nods at the comparison. For two years, he wrote the script with a partner, the Israeli-American filmmaker Oren Moverman, and trained for months for his role. He still feels a bit uneasy with it all: "You imagine things and suddenly the cast has nothing to do with your imagination."

But he is happy that most of the cast is made up of nonactors. He is also proud of the film's early success—it debuted at the 2016 Tribeca Film Festival, where it won the "Best International Feature Narrative" award. At Berlinale, it won an Audience Award. He is excited for it to be released in the United States.

He identifies as a "Palestinian artist and activist—don't ask me which is more." His goals are clear: "I wanted to build myself as a cultural figure who can do political activism and write scripts and act and rap and write music."

A few days later, I meet him again, at a benefit event in the garden of a museum in Jaffa. The audience of elderly wealthy people is not prepared for Tamer. Though he seems to me less than enthusiastic as he goes to the stage, he is a professional. There is no DJ, and he sets up the sound via a laptop himself. But once the beat kicks in, Tamer is all star, giving the music everything he has. Even a few white-haired heads manage to bob along.

BACK IN THE OLD CITY OF JERUSALEM, I MEET MUZI RAPS. HE'S A heavyset young man wearing a Dr. Seuss T-shirt that says GOOD TO THE LAST DROP, with a black cap with gold block print spelling out BAD. One might consider him the Busta Rhymes of Palestinian hip-hop, a sort of easy-smiling trickster. His name is Mustafa Jaber, and he's performed under a variety of stage names, including We Are from Here.

Muzi looks around wistfully as he smokes. He is on his way to a new life, moving to Berlin to work with refugees on their music, in the coming months. His day job is construction work, but he's aiming to set up a music production company.

The easy grin and goofy style is misleading—he grew up a troublemaker, he says, fighting a lot, and was arrested numerous times. He has seven brothers, one of them his twin, whose idea it was to perform hip-hop to begin with.

In 2006, his first album, *My Town,* came out, followed by a second in 2009 called *The Beautiful Life*. "The first one was an issue as it had racist raps against Israelis, so for the second we shifted the focus to the military." His third album, *Who Are You*, is due out at the end of 2016. "It's about police in the Old City and the relationship between police and guns," he says.

Like Tamer, Muzi was influenced by rappers like Tupac, Biggie, Eminem, and Kanye, but in the new album, he says, there are dubstep and techno elements too. Muzi has played for raves (including one, in 2011, with an audience of forty-five thousand) and he is into unlikely fans and scenes overlapping with his.

In 2014, he and his twin performed on a TV show called *Best Talent of Palestine*, and won second place, which put him on the radar of a broader audience. He wasn't just a local kid anymore. While he raps mostly in Arabic, he's open to doing more in English, and he's now learning Hebrew too.

When I ask Muzi if he is an activist, he grows serious, even tough, nodding emphatically. "Before, no," he says. "Now, hell yeah. For sure."

THEN THERE'S THE "FIRST LADY OF ARABIC HIP-HOP." SHADIA MANSOUR was born in 1985, her parents both Christian Palestinians originally from Haifa and Nazareth. She performs in a traditional Palestinian embroidered *thobe* that covers the whole body. Every song is political. Her first single, *"Al Keffiyeh Arabiya"* ("The Keffiyeh Is Arab"), featured rapper M-1 of Dead Prez and was something she felt she had to write when she discovered an American-made blue-and-white-colored Arab scarf with Stars of David on it. Mansour introduced her song onstage in New York by saying, "You can take my falafel and hummus, but don't fucking touch my keffiyeh."

Mansour is a natural lyricist and storyteller. "I got into hip-hop in the mid-nineties," she says. "I was an Arab Palestinian, born in the West, searching for a language that demarginalized or uncategorized me. Hip-hop gave me a head start to speak up for myself and in my own voice. It was the realness and audacity that made it easy for me to relate to and a great way to fight cultural exile that was often unnoticed, unobserved, and unchallenged."

She has broken many glass ceilings—the Arab one, the Palestinian one, and of course the female one. "I think that Arabic hip-hop has come a long way in terms of solidifying its place as a legitimate genre in music. When I came on the scene, Palestinian hip-hop was fairly new, you could say it was an introduction to this new addition to Arabic hip-hop (after Moroccan and Algerian hip-hop). I'm of the generation that put Arabic hip-hop on the map. I came on the scene with the intention to represent Arabic hip-hop, to create the foundation for and transforming it to a genre where women, whether they choose to be lyricists or not, can feel Arabic hip-hop represents them."

When I ask her if she thinks she's an activist, her answer is eloquent. "I personally see activism as an art form in itself, from the way that people express themselves, bringing political, social, or economic issues to people's attention, to the way that action itself can unite, impact, and inspire different people and build bridges among them in the same way that music does."

THE FIRST TIME I SAW THE SLOGAN *HIP-HOP IS NOT DEAD; IT LIVES IN PALestine* was in New York, many years and lives ago, when I was a young hip-hop journalist. The show was Wu-Tang Clan's, and I can't remember what the person wearing the T-shirt looked like, just those words.

Back at the airport after a week in Israel-Palestine, I see the shirt on a teenager who passes by quickly. As I wait for my plane, I think of the strangeness and beauty of being in a region where it's so easy to meet the first and best of their kind, where no matter how famous they are, people are eager to share their stories. A place where to be seen and heard is not something you take for granted, a land where everyone is a storyteller, a world where anything good that happens is a blessing never to be taken for granted. I think of how I stopped writing about hip-hop in the 2000s, when radio rap became more and more about wealth, about luxuries like mansions and fancy cars, and less and less about community troubles and life on the streets. In Palestine, every rapper has a subject, every human has a theme. It is strong, impossible to ignore. Their topics are so urgent, their content so substantial, their message so clear. Injustice doesn't get much clearer than that.

On the way out, my interrogation was smoother, the only hold-up a disagreement about just how many ounces of liquid were in the bottle of face oil in my carry-on. On the plane, I think about the young street kids in Hebron, trying to sell me bracelets and tugging at my purse. I think about the settlers just steps away with their curses and the hot spit they aimed at me, but that landed on their own sidewalk. I think about a Palestinian teenage poet I met, who was planning to study in America for a summer, and who lives with his parents and family—and a group of strangers: one day Israeli settlers showed up at their door with furniture, moving in, claiming half the space as their own. I think about floating in the Dead Sea and looking across to Jordan, so close. I think about the guns I saw, the barbed wire, about the constant threat of violence. I wonder how Muzi's new record is doing, if Tamer's film will be well received in the United States, and whether, for Shadia, being a female or Arab constitutes more of a barrier to success.

As we take off into the sky, I think of my Iranian-ness and my American-ness, and how the two sides of my hyphen challenge each other continually, how so much of my identity has not just been "a problem" in Ben Gurion Airport but pretty much everywhere. I wonder if there will be a time that I can exist outside of those identifiers, what it even means to put those in words. Every thought I have is met with the echo of Tamer's lyrics from his song "Letter from Prison": "I wish bravery was a choice we make and not something we're forced to be."

OCCUPATION'S UNTOLD STORY

FIDA JIRYIS

I 'LL TAKE IT!" I SAID, AS I GLANCED AROUND THE EMPTY APARTMENT.
The lady did not smile or show any sign of agreement. I was
beginning to feel uneasy. She'd looked up at me questioningly as I
knocked on the open door of her office a few minutes earlier. "Yes?"
she'd enquired, cautiously. Something about me must have given me
away.

"Good morning!" I said, as brightly as I could. The group of new
buildings was in a perfect location, halfway between my village and
Nahariyya, a small, seaside town in the Galilee. I'd be close to my
parents, my work, and the beach at the same time. I'd driven past
many times as they were under construction, and, as soon as they
were advertised for rent, I couldn't wait to try my luck. I'd finish
work every day and go jogging on the beach . . .

"Can I help you?" the lady asked, still measuring me up.

"Yes, I'd like to see one of the apartments you've advertised for
rent."

My accent gave me away; I was an Arab. She looked uncomfort-
able. I was used to this kind of reticence, though. I'd just smile and
pretend I didn't notice.

She fiddled around with a bunch of keys and escorted me out of the office, toward one of the buildings. "We have one here . . ." she said.

One? *Lady, the complex is still almost empty,* I thought.

I was a little disappointed when she opened the door. The apartment was bright and new, but it was very small. "Do you have anything larger?" I enquired.

"No, this is all that's available."

"Okay." One couldn't argue with the system. Well, I could, but it was unlikely I'd get anywhere. So I tried to put a smile on instead. "I'll take it. How much is the rent?" I asked, brightly.

"Uh, I need to ask you something first. Where are you from?"

This being Israel, I didn't pause to think of the inappropriateness of the question. "Fassouta. It's a village about twenty minutes from here. Near Ma'alot," I ventured, in reference to a Jewish town near my village, for referencing other Arab towns would have been useless.

"Right . . ." She nodded, frowning. "I'll need to ask you, then, to bring two references with your application, then I'd need to check with the neighbors."

"The neighbors?"

"Yes. I need to ask them if it's okay for you to live here, because, well, no apartments have been given to Arabs here. But if the neighbors are okay with it, we can proceed. I'll just put the application through, quietly," she added, lowering her voice, to imply that she would have to invoke an exception.

I swallowed, thanked her, and left. That was the end of it. I wasn't about to get permission from the neighbors to rent an apartment. It was also one of the many reasons that I found myself, not so long after, moving to Ramallah in the West Bank, part of the occupied Palestinian territory.

The attitude expressed by the woman is a standard illustration of how I and more than one and a half million other Palestinians living in Israel are treated by the state. We do not live in the West Bank and Gaza, but in Israel itself, in the Galilee in the north, the Triangle in the center, and the Naqab (Negev) in the south, all areas of Palestine that were attacked by Jewish militias in 1948 and that subsequently became Israel. We are the Palestinians and their descendants who remained in our country after this initial onslaught. After the wiping out of Palestine, the new state of Israel, created on its remains, had to contend with about 15 percent of the Palestinian population whom it did not manage to drive out with the others. Instead, it imposed Israeli citizenship on them and put them under harsh, military rule for eighteen years, until 1966, to try to squash any Palestinian identity or calls for justice, and to prevent any Palestinians it had ousted from returning. Israel abolished this military rule before its 1967 war and its occupation of the West Bank and Gaza, after which it imposed its military rule on those territories. Meanwhile, it figured that it was stuck with the Palestinians living inside its borders and that it had to start "integrating" them into Israeli society. Fifty years later, this effort has failed dismally, and we are now twenty percent of Israel's population.

Most people living outside Israel, and even Palestinians in the West Bank and Gaza, don't know much about Palestinian citizens of Israel. We are assumed to be the same as citizens of any other country and to be able to live normal lives. On the surface, we are far more "privileged" than our brethren in the West Bank and Gaza; with our Israeli citizenship and passport, we can vote, we have access to good education, public health care, and social benefits, and we can easily travel around the world, except for some Arab countries. We do not live in militarily occupied zones shredded by checkpoints, under the constant threat of clashes, Israeli army incursions, and Jewish settler violence. We are free to study almost anything we choose, with the knowledge that we live in a large job market that should absorb our skills.

But, in reality, this is only the facade of a system of rampant, structural, and institutionalized discrimination.

As Palestinians—on whichever side of the Green Line we live—we spend every minute of our lives in the country paying for the fact that we are not Jewish.

Whether in Israel or the West Bank (I'm prohibited by Israel from reaching Gaza, an hour's drive away, while Jewish Israelis are prohibited from entering Gaza or parts of the West Bank by Israeli law),

I open my eyes each morning to remember the reality of my being a second-, or maybe a third-class citizen, unwanted, oppressed, discriminated against, and inferior—the ugly duckling in a murky pond. I am tolerated, at best, allowed to live here because, well, Israel hasn't figured out a way to get rid of me yet.

When I lived in my family's village of Fassouta, in the Galilee, I was reminded every morning as I drove to work of my people's dispossession at the hands of the state. First, I had to drive through the remains of Suhmata and Dayr El-Qasi, two Palestinian villages that used to lie next to mine and that were depopulated and destroyed in 1948. Suhmata is a mass of shrubs today, with some stones jutting out that survived the Israeli bulldozers' ploughing the village into the ground at the time. Dayr El-Qasi has, in the miracle of Israel's creation, turned into Elqosh, a Jewish community, some of whose residents live in a few of its houses that were not destroyed, perhaps because these residents immigrated from Yemen and Kurdistan and appreciated the Arab architecture that the Palestinian owners who fled left behind—an irony that is a cause for reflection in itself. The Palestinians of Dayr El-Qasi and their descendants have lived in refugee camps in Lebanon ever since. They're stateless refugees about an hour's drive away from what used to be their home. Meanwhile, the people of Elqosh graze their cows, keep chicken coops, grow vegetables, and cultivate fruit orchards, with far more banal cares. They even pop in to Fassouta to do some petty trade and see a doctor or a dentist.

The Palestinians of Suhmata were also driven out, though some managed to remain and became internally displaced persons, that is, refugees in their own country. Some of them live in Fassouta and other nearby villages that survived. They flock to the site of Suhmata once a year, on Nakba Day, to commemorate their village that used to be. One has to wonder what is more painful—being totally removed and far away, or having to drive by one's village every day and see its ruins, while not being allowed to return to it.

Tens of other villages in the Galilee and hundreds more throughout Palestine suffered the same fate. I thought of their people, knowing that it was only through a fluke of fate that I wasn't in some miserable refugee camp with them, just one or two hours away, where millions of Palestinians suffer with no hope of coming home. My village is very close to the Lebanese border, and each time I looked over the hills into Lebanon, I would have the surreal feeling of them being so close, yet so far away. Meanwhile, the people who blatantly took their homes and lands lived right next to me, and I had to see them every day going about their business as usual. There doesn't seem to be much security for the Palestinians remaining, either; some members of the Israeli government and of various academic and intellectual circles in Israel have regularly called for the expulsion of Israel's Arab citizens through "demographic transfer"—code for forced displacement—and other notions, the ultimate aim being to achieve the "purity" of "the Jewish state." This is done publicly with no shame or reprisal.

After passing Dayr al-Qasi and Suhmata, I drove by Kfar Vradim, an opulent Jewish community boasting rows of neat villas, lush gardens, fountains, and wide pavements, contrasting sharply with our narrow streets full of potholes and our village completely lacking such amenities. In fact, the differences between Arab villages and Jewish communities in Israel, often lying right next to each other, are so marked that one can immediately tell which is which, just at a glance.

There are two, equally painful reasons for this. The first is that Palestinian villages evolved organically over hundreds of years, before modern zoning and municipal planning. Palestine and other Middle Eastern countries were never about mass construction of tidy neighborhoods. Their communities and dwellings evolved out of a slower, more organic, deeper connection to the land. These new Jewish communities, by contrast, were built in a planned, methodical way, their homes neat copies of each other, like recently built communities in the West. They seem to have fallen from the sky, in place of the destroyed Palestinian villages, and I see only ugliness in all this beauty and order, because I am reminded when I look at these communities of their unnatural incursion on this land. My mind unwittingly turns to how they came about—by military force and land grabs, and at the cost of ousting another people and taking their place.

Second, the Israeli state budget allocated for infrastructure and economic development in Arab towns and villages is a fraction of that allotted to Jewish ones. So are budgets for health, education, housing, and employment; the list goes on. There is a caveat that the state uses to propagate this practice: government budgets are allocated to each local authority based on the amount of tax revenue collected by that authority, including business and property taxes. With the number of employment initiatives and businesses in Arab municipalities being a bare minimum, the taxes collected are also small, compared with those collected in government-aided Jewish communities. Thus, rather than funding economic development projects in Arab areas, the government allocates smaller budgets to them—in proportion to their economic output—and the vicious cycle continues.

Palestinian citizens of Israel are in a sorry state, the perpetual underdogs of the system. In 1966, my father, Sabri Jiryis, wrote *The Arabs in Israel*, a book that became a landmark document about the Palestinians in Israel and their systematic oppression by the state. Sadly, the core message of the book still applies today, fifty years later. Israel's military regime inside the state itself has long ended, but its attitudes toward its Palestinian citizens are largely the same. We are seen as the enemy, a fifth column, a demographic threat. Our supposed equality enshrined by law translates to a system of institutionalized discrimination against us that spreads its tentacles into every aspect of our lives. Few in Israel question this discrimination, and only the long-battered civil society organizations put together one report after another. For me, it was another fact of life that I swallowed, and drove on.

By the time I got to work, I'd already sunk into that deep state of alienation that marks every breath I take in this country. My work interactions added to the mix. I could never overcome my intimidation at working with Israelis, no matter how hard I tried. I was the only Arab among thirty or so Jewish employees, but it wasn't this that intimidated me: it was the feeling I had every day that I was "lucky," somehow singled out, to be there—as though I had no right to such a job. Although many Palestinians, all Israeli citizens like myself, hold professional jobs in Israel, the majority are systematically poorer, forced, for generations, through practices of the state, to survive through menial or marginal work. Construction, for example, is one of the largest industries to employ Palestinians in Israel, as is manufacturing. Palestinians are largely excluded from senior or well-paying positions in private corporations or public institutions; few Arab engineers are hired, for example, into the Electricity Authority or the telecommunications companies, and they are completely excluded from the defense and aviation industries, among others. I had been so conditioned to the near impossibility of finding a good job as a Palestinian that, when it happened, I could hardly believe it. My family and friends were astounded when they asked about my salary; what was normal by Jewish standards was considered a fortune in our community.

At the job, little glimpses of reality quickly began to show. I often overheard my Jewish colleagues talking about their military service. Most of them were called away for a few weeks from time to time to do reserve army duty. There were heated political discussions about the recent Oslo accords and the relationship with the Palestinians. Throughout all this, I was silent and extremely uncomfortable. I was born in Lebanon, and, in 1983, when I was ten years old, I lost my mother to a bombing of the Palestine Liberation Organization Research Center in Beirut, in the fallout of the Israeli invasion the year before. In 1995, I came to Israel as a result of the Oslo accords. I couldn't help wondering, as I gazed around the room at my colleagues, how many of them had served in Lebanon during the invasion that I'd lived through there. But I pushed these thoughts away. I was back here now, I needed a job and had to start my life.

As though to soften some of my alienation, a friendship blossomed with an older British colleague, with whom I found much to connect and laugh about. She was Jewish and had immigrated to Israel as a teenager and married a local Israeli. One day, I invited her and her husband to my home in Fassouta. She gladly accepted and they came, but the visit turned out to be tense and uncomfortable, for a reason I couldn't immediately grasp. The conversation was strained, each topic I brought up received a lukewarm response, and they ate and left as quickly as possible. I cleared the plates away afterwards, feeling puzzled and deflated. At work the next day, she apologized to me, telling me that her husband had served in a high rank in the Israeli army and was uncomfortable visiting an Arab home.

I was stunned by her forthrightness, but appreciated the truth. With the exception of a few cities, Palestinians and Jewish Israelis live deeply segregated lives in Israel. This creates a real problem for some Palestinians, whose towns and villages are prevented from natural expansion by the Israeli government, as most of their lands were seized in 1948 and the remainder were classified as "state land." The government imposes strict zoning conditions and does not easily permit the expansion of building zones within the municipal boundaries of Arab towns and villages. Thousands of Arab homes are under the threat of demolition by the state for being located outside the permitted zones. Fassouta, my village, for example, has 11,000 dunums (1 dunum equals 1,000 square meters) within the jurisdiction of its local council, yet only 650 dunums have been approved by the government for new building expansion since 1988. The result is overcrowding and having to leave and find homes elsewhere. But many Jewish communities forbid Palestinians from living or even working in them, and some Palestinians have had to resort to lawsuits to secure the right to buy an apartment if they happen to have Jewish neighbors. We are treated as pariahs, unwanted and unwelcome. In a recent example, a Jewish member of parliament advocated the separation of Arab and Jewish women in maternity wards of hospitals, and several medical institutions are reported to have taken heed.

One day, a man I will call Moshe, one of my colleagues at work, stood in the doorway of my small office, beaming, coffee cup in hand. He had been friendly to me from day one. We exchanged small talk about work. He leaned against the door, studying me quizzically as he sipped his coffee. Then he said, rather thoughtfully: "You're not like other Arabs, eh? You've made something of yourself."

I paused. I wondered if he thought he was paying me a compliment, in singling me out from my "crude, backward" race. How was I supposed to reply?

"I tell you, you Christians," he continued, sticking his head in a little closer and lowering his voice, as though sharing a highly valued secret, "you're different. We have no problems with you!"

I blinked. So I was getting two compliments, it seemed, and Moshe was taking it upon himself to give me the stamp of approval on two accounts, including not being Muslim. I stared, thinking of the number of ways in which these remarks were wrong, and how they would be received in any other country, and utterly failing to experience the gratitude that they were meant to produce.

At the end of the workday, I arranged to meet my cousin for a trip to a mall in Haifa. We chattered in her little car, Arabic music playing, exchanging village gossip and news of the upcoming wedding season. For a while, I was transported out of the reality of the country to a world where I lived in my own homeland, Palestine, unencumbered by racism and discrimination.

But the reality shattered, as it always does, the minute we drove into the mall's parking lot. Hebrew signs were everywhere. Inside the mall, there wasn't a single sign in Arabic, though it served mostly Palestinian shoppers from the surrounding Galilean villages, and though Arabic is the second official language of the state. We walked into a shop and felt that familiar nervousness in speaking our language.

But I wasn't about to talk to my cousin in Hebrew. As we perused the clothing, we chatted in Arabic, though our voices subconsciously dropped. Seeing an assistant, I pointed to a dress, asking her for the right size to try. "Those are the last pieces!" the sour-faced woman snapped and walked off.

I turned away uncomfortably, but, this being Israel, we weren't surprised by the rude response. People's rudeness is a known characteristic of the country, and, for some reason, it evokes a national reaction of humor among Israelis rather than disbelief. But there's the chutzpah of Israelis' dealing with each other and the rest of the world, and there's a "flavored" chutzpah, loaded with a tacit sense of dislike and contempt, for dealing with Palestinians. Thus, when a more cheery-looking assistant bounded up to us to help, we were grateful.

Grateful, you see, for being treated like human beings, "despite" being Palestinian.

I tried on the dress. "Wow!" the assistant exclaimed as I came out of the fitting room. Okay, so I understood she was flattering me because she wanted to sell, but I smiled, nonetheless. Then she added: "You're so beautiful; one would never think you were an Arab!"

I returned the dress and walked out, my cousin and I shrugging our shoulders. It is not possible to live for even one day in Israel and forget that we are *us* and they are *them*—and we may never be accepted as being equal to them. In fact, in most of my interactions with Israelis, I feel a vibe of barely concealed hostility, cautious suspicion, or, in the best case, like Moshe, an attitude of benevolent tolerance of us, the indigenous natives, toward whom they are being generous in allowing us to stay on our land.

As my cousin and I lined up for burgers, I glanced curiously at the Jewish Israeli family near us, crowding at the shawarma stall. I wondered how it was that Palestinians didn't seem to exist in this country, but Palestinian food was so sought after. The shawarma had a kosher label, too. We're bending over backward trying to integrate, but I think the state would be happy if we operated our falafel and shawarma stalls and just faded into the background after that.

Because, for Israel to face the weight of its actions against us, right from its foundation and through till this moment, is a tall order, one that no segment of Israeli society is ready to face.

Fast forward a few years, and I returned to the United Kingdom to do my MBA. But the sinking feeling hit me as soon as I graduated and landed back in Tel Aviv. At home in Fassouta, I was back to the old drawing board: looking for a job. The old monster resurfaced. I still had an Arab name and still had no army number to supply; as Palestinians, we're exempt from military service in the Israeli army. Months later, I still had no job. Finally, in desperation, and with mounting debts to pay off, I took a job that I didn't want. We don't have the luxury of self-actualization in this country, I bitterly realized—it's survival we have to worry about.

The job was in Karmiel, which is, again, a Jewish town in the Galilee built on land confiscated from three Arab villages: Deir al-Asad, Bi'na, and Nahf. I blocked this out daily as I went to work; I desperately needed the job, and I also needed the strength to cope with the mental and emotional trauma of being back in the country, which was, by now, getting steadily worse. The second intifada was raging in the West Bank and Gaza, and, every night, I went home to watch the horrors unfold on the news. I had nightmares of bloodied corpses and wails of victims' families. During the day, I could barely focus on anything. That period was one of indescribable stress and agony to me and to other Palestinians, as we watched our people in the West Bank and Gaza being attacked again on such a scale, all of us helpless to do anything to stop it.

At work, I'd hear my Jewish colleagues talk about "battering them," and gleefully discussing Israel's victories against its enemies. I couldn't respond with a single word; again, I had to keep my job, and things were so tense in the country that the atmosphere was like a taut wire about to snap. A few days later, another colleague, in her late twenties and of the same age as me, announced loudly at the lunch table that her government was making a mistake in not "going in there [to the West Bank] and obliterating everything—people, trees, cats, dogs, *everything*—and solving the problem once and for all."

The alienation is, of course, present on a communal level, not just a personal one; shortly after, there was another Israeli Independence Day to live through. Each year, on this day, many Palestinians are overtaken by such depression and despair that we elect to simply stay home. The day of celebration for Israelis marks the memory of our *nakba*, the loss of Palestine and the dispossession of our people. While Jewish Israelis are out flag-waving, having parties and barbeques on what was Palestinian land, we are commemorating our destroyed villages, remembering our dead and those who cannot come home. Each year is a painful reminder that another year has gone by in this tragic predicament. The entire country is plastered in Israeli flags for weeks before and weeks after, at a dose even higher than usual; Israel seems to have an obsession with hanging its flag everywhere, as though to make a point, perhaps to feed its own, insecure national psyche.

I often wonder at our sheer will to survive, as a people, in a system so ruthless in trying to negate our existence. For decades, it was illegal to raise a Palestinian flag in Israel. To this day, Palestinian citizens of Israel are not even referred to as Palestinians by the Israeli establishment, but by a great oxymoron of a term, "Israeli Arabs," carefully concocted to imply that Israel was always there and we were always a minority group within it, and equally, to firmly keep erasing our Palestinian identity and make us nameless "Arabs," a race that includes citizens of twenty-two countries. Worse, after several decades of this harsh indoctrination, even we have sometimes stopped referring to ourselves as Palestinian—not surprisingly, given that the word was tantamount to asking for a prison sentence. Several more names have been created to describe us, some kindly by our Arab brethren, among them "1948 Arabs," which curiously ties an entire people to a single date; "Arabs Inside the Green Line" (of armistice in 1949 between Israel and its neighboring Arab countries; can you imagine using this definition to introduce yourself to someone?); and my favorite, "Arabs of Inside," which would evoke a naturally puzzled response of "Inside what?" by anyone outside this mess. "Inside Israel, of course," we would answer, as though this should be obvious. The reason for all these names is as pitiful as it is useless; it lies in the refusal of some Arabs to recognize Israel and, thus, to call it by its name—another case of sticking one's head in the sand.

Battered by the force of all this, the Palestinian citizens of Israel are still trying to come to terms with their own identity, shattered to oblivion by a foreign power. In recent years, we've begun to cautiously say we're Palestinian again, as the wheel continues to grind on successive decades of Israeli oppression and our patience wears thinner and thinner.

Israel's attempts to sweep us under the carpet, of course, and its severe discomfort at acknowledging our identity, both stem from its refusal to acknowledge the wrongs it has done and continues to do against us, or to realize the impossibility of its project of being a "Jewish state." The Palestinians live in this country, and they lived here long before the Zionist project decided to expropriate it and create Israel in its place. Today, the Palestinians living inside Israel are citizens of it, but Israel is not a state for all its citizens—it is, by its own proclamation, a state for Jews. Though the word *only* isn't at the end of that definition, Israel's practices very much imply that it is a state for Jews only. Its biggest fear seems to be in relinquishing its racist dogma and becoming a binational state, or a state for all its citizens.

When, faced with the discomfort at my presence that I encountered daily at work, on the bus, in the mall, and in government offices, I reflected on Israel's self-definition of being Jewish and democratic, touted so shamelessly by a supposedly modern country with a parliament, a president, a prime minister, and a claim to democracy, my first, instinctive question was, What if you're not Jewish?

The answer, from the state's actions toward me each day that I lived there, seemed to be, Well, then you should leave.

Eventually, I did. I packed my bags and moved to Ramallah, in the West Bank, part of the occupied Palestinian territory, in a desperate attempt to stay in my homeland but distance myself from the oppression of living in Israel. Together with other Palestinians who moved here, we yearned to feel some reclamation of our identity and live in our own self-governance, seeking any scraps of dignity and relief that we could forage in this country.

We came out of the frying pan and into the fire.

For me, it took a while for this to register. My initial reactions on visiting Ramallah were euphoric, completely detached from the reality that I had yet to discover. My heart fluttered with the Palestinian flag that I saw on rooftops and in front of official buildings. I gazed at government ministries with a sense of pride; here were hints of Palestinian sovereignty, here was a fragment of Palestine, all was not lost! There were no Hebrew signs where I lived. People spoke Arabic and were friendly and welcoming. It was almost like coming to a different country.

It was. But it was no tourist destination.

My daily diary here is another side of the same coin, that of Israeli military control and dispossession of Palestinians. Here, it's much more blatant, in our face. It's in the humiliation and endless waiting time at the checkpoints, in the bitter, daily environment of violent clashes, in the sprawling, illegal Jewish settlements gobbling up our land, in the frustration of movement restrictions, in the constant feeling of insecurity. It's in watching my people every day, choked by a foreign occupier, being unable to grow our economy and living a warped existence of barely making ends meet, at the mercy of international aid. It's in generations that find rising unemployment and costs of living, no hope for a better future, and no peace on the horizon.

In fact, the Palestinians are doing Israel a historic and colossal favor in calling this an occupation. The definition of a military occupation as a temporary state of affairs has long stopped to apply here. After half a century, more than a hundred illegal Jewish settlements, and over half a million Jewish settlers illegally squatting in the West Bank, what is happening far exceeds an occupation; it's a structured, systematic dispossession of Palestinians just like that of 1948, only at a slower, yet equally ruthless pace. As more Palestinian land is lost and Palestinians are pushed into tighter and tighter ghettos, choked by a horrendous separation wall snaking through their lands and cutting them off from their families, fields, schools, and work, as they are forbidden from using many roads, and as they continue to be the target of random killings and sometimes mass arrests, Israel has already created facts on the ground that make the realization of a truly independent and viable Palestinian state impossible.

I have always found it curious, however, how both Palestinians and the international community have come to view this military occupation as an isolated problem, removed from the historical context of the *nakba*: the founding of Israel on 78 percent of historic Palestine, the dispossession of around 85 percent of the Arab, Palestinian population of this part of the land, and the ethnic cleansing and destruction of more than four hundred Palestinian villages. The occupation did not fall out of the sky on these territories, the West Bank and Gaza. The occupation is only an extension of Israel's founding principles, its violent beginnings, its dogma of being a national home for the Jews, and its historical attack on the Palestinians with the aim of driving them out of their homeland to fulfill its aims.

To really look at ending the occupation, the issue at hand is much larger; it's in Israel's self-definition, its expansionist goals, its attitude toward non-Jews, and its actions over the last sixty-eight years that attest to all this. Inside Israel is a system in which Palestinians are afraid to speak Arabic in public, in which, in recent years, like our brethren in the West Bank who are frequently shot and killed at checkpoints, we may be killed in the street at the mere suspicion of a soldier or policeman, in which we have to grovel for work and be grateful for any crumbs thrown our way, and in which we have to carve out a dignified existence against a monster of a state that openly calls for our expulsion or "demographic transfer." On either side of the separation wall, one can only wonder at the sadistic ingenuity with which Israel has woven an airtight system around us to suffocate every aspect of our lives—while it relentlessly pursues its goals of more Jewish settlement and more and more grabbing of Palestinian land and resources for Israeli-Jewish-only benefit.

Essentially, in moving to Ramallah, I did not make a choice. For Palestinians, the choice of life in Israel or the West Bank is a choice between two systems of Israeli aggression, different only in their manifestations. Both are just as deadly and soul crushing. Both attempt to negate us, to treat us with condescension and contempt, and to turn us into victims of state oppression in our own homeland. Both refuse to acknowledge our rights and dignity as a people, a people whose country and self-determination were stripped from them and who are losing all hope that there is a way out of this mess.

I NEED ANSWERS, AS DOES EVERY PALESTINIAN, FROM ANYONE WHO SAYS he or she loves Israel.

AN UNSUITABLE PLACE FOR CLOWNS

ARNON GRUNBERG

1.

In 1982—I was eleven at the time—my older and only sister, Maniou-Louise, made aliyah. That is to say: she moved to Israel, her Zionist dream fulfilled. She gave up studying medicine at Amsterdam's Free University and went to study psychology at Bar-Ilan University in Ramat Gan.

Both of us belonged to the Zionist-religious youth group Bnei Akiva, the motto of which was *Torah Ve'avoda* ("Torah and Work"). I attended the meetings with a healthy degree of reluctance, not because I was opposed to Zionism, but because I thought the clubhouse (*mo'adon*) was dirty. There were mice in the building, and I was afraid of mice. The shared meals were lousy too, the other members seemed unfriendly to me, or I was afraid of them, sometimes a mixture of both, and I considered the propaganda for both the state of Israel and for God to be all too transparent. I still remember clearly, though, that one Saturday evening in winter, under the watchful eye of the *madrich* (club leader), we viewed a feature film. It was about the Israeli intervention to free passengers taken hostage at Entebbe airport in 1976. I liked the movie. Not that it made a Zionist out of me (to the extent that I wasn't already a Zionist unawares), but this propaganda was at least entertaining; something that cannot be said for most of the other Bnei Akiva propaganda—or for propaganda in general.

I'd had a religious upbringing—my father was an agnostic, but my mother adhered to Jewish tradition—and was getting ready for my bar mitzvah. I went to the synagogue every Saturday and stuck to a more or less kosher diet, because all these things were expected of me. I underwent Judaism and Zionism in the same way that I would later undergo my high school Latin and Greek classes.

In the summer of 1982, my mother and I accompanied my sister to Israel. She began attending an *ulpan*, a language-immersion program, where she perfected her Hebrew, and I spent entire days walking with my mother around Jerusalem. We also took day trips to Bethlehem and Hebron, cities that were still accessible to tourists of all nationalities at the time. The occupied territories were not occupied, at least not according to my mother and sister.

Because I thought it was expected of me, I wore a yarmulke there, something I never did back in Holland. I even put on an *arba kanfot*, a ritual prayer garment worn under one's clothes. The tzitzit, the tassels, hung out from under my T-shirt. I looked the way a dedicated member of Bnei Akiva is supposed to look.

One hot afternoon my mother and I visited Hebron, in the company of a group of other tourists, most of them Americans. The trip included a visit to a glassworks. As I was standing there watching one of the glassblowers, the man turned around slowly and gave me the once-over. His once-over lasted a few seconds. Then he spit on the ground beside my feet.

My mother hustled me away. I looked over my shoulder and saw that he was leaving the other tourists unmolested, at least as far as spitting went.

What had he seen in me? A staunch member of Bnei Akiva, which is to say: His and his people's enemy?

"Did you see that Palestinian?" my mother said. "Did you see the hate in his eyes?"

It was the first time I had ever been conscious of seeing a Palestinian. I didn't understand why he would hate me, when I didn't hate him.

A few weeks later at Ben Gurion Airport, my mother and I took leave of my sister. She had found a room on campus at Bar-Ilan and was ready to get on with her new life. She had also changed her name to Ma'anit, and to me she said: "You already have an Israeli name. You won't have to change a thing when you get here." She was undoubtedly trying to say something nice, but I considered it a dubious honor. In the Netherlands I was always explaining that my name was neither Anton, Arnold, nor Aron.

Back in Amsterdam I took off my yarmulke and my *arba kanfot*. My parents thought that was a good idea too. "Not everyone needs to see that you're Jewish," my father said.

At the synagogue, an older gentleman asked me if I planned to move to Israel later, like my sister. "No," I said. "I want to become a clown."

Somehow I had understood that the Jewish state was not a suitable place for clowns.

2.

It is Sunday, June 5, 2016, and I am attending the Yom Yerushalayim (Jerusalem Day) parade in Jerusalem. It's the first time I've been to one of these parades, though by now I've visited Israel close to thirty times. On Yom Yerushalayim, people celebrate the "reunification" of Jerusalem, one of the side effects of the Six-Day War. There is, of course, another side of the story: where one party sees liberation, the other sees occupation, repression, and ethnic cleansing. And that is exactly why I'm here, to shed some light on that other account. The crew of a Dutch current-affairs program is tagging along after me. The program's producers think that's interesting, a Jewish writer visiting the occupied territories at the invitation of the NGO Breaking the Silence. A story with a special twist, because that writer also happens to have a sister who lives in a settlement (Dolev). But am I a Jewish writer? Much more preferably a European writer, in fact, one currently living in America. What I did at the age of eleven is actually what I am still doing, albeit more handily and perhaps more ironically: I am adapting. If they expect me to play the part of the Jewish writer, then that's what I'll do.

We cross the old center of Jerusalem, where many of the Palestinian shopkeepers on Al Wad street have been told to close their shops for the day. If they don't, the police won't be able to protect them from the crowds celebrating Yom Yerushalayim; the procession always crosses the Old City and ends at the Wailing Wall. With the help of an interpreter, one of the shopkeepers tells us that they are all closing up for the day, to keep their inventory from being wrecked and pillaged. In a country under the rule of law, one would expect the right of ownership to be protected against vandals and angry crowds, but everything is different around here; different at least from New York, Amsterdam, or Berlin. I am here to demonstrate that in this place everything is different. Or isn't it?

In discussions, in articles, in books about what we'll refer to for the moment simply as the Conflict, it is always the uniqueness that is emphasized, the uniqueness of Israel, the uniqueness of the conflict. Couldn't it be that this perceived or perhaps even actual uniqueness has come to serve as a smoke screen? By appealing to one's own unicity, after all, one gives oneself the right to step out of line.

The real parade still has to begin, but already the occasional group of singing and dancing young people passes by, carrying big Israeli flags. There is something intimidating about them, but then a flag-waving crowd has a tendency to become intimidating soon enough. The hysterical, nationalistic exuberance makes me think of soccer fans, something I will remark on later on Dutch television. After that broadcast a lady will pointedly remind me that the Palestinian-Israeli conflict is not a soccer match. She is implying that I don't take the conflict seriously, that I am playing it down, that I refuse to see the consequences, that I make normal that which ought not to be made normal. She is partly right: the conflict is not a soccer match, there is more at stake here than a victory at the end of a soccer match.

But associations often serve to clarify. Nationalism in postwar

Europe was, for a long time, mostly a by-product of soccer matches, something for which Europeans cannot be grateful enough, if only because it's not at all guaranteed that things will stay that way.

In any case, the lady touched on a sensitive point: marching through the streets with flags may be intimidating, but I also have a hard time taking it seriously. In order to truly understand this conflict, doesn't one also need to take nationalism seriously? Wouldn't it be arrogance to claim that nationalism is an atavistic custom? To accommodate the makers of the television program, I talk to a couple of girls I see walking down an alleyway, settlers from the look of them, or at least members of Bnei Akiva. It's good to be wary of generalizations, but in Israel especially, ideology goes hand in hand with explicit and often also implicit dress regulations.

Even the simple question "Where do you girls come from?" turns out to elicit suspicion.

"We belong here," one of the girls says rather aggressively. "We're not coming from anywhere."

She makes my innocent question sound as though the one posing it wants to drive the Israeli Jews into the sea or send them back to their countries of origin.

I make it clear to them that there was no ulterior motive lurking behind my question; only then are they prepared to tell me that they come from Hebron.

Settlers. A word that can sow confusion, as though there were only one sort of settler. Is my sister a settler? Absolutely. On top of that, ideologically, she is also convinced of being in the right. She is not there because the houses in Dolev are so inexpensive and the gardens so green. She is there to protect the country against the enemy. Because it is her country, because the Torah says it belongs to the Jews.

Her country, not my country. Does one need to have a country? Can you be a guest everywhere you go? Or has the past proved that a worldview like that is ultimately untenable?

A few years ago, a Dutch political commentator claimed that the Palestinians have the right to put up armed resistance against settlers, and that they also have the legal right—according to his interpretation of military law, at least—to kill settlers. I was able to follow his legal reasoning, but the person of my sister made this rather abstract train of thought awfully personal. Did anyone have the right to kill my sister? Of course not. I would actually venture to doubt whether it would be morally correct to sacrifice one's sister, even if that sacrifice would bring peace. I have no real trouble advocating the principle of solely nonviolent protest and civil disobedience, but principles often tell us something about the privileges of the one who falls back on them.

When the girls from Hebron see the cameras, they tell me that they don't trust the foreign media. Yet another principle: The foreign media are against us. All media are against us, except the media of which we approve. I do my best to summon up the bit of Hebrew I remember from my youth. My first name also works to my advantage. Maybe I'm not the enemy after all.

Yes, they are willing to talk for a few moments. Not long, they're in a hurry, they have to celebrate the liberation of Jerusalem. There is so much to celebrate and to commemorate. The molding and maintenance of collective memory is an effective instrument used by all nationalistic propaganda machines.

Then the girls see Yehuda Shaul, cofounder of Breaking the Silence; they recognize him. If they were Christians, you might say that in Yehuda Shaul they see the Antichrist. That's the way they look at him. That's the way they recoil. That's how horror stricken they are. But in Jewish mythology the devil plays a very minor role. Let's say that in Shaul they see a serpent to whose forked tongue no one should be exposed. They shout a few terms of abuse and, as they move away, they warn other girls not to talk to me. I'm with Shaul, which makes me a serpent too.

A few hours later I find myself in the western part of the city, where at that moment the demonstration is reaching its apogee. The parade opens out before my eyes. My initial association had been with a soccer match, but now I'm reminded of the Soviet Union, China perhaps. As though the state offers the citizen an invitation to nationalistic enthusiasm and the citizen cannot refuse the offer. But the state here is Bnei Akiva, and probably those yeshivas associated with it.

I see a couple of families, but mostly young girls and boys between the ages of twelve and twenty, dressed in almost identical white shirts and blue trousers (the semiofficial Bnei Akiva uniform). They are marching around. Or rather, they are marching on the old city center.

You could also say that it's like Carnival, only without the floats and the admixture of alcohol and eroticism. There is no eroticism around here, this ecstasy has nothing to do with lust.

I used to be a part of this. I was a member of this club; mostly, I have to admit, because my sister was such a confirmed and fanatical member herself, but still. Could I have become one of these singing and dancing nationalists? No, that's impossible, and to reach that conclusion you don't even have to be a fanatical believer in free will. I simply didn't have what it takes to be a Jewish nationalist—I wanted to be a clown.

A young man who speaks fairly good English is willing to answer a few questions. He tells me that he runs a blog on which he publishes the truth about the Conflict, then he launches into a jeremiad against the media, all of which he says are against Israel. Against Jews. Anti-Semites. As a representative of the foreign media, I of course am an anti-Semite too, maybe without even knowing it, but that doesn't matter. No nationalism without paranoia, but the religious-tinted nationalism in Israel seems almost impossible to distinguish from paranoia.

The hostess of the Dutch TV program butts into the conversation; she seems to feel that I am not doing enough to interrupt the flow of slurs and insinuations.

"He's Jewish too," she says, pointing at me.

I have been unmasked. The young man looks at me nonchalantly and says: "Then he's a self-hating Jew."

The conversation is bogging down. Anything I say is suspect by default; I, after all, am the self-hater. In the Netherlands too, by the way, non-Jewish Dutch people often level such accusations against me, especially when I claim in a newspaper or magazine that Islam is not identical to terrorism. Some Dutch people seem to think that Jews are obliged to hate Muslims; if they don't, then they must be self-haters.

After a short coffee break—I've had my fill of this depressing parade—we take off to find the counterdemonstration.

Atop a little rise, cordoned off by police, stands left-wing Israel. A few hundred people. About one policeman to every ten demonstrators, I'd say.

An older lady, originally from South Africa, blames the meager turnout on indifference. "Lots of people share our views," she says, "but they stay at home. I come out, and I will as long as I have the strength to do so."

A young girl explains that the counterdemonstrators are also waving Israeli flags to show that the flag is not the exclusive property of Bnei Akiva and other religious right-wingers. "It's our flag too," she says. The paltriness of the counterdemonstration alone is enough to induce melancholy. On my way to the exit—crush barriers have been used to set up obvious entrances and exits—I see young men approaching in what are unmistakably animal costumes. They looked like they're stoned, but I can't be absolutely sure.

The counterdemonstrators in animal costumes start in on a sort of animal dance. Are these the clowns? Could I join up with them?

We walk toward the Old City. In the special set of grandstands set up for the press, to separate the journalists from the demonstrations and probably to give the journalists a clear view of any disturbances, a few photographers are still standing around. The parade is over. Few or no disturbances this year. "It's the same thing every year," says the lady from the TV program, who has been working as a correspondent in Israel for some time now. "It's also a kind of performance. A play." It sounds as though she's trying to comfort me, but it doesn't comfort me.

3.

Early Tuesday morning we find ourselves at the Qalandiya checkpoint. "We" being a handful of writers and a photographer. This is the checkpoint where thousands of Palestinians cross the border each day on their way to work in Israel. There are also thousands of other Palestinians who work illegally in Israel, under even worse conditions than those who do so legally. Almost everywhere that a state closes its borders, illegal aliens cross those borders to be exploited as workers in the land of their dreams, or at least in a place where they hope to be just a little less worse off than they are at home.

We're here with Hannah Barag, an Israeli lady in her eighties who is a member of Machsom Watch, an organization composed of about 250 Israeli ladies of a certain age. The organization's activities include going to checkpoints where Palestinians cross the border (which is not supposed to be called a border), in order to monitor what takes place there. Ladies of a certain age, because younger women, Barag tells us, have a job or a family and can't spend hours standing at a checkpoint.

Barag says: "What you see here is the evil bureaucracy of the occupation. To keep a people under your thumb you don't need a soldier on every street corner, all you need is the evil bureaucracy."

I look at the men, all men, standing in line before the gates that open and close at the push of a button and allow them to approach the counter. As soon as the gates open the men start running, fearing that otherwise they will be late for work.

The fences, the gates, the silent yet desperate shoving in line, remind me of cattle in a pen, but I suppress that thought. Some metaphors obscure rather than clarify.

Barag explains that, with no prior notice, Palestinians can have their names put on a list that will result in them losing their permits to work in Israel. "There are different kinds of lists," she says. "The first kind is put together by the internal security service, the Shabak; there are about 350,000 Palestinians on that one. The Shabak doesn't check up on everyone individually, so often the service itself doesn't even know who's on the list. In other words, not everyone on the list is a terrorist; in fact, most of the people on the list have nothing to do with terrorism. You can get your name off the list, but that involves a complicated bureaucratic procedure. To appeal a scond time, you have to wait a full year. If you make your appeal one day too early, you have to wait another year on top of that. There are lawyers who make money off of that."

As I listen to Barag talk, looking at the seemingly endless line of waiting men and thinking about the lists on which one can end up quite mysteriously and never—or only with great difficulty—get off again, it occurs to me that this is indeed the subtlest weapon for repression, but a substantial one at that. The bureaucratic monster, barely in need of violence anymore to effectively bend others to its will. The demand for prisons and military trials that remains is at most an indication that the bureaucracy has not yet achieved 100 percent effectiveness.

A little more than a month later I call Barag to ask whether anything has changed since our visit. "Not much," she says. "There have been fifty-eight thousand work permits rescinded. That's new. It doesn't have all that much to do with the attacks. It's the work of the new Israeli defense minister, Lieberman. He's a strong believer in the efficacy of collective sanctions."

She tells me about the fourth "security list," a fairly recent invention. That list is composed, according to Barag, of Palestinians who are being collectively punished. No attempt is made to uphold even the pretense of guilt or of having committed an offense.

"But I don't think that fourth list will be too long lived; Israeli employers are protesting against it. They can't do without the cheap labor," Barag adds.

Economic interests are sometimes, but unfortunately not always, at loggerheads with the fundamentalist faith in the efficacy of collective punishment. Barag reminds me of my mother; the same slenderness, the same fervor, she is just as small as my mother was, but my mother would never have stood at a checkpoint trying to protect Palestinian workers against injustice. Or to document that injustice at the very least, to be a witness to the evil of the bureaucracy of occupation, as Barag puts it.

"There is one major Catch-22," Barag had said on that Tuesday in June, standing at the center of a little group of writers. "If you want to get a work permit, you need an Israeli employer. But how do you find an Israeli employer if you're not allowed to enter Israel?

There's a huge black market in work permits, people who know people. *Machers* is the Yiddish word for them."

The Israeli philosopher Avishai Margalit draws a distinction between witnesses and moral witnesses. The moral witness must not only perceive the injustice, but also have suffered under it himself or be willing to actively oppose it. Am I a moral witness? I doubt it. Does writing make me a moral witness? Not nearly enough. I feel, in fact, more like a sightseer at the scene of a disaster than a moral witness. A distasteful feeling.

Barag says that the checkpoints often open late, so that the workers once again arrive too late for work. When Machsom Watch observers see that, they call the checkpoint commander, and sometimes that helps. "We started Machsom Watch in February 2001," Barag says. "I find it hard to say exactly what we've achieved. At first, a normal wait in line took three or four hours; it's down to an average of ninety minutes now, but that's also because the system has been computerized. At first the gates opened at six, now they open at four. Does that mean you've achieved something? You haven't changed the system, but you *have* made the situation more livable."

Her organization has also helped dozens of Palestinians get their names off the list of those who supposedly pose a terrorist threat or who have been denied a work permit for some other reason.

Caprice, the byproduct of unbridled power.

There is a separate gate for women and children. "They call this the humanitarian gate," Barag says, "but I don't know what's humanitarian about it. This gate is open only from six to six forty-five, but they usually don't open until a quarter past six."

A female soldier—"I know her," Barag says, and her intonation makes it clear: this young woman seems to revel in the power and the arbitrariness—is parleying with a Palestinian woman from behind the bars of her counter.

"We're not changing the system," Barag says, "but I think the system is going to collapse. That's my personal opinion. Something's brewing, a new crisis. We already have a former president and a former prime minister in prison, and that didn't bring down the system.

But one day it will fall. Maybe I'm overly optimistic, but you need hope in order not to let this system crush you."

An hour or two later we leave the checkpoint. We've seen enough. There is still a long line of Palestinian workers.

In 2007 I wrote a feature article about the Israeli army. I was given a tour along a section of the wall that the Ariel Sharon government had started building at the time of the second intifada. A helpful press officer explained to me how successful the wall was in the fight against terrorism. I can't escape the impression now that the wall was also built to more effectively control a population, and to provide Israeli employers with cheap labor. Closing borders will often result in all kinds of refugees crossing the border in the hope of a better life and work. And the illegal employee is the cheapest and easiest to exploit. As Barag put it: "When Gaza was shut off, we had to bring in Chinese workers, but lots of Israeli employers prefer Palestinians."

Back at the car, I start wondering how we can distinguish terrorism from legitimate acts of resistance. According to some Bnei Akiva adherents—and I'm afraid they're not the only ones—no single Palestinian act of resistance against the state of Israel is legitimate, not even the most peaceful one.

And can we still go on believing that the occupation is the problem, that the problem will go away when the settlers go away, that the evil bureaucracy will disappear then too? The faith in the two-state solution is seeming to me more and more like a ritual devoid of all meaning.

I was already skeptical in 2007 while doing that feature article about the Israeli army, but at the Qalandiya checkpoint the skepticism gels into a question: Is this the Zionist dream for which my sister left the Netherlands in 1982? More like a Zionist nightmare. Barag says: "You have to do something, especially at my age, because otherwise you just sit around thinking about your little aches and pains and your next doctor's appointment."

The next evening, at a restaurant in Tel Aviv, the Israeli writer Nir Baram will tell me: "For as long as I can remember, people have been shouting that the status quo cannot be maintained, but I fear the status quo can be maintained for decades still."

Decades. Barag sees that differently; in view of her age, though, she's in more of a hurry.

Is Qalandiya worse than other checkpoints in other countries where people are repressed and exploited? Is the Israeli system worse than the comparable systems still rife on this planet? Are these questions even relevant?

Is it true what Bertolt Brecht said, that everyone should speak about his own disgrace? And even though I don't live in this country, is this my disgrace?

4.

I'm sitting in the hotel lobby, across from Gerard Horton and Salwa Duaibis of Military Court Watch. They are going to accompany me to Ofer, a military court and detention center in the West Bank, close to the border between Palestinian territory and the territory claimed by Israel.

Before we leave, though, Horton explains what their organization does. Military Court Watch documents the treatment given to minors in Israeli military detention. "The things minors are subjected to in the military detention system are more or less the same things undergone by defendants who are of age."

Minors from the age of twelve on can be considered criminally culpable, both in Israel and before the Israeli military courts in the Palestinian territories, and be subjected to sentencing and sanctions.

Horton says that many minors report being subjected to ill treatment upon arrest. Most are blindfolded and handcuffed, and many are made to lie down on the floor of military vehicles, thereby increasing the chance of injuries. Many are threatened and intimidated during interrogation. People fail to tell the underage prisoners that they have the right to remain silent in the overwhelming majority of cases.

I'm reminded of Hannah Barag. When they know they are being observed, those in power have the tendency to act with a little less capriciousness.

Horton, an Australian corporate lawyer—he came here almost eight years ago to do volunteer work—says: "If you want to maintain control over a population the size of that in the occupied territories, you have three possibilities: kill them all, drive them away, or repress them. Israel has chosen for the least terrible of the three."

I wait to see if something else is coming, I study Horton's expression but detect no trace of irony.

"When it comes to taking Israel to court at the International Criminal Court in The Hague, people often talk about the Gaza War, but that would be a fairly complicated and rather unclear case. However, under the fourth Geneva Convention, Palestinians from the occupied territories are not to be locked up in prisons in Israel. In fact, however, this has been taking place on a large scale for nearly 50 years."

"But do you think Israel will ever be taken to court in the Hague?" I ask.

Horton shrugs. "Israel isn't a party to the Rome Statute of the ICC, but Palestine is. The prosecutor is working right now on a preliminary investigation considering multiple issues. You can't rule anything out."

Horton says the military trials don't correspond in many respects with what is considered a fair and impartial hearing. More than 99 percent of all defendants are convicted. When Palestinian lawyers attempt to organize boycotts of the courts, the prosecution seeks much tougher sentences.

We take the car to Ofer. In a sort of courtyard there, Palestinians are waiting to sit in on the trial of a family member. It is Ramadan, so the Palestinians there are not eating or drinking.

After half an hour we are let in to attend a hearing.

Three defendants, men who look to me to be somewhere in their twenties, are sitting next to each other on a bench. There is a guard beside them. He looks bored. His tzitzit is hanging out of his uniform. Could he have once been a member of Bnei Akiva?

The prosecutor, interpreter, and judge are all soldiers. A Palestinian lawyer wearing a white shirt is discussing something with his clients. The prosecutor is a woman. Salwa Duaibis says: "The interpreter is a Druze, I can tell by the way he speaks Arabic."

One of the defendants is said to have thrown rocks at soldiers, but he says he was only in the area when rocks were thrown. The average sentence for throwing rocks is six months. A female defense lawyer comes in. The judge starts joking with the prosecutor. The female lawyer says it is inappropriate for the judge to laugh. The judge defends his right to laugh.

The other lawyer is preparing a document for signing. The defendants sit there, uninterested, almost bored. As though they've already given up on the whole thing. After half an hour, we give up too. We walk around, trying to find a trial with an underage defendant, but there aren't any at the moment. It is lunchtime.

5.

On Friday morning I pay a surprise visit to my sister in Dolev. She has seven children and, these days, six grandchildren; all Bnei Akiva members, each a little more fanatical than the next. When my father died in 1991, my sister was in an advanced state of pregnancy. She wasn't allowed to fly, she was living in Kfar Darom, a settlement in Gaza. That is why my father is buried in Jerusalem. My mother wanted to be buried close to my father, so she has been in Jerusalem too since 2015. That is how my parents happen to be buried in a graveyard in Israel without ever having lived here.

My father, born in Berlin in 1912, survived the war by going into hiding at a number of addresses. My mother, born in Berlin in 1927, survived the war in a number of camps. Unconditional loyalty toward Israel went without speaking for them, but they never seriously considered emigrating. My father always said it was too hot in Israel, and my mother said she would go there when she was very old.

In the end, she went there as a corpse.

When I cross the threshold at my sister's—the house never fails to remind me of the Bnei Akiva clubhouse in Amsterdam—she hugs me. She doesn't ask what I'm doing here. I don't tell her either. That seems better to me. We go to the garden and play Ping-Pong.

Outside the house, a Palestinian taxi driver is waiting for me. He says he drives to Dolev fairly often, to pick up nurses who work at a hospital in Jerusalem.

"Have you been to visit Mama?" my sister asks.

"Not yet," I reply.

Are the Jews safer because Israel exists, the way my parents thought? I have my doubts. Is living in Israel a religious duty for a Jew, the way my sister thinks? Aren't such duties, religious or no, the start of all intolerance?

While we're playing, I think about Hebron. On Wednesday I went there with a couple of other writers. There was nothing about the town that reminded me of the place I visited with my mother in 1982, where I caught my first conscious glimpse of a Palestinian at a glassworks.

As we were walking through the ghost town, a settler approached us; he had recognized Yehuda Shaul, the settlers' Antichrist. The man began screaming and cursing. I don't know whether he spit as well. Israeli soldiers came to stand between us and the settler. For a moment the man reminded me of that glassblower back in 1982, but even angrier, even more enraged.

In his book *The Portage to San Cristobal of A.H.*, which the author refused to have published in Germany, George Steiner writes about a fictional Adolf H. who is put on trial in Brazil after the war. Adolf H. claims that he brought the Jews home, that Zionism only became truly viable thanks to him, the Messiah.

A gruesome thought. But however speculative it may be, the question remains: Without the Nazis, would there have been a state of Israel? In his book *My Promised Land*, the *Haaretz* journalist Ari Shavit also writes: "But at the end of the 19th century the Jews realized that however much they loved Europe, Europe did not love them."

If the Europeans had hated the Jews a little less, Hanna Barag would not have had to stand at a checkpoint at four in the morning and document the evil bureaucracy. At the same time, I realize that Barag is living proof that the real, existent Zionism is more than that evil bureaucracy alone.

Maybe Barag is right when she says that the system will collapse, even sooner than we may think; nevertheless, playing Ping-Pong with my sister, I know that the collapse of one system does not necessarily mean that the system that takes its place will be that much better.

(Translated from the Dutch by Sam Garrett)

JUSTICE, JUSTICE YOU SHALL PURSUE

AYELET WALDMAN

T'S PLEASANTLY COOL IN THE SHADE BENEATH THE WIZENED CYPRESS tree in the bedraggled front garden of the Youth Against Settlements community center, on a hill in Tel Rumeida, in the city of Hebron. A boy of sixteen, whom I'll call Karim, serves me a glass of Arabic coffee from a battered tin tray. I've come to interview him about his arrest and incarceration in Ofer Prison six months ago, but for a few moments we sip our coffee, make jokes about how much sugar I take (a lot), and enjoy the view. Amid the stone houses in the distance is a ribbon of empty white: Shuhada Street, on which Karim is forbidden to tread, because he is Palestinian and the once bustling market street is reserved for Israelis and those with international documents.

With me as I talk to Karim is Issa Amro, a community organizer who has turned his home into this community center. Issa holds youth meetings and teaches lessons here at the center, at least when he's permitted to. Issa's unwavering commitment to nonviolent resistance drives Israeli military officials crazy, and for years they have waged a campaign against him and his community center.

In a conversation with US officials that was revealed by WikiLeaks, Amos Gilad, the director of the Political-Military Affairs Bureau at Israel's Defense Ministry, said, "We don't do Gandhi very well." Shooting a person in a suicide vest, a person with a gun, even a child with a knife, is easily justified as self-defense. But a man whose weapon are his words, who can convince a young person to put down her gun or her blade and resist with tools learned from the example of the Reverend Martin Luther King Jr. and, yes indeed, from Gandhi—what do you do with him? Issa has been arrested and detained so many times that when I asked him the number, he could only shrug and smile. Periodically, the military declares his home a "military zone" and prevents anyone other than Issa himself from entering. But whenever they are allowed, the young people of Hebron come to listen to Issa's lessons about the pointlessness of stone throwing and knife attacks and the power of his alternative path.

The community center, Issa's home, sits right above an army checkpoint and right below the house of Baruch Marzel, an American-born settler with views so extreme that even among the right wing of Hebron he can fairly be deemed a fanatic. Marzel has called for targeted assassinations not only of Palestinian terrorists, but of left-wing Israeli Jews. He has railed against gay people and against Jews who marry non-Jews. His arrest record rivals that of Issa, though unlike Issa's his arrests have been for assaults: attacks on Palestinians, on leftist Jews, on reporters, on Israeli police officers. In 2013 Marzel broke into Issa's home and violently attacked him. Only two years later was Marzel finally charged for the crime. Unlike Issa, however, Marzel did not face military prosecution. In the areas of occupation, Israeli citizens and Palestinians, even those who reside in the same West Bank cities, even those charged with identical crimes, are subject to two different legal systems. Palestinians are governed by strict military law and prosecuted in military courts, yet Israelis experience the broad protections of the country's civilian judicial system. As the US State Department's Country Report on Human Rights Practices for 2015, published in April 2016, noted, the imposition of these two separate but unequal systems of law to people based on identity gives rise to discrimination and injustice.

In the fall of 2015, tensions escalated in Hebron and in the rest of the West Bank. A wave of stabbings, shootings, and car rammings overtook Israel and the West Bank. Thirty-six Israelis were killed in attacks by Palestinians, and three citizens of other countries, including two Americans, were killed. One hundred and forty Palestinians were killed carrying out attacks against Israelis, and a further eighty-two Palestinians were shot by Israeli forces during clashes. Issa was finding it ever more challenging to convince the children with whom he worked of the merits of nonviolence. One day, alerted by a neighbor, he rushed to a doorway where an eighteen-year-old Palestinian girl huddled, a knife in her hand, ready to stab the next Israeli she saw. Issa convinced her that there were ways to resist the occupation without taking a life and in the process throwing away her own. Shaking, she dropped the knife and accompanied him to Palestinian security officials, who took her into custody.

Inspired by this incident and others, in November Issa called the young people together for an urgent refresher on the principles of nonviolence, and how to behave if detained. "Don't give the army an excuse to shoot you," he said. Be polite and calm. Don't resist. He gave them the contact information for an attorney, one of the group of human rights lawyers, some of them Israeli, who have rallied to his cause. The speech as he recounted it to me reminded me of one I used to give to my clients years ago when I was a public defender. Be polite, calmly ask for your attorney and your parents. Answer no questions, make and sign no statements.

According to military authorities, 861 Palestinian children were arrested by the Israeli Defense Forces in 2014. This figure understates the true figure, as it does not include children detained by the IDF and released after a few hours, without being registered into military detention facilities. Most of those children were between the ages of twelve and seventeen, though the youngest child ever to be detained by the IDF, a boy from Hebron, was a mere five years old. According to Military Court Watch, an NGO that monitors the treatment of Palestinian children in Israeli jails, prisons, and courts, which receives its data from the Israeli Prison Service, "at the end of April 2016, 414 children (12–17 years) were held in military detention. This represents a 93 per cent increase compared with the monthly average for 2015. The latest data includes 12 girls; three children under 14 years;

and 13 children held without charge or trial in administrative detention." At sixteen, Karim was among the younger teenagers gathered in Issa's garden. And yet he had already been arrested three times, though each time detained only briefly.

The first time Karim was arrested, he was thirteen years old. He and his sister were walking near a checkpoint when a car came within a hair's breadth of running them down. Karim, frightened, lifted his hand to ward off the vehicle. It screeched to a halt and a settler leapt out of the driver's seat and began punching the boy. The police arrived and arrested not the man beating the child, but the child being beaten. The settler went on his way. Karim spent four hours in police custody.

Three years and one more arrest later, Issa's lecture felt not merely relevant, but urgent. Normally, Karim had a hard time sitting still. He'd pop up from his seat, get distracted. But that November night, he sat, rapt, unmoving, for nearly an hour, almost as if he knew what was about to happen.

There was the sound of footsteps, a rustling, and then the pop of flares. In the sudden, brilliant light Issa and the young people found themselves surrounded by Israeli soldiers. The commander peered at the youths one after another, and then pointed at Karim. He was the one they wanted.

The soldiers took Karim aside and searched him. At this point Karim told me he felt relatively unconcerned. He assumed that he was merely the first of the group to be searched, and that the others would soon follow. However, once he'd been thoroughly frisked, the commander said, "*Yalla*," Arabic for "Let's go," and motioned for Karim to start walking.

"Where are you taking me?" Karim asked in Arabic.

"Quiet," the commander told him in Hebrew. Issa offers Hebrew lessons at the community center, to arm the children with language, but Karim's is rudimentary at best.

The soldiers led Karim down the hill and out onto Shuhada Street, a strange experience for a boy who'd never been allowed to walk there before. They stopped in front of the imposing, gorgeously renovated Beit Hadassah, a Jewish settlement and museum built on the site of a medical clinic that nearly a century earlier had served the small Jewish community of Hebron. In 1929, Palestine, then under British rule, was engulfed in riots, and sixty-seven Jewish residents of Hebron were massacred by their Palestinian neighbors. The British subsequently moved the rest of the Jewish community out of the city. For the next fifty years, Hebron was exclusively occupied by Palestinians, though after the Six-Day War the Israelis built a large settlement on its outskirts. In 1979, a group of religious Jewish settlers, mostly women and children, stole into the heart of Hebron in the middle of the night and illegally occupied Beit Hadassah. The Israeli government went on to sanction their settlement.

The commander exhibited Karim to two soldiers who were standing in the middle of the street out in front of the elaborate building. The first soldier shrugged. "Maybe it's him. Maybe it's not him," he said. The second soldier, an Arabic-speaking Druze, insisted that yes, Karim was the one they were looking for. He then poked the other soldier, who hesitated a moment, then shrugged his shoulders and agreed. Yes. They had the right boy.

A few moments later, a border police officer arrived. This officer was also Druze, and he spoke to Karim in Arabic. He showed Karim a long knife with a black handle. "Karim," the officer said, "admit that this is your knife."

It was when he saw the knife that Karim panicked. They could imprison you for a knife. They could shoot you. Terrified, he violated the rule Issa had laid down. He spoke. "No! No!" he insisted. He'd never seen that knife before. He had no idea whose it was or how it came to be on the ground in front of Beit Hadassah.

In 2010, the Office of the Israeli Military Advocate General instructed army commanders that when dealing with minors, they should always tie hands from the front, unless security considerations require tying their hands behind their back. Karim was compliant. Nonetheless, the soldiers zip-tied him with his hands behind his back. The rules also require the use of three plastic ties—one around each wrist and one connecting the two—to avoid pain. On Karim, the soldiers used a single tie. Evidence collected by Military Court Watch suggests that Karim's treatment is typical. Commanders in the field routinely violate both international standards and the IDF's own rules regarding the restraint of children.

As the police officer loaded Karim into a jeep, settlers began pouring out of Beit Hadassah. Their faces contorted with rage, they began shrieking, "Terrorist, terrorist!" *Be quiet*, Karim told himself. *Be calm, so you won't get hurt.*

In 2013, after UNICEF recommended that the blindfolding or hooding of children be prohibited, the IDF legal adviser for the West Bank reminded all commanders that blindfolding is only permitted when there is an explicit security need. Nonetheless, when Karim arrived at the police station, he was blindfolded. This is a consistent pattern: the IDF responds to international pressure by establishing appropriate rules and procedures, which are routinely violated without consequences.

Issa, meanwhile, had followed Karim and the soldiers down to Shuhada Street, though of course, because he is Palestinian, he was not permitted to go as far as Beit Hadassah. He stood, watching from a distance, until Karim was taken away. Then the soldiers came up to him. Issa asked them why Karim was arrested, but the commander raised a hand, silencing him.

"Was the boy found in your house?" the commander asked.

"You know he was," Issa told them. The soldiers had been in the garden when Karim was arrested, and they knew Issa well. They knew the house belonged to him.

"You are arrested for harboring a terrorist in your house," the commander said.

"What terrorist?" Issa asked. "Who is the terrorist?"

Karim, the commander said, had walked up to the soldiers in front of Beit Hadassah, a knife in his hand. Frightened, the boy had dropped the knife and run up to Issa's house.

"When?" Issa asked. "When did this happen?"

"Five minutes before we arrested him."

Issa tried to explain that the boy had been with him for the previous hour, that it could not be Karim who had dropped the knife. But the exercise was futile. More than futile, it was a farce.

The soldiers arrested Issa, handcuffing and blindfolding him.

They brought him to the police station where they were holding Karim and shoved him into a bathroom, seating him on the toilet. Issa sat there for the next four or five hours. Periodically a soldier would open the door, cock his weapon so that Issa could hear it, and then leave.

While this was happening, Karim was being held in the same base, sitting outside on the ground, blindfolded and zip-tied. He was neither given water nor allowed to use a bathroom. Eventually, after what Karim estimates is about four hours, the police officer returned and led him to an interrogation room.

The interrogator removed Karim's blindfold and the zip-tie that was cutting painfully into his wrists. He began asking Karim questions, none of which had to do with the knife. What the interrogator wanted to talk about was Issa Amro.

Tell us about Issa, the interrogator asked. What does he do? Whom does he talk to? What does he tell the young people at the community center?

Karim refused to answer the questions. Instead, he asked the interrogator to call his parents. He also asked to speak to the lawyer, whose name he fortunately remembered. UNICEF recommends that interrogations of minors always take place in the presence of a lawyer and a family member. This is not a standard the IDF accepts. As the US State Department report noted, 96 percent of Palestinian children report being denied access to an attorney during or before interrogation. Unusually, however, in the face of Karim's valuable insistence on his rights, instilled in him by Issa, the interrogator did indeed put Karim on the phone with a lawyer, who reaffirmed the boy's right to remain silent.

After this, Karim was taken out of the interrogation room. His blindfold was put back on, more tightly this time. He was zip-tied, also more tightly. The soldiers placed him in a chair, and then pushed him from the chair onto the ground. Then they started beating him.

Up until the late 1990s, Israeli Shabak interrogators routinely used physical violence, even torture, against Palestinians. In September 1999, the Israeli high court banned the use of physical means of

coercion in interrogations, though it made an exception to the pro-
hibition for cases involving a "ticking time bomb," which interroga-
tors have continued to use to justify abusive interrogation methods.
B'Tselem (the Israeli Information Center for Human Rights in the
Occupied Territories) and HaMoked (the Center for the Defense of
the Individual) have documented a myriad of continued violations
of human rights and international law. According to their reviews,
prisoners are held in miserable conditions, fed so poorly they lose
weight during detention, subject to solitary confinement, and denied
hygienic items like toilet paper. They are forced into stress positions
and bound, sometimes for days at a time. And they continue to be
beaten. UNICEF, official IDF policy, and the Geneva Convention
all prohibit the beating of detained children. And yet, as has been
noted in the US State Department report, 61 percent of detained Pal-
estinian minors suffer physical violence during arrest, interrogation,
and detention. Children like Karim report being punched, kicked,
forced into painful positions, and more.

When the beating stopped, a soldier pressed a cup of water into
Karim's hand, but though he was parched, he refused to drink. With
his eyes blindfolded, he couldn't tell what was in the cup, and he'd
heard stories of boys being forced to drink the soldiers' piss.

For the rest of the night, Karim was left outside in the cold. At
some point, an Arabic-speaking soldier put a jacket over him, but it
was quickly taken away. Later on, a kindly female soldier brought
him inside to a warm room, but almost immediately a male soldier
took him back out. Finally, in the morning, Karim was loaded into
a jeep and taken to the army base at Kiryat Arba, the settlement out-
side Hebron. There a physician checked his body for bruising and
took a medical history. Karim spent the next night in the detention
facility at Gush Etzion. This facility is for adults, not minors. The
next day, Karim was transferred to Ofer Prison. The day after that,
he went before a military judge.

Extrajudicial administrative detention, where prisoners are held
for up to six months, with the possibility of indefinite renewals, is
routinely used against Palestinian adults. In December 2011, in re-
sponse to international pressure, the IDF stopped issuing administra-

tive detention orders against children, though that fall, as the violence in the West Bank escalated, they once again began detaining some children without trial. Karim, however, avoided the purgatory of administrative detention. In the six days he was held, he went to the military court three times.

The military court at Ofer Prison is a dusty complex of portable structures. The courtyard in which families wait is walled in by Perspex panels bolted together, separating the waiting area from the trailers that house the miniature courtrooms. In one corner is a makeshift snack bar with a Hebrew sign, its menu and prices written in Arabic. On the morning I visited, no one lined up to buy the Hello Kitty ice cream or sesame seed *bourekas*, and the vendor entertained himself by playing Kanye West's "Power." There is about the place an air of helpless patience and boredom, women and elderly men trying to pass the time by doing nothing as they wait to witness their sons and daughters, husbands and wives, be tried and sentenced.

The Ofer court seems like a temporary facility, tossed up to accommodate an urgent need. This is appropriate, given that international law is premised on the concept that military occupation is temporary, and that the military legal system is meant to exist only briefly, during occupation. And yet the failure to construct permanent facilities is curious, given that this temporary occupation has now lasted fifty years, with no end in sight. In contrast, most Israeli settlements, even those constructed hurriedly, often in the dark of night, quickly assume the prospect of permanent structures.

Karim had a hard time understanding what went on during his court hearings. Even now, months later, he wasn't exactly sure what had happened. The proceedings were held in Hebrew, with an Arabic translator. He described the translator to me as a young uniformed soldier who sat playing with his smartphone. Karim told me, "He speak the lawyer ten words; the translator tells me one word."

Gaby Lasky, a civil rights attorney and a progressive member of the Tel Aviv City Council, who along with colleagues represented Karim in this case, told me that she once won a case at the Salem court in the northern West Bank. At the announcement of the not guilty verdict, the translator, an Arabic-speaking Druze, looked puzzled, and then stopped the proceedings. He couldn't remember or did not know how to translate the word *acquittal* to Arabic and had to ask one of the lawyers in the courtroom.

The conviction rate in the IDF military courts is above 99 percent (as of 2011), with the vast majority of young offenders taking plea bargains. They plead guilty not because they necessarily committed the crimes of which they are accused, but because children are routinely denied bail. In the occupied territories, if a child is charged, for example, with throwing stones, and insists on his innocence, he is likely to spend four to six months in jail awaiting a hearing. But if he pleads guilty, he will serve on average a three-month sentence and then go home.

Many things made Karim's case different from that of the typical Palestinian child accused of a crime. Karim was well trained. He knew not to answer questions and had been drilled to expect and demand his rights. Because of his relationship with Issa, who was the 2010 winner of the UN's Human Rights Defender of the Year in Palestine award and is well known in human rights circles, Karim had an Israeli lawyer. Most important, his case attracted the attention of the Israeli media. For all these reasons, though he was held without bail for a number of days, eventually Karim's case was dismissed without indictment.

Issa believes that the boy was arrested as part of a campaign of harassment and intimidation directed at him. He is convinced that the arrest was primarily for the benefit of Baruch Marzel, who appeared at the community center at the same time as the soldiers. At Marzel's side was an American settlement supporter. Marzel and the visitors from America set up an encampment around the community center, complete with tables and chairs. When Issa returned from detention and notified the army that the settlers were trespassing on his land, he was told that they had obtained a permit for a protest. This was not true. Even in the West Bank one cannot get a permit to stage a protest on another's private land. The extremists surrounded Issa's property for twenty-four hours, at all times accompanied by Israeli soldiers. Though Gaby did not feel comfortable speculating about the arrest, about whether there had ever been a boy with a knife, she did tell me that it would not have been the first time in her experience that the IDF had arrested a nonviolent activist without justification. Nor would it have been the first time that the IDF engaged in the theatrics of oppression for benefit of the settlers.

As frightened as Karim had been, as miserable was the experience of being arrested, he was conscious that things could have been a lot worse. Unlike most young arrestees, he didn't go through the terrifying experience of being roused from his bed in the middle of the night. Another teenager, whom I'll call Mahmoud, described to me this more typical experience. Mahmoud's family woke one night to the sound of loud banging and shouts. Knowing that their door would be blown off its hinges or kicked in if he didn't move quickly to open it, Mahmoud's father leapt out of bed, stumbling over his children sleeping on mattresses on the floor. This was not the first time the family had been woken in this way. When I asked Mahmoud's mother how many times the IDF had shown up at their home in the middle of the night, the doe-eyed thirty-nine-year-old mother of nine shrugged.

"Ten?" she said, hazarding a guess.

I was aghast. "Ten? Is that common?"

"In this village?" she said. "Yes."

Mahmoud lives in a village called Beit Fajjar, a center of production for a type of limestone known as *meleke* or Jerusalem stone, depending on whether you're Palestinian or Israeli (in Israel-Palestine, even the rocks are political). His father, like most of the men in the village, is employed as a stonecutter. The village is close to Kibbutz Migdal Oz, part of a cluster of Israeli settlements known as Gush Etzion, so close in fact that the young Israeli peace activist who had accompanied me to Beit Fajjar stopped on Mahmoud's family's doorstep, shaking his head in surprise.

He pointed at a nearby hillside. The building we saw belonged to a women's seminary on the kibbutz where his wife, a human rights attorney, had studied when she was younger.

"I had no idea that it was so close," he said.

Curious to see how far apart the two villages were, I input their names into Google Maps. I judged the distance as no more than a couple of kilometers apart, and I could see clearly the road that connected the two. Google, however, was stumped. *Sorry, we could not calculate driving directions from Migdal Oz to Beit Fajjar.* Nor could it calculate walking distance, though I could have set out across the paths and fields and reached the kibbutz in less than half an hour.

We turned back to the house. Parked in front of the house was a beat-up old car. On the bumper was a Hebrew sticker: JEWS LOVE JEWS.

"It's a right-wing Israeli Jewish unity thing," my friend told me.

"But why is it on a car in a Palestinian village?"

He shrugged. "His family must have bought a used car from someone in one of the settlements."

Before I began interviewing arrested children and the lawyers who represent them, I assumed that the arrests were merely military responses to criminal behavior like rock throwing and stabbings. What I came to understand was that the arrest of children like Mahmoud is more than a series of responses to specific incidents. It's an integral part of the system through which the IDF ensures the safety of the settlers.

About four hundred thousand Israeli settlers live in the West Bank, a conflict zone. They have built houses and schools, opened shopping malls, and founded tech companies, all the while surrounded by approximately 2.9 million Palestinians, who consider them to be invaders and enemies. Over the last seven years of occupation, the average number of settlers killed each year has been less than five. When one stops to consider both the closeness of these communities and the extent of the enmity, what's striking is not the fact that there have been occasional outbreaks of violence, but that more Israelis have not been killed.

The relative safety of the four hundred thousand settlers (and the two hundred thousand more in East Jerusalem) represents a remarkable Israeli military achievement, one accomplished by means of a two-pronged system of control: collective punishment and mass intimidation. The arrest of children like Karim and Mahmoud serves both ends.

The majority of the Palestinian children arrested or detained by the IDF every year live in villages that are, like Beit Fajjar, within two kilometers of an Israeli settlement. It is in these villages where the IDF must be most proactive in order to protect the surrounding settlers. It must come down hard on any infraction in order to intimidate the population as a whole. To do so, it has at its disposal a wide variety of restrictive laws. In the West Bank, any gathering of more than ten people is considered a protest, and all protests are forbidden.

The IDF discourages resistance by responding firmly to each incident, be it stone throwing or, in Mahmoud's case, the attempt to set fire to a field that the IDF has co-opted as a firing range. When an incident occurs, the not unreasonable assumption is made that the guilty party or parties are boys and young men between the ages of twelve and thirty. The Israel Security Agency, also known as Shin Bet or Shabak, possesses a wealth of information about every Palestinian village within the close proximity of a settlement. Shabak officers know who the residents are, what their political affiliations are, who has an arrest record or has been previously detained. More important, the Shabak has a stable of informants, including children, recruited either through inducements like the proffering of work permits to their fathers, or through threats. Shabak officers have been known to threaten the arrest of sisters and mothers if their targets hesitate to become informants. Estimates are that there are tens of thousands if not more informants in the West Bank. This vast informant network not only provides information, but also disempowers resistance by sowing distrust within communities. It is difficult for people to organize when they do not know whom to trust.

Mahmoud's name was likely given to the Shabak by an informant. The Shabak officer then added it, along with others, to an arrest list. It was the local IDF commander's job to find and arrest Mahmoud and the other boys on the list.

Mahmoud dropped out of school when he was young. He is thus easy to find: he is almost always at home. Nonetheless, the IDF arrested him and the other boys on their list in the middle of the night.

Night raids are terrifying, especially to children. Moreover, continual sleep deprivation causes tremendous psychological harm. For these reasons, in 2013, UNICEF recommended that arrests of minors be carried out during the day. In response, the Israeli military introduced a pilot program in which minors would receive written summons to appear in court rather than arrested in the middle of the night. The program was suspended within half a year and appears now to be discontinued, though even during the period when it was in effect, these summonses, meant to alleviate the trauma of middle-of-the-night raids, were often issued in a way that made a mockery of the program. For example, Military Court Watch documented a case in March 2015 in which a military unit banged on a family's door at two in the morning to issue a verbal summons to their fourteen-year-old son. Nearly half of the arrests of Palestinian children continue to be made in the middle of the night, inspiring fear and terror, especially among children.

The IDF engages in night raids in part because they are safer. If soldiers roll into a village when people are sleeping, they are less likely to encounter resistance. But equally important is the fact that night raids degrade the fabric of society and subdue the population. Being woken again and again in the middle of the night is exhausting and demoralizing for the entire family and for their neighbors, not merely for the child arrested. Exhausted and demoralized people are incapable of organizing a trip to the grocery store, let alone a campaign of resistance.

On the night of Mahmoud's arrest, after his father opened the door, soldiers, as many as ten of them, streamed into the house. Lights attached to the ends of their weapons lit up the room, dazzling the eyes of the nine children, whom they dragged from their beds. The soldiers were masked, their faces covered in black cloth. These masks, part of an IDF soldier's military-issued kit, have become a feature of Israeli raids, as soldiers seek both to terrify and to avoid being recognized on social media.

Mahmoud's family is poor. Eleven people live crammed into a few small rooms. At night some of the children sleep on the worn and faded foam couches flanking the walls of the bare front room. In a cage hanging from the ceiling are two small birds, which chirped throughout my interview with Mahmoud and his family. Listening to the birds, I wondered if they were struck silent when the soldiers dragged the family from their beds and gathered them in this room or whether they'd continued their merry chirping. During our interview, Mahmoud's older sister served me bitter coffee, and then when she noticed that I took only the smallest of sips, a glass of pink juice so sweet that it made my teeth ache. As we spoke, Mahmoud's mother dandled his infant brother on her knee. The baby was shy, but when Mahmoud leaned over and kissed him lightly on the cheek, he smiled and patted his brother's face with a plump, sticky hand.

When the soldiers burst into the house, the baby began wailing frantically. Mahmoud's parents, panicked at the prospect of one or more of their children being arrested, shouted at the soldiers, adding to the cacophony. Over the hubbub, the commander read Mahmoud's name from a scrap of paper.

Like Karim, Mahmoud's hands were zip tied, in his case so tightly that for three days his wrists were bruised and red. He and another boy from the village, a twelve-year-old, were loaded into a troop carrier and taken to a nearby police station. In a strange way it was a comfort to Mahmoud to be with the frightened young boy. It forced him to take on the role of older brother, to comfort and reassure.

For days Mahmoud was interrogated. He was given very little water and food. He was blindfolded and yelled at, slapped and pushed. The interrogators demanded that he confess to attempting to set fire to the field, to throwing stones, and to a variety of other crimes. Beit Fajjar is a town notorious to the IDF. The young men and boys of Beit Fajjar not only throw stones at passing cars, but they have fired weapons at them, and have even set pipe bombs. They make these pipe bombs using gunpowder gleaned from spent Israeli shells that they collect on firing ranges like the field Mahmoud was accused of setting alight. The interrogators asked Mahmoud if he had ever made or thrown a pipe bomb.

Though Mahmoud insisted to me that he remained stoic in the face of interrogation, I could not help but wonder if he was blustering. It is a rare adult who can withstand interrogation for long, and Mahmoud is only seventeen, and illiterate. Though interrogators are required to inform minors of their right to silence, only a small minority of minors report hearing a warning. Moreover, even when they are informed of their right to silence, it's often in a way that precludes exercising it. In one case, a child told Military Court Watch that after one interrogator told him he had a right to remain silent, another told him that he would be raped if he did not confess. On his own with the interrogator, it's likely that Mahmoud, like the vast majority of arrested children, made an incriminating statement.

Eventually, Mahmoud was taken to Ofer Prison and brought before a military judge. The Israeli military provides no legal services to detainees in the West Bank, not even to children. Representation thus falls to the Palestinian Authority or to NGOs supported by contributions from the United States and Europe, and to private Palestinian attorneys who eke out a living ushering children like Mahmoud through the military court system. The lawyer Mahmoud's parents hired, whom he did not see until he arrived at court for the first time, told him to "confess and apologize." He would pay a fine and serve a minimum sentence. Fighting the charge would only result in a much longer sentence, a larger fine, and increased attorneys' fees. Eventually, the family managed to scrounge together enough to pay the lawyer and the fine, and Mahmoud was released.

When he got out, however, there was no one waiting for him. The village had been closed by the IDF. The closing of shops and roads after an arrest, the imposition of what amounts to house arrest on an entire village, has proved effective at controlling the population. With their livelihood threatened, shop owners and others turn on families they suspect of engaging in acts of resistance. Whether those accused in fact committed the offenses is less important than the creation of a general climate of fear, anger, and distrust that quashes rebellion. That this type of collective punishment is a war crime has not dissuaded the IDF from frequently engaging in it.

Mahmoud thus made his way home from Ofer Prison alone. In the wake of his arrest, his mother tells me that Mahmoud was initially quiet. He stayed in bed, sleeping. He avoided his friends and family. But eventually he began arguing with his parents. He told them that he was angry at them for paying his bail, but the anger seemed to his family more an expression of power than a specific complaint. To this younger son, having been arrested felt like a rite of passage. Since his arrest he has begun feeling and acting like a man with the right to control his family, especially his older sister.

Though Mahmoud's sister laughed when she described his behavior, she was clearly frustrated by it. "He practices his authority on me!" she said. "He refuses to let me out of the house. He won't let me use my phone. He says my friends are a bad influence."

To these complaints Mahmoud replied with a smile and a shrug.

Karim, younger than Mahmoud and with Issa's example to guide him, would never attempt this kind of control over his own older sister, herself a political activist. If anything, he is deferential to her. Both boys are quiet, but Karim's silence feels to me like a boy's shyness, rather than a teenager's surliness.

My conversation with Karim in Issa's garden is interrupted by a squad of Israeli soldiers. Somehow alerted to my presence in the garden—perhaps by Baruch Marzel or one of the members of his household, who seem perpetually to be perched in their windows, glaring down at the community center—the soldiers demand to see my papers and the papers of the young peace activist who accompanies me. We were careful to verify ahead of time that our presence was permitted, and our familiarity with the various orders regarding military secure zones seems to annoy the commander.

While they rifle through our documents, Issa shows the soldiers how the electrical wires to his home had been cut the night before. The commander initially gives him an argument. Perhaps the wire frayed? Issa shows him the clean slice. Perhaps Issa did it himself, the commander says. By then I have taken out my phone and am taping the interaction. A young soldier tells me not to record his face, and I apologize but continue. He turns his back to me and shrugs his shoulders up to his chin, as if to hide within his own body. I feel a flash of pity for this young man, very nearly a boy himself. For most IDF draftees, service in Hebron is a function of bad luck, not choice. Perhaps this young man, like the one escorting me, will be so infuriated and horrified by his experience in Hebron that he will become a peace activist himself.

Eventually, Karim and I leave the garden and walk through the high brush to his house. He lives very close to Issa, but the road between the two houses is blocked by settlers, so to get from one to the other we must navigate a circuitous path, up and down and around until I'm no longer even sure where we started. When we reach his home, he introduces me to his mother and his lively older sister, who take me into their main room, and sit with me on large foam couches like the ones in Mahmoud's family's house. It is Karim who goes into the kitchen to prepare coffee and juice, not his sister, even Karim who rushes into the bathroom to prepare a bucket of water for me to use to flush the toilet. Baruch Marzel, in his house perched directly above, can turn on his taps any time of the day or night, but Karim's family's water runs only a couple of hours a day. I use as little as possible, to spare them having to haul more.

After a while Karim and I take leave of his mother and sister and head down the hill, where Issa has met up with the group of writers with whom I came to Hebron. Karim and Issa lead us on a walking tour of their beleaguered city that begins at one checkpoint, at which Issa is stopped, trapped for nearly a quarter of an hour in the turnstile like an animal in a cage, while the soldiers laugh and make a show of ignoring our pleas for his release, and ends in another, where Karim is pulled aside.

"What are you doing?" I ask the police officers, themselves young men only a few years older than Karim. "Why are you stopping him?"

They refuse to answer my questions, just continue to search and question Karim. Issa begins arguing with the police officers, to no avail.

"Are they arresting Karim?" I ask Issa. "He hasn't done anything!"

Issa kindly refrains from stating the obvious. Instead he says, "I think it's best if you go."

"You want us to leave?" I ask. "But won't it be safer for Karim if we stay?"

"I think they will hold him until you leave. And then they will let him go."

I look back at Karim, whose expression bears the same implacable stoicism I saw on Issa when he was trapped in the turnstile.

"Good-bye, Karim!" I call out.

He smiles and waves.

TWO STORIES, SO MANY STORIES

COLUM MCCANN

*"What is the source of our first suffering?" It lies in the fact that
we hesitated to speak. . . . It was born in the moment when we
accumulated silent things within us.*
—GASTON BACHELARD

COME NOW. QUIETLY. ALONG THIS SUSPENSEFUL STREET. IT IS
early evening and there is a November chill. Two or three
stars hang perilously over Beit Jala. The lights of Bethlehem
seep yellow in the distance, fading into the dark hills. Tighten your-
self a little against the cold. Watch your breath make a little argument
against the gathering dark. Up the hill. The shops are closed. The day
draws itself into silence: no church bells, no call of the muezzin. A
couple of cars and a motorbike are parked outside a four-storey apart-
ment building. Come now, past a building site, around the side of the
apartments, up the outside stairwell. Careful. It is not well lit. A hint
of light reflects from the white brickwork. Nothing fancy. Nothing
ruined either. The walls are bare. A place you could find just about
anywhere. The fluorescents flicker in the ground-floor stairwell. You
take in the smell of stale smoke. The sharp tang of coffee. No elevator
here. You climb the stairs. One flight, two. Your footsteps echo. The
sign on the door reads PARENTS CIRCLE. You step inside. More colour

here. More brightness. Music from the radio. Posters on the wall. Inside, at the head of a long table, sit two middle-aged men. One dark skinned, one pale. One thin, the other robust. They sit close to each other, shoulders almost touching. Bassam Aramin and Rami Elhanan. They lean forward to speak. Gather around. Come now. Listen. The darkness outside is descending.

"My name is Rami Elhanan. I'm a sixty-six-year-old graphic designer, a seventh-generation Jerusalemite. My mother was born in the Old City of Jerusalem, from an ultra-Jewish, ultraorthodox family. My father came here in 1946, after spending one year in Auschwitz. He was a quiet man. He tried to make a life here. He was very badly wounded in the '48 war in the Old City. My mother was the nurse who took care of him. They fell in love and had a family. Things were straightforward enough, I suppose. I grew up, an ordinary kid, a Jew, an Israeli, a human being.

"The story I want to tell you starts, and ends, on one particular day of the Jewish calendar, Yom Kippur. For us Jews this is the day when we ask forgiveness for our sins. On this very day forty-two years ago I was a very young soldier fighting the October '73 war in Sinai. Like any war, it was a horrible thing. I eventually fought in three wars. No good thing comes from any war. But in '73 we started it with a company of eleven tanks—and finished it with only three. My job included bringing in ammunition and taking out the dead and wounded. I lost some of my very close friends. I saw their stretchers turn red. I emerged from the war angry and bitter, a disappointed young man with one determination: to detach myself from any kind of involvement or commitment.

"I got out of the army and finished my studies at Bezalel Academy of Art. I got married and I had four kids. One of these children was my daughter, Smadar. She was born on the eve of Yom Kippur, in September 1983, in a hospital in Jerusalem. Her name is taken from the Bible, from the Song of Solomon, grape of the vine, the opening of the flower. A sparkling, vivid, and joyful little girl. Very beautiful. An excellent student, a swimmer, a dancer too. An amazing child; we used to call her 'the Princess.'

"My three boys and this little princess, we lived what seemed to be a perfect, sheltered, secured life in Jerusalem with our house in the Rehavia neighbourhood. My wife, Nurit, taught in the Hebrew University. In a way, you could say that we lived inside a bubble, completely detached from the outside world. I was doing graphic design—posters and ads—for the right wing, for the left wing, whoever paid money. Life was good. There weren't many complications.

"And this went on, until about eighteen years ago, on the fourth of September, 1997, when this bubble of ours was shattered into millions of pieces by three Palestinian suicide bombers, who blew themselves up in the middle of Ben Yehuda Street, in the center of Jerusalem.

"I have told this story so many times, but there is always something new. Memories hit you all the time. A butterfly. A book that is opened. A door that is closed, a beeping sound. Anything at all.

"They killed five people that day, including three little girls. One of these girls was my Smadari. It was a Thursday afternoon. She was out buying books.

"At first when you hear about an explosion, any explosion, you keep hoping that maybe this time the finger of fate will not turn towards you. Then gradually you find yourself running in the streets trying to find your daughter, your child, your Princess—but she has completely vanished. You go from hospital to hospital, from police station to police station. You do this for many long and frustrating hours until eventually, very late at night, you and your wife find yourselves in the morgue. This finger, it points at you, right between your eyes, and you see this sight which you will never be able to forget for the rest of your life. Your daughter. On a steel tray. Your daughter. Fourteen years old.

"The funeral was held in Kibbutz Nachshon. Smadar was buried next to her grandfather, General Matti Peled, a true fighter for peace, a professor, a Knesset member. People came from everywhere in this mosaic of a country, Jews and Arabs, representatives of the settlers, representatives from the parliament, representatives of Arafat, from abroad, everywhere.

"And then she is buried. Your daughter. Smadar. Grape of the vine.

"You come back home, the house is filled with thousands and thousands of people coming to pay respect to you, offering condolences. These are the seven days of shivah. You are enveloped by these thousands of people in a very clever, traditional way of easing your way back to the new life. On the eighth day, everybody goes back to their normal, everyday businesses, and suddenly you're left alone. Without your daughter. She is not there. She is just not there.

"You need to wake up, to stand up and face yourself. You have to make a decision. What are you going to do now, with this new, unbearable burden on your shoulders? What are you going to do with this new personality of yours, which you never thought could have existed? What are you going to do with this anger, that eats you alive from within?

"There are only two ways to choose; the first one is obvious. When someone kills your fourteen-year-old girl, you are so angry that you want to get even. This is natural. This is human. And this is the way most people choose to go—the way of revenge and retaliation. This way creates this endless cycle of violence which never stops. A bullet leads to another bullet. A suicide bomber to a rocket-propelled grenade.

"But then after a while you start thinking and asking yourself questions, you know: We are human beings, we are not animals, we can use our brains. And you ask yourself, Will killing anyone bring my daughter back? Will killing the whole world bring her back? Will causing pain to someone ease the unbearable pain that you are suffering? Well, the answer is easy. Dust returns to dust. That is all.

"Foolishly, at the beginning, I thought I could go on with my life, pretending as if nothing had happened. I tried to lead a normal life, go back to my studio. But nothing was normal anymore. I wasn't the same person.

"She was gone.

"So in a very gradual, complicated process, you come to the other option, which is the much more difficult option: trying to understand what happened to your daughter. Why did it happen? How could such a horrible thing take place? What could cause someone to be that angry, that mad, that desperate, that hopeless, that he is willing to blow himself up alongside a fourteen-year-old girl? How can you possibly understand that instinct? And then, the most important question of them all: What can you do, personally, in order to prevent this unbearable pain for other people, other families? Well it's not easy, it takes time.

"About a year later, I met a man who changed my life completely. His name was Yitzhak Frankenthal, a religious Jew, you know, with a *kippa* on his head. And, you know, we tend to put people into drawers, stigmatize people? We tend to judge people by the way they dress, and I was certain that this guy was a fascist, a right-winger, that he eats Arabs for breakfast. I prepared myself to fight him, to argue with him, but we started talking and he told me about his son Arik, a soldier who was kidnapped and murdered by Hamas in 1994. And then he told me about this organization that he created—people who lost their loved ones, but still wanted peace. And I remembered that Yitzhak had been among those thousands and thousands of people who came to my house a year before during those seven days of shivah, and I went crazy. I was so angry with him, I asked him, How could you do it? How could you step into someone's house who just lost a loved one, and talk about peace? How dare you?

"And he—being the great man that he is—was not insulted by my rage. He just invited me over to watch a meeting of these crazy people, and I got curious. I said okay. I went to see. I stood outside. Very detached, very cynical. As I always am. And I watched those people coming down from the buses.

"The first group to come down from the buses were, for me—as an Israeli—living legends. People I used to look up to, admire. I had read about them in the newspapers. They had lost loved ones and were searching for ways of peace. And I never thought that one day I would be one of them. I saw peace activists, Holocaust survivors, so many others.

"This took the lids from my eyes.

"But then I saw something else, something completely new to me, to my eyes and to my mind, to my heart, to my brain. I was standing there, and suddenly I saw some Palestinian bereaved families walking towards me. This flabbergasted me. The enemy. They were shaking my hand for peace, hugging me, crying with me. I was so deeply touched, so deeply moved. It was like a hammer on my head cracking me open.

"This was extraordinary. An organization of the bereaved. But even more extraordinary, they were both Israeli and Palestinian. Together. In one room. Sharing their sorrow. What sort of madness is this?

"I remember seeing this old Arab lady coming down from the bus, in this black, traditional Palestinian dress. And she had a picture of her six-year-old kid clutched to her chest, exactly like my wife carrying the name of our daughter, Smadari, on hers.

"You see, I was forty-seven years old at the time, and I'm ashamed to admit it was the first time in my life, to that point, that I'd met Palestinians as human beings. Not just workers in the streets, not just caricatures in the newspapers, not just human transparencies, not just terrorists, but human beings—human beings—people who carry the same burden that I carry, people that suffer exactly as I suffer. An equality of pain. I'm not a religious person—I have no way of explaining what happened to me back then. All I can tell you is that from that moment until today, I have devoted my life to going everywhere possible, to talk to anyone possible, people who want to listen, even people who will not listen, to convey this very basic and very simple message, which says, We are not doomed.

"And you can quote me on that."

THE WORLD PRESENTS ITS IRONIES AT THE ODDEST TIMES: FROM OUTSIDE, the sound of a police siren ripping along Virgin Mary Street.

"They've come to get you," smiles Bassam, glancing at Rami.

"Oh they can have me," says Rami, his face moving wide into a grin.

It is not entirely out of the realm of possibility, since Rami, as an Israeli, is here illegally: he is not allowed to travel into this part of Beit Jala. He doesn't care. He gets here on his motorbike, taking backroads if he must. There are always ways around the checkpoints.

All the walls—even that Wall, a few hundred yards away, snaking its way towards Bethlehem—are breachable. Bassam, too, needs a special permit to enter Israel.

The siren fades away and we are left with the fluorescent hum of the lights above.

On the table there is coffee, some small pastries, a number of green napkins. Rami and Bassam have sat by each other thousands of times, telling the same story to anyone open enough to listen.

Most stories eventually die by repetition, but not theirs. Their stories are kept alive by the brutal reality that people are still dying outside the windows. The only way they know how to confront this is to share their experience—and so they do so over and over again. They have learned that the art of the story is getting others to listen: schoolchildren, dignitaries, teachers, army officers, fighters, politicians, you, me. It is unthinkable to them that they could live without the ability to tell their stories. They are, in a way, learning how to restore themselves at the same time. They braid in and out of each other, woven on a loom of possibility. They have found something beyond grief. And so they somehow vault death. It is as if they have stepped forward from the pages of the *Mu'allaqat*: Is there any hope that this desolation can bring me solace?

The two men glance at each other. One can't help but feel that there is someone else telling their story too. One child went out for books. The other—as you will soon discover—went out for candy.

"My name is Bassam Aramin. I'm a terrorist. Just kidding. Or maybe I'm not kidding, that's how many people see me, many people want it to be true. When I was a kid, I thought it was a punishment from God to be a Palestinian, or a Muslim or an Arab, because it's very difficult to grow up under occupation. People you don't understand, in a language you don't understand, they come to your village and occupy. Suddenly you become a fighter or a warrior, which is not your dream, not your mission.

"It's a tragedy that as Palestinians, we need to prove that we are human beings. Not only to the Israelis, unfortunately it's also for the

Arabs, for our brothers and sisters. To the Americans, to the Europeans too. We have to prove that we are human beings. Why is that?

"When I was a kid in Hebron I fought the occupation by raising the Palestinian flag in our playground. To make the Israelis crazy. They hated us raising our flag. We never felt safe. We were always running from jeeps to avoid the soldiers beating us. Our homes were invaded and children I knew were killed. At the age of twelve I joined a demonstration where a boy was shot by a soldier. I watched this boy die in front of me.

"From that moment I developed a deep need for revenge. I became part of a group whose mission was to get rid of the catastrophe that had come to our town. We called ourselves freedom fighters, but the outside world called us terrorists. At first we just threw stones and empty bottles, but when we came across some discarded hand grenades in a cave, we decided to hurl them at the Israeli jeeps. Two of them exploded. Luckily no one was injured, because we didn't know how to use them properly, but we were caught and in 1985, at the age of seventeen, I received a seven-year prison sentence. It's a long story; a long seven years.

"We had a mission in jail, because the Israelis had a mission too. Their purpose was to kill our humanity. Our mission was to survive and to protect our humanity because we are human beings. On October 1, 1987, over a hundred of us—all teenage boys—were waiting to go into the dining room when the alarms suddenly went off. About a hundred heavily armed soldiers suddenly appeared and ordered us to strip naked. A very embarrassing thing, to be stripped of everything, first our dignity, then everything else. They beat us until we could hardly stand. I was held the longest and beaten the hardest.

"What struck me was that the soldiers were beating us without hatred, because for them this was just a training exercise and they saw us as objects. We were not human.

"As I was being beaten, I remembered a movie I'd seen the year before about the Holocaust. At the time I'd been happy that Hitler had killed six million Jews. I remember wishing that he'd killed them all, because then I would never have been sent to prison. But after a few minutes, I found myself secretly crying in sympathy with those people, naked people. I'm a very simple man. I tried to convince myself that it was just a movie; there are no human beings that would do this to other human beings. It seemed impossible.

"It is always very difficult to recognize that pain of your enemy—in our case, the Palestinians, to recognize the pain of the Israelis, or the Jews who occupied us. For us the Holocaust was a big lie. So we chose not to know, and to deny it. But this movie, it pushed me to understand them. I found myself crying and feeling angry that the Jews were being herded into gas chambers without fighting back. If they knew they were going to die, why didn't they scream out? I tried to hide my tears from the other prisoners: they wouldn't have understood why I was crying about the pain of my oppressors. It was the first time I felt empathy.

"But now—as I was being beaten a year later—I remembered the movie and I started screaming out at them: 'Murderers! Nazis! Oppressors!' And as a consequence, I felt no pain.

"This beating made me realize that we had to preserve our humanity—our right to laugh and our right to cry—in order to save ourselves. I also slowly realized that much of the Israeli oppression was because of the Holocaust, and I decided to try to understand who the Jews were. This led to a conversation with a prison guard. The guards all thought of us as terrorists and we hated them, but this guard asked me, 'How can someone quiet like you become a terrorist?' I replied, 'No, you're the terrorist. I'm a freedom fighter.'

"He was from a settler family, but he really believed that we, the Palestinians, were the settlers, not the Israelis. I said, 'If you can convince me that we are the settlers, then I'll declare this in front of all the prisoners.' He was shocked. He said he never met anyone like me before.

"It was the start of a dialogue and a friendship. The start of a discovery. Some months later the guard came back and sat down to talk to me. His face was changed somehow. He said he understood now that we were not the settlers. We were the oppressed. He had not recognized this before. He even became a supporter of the Palestinian struggle. From then on he always treated us with respect. He allowed me to drink tea from a glass, not plastic, and once even smuggled in two big bottles of Coca-Cola, which I shared with the other prisoners. And he protected me from the other soldiers when they went to beat me, shouting, 'He has a weak heart! If he dies it will be on your heads.'

"Seeing how this happened without force—through simple dialogue—made me understand that the only way to achieve peace was through nonviolence. Our dialogue enabled us both to see each other's purity of heart and our good intent.

"Does this sound impossible? I don't care. Nothing is impossible.

"I got released in 1992 and I still believed in our armed struggle. It was the time of the Oslo accords and there was a great feeling of hope for a two-state solution. But it never happened because the politicians said we weren't ready for it. I think if I hadn't had such strong beliefs and principles, anger and hatred would have taken over again. There was no conflict like our conflict. We would never solve it, we would continue hating each other forever, even if it's not written in the Quran and in the Bible.

"In 1994, I had my first child. When you think as a father it's a different issue, because you have more responsibility. Not because you became a coward. But sometimes you go to the other side, because for your kids you want to sacrifice yourself in a different way. I saw Palestinian kids throwing flowers instead of stones when the Israeli troops were leaving Jenin. All of this led me to totally change my mind. I decided that peace would only work if we could begin to make a connection with the Israelis. Because for more than one hundred years we have tried to kill each other, defeat each other, tear each other apart. And what do we have? Israel is not safe, and Palestine is not free. And every day, every week, every year, more blood, more pain, more victims, and we don't even think about it.

"So I decided my son will never go to the Israeli jails, and he will never throw stones. Then I started to be active in my society, on the Palestinian side, saying that we need to change our way to try to achieve our goal.

"Don't get me wrong. It's the same goal: it's to end the Israeli occupation. We'll never accept it. We will never accept it even after one thousand years. But we have to do it differently. We have to use the force of our humanity. A new sort of strength.

"It wasn't until 2005 that some of us who believed in nonviolence started meeting in secret with former Israeli soldiers, the refuseniks. I was among four Palestinian representatives. You can't imagine the first meeting. Here, in another part of Beit Jala. For us they were criminals, killers, enemies. And for them, we were the same. We were meeting as true enemies who now—somehow—wanted to speak.

"One of them, in fact, was Rami's son, Elik. That's how our families met.

"These young Israelis were refusing to fight, not for the sake of the Palestinian people, but for the sake of their own society, their own morality. We too were not acting to save Israeli lives, but to prevent our society from suffering even more. It was only later that we both came to feel a responsibility for each other's people.

"Essentially we discovered that we were the same. We realized that we wanted to kill each other to achieve the same thing—peace and security! Of course, each one has a different point of view: they are occupiers; we are under the occupation. We have the right to resist, and to use our struggle. But in the end we are dying, we are killing each other. We had to find another way to survive together.

"This took time. It took dialogue. We needed to know one another. As I have always said, it's a disaster to discover the humanity and the nobility of your enemy—because then he is not your enemy anymore.

"It didn't happen from the first meeting. It took more than a year of meetings. We started an organization called Combatants for Peace. In the first year we had three hundred members, now we have more than six hundred. Maybe the story could have ended there.

"But my story has a much darker side to it. On January 16, 2007—two years after Combatants for Peace was founded—my ten-year-old daughter, Abir, was shot and killed in cold blood by a member of the Israeli border police while standing outside her school with some classmates. She was shot with a rubber bullet. An American-made rubber bullet. An American-made M16. There were no demonstrations or violence or intifada going on. She was just shot.

"The world was appalled by the details of what happened, not least that she had just bought candy at the store. Some details are awful, but sometimes I think that she hadn't had time to eat it. Just that. She did not have time to eat the candy.

"Ten years old. A bullet to the back of the head. She fell flat on her face.

"It took me four and a half years to prove in the civil court that my daughter had been killed with a rubber bullet. My goal has been to bring the soldier responsible to trial, but the Supreme Court decided after four and a half years there was no evidence, so they closed the file for the fourth time. I believe in justice, and many hundreds of my Israeli brothers and Jewish brothers around the world support me. I want to bring this man to justice because he killed my ten-year-old daughter; not because he's an Israeli and I'm a Palestinian but because my child was not a fighter. She was not a Fatah or Hamas member. She was out buying candy. For there to be reconciliation, and for me to consider forgiveness, Israel has to recognize such crimes.

"Abir's murder could have led me down the easy path of hatred and vengeance, but for me there was no return from dialogue and nonviolence. It eventually pushed me to finish my master's degree in 2011 on the Holocaust in a program in England. And to do this work for peace. After all, it was one Israeli soldier who shot my daughter, but one hundred former Israeli soldiers who built a garden in her name at the school where she was murdered."

IN 1993 THE ALGERIAN POET TAHAR DJAOUT WAS GUNNED DOWN BE-cause—in the language of his attackers—he wielded a fearsome pen. Shortly before he was killed he wrote: "If you keep quiet, you die. If you speak, you die. So, speak and die."

The Algerian knew what all men and women finally know: that stories can pry open our rib cages and twist our heart backwards a notch. They can aim a punch at the back of your brain. They can dolphin themselves up out of nowhere and connect us. They are a foothold against despair. They can make the silence breathe.

Djaout was aware—like Bassam, like Rami—that speaking up and telling stories can make the world a wider place: we become alive in a body, a time, a feeling, a culture, an adventure that is not our own. We get dragged out of our stupor. We speak of experience, however bitter or lacerating. In telling our stories we oppose the awful cruelties of the times and present to the world the profoundest evidence of being alive. At the same time, most of us know that the suffering of the present and the evil of the past are unlikely to be redeemed by a future era of universal happiness, but that doesn't take away the need to listen. And to be listened to.

One story is so many stories.

So, speak and live—at least until you don't.

"IT IS NOT OUR DESTINY TO KEEP KILLING EACH OTHER IN THIS HOLY land of ours forever," says Rami, looking across at Bassam, shaking his shoulder. "Even me and this terrorist here."

Bassam grins back at the man he calls his brother.

"The thing I had to learn to understand," continues Rami, "is that the killer of my daughter is a victim too. He is a victim in many ways, even a victim of himself."

"There is nothing worse than losing a child," says Bassam. "Especially because Abir and Smadar were not fighters. They did not know anything about the war. But you discover that there is no revenge, no point in revenge, because you will never meet your daughter again, not on this earth anyway. It's ongoing pain, forever, twenty-four hours, every single day of the year. You need to learn how to live with your pain. We don't want revenge; we want justice."

"Most of us Israelis sit in the coffeehouses in Tel Aviv, and we don't look two hundred meters under our noses what is going on," says Rami. "The ordinary Israeli needs to know that occupation pays a price. The Palestinians know the price. There is not a single Palestinian house—not a single one—without a dead, without a person wounded, without a prisoner. They live it every instant of their lives. But we Israelis, we don't want to know. We turn away. We go to the beach. We go to our discos. And in the meantime, the occupation is on, atrocities are on, checkpoints are on, and the settlements—there are more and more and more of them. This is the aim of the occupation: to prevent any possibility of a solution. This is the main purpose of the settlements, and sometimes I'm afraid they have won. I'm afraid that today, to dismantle this war will be difficult, and we will have to think about new ways how to deal with it."

"We want to spread a very simple message," says Bassam, "that we need to share this land with the enemy, as one state or two states or five states or five hundred, otherwise we will share the same lands to dig graves for our kids and our people. The Israelis will never give up their safe place, and we Palestinians will never give up our freedom and our dream to create our own state."

"I am speaking as a son of an Auschwitz graduate," says Rami. "Seventy years ago they took my grandparents to the ovens in Europe. And the world did not lift a finger. And today, seventy years later, while we are massacring each other, the world keeps standing aside. This is a crime! I cannot say it loud enough. This war is a crime against humanity. And standing aside while this crime is being committed is also a crime. Now I don't ask of people to be pro-Israeli, or to be pro-Palestinian. I demand of them to be pro-peace, to be against injustice, and against this ongoing situation in which one people is dominating another. My personal message is that as a Jew—a Jew with the utmost respect for my people, for my tradition, for my history—ruling and oppressing, and humiliating, and occupying millions and millions of people for so many years, without any democratic right, is not Jewish. Period. And being against the war is not anti-Semitism of any shape or form."

The electricity continues to shoot between the two men, their voices helixing together.

"We need to learn how to live side by side. The main word—the most important word—is the ability to respect the other side. Respect. There is no other alternative. All the others are technical issues: how to prepare a life that will enable you to get up in the morning, send your kid to school, and get him back in one piece."

"Don't call us naive. Don't call us sentimental. We can change it; we can break, once and for all, this endless cycle of violence and revenge and retaliation. And the only way to do it is simply by talking to each other. Because it will not stop unless we talk. I believe deeply that you can teach yourself to listen. I believe deeply that once you listen to the pain of the other, that you can expect the other to listen to your pain. And then, only then, together we start this very long journey, towards reconciliation, and maybe some kind of peace at the end. This is a very long, bumpy road—no shortcuts—but this is the only way possible, because the other way leads nowhere. The price of the other way is really too horrible."

"So this is what we are trying to do, my dear brother beside me, here, and the seven hundred family members of this unique organization of ours, Parents Circle. We bang our heads against this very high wall of hatred and fear that divides these two nations today, and we put cracks in it. Cracks of hope. Small cracks. Tiny ones even. A spiderweb of them. There is no alternative, the alternative is really too horrible. Do we get disappointed? Yes, every day we are disappointed. But the deeper the engagement, the greater the ability for disappointment. This is a simple truth. We must. We absolutely must."

"We need to meet each other on the ground, to enjoy this land, otherwise we will meet each other under the ground. In the graves. In the dirt."

"I always quote Martin Luther King: 'In the end we will remember not the words of our enemies, but the silence of our friends.'"

"We need to tell stories."

"We need to hear stories."

"Listen to one another."

"Not underground."

"Up here . . ."

"You can't overcome hatred with more hatred."

"We refuse to be enemies."

"You must understand: there is no difference between me and my brother here. We are not talking two different narratives."

"What makes us so close is the price we both paid."

"We have an enormous ally on our side, which is the power of our pain."

"And in the end we will win them over with our humanity."

"You can quote us on that."

"Both of us."

OUTSIDE THE DARKNESS HAS DESCENDED. NIGHTTIME IN BEIT JALA. YOU reach for a green napkin on the table. A souvenir on which both men have signed their names. On it they have written their names and the words *Harness the power of pain.*

You walk out of the office and down the apartment block stairs. The sky is fierce with stars. Rami and Bassam stand together. They kiss four times on the cheek. Rami gets on his motorbike. He will have to negotiate the checkpoints and pass the Wall on the way home to Jerusalem. It doesn't worry him: he will have no trouble, he knows the way.

"There are only two types of people who can get past that Wall— the peacemakers and the terrorists."

He pulls on his helmet and waves good-bye to Bassam.

Bassam lights a cigarette and walks up the hilly portion of the street towards his car. He too will drive to Jerusalem. He will take a different road, the only one he is allowed to take back to his home in Anata, driving south at first, forced, for a while, in the wrong direction. He has a slight limp. You think for a moment that it might have something to do with the way he was beaten in prison, but you find out later that he contracted polio as a child. He was given a shorter prison sentence for his attack as a juvenile because he only posed as a lookout. He was unable to run fast. He might have spent twice as long in prison but for that.

Another irony, another siren on Virgin Mary Street.

Bassam bends down to the car door, inserts the key, climbs in. The rear lights of Rami's motorbike top the hill.

The two men go in opposite directions, the lights of their vehicles spraying in the dark. They will be back again in a few days, to tell their stories again. Again and again and again. Until their dying days. Or until the days themselves are dead.

You can probably quote them on that, but for now they are gone.

H2

MAYLIS DE KERANGAL

LEAPING OVER, SLIPPING ALONG, CLIMBING UP. NOUR HURRIES through the night and I follow close behind. She cuts across the fields, reaches a stone enclosure, and pushes open a metal door to reveal a messy courtyard surrounding a house with dark windows, finds an opening in the wall opposite, and climbs a mound of dirt and rocks that turns into a path. I can't see a thing, and I am careful not to let her get too far ahead, to keep the pale glimmer of her pink headscarf in sight. A hole to be jumped over, then a slope of stones and roots to fumble down, trying to find handholds. Nour turns around, takes my hand to help me down—her own, delicate as a child's, is impressively strong. This leads us to a second rear courtyard, identical to the first—same cement floor, same darkness pierced by cold light, same beat-up, broken-down objects scattered randomly about—and again the same diagonal route, again the gap in a wall, again the dirt track. Nour turns on the flashlight on her cell phone, a glowing Samsung, and now the beam of light cuts a trail for us, makes the black beetles scuttle away and reveals the dust on the leaves of the bushes. The vegetation has become thicker. Nour protects her face, ducks her head so as not to catch her scarf in the branches, and I watch my step too. Finally the thickets become sparser, the grass reappears in the moonlight, these are the last few yards, somewhere very near a dog unleashes a fit of furious barking and I sense the young girl speeding up. She races up a staircase and jumps into a third rear courtyard, the door of the house is open, we go inside.

Nour. She is a young girl of twenty-two who looks sixteen. Our eyes met for the first time in front of the building that houses the facilities of the Youth Against Settlements organization on the heights of Hebron. An expressive face framed by a pale pink headscarf, dark eyes, doe-like lashes, pearly skin, delicate hands with polished nails, an upright, proud figure. What immediately strikes me is the restrained intensity she possesses, the determination and wisdom apparent in her every gesture, in her every word, spoken in her slow and perfect English. She is someone who, for example, will always pause before responding, for a while, two or three seconds, and this pause, borne of a desire to nuance or from a sense of reserve, imbues her words with resolve. It is with her, in her family home, that I have come to spend these three days.

Wi-Fi. Inside the house is bare, basic, tiled, and spacious. Nour's parents, Hisham and Fatima, are in the living room with her little sister Aisha. Big armchairs are placed side by side against the walls all the way around the room. The father has folded up his long legs and is sitting cross-legged, his computer on his knees; the mother is braiding her little girl's hair, who is fidgeting at her feet. Nour goes over to kiss them. She has taken off her scarf and her long dress and appears now as a teenager, her hair in a bob, dressed in long shorts and a gray cotton T-shirt. The evening stretches out in familial intimacy; it is quiet, the boys aren't home yet. *Times are difficult here*: Hisham, the father, whom Nour affectionately calls Baba—*daddy* in the local Arabic dialect—rolls his *r*'s and mops his brow, his eyes weary, his skin pallid, his smile sad. I notice his lifeless hand. Learning that I am French, he tries a Skype call with one of his cousins who lives just outside Toulouse while Nour sends WhatsApp messages and Aisha, curious as a cat, circles around me. At around eleven o'clock the mother serves us tea and cakes, then we look at photos of the eldest daughter, who lives in Jordan, in Amman. It gets later; the little girl is sent to bed, but she drags her feet, returns, demands that we take photos using a homemade selfie stick. I like how she seizes the slightest opportunity to play, laugh, have fun, stay with us, and with me, the main attraction for this evening. The boys are late, it seems. The parents cannot go to sleep without knowing they are home, they are anxious, it is dangerous outside. Outside is the Tel Rumeida district in the H2 zone of Hebron, and it is not a particularly safe place for young Palestinian boys.

Enclave. Hebron is the largest city in the West Bank. Since the ratification of the Hebron agreement in January 1997, the city has been split into two separate yet twinned sectors. The first, named H1, covers 80 percent of the agglomeration and contains more than 160,000 Palestinians; it is under the control of the Palestinian Authority. The second, H2, comprises 20 percent of the city's territory, with around 40,000 Palestinian inhabitants and around 800 Israeli Jewish settlers living in several settlements; it is controlled by Israel which, according to the agreement "will retain all powers and responsibilities for internal security and public order. . . . In addition, Israel will continue to carry the responsibility for overall security of Israelis." In fact, zone H2, although located in the heart of Hebron, is today under the sole jurisdiction of the IDF, the Israel Defense Forces. It is an enclave.

Map legend. I open the map. Area H2 comprises the eastern limit of the city of Hebron, forming a spike to the west that suddenly jabs into the city to enclose the Jewish cemetery. Its perimeter includes the Old Town of Hebron, the Cave of the Patriarchs, and the Casbah, as well as the different Jewish settlements (excluding the large settlement of Kiryat Arba to the east), and other smaller establishments located in the historical center. These include Beit Hadassah, Beit Romano, Admot Yishai (the Tel Rumeida settlement), and Avraham Avinu, colonies inhabited primarily by religious Zionists in favor of the annexation of the Palestinian territories. The area thus delineated comprises different zones, crosshatched with lines and dotted with symbols explained by a large map legend— the abundance of icons is yet another indication of this complexity. I focus on movement within this space, on the regulation of access to public roads which in themselves give an indication of the tension that prevails here: there are "sterilized" roads, like an exsanguinated body, or, rather, like the sterile field established around the body of a patient in an operating room: closed shops, empty houses, Palestinian vehicles banned; there are the roads where no Palestinian vehicles are permitted but that Palestinians can still use on foot; and finally, there are the roads barred to all Palestinians, whether by vehicle or on foot. To these restrictions are added the zones around Jewish settlements where Palestinians are forbidden to enter, as well as the twenty or so checkpoints, mobile and otherwise, the roadblocks, the watchtowers, and all the other boundaries that cover the area. These blocked, restricted, monitored routes concern only the Palestinian population of H2. As for the Jewish settlers, they can travel freely around the sector, whether by car or on foot. The soldiers ensure their safety. As I examine the map, the title of a famous essay by the geographer Yves Lacoste comes to mind: *Geography serves, first and foremost, to wage war.*

Ballerina pumps. The route Nour took at night on her way back from an evening out in the nearby hills, like a mountain goat, her black ballerina pumps springing through the darkness, is consistent with the logic of detours and dodging. A parallel network of movement is reactivated, occupying the forgotten interstices at the back of the houses and the breaches in the walls, devising a leafy, crowded, backstage world where one slips along more than one walks, where one climbs up, leaps from one wall to another, one roof to another, where one cuts across the fields. This "circumventory resistance" denotes both the stranglehold of the occupation on the territory and the vitality of the Palestinians who live there.

Brothers. Marwan, the elder brother, comes home around midnight. He arrives wearing a sweatsuit in the colors of the Hebron football team for whom he is a professional player, kisses his parents, shakes my hand, and goes straight to bed, worn out by training. I can feel the parents starting to relax. Later, in the girls' room, lying on a little bed between Nour and Aisha, I hear the other brother, Hafez, arrive, the mother's voice, and then the little band of light beneath the door goes out. Everyone is at home now, the house is still, the parents are sleeping. Hafez's arrest in the fall of 2015 by Israeli soldiers looking for the perpetrator of a knife attack on a Jewish settler has taken its toll, even though the young man was ultimately freed without even having to pay a fine, a thing sufficiently rare that Nour mentions it to me several times. The young girl recounts this episode in simple terms, subtly hints at the misery that reigned in the household at that time, the uncertainty and the anguish.

Smartphone. Nour's face is illuminated in the dark by the bluish screen of her cell phone. Her fingers fly across the keypad, her eyes shining. I wonder if she is in love. I wonder if she would like to go away, to leave H2, this girl who has already traveled around Italy and Ireland, who said to me: *You can go where you want in the West Bank, and me, I just can't move freely in my own country.* Then, laughing: *Please, take me in your bag if you go to Gaza!* Later on, when I wake up, a moonbeam shines across the bedroom and I watch her sleeping on her back, like one who does not fear the night, sovereign, her long, thick lashes absolutely still, while her little sister shifts on her stomach, wriggling, talking in her sleep, a kitten.

Morning. In the morning, the house fills with the voices and noises of a family. Fatima, the mother, got up at five a.m. to pray, prepared the coffee, spread out sheets of newspaper on the living room rug where the breakfast foods are laid out—a cup of olive oil, pitas, tomatoes, olives, *labneh*, and those hard-boiled eggs she shells at high speed and hands to each of us in turn. She warns me there is no water to wash this morning. We will have to wait. Nour is kneeling on her bed, putting on her eyeliner in front of the mirror as she mutters imprecations against Aisha, buzz off. I meet Hafez, Nour's younger brother, the one who wants to be a veterinarian and who describes to me at length the horses he saw last week in a paddock to the south of the city, in the same precise and slightly drawling English as his sister. Same long lashes too.

Little bicycle. The house is cool but already the sun is beating down. Outside, Aisha twists and swerves around the house. The holidays have begun, she's keeping herself occupied. With a wave of her hand she shows me which way her school is, in Tel Rumeida, she goes on foot, she too makes a little path across the hill and passes in front of the settlers' houses. She has always lived in this hostile neighborhood. I look at her. She is on a bicycle cycling backward and forward on the kind of cement sidewalk in front of the house, both—

the bicycle and the track—far too small, far too narrow for this lively little girl who is already big, always moving, and the scene is made all the more upsetting because it would be unimaginable for this girl to go for a ride in the street—Aisha is a child of H2.

Home. Nour's family, which used to live in the other part of the city, moved to Tel Rumeida in 2003. An uncle let her father know that his house would soon be vacant and asked him to come live in it. It was the opposite of the usual journey made by Palestinian families in the area who, weary of living in H2, leave the zone and move to H1, abandoning empty houses, shops, and offices, which are coveted by the settlers, who often waste no time in squatting in them. I wonder what discussions this decision may have provoked between the parents, who already had four young children at the time and a fifth on the way. I imagine their hesitation, given the danger, the periods of strict confinement during the intifada, the perpetual difficulties of daily life in occupied territory: gas and water are supplied to the Palestinian houses in H2 by the services of the Palestinian Authority, and to deliver to the houses the trucks use designated corridors lined with security fences, the access to which is strictly controlled by the Israeli army. All the same, they were knowingly taking a risk, a leap in the dark. I talk to Nour about it, and she shakes her head and simply says that the hardest thing for her mother was to leave her family, who still live in the town of Halhul, north of Hebron. But that her parents did what had to be done—her little chin quivers.

Occupation. The old Palestinian neighborhood of Tel Rumeida, to the west of Hebron and to the southwest of the Casbah of Shuhada Street, has since 1984 been the location of an Israeli settlement, Admot Yishai, composed of around ten families. The property rights to the land and the houses lie, here as elsewhere, at the heart of a violent conflict between the two communities. These lands and these dwellings, which are farmed or owned by old Palestinian families, are the subject of claims by the settlers, who argue a prior Jewish presence based on archaeology: Tel Rumeida is also the oldest site in Hebron. Or else they base their claim on title deeds—in reality ninety-nine-year leases—acquired in 1811 by a rabbi of Egyptian origin with whom the current settlers share no family ties whatsoever.

Desert and tomb. I am sitting in front of a souvenir shop, a few meters away from the checkpoint that controls the ascent to the Cave of the Patriarchs, in the Old Town. It is deserted here. There is no one in the streets, no one in the square, except for the soldiers on guard duty, two or three boys hanging around, a few old Arab men drinking tea beside me, a small group of tourists who have emerged from a white van with its curtains drawn, and a pair of girls with rucksacks who are sipping freshly squeezed orange juice. The sun is blazing, not a cloud in the sky. On the other side of the road, a Palestinian family—a couple with their three children—is waiting in the shade beneath a tree, while their papers are inspected in the armored hut that serves as a checkpoint. There is a feeling of emptiness made all the more paradoxical by the fact that the Cave of the Patriarchs is an important place for both Judaism and Islam. According to religious tradition, major biblical figures are buried here in the Cave of Machpelah—Abraham and his wife Sarah, but also his son Isaac, and Rebecca, as well as his grandson Jacob, and Leah—and it is the second-holiest place of Islam in Palestine, after the Temple Mount/the Noble Sanctuary of Jerusalem. Hordes of pilgrims should be thronging here. I wonder where the inhabitants are, where the life has gone.

Cohabitation. The Muslims and the Jews—the latter always forming a small minority community—lived together in Hebron for four centuries under Ottoman rule (1517–1917), and then under the British Mandate (1917–1947). This cohabitation experienced violent incidents, and broke down in 1929, when sixty-seven Jews were massacred by Palestinians who also ransacked their houses. The Jews fled the town or were "moved on." The memory of this killing is omnipresent in H2, commemorated by numerous street signs. In 1949 Hebron came under Jordanian control and the Jews were no longer allowed to visit the Cave of the Patriarchs. Their "return" to the heart of Hebron began in 1968 and became effective in 1979 when a group of women left the settlement of Kiryat Arba, walked toward the Old Town, entered the Beit Hadassah building, which had previously been a Jewish hospital, and moved in. Hebron became the only town in the West Bank whose historical center was occupied by Jewish settlers, protected by the IDF. Since February 1994 and the massacre of twenty-nine Muslims by a Jewish extremist from Brooklyn, Baruch Goldstein, a long-term resident of Kiryat Arba, the Cave of the Patriarchs, already under Israeli army control, was split into two and access strictly controlled. Moreover, when I get up to go, the Palestinian family is still waiting beneath the tree, in silence.

Ghost town. Further on, Shuhada Street is quiet, our footsteps echo, the atmosphere is leaden. What was once one of the most lively shopping streets in the town, rows of shops squeezed together leading to the different traditional markets—meat, vegetables, fruit—is now a ghost road. In a cruelly ironic twist, the 1994 massacre resulted in an intensification of the military occupation. The security perimeter around the settlements in the center of town was widened, the pressure on the Palestinians increased with systematic inspections and searches, and the vicious cycle was set in motion whereby the shops close—over 1,800 businesses in the area are said to have shuttered—and the houses are abandoned to the settlers' attempts at appropriation. By "sterilizing" Shuhada Street, the settlers are working to connect the different settlements together and to create a secure corridor between the settlements and the Cave of the Patriarchs. I walk past the closed shops, their metal double doors sealed shut, their celadon-green awnings eaten away by rust, their shutters down: it is dead here.

Cages. The windows of the houses along Shuhada Street, like those of many homes in Tel Rumeida, are covered by iron grilles that turn the houses into cages. Seeing my gaze linger on the grim facades, Nour remarks laconically: The gratings are there to protect the inhabitants from the stones the *settlers* throw at us, there are some at my house as well, did you see? The settler houses are located just behind and slightly above her own, scarcely a few meters away. The settlers have sometimes thrown dirty water or garbage. These incidents are indicative of the reality of living in a neighborhood filled with hatred, bound in a strange intimacy: the everyday noises, the shouts of the children, the dog barking, the conversations in the courtyard, you can hear all of it, and the insults too.

Sandals and boots. Today, Saturday, Nour doesn't have class at university but we are heading into H1 all the same, to the other part of the city to attend a meeting of the association founded by the young girl and her friends, Hope for Children in Palestine. I would also like to take the opportunity to buy a pair of sandals because my own are worn out. Nour laughs, perfect timing, this town is actually famous for its shoes, this is where the boots for the Israeli army were made, did you know that?

The Michelin men. On this part of the road leading down to the checkpoint, only settler vehicles are allowed, while the Palestinians must travel on foot. From the bottom of the slope two soldiers on guard duty watch us coming, Michelin men with pale, youthful faces squashed by their helmets, bodies trussed, assault rifles held with both hands. Nour walks by without looking at them, but she tells me: It's ok, those ones aren't too bad. Oh really? Do you know them? She nods, then adds: Each change of unit is an important time for us, the commander's personality, their leadership style, has an impact on life here. She goes on: At the moment the soldiers are from the Nahal Brigade, they behave well, are fairly polite—*respectful*—they don't even shout!—I catch that phrase. The ones before were much less polite, and the ones before them were terrible, their commander was a manipulator whose behavior was constantly changing, he could be violent, shout, shoot using real bullets and then tell us with a smile, okay, it's open, you can go through now.

Intimacy. In Hebron, around 650 soldiers are responsible for the security of some 800 settlers who have come to live in the heart of the city. The soldiers are young, called up between eighteen and twenty years of age for military service lasting three years for the boys and two for the girls. They rarely stay more than three or four months in the same posting in Hebron, as elsewhere, which prevents any relationship from forming with the Palestinians. When, nevertheless, a relationship does develop, it is established on the basis of inspecting and being inspected. In the end you know the faces and you know the names. Domination assumes a human face here: the army is not a nebulous power, a powerful and anonymous armed force imposing its laws, it is this young man here, nervous, sweating uncontrollably in his army jacket, it is that one there, who decided this morning to take his time, or even that one, who dares to ask Nour if she has a boyfriend. The soldiers end up knowing who are brothers, cousins, friends, which ones are students, who works and at what times. The Palestinians also end up identifying the ones who follow instructions to the letter, those who humiliate them, those who answer their questions, those you shouldn't antagonize. It is the intimate side of the occupation.

Pressure point. Checkpoint 56 is a major transit point between H1 and H2. The inhabitants of Tel Rumeida cross it every day to go to work, to seek medical care, to visit people or to go shopping—apart from a tiny minimart near the Jewish cemetery, there's nothing in the neighborhood. In concrete terms, it is a border post set up across an alley and overlooked by a lookout post, while at ground level the area is divided into two lanes. The first, which you take to leave H2, is a simple turnstile door like those found at the exit to the Paris metro. The second, which you take to enter H2, is an entirely different prospect. There is a first holding area, a glass-enclosed counter behind which a soldier inspects the papers—in other words, they call an office to give them an ID number, which is verified with another service, then yet another, before the answer makes its way back the other direction. There is a baggage scanner, onto which you place your bag like the ones you find at the security check in an airport or at the entrance to a prison, then a second holding area, which leads onto the street. So it is access to H2 that is controlled: who gets in and who doesn't. In this, the checkpoint is an embodiment of the occupation, it symbolizes it, makes it manifest. Each crossing reminds the Palestinians of H2 that they are subject to the power of the soldiers, that they are "occupied"; every crossing hits a nerve. Like a pressure point in a congested body, a suffering body, an overflowing body. And the flip side is that here, too, the soldiers are visible, immobile, this is where you can find them if you come looking for them. The checkpoint thus crystalizes the violence of the occupation, and creates a highly volatile space where a simple inspection can quickly turn into a tragedy.

To pass or not to pass, enter/exit. Obtaining a permit requires all your energy when randomness remains the rule. A complex bureaucracy has been put in place: there are dozens of permits. Sometimes the zone is completely sealed off: when Nour's uncle had a heart attack after having been exposed to tear gas, the soldiers wouldn't allow through the ambulance that was supposed to evacuate him to the hospital. He didn't receive treatment in time and didn't survive. In the same vein, pregnant women leave H2 several months before giving birth for fear of being unable to get to the hospital in good time, and becoming, as it were, trapped.

Shrinking world. On the days when she goes to university in H1, Nour goes through checkpoint 56. Sometimes she waits there for over two hours, after which she takes a taxi, which brings her in ten minutes to the university, where she studies English and teaching methodology. Sometimes she has to turn around at the checkpoint and go home simply because today "it's closed." During the period when Tel Rumeida was declared a "closed military zone," the Palestinians had to register in order to receive a number, a number that is checked every time they go through—who is outside, who is inside—and the wait has become unending, humiliating. Enough to discourage all movement. Studying, visiting a friend, running to the store, all of it becomes too much, too hard, too complicated: Nour gives up. Likewise, when I ask her if her friends come to visit her in H2, she shakes her head: no, one of them went through the whole process once, was set upon in the street, got scared, and she never came back. So, there are days when Nour doesn't leave the house, days when her world shrinks to four bare walls.

Another world. On the other side is H1, and it is another planet. Massive traffic jams, a cacophony of klaxons, air-conditioned malls, traditional corner shops, people everywhere. This is the Arab street, potent and chaotic. Your senses, the way you move your body, how fast you move, all of it has to adapt, to solicit other reflexes, as though this were another environment, another atmosphere. We make our way along the packed sidewalks, weave between the guys waiting in the shop doorways. I am looking for gifts for Fatima, a perfume, a bag, I don't know. Nour guides me. She chose her outfit carefully for going into town, wearing a long red dress and a flowery headscarf identical to those of her best friend whom I meet later: they are twins, it makes them laugh. Nour takes makeup lessons every Saturday in Bethlehem, one of her uncles brings her in his car. There, she learns how to put on mascara, to apply eyeshadow, to blend foundation. She meets up with friends, tries out the products and the techniques: I'm doing this just for myself, I don't want to make a career of it. I like the fact that this young girl puts time and effort into her beauty, that the earnestness of her activism gives way to this levity that is so precious when one lives here, a shopping trip, a fit of laughter, a *shisha* pipe shared with friends at the Orange Café. A hit by Adele sung at the top of her lungs while dancing with Aisha in the half light of their room.

Cameras. Nour first became involved with B'Tselem, an Israeli organization opposed to the occupation, one of whose protest activities involves giving cameras to Palestinians to allow them to film the abuses they are subject to in the occupied territories, then bear witness to them on social media.

Hand. Nour's family was given a camera but, as the young girl explains, filming the assaults turned out to be difficult: by the time they were alerted, grabbed the camera, and got to the location, the attack was already over. Nour recalled the story of how Hisham, her father, was injured during the first intifada. On that day some Israeli soldiers summoned her father to go and take down a Palestinian flag at the top of an electrical pole, threatening to kill him if he didn't obey. Then that nightmarish scenario: the father first refuses, then finally climbs, gets electrocuted, falls, his left hand useless from then on, to such an extent that he can no longer work as a joiner.

Nonviolence. Later on, at around sixteen years of age, Nour joined Youth Against Settlements, a nonviolent association founded by Issa Amro and based in Tel Rumeida. Issa is a major figure in the resistance to the occupation and a close friend of Nour's family, to whom he was a great help after Hisham was injured. Today we're celebrating: the association's center has once again opened after having been forced to close for six months by the army, and the activities are starting up again. They are preparing a demonstration to support the reopening of Shuhada Street, an intervention to protect a Palestinian home, and, as always, seeking to counteract, to ward off, to anticipate the insidious process of colonization spreading little by little all over the sector. The young boys who are present have all had dealings with the occupying army. Nonviolence is not the most obvious form of resistance, and it is also a form of education.

Evening. The sun goes down over Hebron, a golden light gilds the olive trees of Tel Rumeida, and the voice of the muezzin rises, floats over the city, and amplifies the sky. The countryside is so peaceful that it tears you apart, and the thought that it could be the site of such unending violence seems unreal to me. We smoke a *shisha* pipe on the central terrace of the association. Aisha is there, acting the clown, Nour is looking at photos of the demonstration for the reopening of Shuhada Street, while at the end of the little concrete alleyway that leads to the center two Israeli soldiers are stationed in a watchtower. Some young boys have gone down to the field below the house and are improvising a hockey match using brushwood collected from the bushes as sticks. They run, chase after one another, overtake each other, play, laugh, shove each other, having a great time, free, like escaped horses.

Post. The day after I leave Hebron, two Palestinians from the southern districts of the city open fire on the terrace of a café in Tel Aviv, killing four people and injuring eight others. The Israeli government cancels eighty-three thousand travel permits for Palestinians at the beginning of Ramadan. Violent, explosive, and fragile, Hebron, its hills, its districts, its ghettos, are under pressure. The town seems to be at the epicenter of Palestinian uprisings. I leave a message for Nour on WhatsApp. Everyone is here, it's okay, don't worry.

(TRANSLATED FROM THE FRENCH BY DÚNLAITH BIRD)

AFTERWORD

BREAKING THE SILENCE IS MADE UP OF ISRAELI SOLDIERS WHO served in the occupied territories. We are the combatants who carried out Israeli government policies in the occupied territories over the past fifty years. We implemented aggressive military mechanisms of control. We strong-armed millions of human beings into submission. We stripped people of their basic rights, their freedom, their ability to determine their own fates.

Our act of speaking out—of "breaking the silence"—is an inevitable reaction to the violence and immorality we witnessed and carried out. It is a personal moral outcry, and a civic outcry. Breaking the silence, for us, entails taking responsibility for our actions, and demanding that the situation be changed. It is an expression of love for our homeland, and of our deep fear for its future.

Our fight began in June 2004, when more than sixty former soldiers organized an exhibition of photographs and testimonies detailing their service in the Occupied Palestinian Territories, mostly from the city of Hebron. The exhibition ignited a political storm in Israel, and led to the creation of our organization Breaking the Silence. From that first exhibition and to this day, we have endeavored to fight against the Israeli occupation by publicizing testimonies of the very Israeli soldiers sent to carry it out. Our testimonies are published in the first person: We describe the things that we saw, the things we took part in, and the daily realities we witnessed; realities that include the grievous and ongoing violation of the human rights and freedom of the Palestinian residents of the West Bank and Gaza.

OVER THE PAST DOZEN YEARS, BREAKING THE SILENCE HAS INTERVIEWED and published the testimonies of more than 1,000 soldiers who served in the occupied territories.*

Silence in regard to the *inherent* immorality of the regime of occupation—which both oppresses Palestinian society and corrupts Israeli society—is rampant in Israeli society and, to a certain degree, in the international community. Through this book, authors from around the world joined hands and hearts with Breaking the Silence in the act of bearing witness, from a place of shared commitment to values of justice, morality, equality, and human rights. The essays in this volume can thus be seen as a collection of *testimonies,* stories about the realities of occupation by those who witnessed it firsthand, and who have chosen not to be silent.

The testimonies of these authors and of the people they met during their visits to the occupied territories are, of course, quite different than those usually publicized by Breaking the Silence.

Breaking the Silence's project of testimony-gathering over the years and the motif of testimony-sharing spread throughout the pages of this book come from opposite directions: the testifiers of Breaking the Silence describe first and foremost the personal experiences of soldiers sent to maintain and carry out the occupation. Through such testimonies, we highlight the IDF's methods of enacting Israeli government policies in the occupied territories. In our book, *Our Harsh Logic: Israeli Soldiers' Testimonies from the Occupied Territories, 2000–2010,* we compiled a wide range of testimonies, alongside an analysis of the IDF's mechanisms for upholding and entrenching the occupation.

THE ESSAYS IN THIS BOOK WERE WRITTEN BY AUTHORS MOST OF WHOM reside outside of the region and many of whom had spent little or no

---

* You can read and watch Breaking the Silence testimonies at http://www.breakingthe silence.org.il/testimonies/database

time in the occupied territories before this visit. Further, during their time here, the authors focused primarily on the stories of people living *under* occupation, rather than those sent to *maintain* occupation. Yet these essays and Breaking the Silence's testimonies ultimately share the goal of telling the truth about what is happening in the occupied territories, and of confronting the occupation by exposing—through direct and personal narrative—the injustices taking place there.

Similar to the testimonies gathered by Breaking the Silence, we hold that the stories gathered in these pages are not simply reports, but are rather actions in and of themselves, actions that have the potential to change political realities.

We are not naive: We are aware that the Israeli occupation is almost as well-documented as it is old, and that the information—including the thousands of testimonies given by testifiers in our organization—is available to anyone with access to the Internet. Still, we are hopeful that this book and the act of testimony-gathering undertaken in its pages will disturb and mobilize its readers, in Israeli society and all around the world, to do what must be done to end the Israeli occupation of the Palestinian territories. We hope it will spark a public discourse both inside Israel and out, and inspire others to speak out.

We are beyond grateful to the editors of this book, Ayelet Waldman and Michael Chabon, for their dedication, vision, and brilliance; to Mario Vargas Llosa, who lent his support to the project in its nascent stages; to the book's associate editor, Moriel Rothman-Zecher, for his invaluable work on this project; to all of the authors who took part in this project, and to the scores of people—Palestinians and Israelis—who contributed to this project, some of whom are mentioned in the essays themselves or in the acknowledgments, and others who are not. We are grateful to everyone who has taken it upon themselves to witness this reality, from up close and from afar, and to break the silence with us, to confront the occupation, and to fight for a better future for Palestinians and Israelis alike.

—BREAKING THE SILENCE

ACKNOWLEDGMENTS

We want to thank Baha Nababta, a generous, huge-hearted person whose optimism that the occupation would certainly come to an end and whose commitment to his community and to justice inspired us, and so many lucky enough to meet him. Baha was killed on May 2, 2016.

This book would have been impossible to create without the help of the following individuals:

Jawad Abu Aisha, Nael Abu Aram, Thawra Abu Khdeir, Kifah Abu Khdeir, Mahmoud Aburahma, Fiaz Abu-Rmeleh, Uri Agnon, Ra'anan Alexandrovich, Arafat Alian Omar Aljafari, Munthar Amirah, Ahmed Amro, Issa Amro, Arab Aramin, Bassam Aramin, Ahmed Azza, Sundus Azza, Sam Bahour, Daphna Banai, Hanna Barag, Tia Barak, Jennifer Barth, Leon Barzarar, Bashir Bashir, Nadav Bigelman, Mia Bengel, Frima Bubis, Jonathan Burnham, Guy Butavia, Sonya Cheuse, Hillel Cohen, Tamar Cohen, Efrat Cohen-Bar, Alon Cohen-Lifshitz, Maggie Doyle, Salwa Duaibis, Bob Edelman, Eila Eitan, Rami Elhanan, Yigal Elhanan, Ori Erez, Dror Etkes, Mary Evans, Ido Even Paz, John Gall, Mary Gaule, Amos Goldberg, Michael Goldberg, David Goldblatt, Shiraz Greenbaum, David Grossman, Avner Gvaryahu, Amira Hass, Nir Hasson, Nirit Haviv, Gerard Horton, Lama Hourani, Eid Hthaleen, Mustafa Jaber, Penny Johnson, Julia Kardon, Shareef Khaled, Mohammad Khatib, Miki Kratzman, Talia Krevsky, Gaby Lasky, Uri Levy, Dana Lotan, Yoni Mandel, Keren Manor, Shadia Mansour, Tali Mayer, Yaniv Mazor, Ilai Melzer, Yehuda Melzer, Omri Metzer, Quamar

Mishirqi-Assad, Yoni Mizrachi, Salah Mohsen, Avi Mughrabi, Hiba Nababta, Azzam Nawaja, Fatmeh Nawaja, Nasser Nawaja, Yuli Novak, Orly Noy, Hagit Ofran, Yudith Oppenheimer, Jonathan Pollack, Fadi Quran, Yotam Ronen, Yaqub Rajabi, Zuheir Rajabi, Eyal Raz, Kate Rosenberg, Kayla Rothman-Zecher, Alon Sahar, Abdul-Hakim Salah, Kela Sappir, Achiya Schatz, Emily Schaeffer Omer-Man, Ronit Sela, Michael Sfard, Ishay Shneydor, Murad Shtawi, Jawad Siyam, Yehuda Shaul, Pnina Steiner, Bassem Tamimi, Nariman Tamimi, Aviv Tatarsky, Mojtaba Tbeleh, Leah Tsemel, Amiel Vardi, Sahar Vardi, Shira Vizel, Nadav Weiman, Erin Wicks, Noa Yammer, Raya Yaron, Roy Yellin, Cesar Yeudkin, Shlomy Zaharia, Ron Zeidel, Oren Ziv.

And the following groups and organizations:

ActiveStills, Al Mezan Center for Human Rights, the Association for Civil Rights in Israel, Batan al-Hawa Popular Committee, Bil'in Popular Committee, Bimkom, B'Tselem, Budrus Popular Committee, Comet-ME, Emek Shaveh, HaMoked: Center for the Defense of the Individual, Gisha: Legal Center for the Freedom of Movement, Ir Amim, Jinba Popular Committee, Kerem Navot, Kufr Qaddum Popular Committee, MachsomWatch, Military Court Watch, Nabi Saleh Popular Committee, the Parents Circle: Bereaved Families Forum, Peace Now Settlement Watch, Susiya Popular Committee, Ta'yaush, Umm al-Khair Popular Committee, Wadi Hilweh Information Center, Wallajeh Popular Committee, Youth Against Settlements, Zbeidat Women's Committee.

CONTRIBUTORS

LORRAINE ADAMS is a novelist and Pulitzer Prize–winning journalist. Her first novel, *Harbor*, on North African Muslims, won the Los Angeles Times First Fiction Award and was short-listed for the Guardian First Book Award. Her second novel, *The Room and the Chair*, took her to Iran, Afghanistan, and Pakistan. She won a Guggenheim Fellowship in 2010 and the Pulitzer Prize for investigative reporting in 1992. She worked for the *Washington Post* for eleven years, and is a regular contributor to the *New York Times Book Review*.

GERALDINE BROOKS is the author of five novels, including the Pulitzer Prize–winning *March* and the international bestseller *People of the Book*. She was the *Wall Street Journal* Mideast correspondent and is the author of a nonfiction work on Muslim women, *Nine Parts of Desire*, which was translated into more than twenty languages. In 2016 she was named an officer of the Order of Australia.

MICHAEL CHABON is the author of numerous novels, among them *Moonglow*, *Telegraph Avenue*, *The Yiddish Policemen's Union*, and *The Amazing Adventures of Kavalier and Clay*, which was awarded the 2001 Pulitzer Prize for Fiction. He lives in Berkeley, California, with his wife, Ayelet Waldman, with whom he edited the present volume.

LARS SAABYE CHRISTENSEN made his literary debut in 1976 with *Historien om Gly*. His breakthrough novel was *Beatles*, which is one of the greatest literary successes in Norway and which continues to speak to new generations. He received both the Bookseller's Prize and the Nordic Council's Literary Award for the novel *Halvbroren* in 2001. This novel also marked his breakthrough to the international market. His works have been translated into thirty-five languages.

MAYLIS DE KERANGAL is the author of several novels and short stories, all published by Gallimard/Verticales. She received the Prix Médicis for *Birth of a Bridge* (Talonbooks, 2010). *Réparer les vivants* came out in France in January 2014 and received rave reviews for its intimate look at the realities and philosophical questions around organ donation. It has been published under the title *Mend the Living* (Maclehose and Talonbooks, 2016) and *The Heart* (Farrar, Straus and Giroux, 2016), and was long-listed for the Man Booker Prize in 2016.

ANITA DESAI was born and raised in India. She is the author of several novels of which three—*Clear Light of Day, In Custody*, and *Fasting, Feasting*—were short-listed for the Booker Prize. She is also the author of two collections of short stories, *Games at Twilight* and *Diamond Dust*. She is a Fellow of the Royal Society of Literature in London and the American Academy of Arts and Letters, and a professor emeritus of the Massachusetts Institute of Technology.

DAVE EGGERS is the author of ten books, among them *Heroes of the Frontier, The Circle*, and *A Hologram for the King*, which was a finalist for the 2012 National Book Award. He is the founder of McSweeney's, an independent publishing company based in San Francisco. He is also the cofounder of Voice of Witness, a nonprofit book series that uses oral history to illuminate human rights crises around the world. In 2014, Voice of Witness published *Palestine Speaks: Narratives of Life Under Occupation*. Eggers is the cofounder of 826 National, a network of eight tutoring centers around the country, and of ScholarMatch, a nonprofit organization designed to connect students with resources, schools, and donors to make college possible. His journalism has appeared in *The New Yorker, New York Times*, and *Guardian*.

ASSAF GAVRON is an acclaimed Israeli writer who has published five novels: *Ice, Moving, Almost Dead, Hydromania,* and *The Hilltop*; a collection of short stories, *Sex in the Cemetery*; and a nonfiction collection of Jerusalem falafel-joint reviews, *Eating Standing Up.* His fiction has been adapted for the stage in Israel's national theater, and optioned for movies. He is the recipient of several awards, including the Bernstein Prize for *The Hilltop*, the Israeli Prime Minister's Creative Award for Authors, and the Prix Courrier International in France for *Almost Dead.* Gavron's latest novel in English, *The Hilltop*, was published by Scribner in the United States in October 2014.

ARNON GRUNBERG was born in Amsterdam in 1971. He lives and works in New York City. He started his own publishing company called Kasimir, specializing in non-Aryan German literature, at the age of nineteen, and has acted and written plays. When he was twenty-three years old, his first novel, *Blue Mondays*, became a bestseller in Europe and won the Anton Wachter Prize. It has been translated into thirteen languages.

HELON HABILA is an associate professor of creative writing at George Mason University, USA. His novels include *Waiting for an Angel* (2002), *Measuring Time* (2007), and *Oil on Water* (2010). He is the editor of the *Granta Book of the African Short Story* (2011). Habila's novels, poems, and short stories have won many honors and awards, including the Commonwealth Prize for Best First Novel (Africa Section), the Caine Prize, and most recently the Windham-Campbell Prize. Habila has been a contributing editor for the *Virginia Quarterly Review* since 2004, and he is a regular reviewer for the *Guardian.* He lives in Virginia with his wife and three children.

ALA HLEHEL is a Palestinian author, screenwriter, and playwright. He has received several awards for his work, among them A. M. Qattan Foundation Competition awards, the "39 Beirut," and the Ghassan Kanafani short stories award. His last novel, *Au revoir Acre*, was published in 2014, and the Hebrew and English translations are in process.

FIDA JIRYIS is a Palestinian from the Galilee based in Ramallah. She is a writer, editor, and freelance business consultant. Fida has contributed short stories and articles to various publications including *This Week in Palestine, Mondoweiss, The Palestine Chronicle*, and *+972 Magazine*, and is the author of *Hayatuna Elsagheera* (*Our Small Life*) and *Al-Khawaja* (*The Gentleman*), two Arabic books of short stories on village life in the Galilee. Her third book, *Al-Qafas* (*The Cage*), will be published in 2017. She has also completed an English women's novel, *Forty-Six Pounds*, which she is seeking to publish, and is currently working on *My Return to the Galilee*, a memoir of her return to Israel after the Oslo accords.

POROCHISTA KHAKPOUR was born in Tehran, raised in Los Angeles, and lives in New York City. She is the author of the forthcoming memoir *Sick* (HarperPerennial, 2017), and the novels *The Last Illusion* (Bloomsbury, 2014)—a 2014 best book of the year according to NPR, *Kirkus, Buzzfeed, Popmatters, Electric Literature*, and more—and *Sons and Other Flammable Objects* (Grove, 2007), the 2007 California Book Award winner in first fiction, one of the *Chicago Tribune*'s Fall's Best, and a *New York Times* Editor's Choice. Her writing has appeared in or is forthcoming in *Harper's*, the *New York Times, Los Angeles Times, Wall Street Journal, Al-Jazeera America, Bookforum, Slate, Salon, Spin, Daily Beast, Elle*, and many other publications around the world. She is currently writer-in-residence at Bard College.

HARI KUNZRU, born in London, is the author of the novels *The Impressionist, Transmission, My Revolutions*, and *Gods Without Men*, as well as a short story collection, *Noise*, and a novella, *Memory Palace*. His forthcoming novel *White Tears* will be published in 2017. His short stories and essays have appeared in diverse publications, including the *New York Times, The New Yorker, Guardian, London Review of Books, Granta, BookForum*, and *Frieze*. He was a 2008 Cullman Fellow at the New York Public Library and a 2014 Guggenheim Fellow.

RACHEL KUSHNER is the author of two novels, *The Flamethrowers* and *Telex from Cuba*—both finalists for the National Book

Award, and a book of stories, *The Strange Case of Rachel K.* She lives in Los Angeles.

EIMEAR McBRIDE studied at Drama Centre London. Her debut novel, *A Girl Is a Half-Formed Thing*, received a number of awards, including the Goldsmiths Prize, Bailey's Women's Prize for Fiction, and Irish Novel of the Year. She occasionally writes and reviews for the *Guardian*, *Times Literary Supplement,* and *New Statesman*. Her second novel, *The Lesser Bohemians*, was published in 2016.

COLUM McCANN is the author of six novels and three collections of stories. Born and raised in Dublin, Ireland, he has been the recipient of many international honors, including the National Book Award, the International Dublin IMPAC Prize, a Chevalier des Arts et Lettres from the French government, the election to the Irish Arts Academy, several European awards, the 2010 Best Foreign Novel Award in China, and an Oscar nomination. His work has been published in forty languages. He is the cofounder of the nonprofit global story exchange organization Narrative 4, and he teaches in the MFA program at Hunter College.

EVA MENASSE is an Austrian-born writer and essayist, living in Berlin. Menasse had a successful career as a journalist, writing for leading German and Austrian newspapers such as *Frankfurter Allgemeine*, *Süddeutsche Zeitung*, and *Die Zeit*. She reported on the David Irving Holocaust-denial trial in London in 2000 and wrote a nonfiction book on it, *The Holocaust on Trial*. The English translation of her first novel, *Vienna*, was short-listed for the 2007 Independent Foreign Fiction Prize in the UK. Her last novel *Quasikristalle* (*Quasicrystals*, 2013) was a bestseller in Germany, and was awarded the Heinrich Böll and Jonathan Swift Prizes. Her work has been translated into more than ten languages.

EMILY RABOTEAU is the author of a novel, *The Professor's Daughter*, and a work of creative nonfiction, *Searching For Zion*, which was named a Best Book of 2013 by the *Huffington Post* and the *San*

Francisco Chronicle, as well as being a finalist for the Hurston-Wright Legacy Award, the grand prize winner of the New York Book Festival, and winner of a 2014 American Book Award. An avid world traveler, Raboteau resides in New York City and teaches creative writing in Harlem at City College, once known as "the poor man's Harvard."

TAIYE SELASI is a writer and photographer. Born in London and raised in Boston, she holds a BA in American Studies from Yale and an MPhil in International Relations from Oxford. In 2005 she published the seminal essay "Bye-Bye, Babar (or: What is an Afropolitan?)," offering an alternative vision of African identity for a transnational generation. In 2011 she made her fiction debut with "The Sex Lives of African Girls," selected for *Best American Short Stories 2012*. In 2013, Selasi's first novel, *Ghana Must Go*, a *New York Times* bestseller, was selected as one of the ten best books of 2013 by the *Wall Street Journal* and the *Economist*. She is currently writing her second novel.

RAJA SHEHADEH is a writer and lawyer who founded the pioneering Palestinian human rights organization al-Haq. Shehadeh is the author of several acclaimed books, including *Strangers in the House*, *Occupation Diaries*, *Language of War, Language of Peace*, and winner of the 2008 Orwell Prize for *Palestinian Walks* (all published by Profile). He lives in Ramallah in Palestine. His latest book, *Where the Line Is Drawn: A Tale of Crossings, Friendship and Fifty Years of Occupation*, will be published in Spring 2017.

MADELEINE THIEN was born in Vancouver. She is the author of a story collection and three novels, including *Dogs at the Perimeter*. Her most recent book *Do Not Say We Have Nothing*, about music, art, and revolution in China was short-listed for the 2016 Man Booker Prize, and won the 2016 Scotiabank Giller Prize and the Governor-General's Literary Award for Fiction. Her work has been short-listed for the Sunday Times EFG Short Story Award and Berlin's International Literature Prize, and her books and stories have been translated into twenty-six languages. The daughter of Malaysian-Chinese immigrants to Canada, she lives in Montreal.

COLM TÓIBÍN is the author of eight novels, including *The Master* and *Brooklyn*. His play *The Testament of Mary* was nominated for a Tony Award for best play in 2013. He is the Irene and Sidney B. Silverman Professor of the Humanities at Columbia University.

MARIO VARGAS LLOSA was born in Arequipa, and also spent parts of his youth in Cochabamba (Bolivia), Piura in northern Peru, and Lima. He made his debut as a novelist with *The Time of the Hero* (1962). His other works include the novels *Conversation in the Cathedral, The Green House, The Real Life of Alejandro Mayta, Who Killed Palomino Molero?, The Storyteller, Aunt Julia and the Scriptwriter, The Feast of the Goat, The Bad Girl, The Dream of the Celt*, and *The Discreet Hero*, and the plays *La Chunga, Kathie and the Hippopotamus*, and *The Young Lady from Tacna*, among other works. He has also published several books of essays. He has been awarded the Leopoldo Alas Prize (1959), the Rómulo Gallegos Prize (1967), the National Critics' Prize (1967), the Critics' Annual Prize for Theatre (1981), the Prince of Asturias Prize (1986), the Miguel de Cervantes Prize (1994)—the Spanish-speaking world's most distinguished literary honor,—the Jerusalem Prize (1995), the Peace Prize of the German Book Trade (1996), the PEN/Nabokov Award (2002), and the Nobel Prize (2010).

AYELET WALDMAN is the author of the book *A Really Good Day: How Microdosing Made a Mega Difference in My Mood, My Marriage and My Life*, and of the novels *Love and Treasure, Red Hook Road, Love and Other Impossible Pursuits*, and *Daughter's Keeper*, as well as the essay collection *Bad Mother: A Chronicle of Maternal Crimes, Minor Calamities, and Occasional Moments of Grace*. She is the editor of *Inside This Place, Not of It: Narratives from Women's Prisons*. She lives in Berkeley, California, with her husband, Michael Chabon, with whom she edited this volume.

JACQUELINE WOODSON is the 2014 National Book Award winner for her memoir *Brown Girl Dreaming*. Her novel *Another Brooklyn* was a finalist for the National Book Award in fiction. She is the author of more than two dozen books for young adults, middle graders, and children. Among many awards, she is also a four-time Newbery Honor winner, a four-time National Book Award finalist, a recipient of the NAACP Image Award, a two-time Coretta Scott King Award winner, and was recently named the Young People's Poet Laureate by the Poetry Foundation. Her book *Miracle's Boy* received the Los Angeles Times Book Prize. Jacqueline was also the winner of the Jane Addams Children's Book Award, and was the 2013 United States nominee for the Hans Christian Andersen Award. She lives with her family in Brooklyn, New York.

PERMISSIONS